MW00464173

W. E. B. Du Bois Institute

The W. E. B. Du Bois Institute brings together leading scholars from around the world to explore a range of topics in the study of African and African American culture, literature, and history. The Institute series provides a publishing forum for outstanding work deriving from colloquia, research groups, and conferences sponsored by the Institute. Whether undertaken by individuals or collaborative groups, the books appearing in this series work to foster a stronger sense of national and international community and a better understanding of diasporic history.

SERIES EDITORS

Henry Louis Gates Jr.
W. E. B. Du Bois Professor of the Humanities
Harvard University

Richard Newman
Research Officer
The W. E. B. Du Bois Institute
Harvard University

RACE AND THE MODERN ARTIST

EDITED BY

HEATHER HATHAWAY,

JOSEF JAŘAB, AND

JEFFREY MELNICK

OXFORD
UNIVERSITY PRESS

2003

OXFORD
UNIVERSITY PRESS

Oxford   New York
Auckland   Bangkok   Buenos Aires   Cape Town   Chennai
Dar es Salaam   Delhi   Hong Kong   Istanbul   Karachi   Kolkata
Kuala Lumpur   Madrid   Melbourne   Mexico City   Mumbai   Nairobi
São Paulo   Shanghai   Taipei   Tokyo   Toronto

Published by Oxford University Press, Inc.
198 Madison Avenue, New York, New York 10016

www.oup.com

Oxford is a registered trademark of Oxford University Press

Library of Congress Cataloging-in-Publication Data
Race and the modern artist / edited by Heather Hathaway, Josef Jařab, and Jeffrey Melnick
   p. cm. — (W. E. B. Du Bois Institute)
Includes bibliographical references and index.
ISBN 0-19-512323-9; 0-19-512324-7 (pbk.)
1. Race relations in literature. 2. American literature—African American authors—
History and criticism. 3. Modernism (Literature) I. Hathaway, Heather. II. Jařab, Josef.
III. Melnick, Jeffrey. IV. W. E. B. Du Bois Institute for Afro-American Research.
PN56.R56   R33   2002
810.9'355—dc21   2002002385

9 8 7 6 5 4 3 2 1

Printed in the United States of America
on acid-free paper

The volume was originally intended to express the joy of scholarly collegiality shared by fellows and associates at the W. E. B. Du Bois Institute for Afro-American Research at Harvard University during their affiliation with the institution. After the sudden and untimely death of Professor Nathan Huggins, the generally revered director of the institute, in 1989, it was natural that it be dedicated to him as a tribute to his excellent scholarship, his skilled and wise leadership, and his genuine friendship.

More than a decade has passed, however, since the idea of the book was first conceived. With a small number of essays by colleagues in hand I, as editor, returned to my home in Czechoslovakia just before the historical turnover took place there—and in the aftermath of the Velvet Revolution I became swamped in service to the rapidly transforming society in a number of novel and previously unforeseen positions, from university rector and alderman of my hometown to senator of the Czech parliament, member of the Parliamentary Assembly of the Council of Europe, and rector and president of Central European University in Budapest. Such demanding tasks emerging in the course of those exciting months and years kept the teacher and researcher in me away from the writing desk and planned literary projects.

Over time, when it became obvious that some assistance would be needed to bring the project to completion, I turned for help to Heather Hathaway and Jeffrey Melnick, both in the capacity of co-editing native speakers and as contacts to a number of contributors of their own younger generation of literary scholars. Thus the present book brings together essays produced by at least two generations of researchers who in one way or another have been associated with the Du Bois Institute—as fellows or colleagues and students or disciples of former fellows—all scholars interested in the field of African American and minority culture, in the problems of ethnicity, and in the complex phenomenon of modernism.

As for the living legacy of Nathan Huggins himself, it may be of interest to note that his personal library was generously bequeathed by his widow, Brenda Smith Huggins, to the Department of English and American Studies at Palacký University, Olomouc, Czechoslovakia, and it became the core of an ever growing collection of books at the Center for Comparative Cultural Studies, in the Nathan I. Huggins Library for American Studies at Palacký University. The ceremonial opening, in March 1993, became an important event not only in the academic world of the Czech Republic but within the international community of African Americanists, who used the opportunity to organize, in the presence of Ms. Huggins, a high-profile international symposium under a Hugginsian title, "The African-American Odyssey," in which a great number of distinguished scholars took part, among them Leon Litwack, Lawrence Levine, Werner Sollors, Alessandro Portelli, Berndt Ostendorf, Fritz Gysin, Maria Diedrich, and Genevieve Fabre, as well as the new director of the Du Bois Institute, Henry Louis Gates Jr. This was also the occasion and venue for the first formal meeting of the newly founded Collegium of African American Research, which has since grown into a very potent community of scholars. All these activities, the participants felt and strongly believed, would have won Nathan Huggins's approval and endorsement. The editors hope that he would have been pleased with the present volume as well.

Our debt to Nathan I. Huggins, to whom this book is dedicated, must by now be self-evident, but I would still like to add a word of grateful recognition of the personal enrichment I experienced during the six months I spent at the Du Bois Institute in 1989. Thanks are naturally due to all the contributors and the co-editors, Heather Hathaway and Jeffrey Melnick, for their work and gentle but steady nudging to move forward with the project. My personal gratitude belongs to Allen Ginsberg for his willingness to sit with me for the two-stage interview, in 1989 and in 1993, for his careful editing of the transcript, and, last but not least, for his friendly consent to have the texts published and included in this volume.

CONTENTS

CONTENTS

FRITZ GYSIN is professor of American literature at the University of Bern, Switzerland, a former president of the Swiss Association for North American Studies and the Swiss Association of University Teachers of English, and a founding member and board member of the Collegium for African American Research. He has written two books, *The Grotesque in American Negro Fiction* (1975) and *Model as Motif in "Tristram Shandy"* (1983); edited *Apocalypse* (Swiss Papers in English Language and Literatures 12, 1999); and published articles on Sterling Brown, Joseph Conrad, Leon Forrest, Charles Johnson, Nathaniel Hawthorne, Langston Hughes, Nathaniel Mackey, George Schuyler, Jean Toomer, Mark Twain, John Edgar Wideman, and Sherley Anne Williams. He is interested in the interface of African American literature and jazz and is working on a book on boundaries in recent African American fiction.

HEATHER HATHAWAY is associate professor of English and co-director of the honors program at Marquette University. She is the author of *Caribbean Waves: Relocating Claude McKay and Paule Marshall* (1999) and is co-editing *Conversations with Paule Marshall* (forthcoming) with James C. Hall. She is currently working on a study of freedom, captivity, and American ethnic identity.

JERROLD HIRSCH is associate professor of history at Truman State University in Kirksville, Missouri. He is the author of *The History of the National Training Laboratories, 1947–1986: Social Equality through Education and Training* (1988) and a co-editor, with Tom Terrill, of *Such as Us: Southern Voices of the Thirties* (1979), and he has written numerous articles on the New Deal's Federal Writers' Project (FWP), the history of American folklore studies, and disability history. Hirsch is completing a book on the FWP and continuing, with Karen Hirsch, historical research on disability among African American slaves and southern textile workers.

JOSEF JAŘAB is professor of English and American literature and director of the Center for Comparative Cultural Studies at Palacký University, Olomouc. He has written extensively about African American literature and culture, modern American and English poetry and fiction, and issues of higher education and research. He served as first chairman of the Czech Fulbright Committee and the Czech and Slovak Association for American Studies and is currently president of the European Association for American Studies. He served from 1989 to 1977 as rector of Palacký University, and from 1977 to 1999 as rector and president of the Central European University in Budapest and Warsaw. At present he is serving a six-year term as senator in the Czech parliament and holds a seat in the Parliamentary Assembly of the Council of Europe.

JEFFREY MELNICK is associate professor of American studies at Babson College. He is the author of *Black-Jewish Relations on Trial: Leo Frank and Jim Conley in the New South* (2000) and *A Right to Sing the Blues: African Americans, Jews, and American Popular Song* (2001). He has also co-edited, with Rachel Rubin, *American Popular Music: New Approaches to the Twentieth Century* (2001).

ADAM ZACHARY NEWTON is associate professor of English and teaches in the Committee on Comparative Literature, Middle Eastern Studies, and Jewish Studies at the University of Texas at Austin. He is the author of *Narrative Ethics* (1995), *Facing Black and Jew: Literature as Public Space in Twentieth-Century America* (1999), and, most recently, *The Fence and the Neighbor: Emmanuel Levinas, Yeshayahu Leibowitz, and Israel among the Nations* (2001). He has published articles in *American Literary History*, *Narrative*, *South Atlantic Quarterly*, *Prospects*, and *Social Identities*, and in several essay collections as well. His current project, a study of writers from Central Europe and the Levant, is entitled *The Elsewhere: On Belonging at a Near Distance*.

ALESSANDRO PORTELLI is professor of American literature at the University of Rome "La Sapienza." He is the author of *The Test and the Voice: Speaking, Writing, and Democracy in American Literature*, *The Death of Luigi Trastulli: Form and Meaning in Oral History*, and *The Battle of Valle Giulia: Oral History and the Art of Dialogue*. His recent book *L'ordine è già stato eseguito*, on Nazi war crimes in Rome, was awarded the Viareggio Book Prize in 1999. He has served as secretary of the Council for African American Research from 1994 to 2001.

RACHEL RUBIN is assistant professor of American studies at the University of Massachusetts, Boston. She is the author of *Jewish Gangsters of Modern Literature* (2000) and co-editor, with Jeffrey Melnick, of *American Popular Music: New Approaches to the Twentieth Century* (2001). She is currently completing a book about immigrants and American popular culture.

JAMES SMETHURST is assistant professor of Afro-American studies at the University of Massachusetts, Amherst. He is the author of *The New Red Negro: The Literary Left and African American Poetry, 1930–1946* (2000) and the co-editor of *Twentieth-Century Americanisms: The Left and Modern Literatures of the United States* (forthcoming). He is currently working on a study of the origins of the black arts movement.

WERNER SOLLORS is the Henry B. and Anne M. Cabot Professor of English Literature and professor of Afro-American studies and chair of the History of American Civilization Program at Harvard University. He is the author of *Beyond Ethnicity: Consent and Descent in American Culture* (1986) and *Neither Black nor White yet Both: Thematic Explorations of Interracial Literature* (1997). The essay included here is excerpted from his book-length contribution to the forthcoming *Cambridge History of American Literature*, edited by Sacvan Bercovitch.

DANIEL TERRIS is director of the International Center for Ethics, Justice, and Public Life and teaches American studies at Brandeis University. He also oversees the Brandeis Seminars in Humanities and the Professions, which provide programs on professional values and ethics using literary texts as the basis of discussion to professionals around the United States. Terris has written on twentieth-century art, politics, and religion.

M. LYNN WEISS is associate professor of American studies at the College of William and Mary. She is the author of *Gertrude Stein and Richard Wright: The Poetics and Politics of Modernism* (1998) and most recently edited and wrote the introductions to *The Jew of Seville* (2002) and *The Fortune Teller*, both by Victor Sejour (2002).

RACE AND THE MODERN ARTIST

■ JOSEF JAŘAB

Introduction

Modernity, Modernism, and the American Ethnic Minority Artist

■

It should not be too surprising that the terms "modern," "modernity," and "modernization" have in the ever growing bulk of critical literature manifested a great deal of openness, indeed a yielding elasticity, when we realize that the very idea at the core of all these phenomena is *change*. And the dynamic changes themselves that our world witnessed through the early as well as the latter decades of the twentieth century have certainly further contributed to the difficulties marking the effort to define the terms, or, at least, to provide a conceptual description that would bring us closer to a better and fuller understanding of the experience or conceits they should describe. As a matter of fact, all the various concepts of the modern not only reflect changing historical circumstances but are themselves in the ongoing discussion becoming gradually more complex, both in content and application.

A clearer distinction between the terms "modernity" and "modernism" was introduced as the debate over *the new* continued, which helps to prevent their being used interchangeably. Some authors, though, still dwell on using the word "modernity," as if in accordance with the Baudelairean *modernité*, to express the quality and mode of modern life and reality as well as the new aesthetics and aesthetic practices (e.g., Matei Calinescu, David Frisby). Those who insist on the practical usefulness of the distinction, however, reserve the concept of modernity (or modernization) for the "process of social and economic development, involving the rise of industry, technology, urbanization, and bureaucratic institutions, that can be traced back as far as the seventeenth century" (Daniel Joseph Singal). So, in broader terms, the history of modernity—as Art Berman, among others, would assert—has in fact become the history of the Enlightenment. Although the term modernism still remains "elusive and protean," as Irving Howe conceded in the 1960s, a consensus seems to be building up that it is, as Singal maintains, "the name of an aesthetic movement inside modernity" and that it "should be properly seen as a culture—a constellation of related ideas, beliefs, values, and modes of perception—that has had a powerful influence on art and thought on both sides of the Atlantic since roughly 1900."[1] This is not to say that precursors of modernism are not to be found by literary and art historians among thinkers, artists, and writers long before the beginning of the twentieth century, wherever and whenever an effort could be observed to create art that challenged the "certainties that had supported traditional modes of social organization, religion, and morality, and also traditional ways of conceiving the human self."[2]

It can also be assumed that only after a clearer differentiation between the terms "modernity" and "modernism" is achieved and established can a study of the relationship between the two concepts be of any value. Astradur Eysteinsson in 1990 warned against "positioning modernism parallel to the tumultuous aspects of modernity," as that could "lead to an unproductive view of its semiotic practices"; Berman in 1994 pointed to social, philosophical, and at times even political tensions that might emerge from a lack of terminological distinction. Surveying its history, we must see that even if modernism can be perceived as a part, if not a product or an advocate, of modernity, still, in the course of time, the modernist artist can also become its critic and adversary. "Modernism accuses modernity of shortsightedness, of which modernism is the overcoming," Berman believes. He continues in his critical rumination: "Modernity had failed to recognize its limitations, its intellectual onesidedness; overcoming this deficiency is both to rectify modernity and to accelerate it. Modernism is modernity's deconstruction of itself . . . Modernism intends . . . not to become a rescuing alternative to modernity, but rather a component of it, its informing structure."[3]

More-comprehensive views of the relationship between progress in the modern world (and also the lack of it, or the threats that appear as the unwanted consequences or side effects of "progress") and the developments of modernist aesthetics offer a meaningful historical perspective allowing, among other things, an ideological investigation that discerns within the modernist movement trends tending toward the political Right or Left; such scrutiny may also assist ways of seeing cultural policies as more distinctly elitist on the one hand and populist on the other. In addition, occasionally attempted chronological divisions of the modernist history into stages such as early modernism, mid-modernism, high modernism, late modernism, and neomodernism may have prompted the sudden leap of some critics into the uncertainty and vagueness of postmodernism (sometimes as a result of their own uncertainty and vagueness); but the introduction of a temporal—that is, historical—aspect could also have made such a leap in the line of development more convincing.[4]

The modernist and postmodernist discourse of modernism as a phenomenon either "outside of history" or "within history" continues; modernism can still be viewed as a product of adversary culture and an aesthetics of subversion and also as a cultural force already assimilated in the environment of commercialism; it can be perceived as a purely aesthetic project and also as an avant-garde political or politicized agency. And there is reason to believe that such debates will go on for years and decades as both modernism and modernist criticism move along with and, often simultaneously, turn against the changes of social, economic, intellectual, and spiritual conditions in the world generally and in specific societies in particular. Although modernism has admittedly become a tradition, it still seems to be able to retain the power of reacting against conformism and conventionalization.

After all, the mission of the modern is as much a rejection of the old as it is an advocacy of the new. According to Stephen Spender, the modern (i.e., the modernist) artist "with his sensibility is committed to the present; with his intellect he is committed to criticizing that present by applying to it his realization of the past."[5] But it became apparent in the course of the twentieth century that the past to be used was often a selective past: a part that was "usable" at one moment and for some artists could become "unusable" later and for others.[6]

In his attempt to define American modernism, Daniel Joseph Singal, like Malcolm Bradbury or James McFarlane, stressed the modernists' rebellion against Victorianism, against the representation of human thought, feelings, and behavior predominantly in rationally conventionalized ways—a rebellion against the rigid categorization of people and societies, especially as far as class, gender, and race were concerned. Indeed, the modernist efforts at the turn of the twentieth century and in its first decades did aim at challenging established categories and breaking dead rules and lines of demarcation in the social and intellectual world as well as in the arts. "What all these various manifestations of Modernism had in common was a passion not only for opening the self to new levels of experience, but also for fusing together disparate elements of that experience into new and original 'wholes,' to the point where one can speak of an 'integrative mode' as the basis of the new culture. Put simply, the quintessential aim of the Modernists has been to reconnect all that the Victorian moral dichotomy tore asunder."[7] Spender also observed that "the modern tends to see life as a whole and hence in modern conditions to condemn it as a whole."[8] It may be worth a reminder that the modernist tendency in the arts to reexamine conventional "wholeness"—thus breaking it into fragments—and to attempt a new integration, a modern and modernist reintegration of the individual's existence and of the society, had also been manifestly informed by the developments and discoveries in the world of scientific knowledge and understanding, involving disciplines ranging from psychology and physiology to physics and sociology.

But was such a program of *novel integration*, which may have sprung from modern minds in America at the turn of the century, a generally desired and a feasible goal, especially in its larger cultural and, above all, social implications? Was the common awareness comprehensive and deep enough to even register what, for instance, integration in the pluralistic society would really amount to; how such a process would be implemented and realized; and who the actors in its unavoidable drama would be? Obviously, even if the modernist claims of an integrative intent were true and sincere, the social scene was hardly ready at the beginning of the twentieth century, and, in fact, neither were the cultural sensitivity and civic mentality of American society mature enough for such dramatic changes.[9] The reality was that "notwithstanding his global ambitions and instinct for domestic reform, [Theodore] Roosevelt remained, as did most of genteel America, thoroughly committed to Victorian values and ideals."[10]

After all, it could not be entirely accidental that artists and young people with modernist feelings and agendas felt "lost" at home. Some of them were not ready to accept the officially pursued or advertised values and tended to leave the United States in the early decades of the century to join temporarily, and a few for the rest of their lives, the modernist activities, groups, and quarters in Europe, above all in Paris and London. After their arrival in the Old World, quite frequently they themselves became decisive players in the modernist scenarios there, as the illustrious examples of such writers in the realm of "high culture" as Ezra Pound, T. S. Eliot, and Gertrude Stein show. But other Americans too made their mark on European modern culture and modernist movements, not even giving up their Americanness as the former ones may have done: They included jazz musicians such as Louis Armstrong and Duke Ellington, dancer Josephine Baker, and fascinating silent comedians from the early Hollywood motion pictures. It is true that within official cultural circles in the United States at the turn of the century, such a role in and effect of American artists on the Old World could hardly be expected, understood, or even wished for; the reactions from Europe must have reflected similar confusion, because the "custodians of culture did not want art to mirror the present but to express permanence and continuity." For official artists, art "was a force for cohesive social ideals, a purveyor of the certitude that seemed lacking in a world that was undergoing extensive economic expansion and social change."[11] It was only later that it became clearer and could be accepted that "America is synonymous with the modern" and "American culture is in the present, in the NOW," as Nathan Huggins put it after he analyzed the uneasy relationship of the (lacking) cultural traditions and the optimistic openness toward the future that are characteristic of American society of our time.[12]

And indeed the rapid technological progress, industrial development, and efficiency that made America gradually more self-confident and attractive at the dawn of the twentieth century could not continue within the old order, or, rather, what was believed to be the order. So, the fact that America could not make a big jump into its modern and a newly integrated self all at once does not mean that in reality the process of integration, the very modern course of Americanization, was not already underway in the United States at the turn of the century. How could it not be with the migration of thousands of black people from the rural south to the urban north, and with masses of immigrants from the Continent pouring into the country every month through the New World's entrance gate at Ellis Island and under the shadow, and the still inviting and encouraging look, of the Statue of Liberty? Like the majority of Americans, these people wanted to partake in the democratic promise of the country and to become its successful citizens, that is, Americans, enjoying the political and material fruits of democracy and industrial development and even claiming loyalty to the founding principles of the nation. Only if unsuccessful and disappointed could and did the people, above all the newcomers, rebel and protest. In any case, whether planned or not, the increasingly mobile and pluralistic population, and what it brought about, evidently became part and parcel of the phenomenon of modernity, if not at times its driving force.

Looking back at the beginning of the twentieth century today, it must be rather disappointing to observe that disproportionately little of the social and cultural experience of the U.S. melting pot was perceived by the mainstream modernist community as particularly modern, or even interesting. Yet, the experience was clearly an exciting feature typical of the modern times—change of country, of place, of home, of language and lifestyle, and of identity, which was sometimes accompanied by changes of name and even of appearance. Mobility, movement, journeys, uprooting, passing, becoming . . . all these manifestations of change brought about by modernity naturally became the subject matter of artistic works produced by minority artists who, however, were regularly, and also by the then-current definition of art and literature, considered parochial, provincial, and marginal. Or nonexistent.[13] As a matter of fact, it took the country a good part of the century to fully realize and meaningfully interpret not only its own history—that is, the history of all the people, those who had already been Americans and also those who were only to join the nation, the people who had the authority of power and property and those who were, often painfully, struggling to step out of the limitations of second-class or even third-class citizenship—but also the very process by which American society was being transformed.

From the vantage point granted to us by the close of the century, we can note as exceptionally relevant in the acquisition of a historical awareness the decades of the 1920s and the 1960s. And it is indeed telling that these two periods proved seminal as well in the development of American modernism. Although it was not fully recognized at the time and in the years following that the decade known as the Jazz Age could have been named so for weightier reasons than the voguish choice of the Lost Generation, the very fact that it was called after jazz was of great cultural and social importance. The rise of the New Negro after World War I became and remained a historical reality, if not for immediate then definitely for later critical considerations. It was, however, only forty years later, during the times of the human rights and civil rights movements, that the relevance of the Harlem or Negro Renaissance, as a manifestation of the growing visibility and the emerging strength of a hyphenated American culture, was fully acknowledged and began to be better understood as a base that could be fruitfully developed and built upon. "Given all the factors in the dialectical construction of canonical 'modernism' and 'modernist' literary criticism within the academy . . . , it should not be surprising that the Harlem Renaissance writers have only recently begun to be considered modernists," admits the literary historian George Hutchinson in his important monograph on that cultural phenomenon.[14]

This being so, we may ask whether such belated appreciation of the national cultural history was not to some extent related to too much focus being turned on the European modernist scene, which consequently led America to a feeling of immaturity and even an undue inferiority complex concerning the arts. Such feelings were expressed not only in the phenomenon of the exiling of American artists to England, France, Italy, and other places in the Old World but also, more important, in the general state of critical thinking in the country. Nathan Huggins spoke of America's "problematic relationship with the modern." As "American critics and custodians of culture were, in their own concept, 'provincials' to a European culture," they measured themselves and their art by a European yardstick and "looked to Europe for their guide."[15] When examining the history of modernism it was not, of course, just legitimate but also reasonable and justified to take into serious account the significance of European thinkers from Friedrich Nietzsche to Max Weber, Sigmund Freud, and Henri Bergson and of scientists such as Albert Einstein, as well as the impact of artists such as Charles Baudelaire, Franz Kafka, James Joyce, Pablo Picasso, Albert Camus, and many more. It is also possible and necessary to define national modernism in reference to the thought of William James, John Dewey, Randolph Bourne, Franz Boas, and Margaret Mead, among others, just as it is vital and fair to consider the influence of artists ranging from Henry James, T. S. Eliot, Ezra Pound, and Gertrude Stein to Eugene O'Neill, William Faulkner, and Langston Hughes. The welcoming appreciation of the American modern reality and modernist culture in European cities certainly boosted the self-confidence of American artists in the 1920s and 1930s, and the early Nobel Prizes awarded to Americans sanctioned their achievements with authority. But it has been, one dares say, the reverse traffic in the art community, namely the frequent movement of European modernist artists to the United States since the late 1930s, that put the final seal on the recognition of the modernist performance of American arts and culture. While it is true that the first massive wave of European modernist architects, painters, musicians, filmmakers, and writers crossed the Atlantic in order to escape the threats and dangers of Nazism, the ingression continued even after the war ended—both from countries in a liberated and free Europe and, whenever possible, from those locked behind the Iron Curtain. Now, at the beginning of a new century, it seems fair and safe to claim that very few modern European artists have not been at least tempted to make the transatlantic trip, and many did. A significant number stayed and actively contributed to the making of American culture, whose relevance and modern nature is no longer doubted on either side of the Atlantic, or anywhere else.

In the spring of 1999 the Whitney Museum of American Art in New York opened the first part of an exhibition of national art and culture from the period 1900–2000. It was boldly called *The American Century*. The organizers—the chairman of Intel, Andrew S. Grove, and the director of the Whitney Museum, Maxwell L. Anderson—did not try to hide their belief that the title should express their own conviction that the American nation did indeed guide the world into the twentieth century, as Henry Luce believed it should and would as early as 1941. This received wisdom concerns American world and global leadership not just in science and technology but in culture and the arts as well. The exhibition indeed offers a fascinating survey of the dynamics of American modernity and modernism; it presents convincingly the products of artistic creation of the first five decades from across America's pluralistic society and reflects quite adequately the very process of Americanization. Visitors could realize more fully than ever before the close and undeniable interrelatedness of this culturally pluralistic society, and in this sense the exhibition may be perceived as a critical judgment opposing the biased or insufficient recognition of distinctive cultural minorities and their contributions to the "mainstream," or, more precisely, their cocreative efforts in defining and establishing American pluralistic culture. But the exhibition may also be read as an argument with the current policies and practice of multiculturalism, which can stress the differences and even borders between American ethnically generated or marked cultures in a rather politicized and therefore somewhat counterproductive way.[16]

It is exactly in the process and even in the aftermath of gradual integration of racial and ethnic groups that the American society can give an important lesson, based both on positive and negative experiences, to the rest of the world, and, above all, to the European continent. When Chantal Mouffe writes that modern citizenship was formulated in a way that played a crucial role in the emergence of modern democracy but has become an obstacle to making it wider and more pluralistic, the deficit mentioned is, no doubt, smaller in the United States than it is in the countries of Western or Eastern Europe, where a political community viewed as "a diverse collection of communities, as a forum for creating unity without denying specificity," will remain a state of affairs hardly achievable in the foreseeable future, above all in the so-called new democracies.[17]

Acceptance of the idea that the twentieth century was the American century does not, therefore, depend on technological achievements only; the course of Americanization as the creation of a nation, or even better, the lesson to learn from the creation of a pluralistic or multicultural society, is of equal if not greater relevance for the country and for the world at large. Du Bois's clear-sighted deliberation over "the color line" as the problem of the twentieth century appears even more justified a prophecy and warning for the twenty-first. Importantly, though quite belatedly and reluctantly, it is has been admitted and the view has been embraced that the realm of the arts has been a powerful agent in the process of shaping American pluralism and deciding what it should be.

It is the premise of this volume that so-called high modernism, as traditionally understood, was not the only valuable reaction of the arts and artists to changes introduced in America by modernity at the beginning of the twentieth century and amplified in subsequent decades. These essays intend to further open up and dispute the uneasy relationship of modernity and modernism with the reality of American cultural diversity and plural ethnicity; it is believed that as-yet unaddressed or unresolved issues do surface in such a discourse, both of a rather general and of a more particular nature that might result from critical treatments of specific authors or specific texts.

Jerrold Hirsch's essay, "T. S. Eliot, B. A. Botkin, and the Politics of Cultural Representation: Folklore, Modernity, and Pluralism," offers a meaningful confrontation of Eliot's skepticism about ethnic pluralism, which the author of *The Waste Land* and "Tradition and the Individual Talent" could see only as a vulgar threat to the Western tradition and its purity, while Botkin optimistically welcomed ethnic diversity as a cultural force and a new hope for American literature and culture to come. The views of these two critics and poets, though different to the point of mutual exclusiveness—one trusting formal literary traditions, the other believing in the power of rural as well as urban folklore—are still justified with respect to their claim to modernism as an artistic mode of expression.

For Botkin, and for some others as well, it was logical to see Jewish immigrants and African Americans as two *American* characters sharing the modern human condition of homelessness and rootlessness. And during the Harlem Renaissance it must have become evident that African Americans would be destined to play in the United States the role of the representative or model minority artist, and also that the entitlement to such a role would be given by the artistic performance and by the behavior of the black artist as much as by the way black art would be perceived and evaluated in mainstream society.

When Alain Locke saw the productive influence of "primitive" African art on European modernists in the early decades of our century, he announced to the young African American artists: "By being modern, we are being African." But Nathan Huggins, from the vantage point of 1988, saw the situation in the following way: "For the Afro-American in the 1920s, being a 'New Negro' was being 'modern.' And being a 'New Negro' meant, largely, not being an 'Old Negro,' disassociating oneself from the symbols and legacy of slavery—being urbane, assertive, militant. Abandoning dialect and the signs of submissiveness in the literature was one way of being a 'New Negro.'"[18] Abandon the signs of submissiveness quite a few of the writers and artists in the Harlem Renaissance did, but Huggins still found in his pioneering assessment the artistic results of the whole movement rather unconvincing because they were marked and limited by the authors' ethnic provincialism. Younger critics, especially David Levering Lewis, Houston A. Baker Jr., Henry Louis Gates Jr., and George Hutchinson, have viewed the crop and the whole phenomenon of the Harlem Renaissance more favorably, though each for different reasons and from a different perspective and vision of both African American and American culture.[19] It is also against the background of a number of interpretations and evaluations of the Harlem Renaissance by some of the critical authorities that the essays in this volume dealing with literary and cultural figures and issues related to that period have been written.

Werner Sollors, himself an established critical authority on issues of ethnicity, pluralism, and modern culture and literature, in his essay "Four Types of Writing under Modern Conditions; or, Black Writers and 'Populist Modernism,'" illustrates a whole range of formal combinations available to American writers who wanted to take a stand on modern changes in society and points out the obvious tendency of African Americans to challenge various imposing social conventions, even though this was not always expressed in modernist terms. Here Berman's maxim that "worldview is not simply placed inside form; worldview is equivalent to form" would be worth a theoretical confrontation.[20] Indeed, this is illustrated by Claude McKay and his use of the conventional sonnet form to express radical and "racialized," that is, Americanized, thought and mood. The essay by Heather Hathaway, "Exploring 'Something New': The 'Modernism' of Claude McKay's *Harlem Shadows*," demonstrates that the personal freedom of choosing his literary form seemed to be for the poet as strong an argument as the choice itself; it was obviously not just a purely literary matter. The poet's move from a rural Jamaican village to an urban—and very modern—American environment radically shaped his creative process.

James Smethurst, in his essay "The Strong Men Gittin' Stronger: Sterling Brown's *Southern Road* and the Representation and Re-Creation of the Southern Folk Voice," presents another challenge to the traditional distinction between modernism and antimodernism. Brown' s manly, southern, rural, racial, and folk-inspired verse is convincingly characterized as "deeply radical and deeply conservative"—an example of modernist criticism leveled at modernism itself, especially when the poet understood and was suspicious of the movement as an advocate of urban life and an agent of mass culture that tended to acquire the genuine cultural products of the Negro and reduces them to commodities. The internal polemic within the community of African American writers and artists, namely the disagreeing attitudes of Sterling Brown and Langston Hughes toward black urban and rural culture and toward black folklore and jazz, mirrored the complexity of the sometimes rather strangely entangled aesthetic, cultural, political, and ideological disputes of the day.

"Waldo Frank, Jean Toomer, and the Critique of Racial Voyeurism" by Dan Terris shifts the focus to the more programmatic affinity of modernism and ethnicity as it emerged in the critical thought and creative work of Waldo Frank and Jean Toomer. The friendly relationship between the two writers, who considered themselves and were regarded by others as "high modernists," manifested their shared commitment to experimentation with style and literary forms and their interest in the southern environment, above all in the southern Negro, as an alternative to the "chaos of industrialism"; but the relationship also confirmed its vulnerable sensitivity in racial issues. Both Frank and Toomer were ready to employ and exploit the condition of black life in the American south as a metaphor, and they did so in their *Holiday* and *Cane*, respectively, but they naturally differed in the scope and depth of knowledge of the environment and familiarity with its culture; they both craved spiritual wholeness, but the moment of real discord appeared in their views of the prospects of ethnic and racial integration in America.

A different way of looking at the phenomenon of American modernism is to recognize how vital "other" elements were for its formation. Lynn Weiss, in her "'Among Negroes': Gertrude Stein and African America," investigates the influence of African American culture on Stein's writing, and most notably on her short story "Melanctha." As American cultural history can confirm, the experience of expatriatism (Stein left the United States for Paris in 1904) often provided impetus for a re-vision of the American cultural and literary landscape. For Stein, the elements of "otherness" presented by African America served as a catalytic agent and creative force in the emergence of a modernist awareness.

Jeffrey Melnick similarly explores cross-ethnic influences of modern writing in his essay, "A Black Man in Jewface." A memoir of a black musician written in an "as-told-to" form and style serves Melnick as the basis for his thoughtful account of the subject of cross-ethnic collaboration. African American and Jewish relations and interactions all through the century present an exciting and complex chapter in the history of Americanization, in the conquest of modernity in social terms and the expansion of modernism in the world of culture. While taking us through Willie the Lion Smith's own grounds for his connections to Jews and Judaism, which were reportedly genealogical, commercial, and mystical, Melnick touches upon a number of instances of fruitful cooperation between the two largest and most visible American ethnic minorities. At the same time, and unavoidably, he opens as well both the real and invented questions concerning the problems of appropriation of materials from black culture—that is, the problem of alleged cultural thefts, which is pertinent above all in the realm of music. Nevertheless, he demonstrates that despite possible tensions, jazz and later also popular music happened to be a productive meeting place of blacks and Jews whose collaboration contributed to the constitution of one of the most successful American cultural products.

Collaboration can lead to a form of cultural hybridity, as Adam Newton shows in his essay, "*Incognito ergo sum*: Riding or Passing under the Sign of the Hyphen in Cahan, Johnson, Larsen, and Yezierska,"—and this is a hybridity not simply of aesthetics but of identity. Offering a close reading of five texts by four ethnic authors—two Jews and two African Americans, two men and two women—Newton illustrates how various writers have presented the ordeals of the "hyphenization" of ethnic Americans. In the language of a postmodern critical discourse, Newton analyzes in his carefully chosen texts (all of them with some autobiographical elements) the presentation of "the modern burden of double consciousness" and elaborates on William Boelhower's opinion that in the socially imposed processes of self-identification, self-recognition, and self-definition by ethnic Americans, the issue "is not ethnicity *per se* but the *uses* of ethnicity in a post-industrial society."

Rachel Rubin, in her essay "A Jewish New World in Jacob Glashteyn's 'Sheeny Mike,'" takes us in another direction by considering the costs of modernity for ethnic Americans. Rubin suggests in this essay that, on one level, modernity has also brought crime. The essay concentrates on a long poem about a Jewish gangster and his death, written in Yiddish in 1929 by an immigrant from Russian Poland. To Rubin, Glatshteyn's literary performance offers a ground for metaliterary investigation into gangster literature of the Old World (such as Isaac Babel's stories featuring Benya Krik) and in America (such as Fitzgerald, Mike Gold, and Daniel Fuchs); it also inspires comments on anti-Semitic literary and social stereotyping and thought on the place of the Jew in modern American literature. As an interesting footnote, her essay suggests that immigrants from Europe acquainted with early avant-garde movements speeded up the emergence of modernist thought and sensibility in America in the early decades of the century.

Alessandro Portelli, in his essay, "Beware of Signs; or, How to Tell the Living from the Dead: Orality and Writing in the World of Pedro Pietri," focuses on the issue of multilinguistic and multicultural interaction in the Puerto Rican community of East Harlem. He explores the relevance of orality in its traditional and electronic modes and the essentiality of sound in modern poetry; he evaluates Pietri's "speaking" poems and urban immigrant poetry vehicles of expressing the "broken English dream"—not without a reminiscence of broken, thwarted or deferred dreams in other minority groups in America. Pietri's proclaimed kinship to Langston Hughes and the beats only enhances the message comprised in Josef Jařab's two interviews (from 1989 and 1993) with Allen Ginsberg, entitled "When All Met Together in One Room," in which the leading poet of the beat generation confesses to the influence that African American music and creativity had on "liberalization" of American poetics and consciousness in the decades following World War II, and in which he expresses his belief that rock-and-roll culture greatly contributed to the end of the cold war and the fall of the communist totalitarian regimes in Central and Eastern Europe. The implication of Ginsberg's viewpoint is that modern American poetry and literature in general are not necessarily rooted in "high modernism," but may come as well from the sources and forces generated by American society's ethnic diversity.

The concluding essay, "Centralizing the Marginal: Prolegomena to a Study of Boundaries in Contemporary African American Fiction," by Fritz Gysin, presents a sociological, psychological, and anthropological understanding of the phenomena of ethnic and racial boundaries as creations of the complex and dynamic process of Americanization. The author contemplates boundaries as proof of conspicuous and vital changes brought about by modernity; he distinguishes a variety of boundaries as reactions to and products of political conditions in the United States, that is, of political arrangements in society at large or of implementation of political strategies of an ethnic or racial community. Gysin then attempts to relate individual boundaries to particular artistic paradigms in works of contemporary fiction by African America writers of both modernist and postmodernist aesthetics. From his essay, as well as from the volume in its entirety, it should be evident that although ethnicity was hardly considered an element of any vitality and relevance in the beginning of the century and was only recognized even as marginal just a few decades ago, there can hardly be any doubt of its centrality in multicultural America today, and in any discourse concerned with the development of modernity and modernism in the country.

■ NOTES

1. Matei Calinescu, *Faces of Modernity: Avant-Garde, Decadence, Kitsch* (Bloomington: Indiana University Press, 1977); David Frisby, *Fragments of Modernity: Theories of Modernity in the Work of Simmel, Kracauer, and Benjamin* (Cambridge, Mass.: MIT Press, 1986); Daniel Joseph Singal, "Towards a Definition of American Modernism," *American Quarterly* 39 (Spring 1987): 7–8; Art Berman, *Preface to Modernism* (Urbana: University of Illinois Press, 1994), 7, viii; Irving Howe, ed., *Literary Modernism* (Greenwich, Conn.: Fawcett Publications, 1967), 12.

2. M. H. Abrams, *A Glossary of Literary Terms*, 7th ed. (New York: Harcourt Brace, 1999), 167.

3. Astradur Eysteinsson, *The Concept of Modernism* (Ithaca, N.Y.: Cornell University Press, 1990), 6; Berman, *Preface to Modernism,* 7–8.

4. Berman, *Preface to Modernism,* chaps. 2, 3, and 8; Frederick R. Karl, *Modern and Modernism: The Sovereignty of the Artist, 1885–1925* (New York: Atheneum, 1985). Karl considers postmodernism "more a term or tag than a movement"; in his view, it is an evolution from modernism, "solidly based on the practices we have associated with Modernism for almost one hundred years" (401). More radical periodizations of modernism may interpret postmodernism not as a continuation, as the latest stage of the movement, but rather as an aftermath of a crisis of both the modern world and modernism itself, which still does not mean that modernism and postmodernism are being necessarily pitted against each other. Cf. Henry A. Giroux, ed., *Postmodernism, Feminism, and Cultural Politics: Redrawing Educational Boundaries* (Albany: State University of New York Press, 1991).

5. Stephen Spender, "Moderns and Contemporaries," in Howe, *Literary Modernism,* 49.

6. Cf. Van Wyck Brooks, *America's Coming of Age* (New York: B. W. Huebsch, 1915); Russell Reising, *The Unusable Past* (New York: Methuen, 1986).

7. Singal, "Towards a Definition," 10–15. Cf. also Malcolm Bradbury and James McFarlane, eds., *Modernism: 1890–1930* (Harmondsworth, England: Penguin, 1976).

8. Spender, "Moderns and Contemporaries," 48.

9. In this respect, it is revealing to compare two novels, John Dos Passos's *The Forty-Second Parallel* and E. L. Doctorow's *Ragtime,* in which both authors cover the history of America in the early twentieth century, to see how awareness of the ethnic reality and of the contribution of ethnic groups to American culture has grown over the decades.

10. Barbara Haskell, *The American Century: Art and Culture, 1900–1950* (New York: Whitney Museum of American Art in association with W. W. Norton, 1999), 11.

11. Ibid.

12. Nathan Irvin Huggins, *Revelations: American History, American Myths* (New York: Oxford University Press, 1995), 159.

13. When as late as 1950 F. O. Matthiessen, a scholar responsible to a great extent for the creation of the American literary canon from the modern viewpoint, put together *The Oxford Book of American Verse,* a volume of more than 1,100 pages that covered a period ranging from Anne Bradstreet to Robert Lowell, he did not find one line by a black poet worthy of inclusion. Although in the introductory essay Vachel Lindsay was praised for his "exciting use of jazz rhythms and the cadences of revival hymns" (xxx), not a single mention is made of Langston Hughes. The situation is similar in the field of thought and ideas: it is truly difficult to imagine today how a critic with as well developed a social sensitivity as Vernon Louis Parrington could write his *Main Currents of American Thought* in 1927 without one reference to Du Bois and his work, especially *The Souls of Black Folk,* to say nothing about other black thinkers, such as Booker T. Washington or Alain Locke.

14. George Hutchinson, *The Harlem Renaissance in Black and White* (Cambridge, Mass.: Harvard University Press, 1995), 118.

15. Huggins, *Revelations,* 158.

16. Cf. Nathan Glazer, *We Are All Multiculturalists Now* (Cambridge, Mass.: Harvard University Press, 1997). The author presents a balanced analysis of multiculturalism and its potentials and threats, above all in the world of American education.

17. Chantal Mouffe, "Toward a Radical Democratic Citizenship," *Democratic Left* 17, no. 2 (1989): 7. As for the present situation in Eastern Europe, cf. Josef Jařab, "Race Relations in Europe and in America," in *Living with America, 1946–1996,* ed. Cristina Giorcelli and Rob Kroes (Amsterdam: VU University Press, 1997), 287–294.

18. Alain Locke, quoted in Henry Louis Gates Jr., "Harlem on Our Minds," in *Rhapsodies in Black: Art of the Harlem Renaissance,* ed. Joanna Skipwith (Berkeley: University of California Press, 1997), 165; Huggins, *Revelations,* 162.

19. Cf. Nathan Irvin Huggins, *Harlem Renaissance* (New York: Oxford University Press, 1971); David Levering Lewis, *When Harlem Was in Vogue* (New York: Knopf, 1981); Houston A. Baker Jr., *Modernism and the Harlem Renaissance* (Chicago: University of Chicago Press, 1987); Henry Louis Gates Jr., "The Trope of a New Negro and the Reconstruction of the Image of the Black," *Representations* 24 (1988): 129–155; Hutchinson, *Harlem Renaissance in Black and White.*

20. Berman, *Preface to Modernism,* 28.

T. S. Eliot, B. A. Botkin, and
the Politics of Cultural Representation

Folklore, Modernity, and Pluralism

■

T. S. Eliot (1888–1965) and B. A. Botkin (1901–1975). What can be the purpose of juxtaposing these two individuals, the former the most famous of twentieth-century poets, the latter a folklorist unfamiliar to most readers? Readers who recognize Botkin's name—probably as the author of a series of popular folklore treasuries—will still no doubt wonder about the purpose of such a seemingly awkward contrast. Few are likely to know Botkin began his career as a poet interested in folklore. And those who know some biographical data about these two figures, one the descendant of an old New England family, the other a child of Jewish immigrants from Lithuania, will probably find the idea of discussing them together even more puzzling. By background and choice, Botkin represented much of what Eliot detested about modernity—although it is unlikely Eliot knew about Botkin. Botkin, however, like all poets writing in the English language after the publication of *The Waste Land* (1922), thought about Eliot.

Eliot's family could trace its origins to New England ancestors who were merchants and ministers, and beyond that back to England. Botkin, born in Boston in 1901, wrote that he knew nothing about his ancestors except that they were Lithuanian Jews. Eliot, born in St. Louis in 1888, was part of a firmly established American family that had worked its way into the geographical heart of the country. From there, Eliot, an insider, would work his way out of American culture, back to Europe. Harvard, which Eliot attended from 1906 to 1909, was a stepping-stone in that direction. For Botkin, an outsider, Harvard, which he attended from 1916 to 1920, was a way of entering America. From Harvard he moved deeper into the provincial heart of the country. In 1921 he accepted a position in the English department at the University of Oklahoma. In 1937, when he received a Rosenwald fellowship to study southern and black folklore, he made the journey back from the provinces. He headed not for Europe, but for the Library of Congress in the nation's capital; he was ready to try to reconcile provincialism and cosmopolitanism, romantic nationalism and cultural pluralism. In 1938 he became the folklore editor of the New Deal's Federal Writers' Project (FWP).[1]

There are ways in which Eliot, like Botkin, was also a cultural outsider, a marginal figure. Growing up in the Midwest, Eliot later wrote, he felt like a displaced New Englander and during the summers he spent in New England he felt like a displaced Midwesterner. Nevertheless, he always thought of New England as his ancestral home. He seems to have found the progression over several generations of family history from Puritanism to Unitarianism altogether unappealing. We know from his letters and the early poems that he found neither Harvard nor genteel Boston intellectually or personally satisfying. He tried to find in Boston's poorer neighborhoods what was missing from the circles in which he usually moved, but, writes his biographer Lyndall Gordon, "Eliot . . . found that as life-destroying as the well to do Boston Squares." The early poems confirm that he was repelled by the kind of neighborhoods Botkin was growing up in. The Jews and the Irish—"Bleistein with a cigar" and "apeneck Sweeney"—figure as representatives of vulgar and threatening developments in urban civilization. As much as the manners of polite society, modernist form, particularly in the work of Henry James and T. S. Eliot, either dismissed individuals and groups in a state of transition between cultures as vulgar or treated them in a formal context that separated them from the social context that shaped their lives. According to Gordon, Eliot's attitude toward the urban world was well established before World War I.[2]

Psychologically and physically Eliot removed himself from America. He could find no useful tradition, no usable past, no folklore in his native land—consider that the terms are somewhat interchangeable. In England, as Geoffrey Hartman puts it, Eliot "armed himself with the received past: established religion, classical art, conservative politics." In 1927 Eliot declared himself "Anglo-Catholic in religion, royalist in politics, and classicist in literature." By definition such loyalties could not include America. In many ways, there was nothing particularly new about Eliot's choice. It placed him as part of a "tradition" of American artists who complained about the lack of received tradition, as opposed to those who celebrated an art and nation in the process of becoming, a culture and a vision to be achieved.[3]

Neither Eliot nor Botkin seemed to have had a well-defined sense of homeplace. Botkin recalled that "since we moved almost every time [my father moved his shop], I never sank my roots into any one of our four home towns"—but unlike Eliot, Botkin would portray himself as someone comfortable with that situation. In Harvard English classes Botkin wrote about the immigrant Boston world he knew. His "Autobiography of a Boy" was full of vignettes of vital urban folkways. He was especially interested in the folklore of children and the folk life and lore of the various ethnic and occupational groups he had come into contact with. He was placing himself in creative relationship to the diverse folk among whom he grew up.[4]

By all accounts, it would have been difficult for an Eastern European Jew like Botkin to attend Harvard without experiencing some form of discrimination. Still, Harvard seems to have opened up new vistas. It is difficult to imagine Botkin longing for some of the things that Henry James and Eliot missed in America. A country with no established church, no real feudal heritage, and no real aristocratic tradition seemed a land of promise to Jewish immigrants. Botkin graduated on the eve of a change of admissions policy determined to lower the number of Jewish students, a reflection of a resurgent nativism that characterized the 1920s.[5]

Botkin later recalled that he was influenced by the Harvard professor George Lyman Kittredge, a Shakespeare and ballad scholar, and that undergraduate papers he wrote on Wordsworth and Carl Sandburg had had a major influence on his thinking about the importance of the vernacular in poetry, about how to create a poetic language for the twentieth century. The juxtaposition of Wordsworth and Sandburg suggests Botkin saw the Chicago poet as carrying out and modifying Wordsworth's ideas. Wordsworth advocated creating a new poetic language out of the life and speech of the lowly and rustic. Sandburg intended to include rural and urban-industrial America. Botkin's interest in questions about poetic language and modern life was tied up from the beginning with the politics of cultural representation.[6]

Eliot and Botkin represent contradictory approaches to the dilemmas of defining the meaning of tradition in an America rapidly being changed by the growth of cities and mass immigration. "In these circumstances," Marcus Klein argues, "'tradition' secured a peculiar importance, both for those who wanted to reclaim a privilege [Eliot's situation] and for those who wanted for the first time in their American history to claim a status [Botkin's situation]. In a time of rapid changes, rapid degradations, 'tradition,' was a metaphor for place in the world."[7]

Eliot's particular dilemma was that he found the establishment from which he came as shallow as he found the new Americans filling the cities vulgar. For makers of the modern movement such as Eliot, Klein points out, "it was another cause of their exile that their country had been invaded, occupied, and culturally ravaged by barbarians." Eliot was a key figure in a variety of literary modernism that, in the face of momentous social change, asserted, in effect, that white Protestants "still owned and could defend civilization" against Sweeney and Bleistein, emblematic figures of the decline of the West in Eliot's poetry. Writers like Botkin "were no less exiles of course, than Ezra Pound and T. S. Eliot, et alia, but they were exiled in the opposite direction [for] they were likely to have become exiles from home [the ghettoes created by mass immigration], such as it was, as soon as they had individually conceived of literary ambitions in America."[8]

The response of writers such as Botkin to a modernist literature that regarded them and theirs as a vulgar rabble that would despoil "our cultural heritage" was, Klein insists, to conceive of "a field full of Sweeneys and Bleisteins" as "the folk." The idea of the folk allowed non-WASP writers to subvert the conventional hierarchy, for the folk could "be seen *almost* by definition to be the same thing as the idea of democracy, which later was the *American* 'tradition' if anything was." For Botkin, redefining the term "folk" to embrace American diversity and the new America of cities and factories, as well as the older rural areas, became a lifelong project. In the 1920s and 1930s, Botkin and Eliot were both part of a discourse about the politics of cultural representation.[9]

By comparing and contrasting the careers and views of this seemingly odd couple, it is possible to call attention to the relationship between attitudes toward the folk and folklore and the development of literary modernism. In an American context, attitudes regarding folklore are tied up with views of ethnicity and race, and of urbanization and industrialization. Eliot and Botkin were responding to a set of issues that defined a community of discourse in which they both participated. Botkin's poetry spoke to issues similar to those Eliot addressed, and Botkin's theories about poetry, literature, and the relationship between the individual and tradition, and between tradition and modernity, reveal Eliot's influence, although Botkin arrived at positions very different from Eliot's. Comparing Eliot's and Botkin's ideas reveals how the different ways of looking at modern culture emerged out of the interaction between biography and history, personal need and social structure, and individual vision and social realities.

In the 1920s and 1930s Eliot and Botkin shared a vocabulary that reveals the common cultural issues that concerned them: fragmentation, integration, tradition, individual, myth, and epic. Alienation and homelessness are emotions and ideas they and other modernists dwelled on. The point is not that they directly influenced each other, but that they were both part of a literary discourse centered around common questions. What is the future of tradition in a modern, industrial, pluralistic, and secular world? What language is appropriate for poetry in such a world? What is the proper relationship between the individual and tradition, between the poet and his or her society, between provincialism and cosmopolitanism? Both Eliot and Botkin were dealing with how to adjust to a world in which awareness of a multiplicity of traditions had reached unprecedented proportions and the necessity of recognizing pluralist diversity was unavoidable. To understand their responses also requires giving attention to such anthropologists and writers as James G. Frazer, Lucien Levy-Bruhl, Franz Boas, Paul Radin, Carl Sandburg, and Ralph Waldo Ellison.

By taking a view of modernism that is not confined to a critical canon of modernist poets, it is possible to see how the realities of pluralism, the growth of cities, the spread of factories, and the discovery of the folk affected the development of both American literature and folklore studies. Thus, it is possible, by pursuing this comparison, to focus on how ideas about the folk and folklore influenced the development of Eliot's poetry and literary and cultural criticism. It is also possible to see how the questions Eliot asked could be answered differently. Eliot wrote so well and with such Olympian detachment in his essays that the answers he gave to the issues he addressed seemed to many inevitable and authoritative. He could, however, also stimulate someone like Botkin to develop different answers to these questions.

Comparing these two figures can contribute not only to a better understanding of each of them, but also to a deeper understanding of the relationship between folklore studies and modernism. It can help open up the discussion of modernism. The effort to narrow the term "modernists" to describe only those who took a despairing and pessimistic attitude toward modern life reflects the temporary triumph of a particular critical view. This effort to canonize a narrow line of twentieth-century poets confuses literary assessments with historical developments. It may have been true in the 1950s, as a reviewer for the *New York Times Book Review* recently put it, that "modernism and T. S. Eliot were in, folk poetry and Carl Sandburg were out."[10] It should now be possible to see that all these poets were responding to the processes of urbanization, industrialization, and secularization that supposedly destroyed the organic wholeness of traditional cultures.

Similarly, a comparison of these two figures should also help open up a discussion of the development of American folklore studies. As an academic field, folklore did not receive independent status in universities before the 1950s, and even today only a handful of universities offer a Ph.D. in folklore. The distinguished American folklorist Richard Dorson lamented that the history of American folklore studies did not offer a rich field of study. He argued that this was because "wayward individuals" were typical figures in the history of American folkloristics. He maintained that British folklore studies offered a richer subject for study than did the history of folklore studies in his own country. He contrasted the existence of permanent national folklore institutions in Britain and other European countries with the situation in the United States, where "for better or worse, the genius of American folklore study has expressed itself in the wayward, individual collector." This, in his view, explained why "the history of American folklore discloses no books of theories, no continuity, no consensus, no high order of polemics . . . for there was not enough of a common platform to lead to disagreement."[11]

The language in which Dorson couched his comparison of the history of British and American folklore studies, as much as the argument itself, suggests a strategy for exploring the relationship between modernism and the discovery of the American folk. Listen carefully and you hear echoes of Henry James on Hawthorne and the problems of the American artist in a country lacking in tradition: "no sovereign, no court . . . no aristocracy, no church, no clergy." In James's view, the situation was "almost ludicrous; one might enumerate the items of high civilization as it exists in other countries which are absent from the texture of American life until it becomes a wonder to know what was left."[12]

When American folklore studies are seen as part of the debate about the nature and possibilities of American culture, and about tradition and modernity, one discovers a high order of polemics. Discontinuity, the absence of strong institutions, and individualism are traits many Americans have held to be central characteristics of their culture. For every Emerson or Whitman celebrating an original relationship to the universe, there has been a Henry James or a Van Wyck Brooks to lament the lack of institutions and traditions. Lamenters as well as celebrators sensed that they had to invent themselves, as in Ezra Pound's awed comment about the young T. S. Eliot, "He has actually trained himself *and* modernized himself *on his own.*"[13]

Kenneth Burke (who was interested in the work of both Eliot and Botkin) has suggested that literary works can be viewed as answers to strategic questions, though they are always more than that. Eliot's essays "Tradition and the Individual Talent" (1919) and "The Metaphysical Poets" (1922) and his poem *The Waste Land* (1922) are key examples of his initial answers to the problem of folklore and modernity. *The Waste Land* works out the social implications of what Eliot first offered as literary history. Botkin worked out his position in reviews of Eliot and other modernists, his essay "The Folk in Literature," and his poems "Hometown" (1930) and "Old Man, What Are You Planting?" (1931). Botkin's response to modernity in literary essays and poetry had social implications that differed radically from Eliot's. During the Great Depression, both Eliot and Botkin grew dissatisfied with their initial positions. Eliot's University of Virginia lectures, published as *After Strange Gods: A Primer of Modern Heresy* (1934), fleshed out the cultural politics of his literary criticism and poetry. Botkin's reformulations were developed in such essays as "The Folk and the Individual: Their Creative Reciprocity" (1938) and in the work he did as folklore editor of the New Deal's Federal Writers' Project.[14]

Literary and anthropological studies of folklore in the early part of this century were dominated by an evolutionary anthropology that viewed folklore as a survival from an earlier culture and largely ignored the contemporary context from which the lore was obtained as scholars tried to use it to reconstruct the past. Creative writers, however, were interested in folklore in relation to contemporary culture. They dealt with modern contexts in which they saw folklore as either dying out, being adapted to changing circumstances, or created to meet new needs, depending on their own personal backgrounds, needs, and visions, and the anthropology they had absorbed. Questions about tradition became increasingly important as modern means of mobility, the scientific questioning of inherited wisdom, and the pace of social change were felt to expand the existential burden of self-definition.

For both Eliot and Botkin, the question of whether the folk and folklore could survive in the modern world was tied up with a host of other political and social issues. Did industrialization and urbanization destroy the agrarian-based myths that had given life wholeness and meaning? Did increasing heterogeneity portend chaotic fragmentation? Was folklore something that modernity was putting behind us or isolating on the margins of civilized life? Were survivals all that remained of past traditions, myths, and folklore? Was the modern pluralistic, urban, industrial world, in which geographic isolation was disappearing and new technological media of communication were developing, antithetical to tradition, myth, and folklore? Writers, unlike scholars locked into particular paradigms, tried to give form to what it was like to experience and to feel these issues as part of the landscape of modern life.

Eliot's positions regarding the individual's relation to tradition and the dissociation between thought and sensibility helped shape literary discussion in the 1920s and 1930s. In "Tradition and the Individual Talent" (1919), Eliot dismissed the romantic identification of poetry with the expression of individual personality and insisted that in the process of creation the writer should be engaged in "a continual surrender of himself as he is at the moment to something which is more valuable." The poetic utterance stood in relationship to the whole tradition that existed simultaneously with it. The new poem took its life from the tradition it was part of at the same time that it altered that tradition.[15]

Here is an argument that, in terms of high culture, parallels one school of thought in the debate over the role of individuality, personality, and community in the creation of folk song. Eliot read steadily in anthropology and frequently reviewed books on comparative religion and ritual behavior. Both Eliot's essay and the folkloristic debate are evidence of a pervasive cultural concern about the individual's role as a bearer of tradition, about how the individual could play such a role in the modern world, if indeed that was possible. His mythic account—in his view it was a historical account—of a seventeenth-century disaster that led to the dissociation between thought and sensibility became equally famous. It is now possible to see that Eliot's thesis was yet another variant on the romantic idea that sometime in the past, before the fall, culture had been a unified whole. It contrasted the world poets now lived in with a previous age when the poet's way of discovering knowledge through the use of symbols had been natural, for in that world symbols were more easily understood and readily employed. As Frank Kermode has pointed out, it is less important whether there was, as "Mr. Eliot's supporters have thought, a particular and far reaching catastrophe in the seventeenth century, than that there was, in the twentieth, an urgent need to establish the historicity of such a disaster." A view of large social issues was implicit in Eliot's essays on literature and part of the warp and woof of his poetry.[16]

In Eliot's *The Waste Land* (1922), wholeness could no longer be restored to a fragmented world. Drawing on the anthropological and literary work of James G. Frazer's *Golden Bough* and Jessie L. Weston's *From Ritual to Romance*, he used such myths as that of the Fisher King and the Grail legend to portray a desolate, spiritually decaying modern world and recounted a kind of aborted hero for a modern anti-epic. The shifting central intelligence that tours aspects of modern life can heal neither itself nor the world, which remains a wasteland. In part Eliot's view of urban culture was shaped by his reliance on an evolutionary anthropology rooted in the intellectual world of the late nineteenth century. Only the fragments of richer older traditions, myths, and lore can survive the transition from an agrarian to an urban world, from a homogeneous society to a heterogeneous society. Eliot later found in orthodox Christian tradition a solution to his despair over the fragmentation he depicted.[17]

Botkin worked out his initial answers to questions similar to those that concerned Eliot not in London, but in Oklahoma. Thinking back on his Oklahoma years, Botkin tried to explain the state's attraction for him: "encountering a different and more vital variety of word and deed, I soon found my Harvard accent and 'indifference' breaking down." Oklahoma was a means of shedding the genteel tradition that Eliot had also found desiccated. In various forums Botkin would promote the idea that the allegedly crude life of the provinces was as culturally significant as the culture that was defined in the words of the Victorian poet Matthew Arnold as "the sum total of the best that had been said and thought in the world."[18]

In his Sunday book reviews in the *Daily Oklahoman*, Botkin hoped "to make Oklahoma culture conscious and Oklahoma conscious (a two fold pioneering)."[19]

His reviews showed a broad interest in world literature and an awareness of contemporary trends. In addition to the poetry of Eliot, he reviewed the work of W. B. Yeats, Robert Frost, William Carlos Williams, Wyndham Lewis, D. H. Lawrence, and Sherwood Anderson.

Botkin brooded over evidence of social disintegration, which he attributed to the impact of modern urban-industrial life and scientific achievements on consciousness. Shared myths that had given societies cultural power had lost much of their earlier force. In Gorham Munson, Herbert Read, and T. S. Eliot, Botkin found writers who shared his concern about the "present disintegration," but not his faith in "the integration of the future."[20]

Botkin was also working out his own attitude toward modern poetry. For Eliot he had a grudging respect and a fundamental dislike. He criticized Eliot in terms that partly reflected his reading of Wordsworth. In his view, Eliot's poetry was "part perverse precocity," and part "burlesque grotesquerie with abortive imagism and symbolism at its starting point and mirthless satire as its goal." Botkin objected to "the recondite vocabulary [and] euphuistic circumlocutions." And he wanted no part of what he saw as "the monstrous gestation of a blighted expressionistic philosophy of disintegration and disenchantment," although he did not disagree with Eliot about the present disintegration. "Civilization," Botkin wrote in one of his reviews, "has cut our consciousness into 1,000 wriggling fragments, and science, education, and industry are threatening us with a complete disintegration of the spirit." Botkin longed for both integration and enchantment and had not given up the romantic idea that modern man could work his way forward toward his lost integrity, toward the world as it was before self-consciousness and modernization, before the fall. By looking to folk culture, he insisted, it was possible to find a "unifying and enlarging voice."[21]

Botkin's book reviews reflect his definition of modernism and his attitudes toward the opportunities and dilemmas developments in the literature of the 1920s offered writers. He displayed an ambivalent attitude toward the decade's avant-garde writings, though he was aware of and intrigued by such experiments as the use of theatrical masks and by the deliberate blurring of the distinction between prose and poetry. He had reservations, however, about experiments that "deliberately cultivate difficulty." At times, he thought, "the craftsmanship [of contemporary literary experiments] is far out of proportion to the content"; "experiment and revolt have tended to be standardized, and convention rules our magazine poets with an iron hand." A result of standardized experimentation was that often "the depth of the product varies in inverse proportion to its deftness." For Botkin, Van Wyck Brooks, Lewis Mumford, and Paul Rosenfeld were all "distinguished modernists" whose *American Caravan* volumes, therefore, always contained a "high degree of experiment in both form and content."[22]

Botkin noted that as the 1920s were coming to a close, more and more writers were expressing dissatisfaction with their relation to society and were searching for unifying myths. But he often rejected the proposed solutions. He found Gorham Munson's suggestion that writers turn to the *Mahabharata* as a "new source" fantastic and considered Herbert Read's emphasis on "the literature of the music hall" to be "as fanciful" as Munson's. These and similar suggestions Botkin regarded "as symbol of a growing folk consciousness in art, the ways and means of which must be worked out from the bottom up rather than the top down."[23]

Botkin did not look to the aesthetic achievements of foreign cultures for ways to create unifying myths for his own culture, nor did he look to popular culture—though he found evidence of folk influence in popular culture. It was not in the life and art of an American folk, but in America's diverse folk groups, that he thought the basis for individual and national integration could be found. In the 1920s Botkin began to work out his position that diverse American folk groups had both contributed to and constituted material for a national literature. A national literature, in his view, had to reflect American diversity. Such a literature could serve as both a sign and a promoter of democracy. He was unhappy with either a genteel or a purely experimental writing that did not seek to broaden the subject matter of American literature.

In the 1920s Botkin treated the development of black writers and the treatment of blacks in American writing as a major test of whether the nation's literature reflected both diversity and democratic aspirations. Unlike conservative modernists, Botkin did not see ignorance and vulgarity among those excluded from dominant definitions of Western civilization and American national identity. He stressed instead the value of their folk cultures and the emergence of writers in these groups whose work could become part of the national literature. At that time Botkin worked out his position on these matters primarily in aesthetic terms, though even then there was both an anthropological and a reformist element in his approach. Thus, there is a tension in Botkin's reviews of literature dealing with Afro-Americans, between conventional ways of talking about art, civilization, blacks, and his emerging position. This tension reveals continuity and change in the thinking of liberal intellectuals in the 1920s and 1930s.

Along with many modern writers, Botkin associated a pervasive sense of homelessness with modern social change. To deal with this, modern societies needed new forms of writing and social reform. For Botkin homelessness was an autobiographical fact, and it explains in part his approach and what distinguishes it from those who embraced radical literary innovation and conservative cultural politics; it also helps explain his attitude toward those he saw as excluded and deprived.

Like many of the black writers who participated in the Harlem Renaissance, Botkin initially hailed the work of this school as evidence blacks were making a contribution to civilization and thus now deserved a higher status than they had been previously accorded. For him the implications of such cultural facts supported egalitarianism. Thus, in a 1926 review of Countee Cullen's poems, Botkin found it "significant to note" that the *New Masses* had three black contributing editors who were, he maintained, "taking equal part in the new enlightenment alongside their white brothers." To him the "cultural flowering of the Negro" was a sign of the "bursting of the barriers of repression" and "a force to be reckoned with in our civilization." He listed the names of African American artists past and present to prove "that the Negro has established his place in the brotherhood of the arts." A decade later he rejected the notion that it was individual contributions that earned the Negro the right to respect. The study of contemporary anthropology had led him away from Matthew Arnold's definition of culture and civilization as the history of great individual triumphs of thought and art—the canon of high culture.[24]

Even in 1926 Botkin was an Arnoldian with a difference. The collection and publication of black folk songs was, in his mind, as important as the publication of individual Negro authors. In Cullen's poetry Botkin found not only "sweetness and light," but also "the sigh of the new dawn of an old race, bowed under the sins of the world." Botkin was not counseling resignation. For self-expression was taking place in this "age of 'self-determination of peoples.'" In a way that seems strongly felt, but whose personal implications were not made fully explicit, Botkin linked both his feeling of modernity as homelessness and the aspects of his own rootlessness in his comparison of Jews and Negroes: "The New note [in the poetry of Countee Cullen and other black writers in the 1920s] is one of restless seeking and rebellion akin to that of another 'man without a country,' the Jew."[25] In a review essay in *Opportunity*, the journal of the National Urban League, Botkin wrote:

> It might be asked if the dominant note of all Negro song is not the homesickness of an alien, homeless folk, "po' boy long way from home," a nostalgia born of a racial, traditional and ancestral longing for a home that no longer exists like the Promised Land which the Jews have codified in Zion, and like the heaven of the Christians to which the Negro has transferred his unsatisfied earthly longing. The Negro is restless and unresting, obsessed with the need of seeking and finding.[26]

Botkin published black authors, such as poets Langston Hughes and Sterling Brown (who later became the FWP Negro affairs editor), in the *Folk-Say* anthologies—regional miscellanies of folklore, poetry, and fiction—that he edited between 1929 and 1932. He was especially interested in Brown's efforts to find a language and form that could embody the realities of the black experience. Brown also contributed an essay titled "The Blues as Folk Poetry" to Botkin's second *Folk-Say* anthology (1930). In 1930, when few recognized the blues as either folklore or poetry, Brown heard the folk singing about railroads and city life as well as cotton and floods. Brown drew on the blues form in his own poetry, and some of these poems were first published in the *Folk-Say* volumes. He used the strength of black folk tradition to fulfill his own creative needs. In his most successful poems, he demonstrated what Botkin later called the creative reciprocity between the individual and the folk.[27]

In Botkin's view, the Negro's restless searching was emblematic of the modern condition. More than most groups, African Americans' experience of the transition from slavery to freedom, from an agrarian to an industrial way of life, symbolized "the twentieth century in its mad chaotic forment [*sic*] of freedom." Changes resulting from modern life meant not the death but the adaptation of folk tradition to a new world. The spirituals were "not dying out, but . . . undergoing a secularizing process." Black folk song spoke to a large audience—"all the western world is feeling the urge of this social rhythm"—for it spoke of changes in laboring conditions, a longing for home in a rootless society, and the desire for freedom. Botkin's view that the African American experience was representative of important aspects of the American experience was a potentially radical assumption that held the possibility of transforming the definition of American nationality and identity. It was an idea he placed at the center of his work on the FWP.[28]

The *Folk-Say* volumes Botkin edited and two of the poems he wrote at the very beginning of the 1930s are responses to an ongoing literary discussion about modernity, and Botkin, like Eliot, brought his reading in anthropology to bear on the issues that concerned him. His polemical and programmatic essay "The Folk in Literature: An Introduction to the New Regionalism" (1929), which served as the introduction to the first volume of *Folk-Say*, dealt with the relationship between regional folklore and literature and writers' relationship to their culture. Botkin offered his view of the cultural change that had made the relationship problematic. It was clear that Botkin disagreed on theoretical grounds with those who felt there were no folk in America and with those who felt threatened by diversity: "There is," he argued, "not one folk [in America] but many folk groups—as many folk groups as there are regional cultures or racial or occupational groups within a region." In the 1930 volume, he declared, it is time "to recognize that we have in America a variety of folk groups, representing different racial, regional and *even* industrial cultures" (emphasis added). "Folk-say," a term Botkin coined, implied an ongoing activity. And as he later explained, he was trying put the emphasis on the "*living as well as . . . anachronistic phases*" of folklore.[29]

Botkin's program involved recognizing and overcoming what he saw as an arbitrary division between folklore and literature that obscured the relationship between the two, and, implicitly, a way of overcoming the division between the folk and the writer. He addressed questions similar to those Eliot dealt with in his seventeenth-century disaster myth. Botkin argued that "in the beginning lore and literature were one." The division had been caused by the invention of writing and printing, modern individualism, and private property. He maintained that the real distinction was between "folk literature" and "culture literature." If the division was arbitrary, if "in every age literature moves on two levels" and popular culture borrows freely from folk and high culture, then writers could help reunite the two streams and reestablish a vital relation with the folk tradition—and the folk. Indeed, there had always been "that part of culture literature which brooding over folk materials and motifs, rehandles and recreates them." Regionalism was to provide writers with a way of reuniting the two streams of literature into one, as it had been in the beginning and as it could be in a new way in the future: "By setting the scholar and artist at work upon oral tradition [regionalism] is creating a genuine American myth and fable."[30]

From the beginning Botkin linked pluralism and regionalism: "Ours is an age of taking root and of the resulting conflict and compromise, within a locality, of varied racial stocks and opposing orders of civilization." He was receptive to the anthropology of Franz Boas, which emphasized a plurality of historically conditioned cultures, culture as an integrative force, and acculturation, and which advocated a relativistic outlook in place of an evolutionary hierarchy.[31]

Botkin was searching for both an individual and social reintegration that would overcome feelings of alienation. He thought the creative writer in America could play a crucial role in helping to reintegrate a fragmented reality. In Eliot's wasteland no one could play such a role. Botkin's poem "Home Town" can be read as addressing some of the same questions Eliot confronted in "The Waste Land." "Home Town" at first seems an odd title, for the narrator describes himself as an outsider only at home walking the public streets: "The streets were home to him, one long carouse / In sum and common things."[32] For the person described in the poem, it is shared public places that constitute home.

> And homeless though he felt, the poor defense
> Of houses fell before his conquering sense
> Of proud possession; with the sky and air
> Their lives and property were his to share.[33]

The narrator intends to make this town his home by studying it and giving back what he has learned to his fellow townsmen. He sees more than fragments, more than Eliot's "withered stumps of time" or debris to be shored up "against my ruins":

> Of blowing clothes in which he could divine
> An augury as in the flight of birds;
> Milk-jars on steps—stray fragments, hints, mute words,
> A jig-saw puzzle, scattered, disconnected—
> He pieced together bits that he collected.[34]

Botkin saw himself as helping to make American public space a place where diverse groups could feel at home. Diversity and integration in Botkin's vision were compatible. He was interested not only in the relationship between artist and folk group, but also in ways of interpreting one culture to another through its folklore. One's identity and relation to tradition were in his vision matters of choice and knowledge, not biological inheritance. The *Folk-Say* volumes encouraged creative writers, folklorists, and the folk (through the use of first-person narratives) to take up the task of interpretation—to address a diverse audience and ask them to share a sense of community.[35]

The prefatory poem for the 1931 volume of *Folk Say* expressed a vision of how the cultural component of a pluralistic integrated culture might be created. This Oklahoman, this Harvard man, this Bostonian, this son of Jewish immigrants had defined himself as having a major role to play in fulfilling this vision.

—Old man, what are you planting?
—Good tales—root crops—
And myself who lived them,
In the dark of the moon.
Anything you want to grow in the ground,
Plant in the dark of the moon.

—Old Man, I am planting a fence
A crazy worm fence,
With songs for rails,
With men and regions for songs—
Myself the ground rail—

In the light of the moon
So it will stay on top always
Until it rots—
To bridge the now and the then and the still-to-come,
To climb from hell to heaven.
Anything you want to stay on top of the ground,
Plant in the light of the moon.

Grow down, old man;
Grow in and under, old tales;
Grow up, my songs;
Grow together and in and out, myself, men, and regions—
In the dark of the moon,
In the light of the moon.[36]

Botkin found the study of folklore from the literary and social-science perspectives compatible with encouraging writers to experiment with both form and subject matter. Sounding a modern literary theme, Botkin started *Space* (1934–1935), an experimental little magazine—"There's *Time*, a news magazine. Why not *Space*, which will stand for the very opposite?" One goal, Botkin later recalled, was to deal creatively with "the dislocation of the individual in urban, industrial, mass culture." Part of that dislocation, Botkin and the contributors to *Space* thought, was related to modern anxieties about the very relationship between space and time, between place and history.[37] The mailing announcing the appearance of the magazine had a defiant, mystical, and experimental tone:

SPACE AND THE TWELVE CLEAN WINDS OF HEAVEN

We need more sense of space in living, thinking, and writing. From the conquest and annihilation of space in a time-saving and time-serving age, we must turn to the conquest of time. . . . In form and content the material published in *Space* is plastic, connotative, qualitative, and off the beaten track of both standard and "little" magazines.[38]

In the magazine were essays arguing the merits of Eliot's work, pro and con, the opportunities folk cultures presented writers, and the aesthetic and social implications of regionalism. The magazine published work that played with the possibilities of literary form and the nature of the inexplicable psychology of the individual consciousness—and it had the usual little-magazine quota of inexplicable pieces.

With the coming of the Great Depression, Eliot and Botkin, like many other writers, felt compelled to rethink their views about art and culture. Eliot in the 1930s explicitly described pluralism as a threat to purity. Botkin rethought his earlier views with a more explicit anthropology in mind and a greater sense of social crisis. He also returned in new ways to questions about tradition and individual talent, and about the dissociation of thought and sensibility that had concerned them both (as it does every romantic and every modernist variant on the romantic tradition).

In 1933 at the University of Virginia, Eliot declared: "Some years ago I wrote an essay entitled Tradition and the Individual Talent . . . The problem, naturally does not seem to me so simple as it seemed then, nor could I treat it now as a purely literary one." He now offered concrete reasons for why he saw a wasteland landscape. Industrialism and ethnic diversity, he told his Virginia audience, constituted grave threats to tradition. Thus, the South, being "farther away from New York" and "less industrialized and less invaded by foreign races," had a better chance "for the re-establishment of a native culture" than even his ancestral New England. Tradition, Eliot maintained, could thrive only among a stable and homogeneous population, for "where two or more cultures exist in the same place they are likely either to be fiercely self-conscious or both to become adulterate." In the interaction between cultures, he saw only the possibility of an intense struggle to maintain identity or the corruption and debasement of culture. Eliot told his audience that "reasons of race and religion combine to make any large number of free-thinking Jews undesirable." The remark is significant in a larger context than the issue of anti-Semitism. It embodies Eliot's inability to see anything but fragmentation and cultural decay in the realities of American diversity.[39]

Eliot and Botkin both thought part of the answer to the problem of social disintegration was in creating a sense of place. Botkin, however, thought a shared knowledge of a place's history and diverse population could create a commonly held feeling of identity and possession. This was the approach he and other national FWP officials brought to their study of the United States. Both Eliot and Botkin thought a concrete sense of place provided a balance to the abstract qualities of modern life and the modern nation state. Both thought such a feeling of place could no longer be taken for granted. In Eliot's case, however, the idea of place involved discovering "what is the best life for us not as a political abstraction, but as a particular people in a particular place." For Eliot the idea of place was inseparable from homogeneity. Botkin dismissed Eliot as "a wistful though not uncritical fellow traveler of the Agrarians" and regarded his anti-Semitism as similar to the anti-Negro sentiment of the Agrarians typified in Allen Tate's defense of lynching. Eliot and the Agrarians had, Botkin contended, failed to recognize a crucial fact about place and region: "Geographical relationships are important not as they determine character and culture but as they modify and diversify the social structure that underlies individual character and action."[40]

Underlying Eliot's reformulation was his awareness that the political and economic crisis of the 1930s had heightened the appeal of communism and fascism as a way out. The nature of personality and the role of the individual had taken on a social urgency that made it impossible any longer to limit the discussion to literary issues. Both Botkin and Eliot shared in the 1930s a desire to clarify the writer's role in society. For Botkin the answer was in the creative reciprocity that could exist between the folk and the individual; for Eliot it lay in the relationship between the individual and tradition and orthodoxy.

Eliot rejected an unreflective traditionalism. Only a sentimentalist, he argued, would deny that "in even the very best living tradition there is always a mixture of good and bad, and much that deserves criticism." The measure by which one could judge tradition Eliot called orthodoxy, and "orthodoxy in general," he insisted, "implies Christian orthodoxy." Tradition was an unconscious "way of feeling and acting which characterizes a group throughout generations." Orthodoxy, on the other hand "calls for the exercise of all our conscious intelligence." These terms, he explained, had for him taken the place of the "concepts of romantic and classic." To the problem of the dissociation of sensibility he had found a new solution: in the "co-operation of tradition and orthodoxy is the reconciliation of thought and feeling."[41] Botkin, too, was looking for a reconciliation between thought and feeling, but for him the solution was tied up with exploring the customs and values of American folk groups and making them widely known. Botkin and his fellow national FWP officials measured traditions by their own kind of orthodoxy, which involved egalitarianism, liberal reform, and democratic values.

Modern circumstances, Eliot told his audience at the University of Virginia, had produced both a literary and a social cult of excessive individualism and stress on personality. He disapproved of the "glorification" of novelty and originality "for their own sake." He thought it was disastrous "that the writer should deliberately give rein to his individuality," that he should even cultivate his differences from others; and that his readers should cherish the author of genius, not in spite of his deviations from the inherited wisdom of the race, but because of them. Botkin called such excessive individuality modern egoism and thought it could be cured by analyzing the patterns, symbols, and values that held together American folk cultures. Eliot feared a situation "when morals cease to be a matter of tradition and orthodoxy—that is, of the habits of the community formulated, corrected, and elevated by the continuous thought and direction of the Church—and when each man is to elaborate his own, then *personality* becomes a thing of alarming importance." Botkin expressed similar concerns, but instead of pointing to the church, he claimed the writer could find a nourishing way of expressing his individuality by forging a creative reciprocity with folk groups.[42]

Eliot accepted the anthropologist Lucien Levy-Bruhl's argument that individualism did not exist in primitive societies and that the thinking of primitive peoples differed not in degree but in kind from that of people who were part of Western civilization. He found it compatible with a cultural hierarchy he had always accepted and a useful tool in arguing against Marxism, "the heresy bred within the antithetical heresy of liberalism." The "group consciousness" that Eliot thought would emerge in a Marxist society would be a "reversion to a lower kind of consciousness."[43]

In *The Uses of Poetry and the Uses of Criticism* (1933), Eliot clearly reveals the ways in which his modernism is also a variation on romanticism: "I myself should like an audience that could neither read nor write." The barriers standing in the way of creating such an art, he argued, reflected larger problems in modern life: "The most useful poetry, socially, would be one which could cut across all the present stratifications of public taste—stratifications which are a possible sign of social disintegration."[44] Whether an art that fuses a divided audience can be created is an open question. Botkin thought that a step in the right direction would involve listening to other diverse folk voices—racial minorities and urban workers, for example—allowing them space in diverse forums of communication to be heard. In contrast, in *The Waste Land* one only overhears snatches of lower-middle-class conversation.

In a world of rising fascist powers, Eliot had arrived at a position that equated tradition with orthodox Christianity, despaired over pluralism, and offered little hope of social reform in a period of economic crisis. In sharp contrast, Botkin saw in diversity the hope of cultural renewal. He never used words such as "adulterate," with its implication that there was a choice only between purity and impurity. A different view of tradition, culture, industrialism, and urbanism was at the heart of his effort to redefine the term folklore. In the 1930s he formulated in sharper anthropological terms the implications of ideas that in the 1920s he had thought about primarily in literary terms: the relationship between the individual and tradition and between the writer and society, the dissociation of thought sensibility, pluralism, and cultural integration.

Botkin referred to "eternal, universal human values" but did not indicate how one is to know what these are. In his celebration of differences, Botkin revealed the influence of romanticism on the thinking of cultural pluralists. Since he did not specify how one could determine the eternal values, it seems that like earlier romantics Botkin assumed there was, as he later put it, "an essential unity underlying all men."[45] Beyond that assertion he remained vague. Nor did he address directly the question of how to evaluate different aspects of a tradition, nor how to reconcile conflicting traditions and conflicts between groups with different traditions. In part, the idea of essential unity held out the promise that knowledge and understanding would help eliminate conflict. Eliot rejected all these assumptions and turned to orthodox Christianity for absolute values by which to evaluate traditions. In practice, Botkin evaluated tradition against the orthodoxy of a secular liberal pluralism that Eliot found repugnant.

For Botkin, cultural pluralism functioned in a relativistic way to question the authoritative cultural claims of dominant, mainstream American groups. American art and literature needed what marginal regional and minority groups had to offer. Eliot's disapproval of pluralism was clearly tied to his belief in a cultural hierarchy and the church's claim to authoritative wisdom. Maintaining that Western civilization and Christianity were one and could not be separated without the separation's leading to cultural corruption and decay created no personal problems for Eliot, while it would have for Botkin. By advocating his view of pluralism as a positive value and his approach toward the relationship between provincialism and cosmopolitanism, Botkin was also advocating a view of America that meant that his own ethnic background would not stand in the way of his studying and participating in American life and culture.[46]

There were many who were confident that vanishing folklore was a symbol of progress. Eliot, who believed folklore was dying out but did not share the belief in progress, regarded modern culture largely as a landscape of decayed remnants of the past, an "immense panorama of futility." In the "Folkness of the Folk" and "The Folk and the Individual: Their Creative Reciprocity," Botkin offered an anthropologically informed argument for a new definition of folklore and a new role for the creative writer. He challenged all the major assumptions of the survivalist school that had influenced Eliot and criticized "the tendency . . . to treat folklore from the evolutionary and historical rather than the functional approach," with the result that the lore was separated from the folk who kept it alive and regarded as "anachronistic and static . . . to the neglect of its living and dynamic phases."[47]

Botkin used Boasian anthropology to challenge the idea that folklore survived only among the illiterate and geographically isolated and was destined to disappear. He argued that in the modern world social structure takes the place of geography in creating the isolation and separation that provides the basis for the group identification, from which develops a folklore of the educated as well as the uneducated, an urban as well as a rural folklore. Since "complete isolation is no longer possible," it was important to recognize that a folk group was based not only on isolating factors, but also on "*integration*—a selective, adjusting, and standardizing force from within" (emphasis added). Cultural contact between diverse groups, the acculturation process, and isolation could generate new folklore as "the folk group adapts itself to its environment and to change, assimilating new experience and generating fresh forms."[48]

Botkin argued that given the crisis of contemporary civilization the writer should think of himself primarily in relation to the folk tradition, rather than the literary tradition. In this way the writer would find new values and a role and an audience. The writer, Botkin warned, "cannot do this by writing from the outside looking in and on." Like a good ethnologist, he must be willing to "live the life of the people he writes about. . . . So that when he writes about them he becomes not merely an interpreter but a voice—their voice, which is now his own." From this point Botkin moves in a direction strikingly parallel to Eliot's. Botkin did indeed think the writer would be willing to accept the "loss of sense of authorship" if he understood that "it does not mean extinction but extension and *integration* of personality, through identification with his audience and complete submergence in his materials" (emphasis added).[49]

In Botkin's vision, the writer would contribute to the creation of an egalitarian, democratic, and pluralistic community. The writer's goal should be "not to wipe out but to conserve and strengthen [the folk group's] heritage, by releasing it and making it a living force for differentiation within an integrated society." Here Botkin has rewritten part of his "Old Man, What Are You Planting?" in anthropological terms. He still wanted creative writers to help heal the split between oral and written literature, which in the modern world of print and other technological media constantly interacted with each other: "Now what is fixed becomes floating and now what is floating becomes fixed." Given this movement, Botkin maintained, there would seem to be no valid reason why individual writers could not cross and recross the shifting line between folk and sophisticated expression and bring back at least a basic "integration."[50] Recall that Eliot also thought the modern writer's inability to cross lines was a sign of social disintegration.

In "Tradition and the Individual Talent," Eliot forcefully defended his view that the poet had much to gain from an "extinction of personality," an "escape from personality." In more radical terms, Botkin came close to suggesting that the writer submerge his individual identity in that of the group. Botkin, however, drew a distinction between individualism and mere egoism.[51]

Drawing on the works of the anthropologists Alexander Goldenweiser and Paul Radin, Botkin denied that primitive thought was a lower form of thinking and that primitive people lacked individuality, and furthermore that modern egoism, reflecting "the conflicts and divisions of personality being aggravated by the anarchy and chaos of competitive society," was the same thing as individualism. Botkin turned the conventional Victorian cultural hierarchy on its head. It was a hierarchy that Victorian anthropologists such as James G. Frazer, with their firm distinctions between the savage and the civilized, had helped define. Botkin used Radin to argue that primitive societies had healthier forms of individualism than modern capitalist societies, and that reform in the United States would not destroy individualism. For both cultural and political reasons, Botkin preferred Radin's work on primitive societies to Levy-Bruhl's. Botkin and Eliot's cultural politics thus followed divergent paths.[52]

Botkin attributed the key differences between modern egoism and primitive individualism to writing, machinery, and modern capitalism. These forces had introduced a "greater separation between the subjective and the objective, the worlds of thought and action," than had previously existed. Capitalism had not figured so explicitly or prominently in his earlier explanation of fragmented culture in "The Folk in Literature." And it figured not at all in Eliot's seventeenth-century disaster myth. Botkin, like Eliot, had a theory about the dissociation between thought and sensibility, and in the 1930s he gave it both a more radical and an anthropological basis while still responding to the issues that concerned Eliot and other modernists. For Botkin, a writer who became an interpreter, a voice for the folk, was part of the modernist tradition: "When one has assimilated folk consciousness . . . one becomes like the folk, symbol minded." He held that the distinction between symbol minded in the folk and the aesthetic sense was small if one defined the latter "as identification of subject with object."[53]

In Carl Sandburg's *The People, Yes* (1937), Botkin thought he had found a "great folk poetry that is also significant social poetry." Botkin insisted that Sandburg was "mythopoeic, and all but epic." For Botkin, Sandburg represented a poet who turned to living folk cultures to create an American epic, in contrast to poets such as Eliot, who had, in creating the myths for their anti-epics, relied on materials from dead cultures. Like Eliot, Sandburg also walked through cities—only all about him Sandburg heard the voice of creative folk, and nowhere Eliot's empty walking dead. Botkin saw in Sandburg a poet who had gone to the folk and emerged an individual with values and a voice to express them. He admired Sandburg's effort to create a folk epic of the American people that embodied all its diverse voices. Hearing voices that were both different from and similar to their own, Americans would realize that "Everybody is you and me and all the others / What everybody says is what we all say."[54] Botkin directed the Federal Writers' Project folklore studies with this cultural vision in mind.

Botkin's understanding of modern anthropology and literature led him to the conclusion that life histories could provide artistic and historical insight into both the life of an individual and a group in a state of transition. Transition was the key word. Botkin learned from Paul Radin's denial of the validity of interpretations that saw primitive peoples as existing in a pure and undefiled state before the coming of the Europeans and contaminated and deteriorating thereafter. According to Radin, intercultural contact meant that the tribes anthropologists were studying were living through a rapid state of cultural transition that differed only in degree from that produced by earlier intercultural contacts. Botkin saw that looking at American minorities in this way avoided prejudging the results of acculturation, avoided labeling the process adulteration, as Eliot had done.[55]

In the FWP's interviews with ex-slaves and ethnic minorities, Botkin heard folk experience being presented in the voice of an individual whose account also had potential value as literature or as a source for the renewal of American literature. Botkin insisted the folk and bardic periods were not confined to the past: "Our many folk cultures are not behind us at all but right under us. Below the sur-

face of the dominant pattern are the popular life and fantasy of our cultural minorities and other nondominant groups—nondominant but not recessive, not
static but dynamic and transitional, on their way up." The lives and lore of such
groups, Botkin maintained, needed to be represented in "our" history and literature. In Eliot's poetry the representatives of such groups are peripheral figures who
move toward the center only in menacing ways. In the life histories of minorities,
especially ex-slaves, Botkin heard voices that captured the transition from slavery
to freedom and from rural to urban life that dealt with central aspects of the American folk experience of modernity. He held that such accounts constituted a folk
history, an American saga.[56]

Too often aesthetic judgments are offered in place of intellectual history.
Still, a nagging question remains: Can Botkin's vision of the world produce art of
the same order as Eliot's? Consider that Ralph Ellison was an employee of the Federal Writers' Projects' New York City Living Lore unit. Reading Botkin's "The Folk
and the Individual: Their Creative Reciprocity," it is easy to think of Ellison's Invisible Man, residing underground, not behind us, but right under us, below the
surface—and at the end of the novel, on his way up, affirming pluralist diversity
and life in America as possibility, as a process of becoming, and insisting that his
experience is part of the American experience. In the last chapter of *Invisible Man*,
Ellison uses the same image Franklin Roosevelt employed in a letter to the play-
wright Paul Green: "America is woven of many strands; I would recognize them
and let it so remain."[57]

In *Invisible Man* Ellison found a way to create a work of art that, in its very
structure, wrestled with all the issues that Botkin had hoped federal writers on the
Living Lore units would learn to deal with: the nature of the relationship between
the individual and the folk group, between provincialism and cosmopolitanism,
between tradition and modernity, and between the fact of diversity and the need
for unity. Ellison, as Botkin had advocated, explored the relationship of the individual to a folk group. Like Botkin, Ellison knew that folklore grew and thrived in
the city. Ellison's hero eventually learns that the movement from rural to urban life
is *not* a progressive linear development from provincialism to cosmopolitanism, a
shedding of earlier folkways. To express the creative reciprocity between the individual and his group, Ellison had to create a form adequate to his purpose: "Our
task then is to challenge the apparent forms of reality—that is, the fixed manners
and values of the few, and to struggle with it until it reveals its mad, vari-implicated
chaos, its false faces, and on until it surrenders its insight, its truth." It involved a
struggle to achieve form, and through form "the promise of our lives," as Americans—"diversity, swiftness of change," unity, and "that condition of man's being at
home in the world, which is called love, and which we term democracy."[58]

Once the Invisible Man reconciles his desire for a cosmopolitan worldview
with an acceptance of his folk roots, he is ready in the epilogue to do a jazz solo
flight (like the jazz musician, Ellison uses a Western instrument, the novel, to sing
a folk and individual experience that is both Western and non-Western) on the
themes of pluralism, democracy, and community—themes that were at the heart

of Botkin's work in Oklahoma and as folklore editor of the Federal Writers' Project, but that he had not been able to use to create enduring art. In ways too complex to explore here, the novel can in part be regarded as a description of the impact of changing contexts on folklore texts, an imaginative ethnography raised to the level of epic. While the urban world the Invisible Man walked through was a more frightening and dangerous place than Sandburg ever depicted, it was not Eliot's wasteland, a completely fragmented world devoid of creative possibilities. As Ellison has indicated, he learned from Eliot's use of symbolism in *The Waste Land,* especially the images of death and rebirth, blindness and light, the biblical and mythological symbolism, and what he called its jazzlike rhythms and "its range of allusion . . . as mixed and varied as that of Louis Armstrong." Nevertheless, what the Invisible Man claims to have finally learned by the end of the novel is different on every fundamental point from Eliot's outlook. He has discovered the value of a living, adapting, black folk tradition that continues to provide tradition and forms for living and expressing both the individual and the group experience in a way that transcends fragmentation.[59]

The Invisible Man's final speech ends with a call for his diverse American audience to allow him to establish a relationship between himself and them. To fully exist he needs recognition, an affirmative response to what he sees as his socially responsible call: "Who knows but that on the lower frequencies, I speak for you?"[60] He asks fellow citizens to discover and acknowledge the folk within themselves and without. Ellison and Botkin tell us that answering the Invisible Man's question involves the discovery of the folk and a recognition of the relationships among reform, pluralism, folklore, and the politics of cultural representation.

Perhaps it is ironic that an essay that began with two "sort of" New Englanders end with the discussion of a novel by a black writer from Oklahoma. But one aspect of Ellison's novel is a comment on the New England tradition and the democratic myth. It indicts a false, desiccated version of the Emersonian tradition while reaffirming that part of the tradition that celebrates life as possibility. And for Ellison that sense of possibility is linked to a recognition of pluralism, of the value of diverse folk experiences and traditions. As he put it in *Shadow and Act* (1964), "The small share of reality which each of our diverse groups is able to snatch from the whirling chaos of history belongs not to the group alone, but to all of us. It is a property and a witness which can be ignored only to the danger of the entire nation." A significant part of the experience that concerned Ellison was the "blasting pressures which in a scant eighty years have sent the Negro people hurtling, without clearly defined trajectory, from slavery to emancipation, form log cabin to city tenement, from the white folks' fields and kitchens to factory assembly lines; and which, between two wars, have shattered the wholeness of its consciousness into a thousand writhing pieces." Giving form to such an experience would never have interested Eliot; it was a goal for which his conception of poetry and tradition allowed no space.[61]

Eliot rejected the New England tradition in decline. So did Botkin. Botkin, however, saw himself as contributing to the growth and flowering of "personality and freedom, enjoying what Emerson calls 'an original relation to the universe'." All around him he saw "folklore in the making." Eliot had (to paraphrase his remark about Henry James's mind) created a view of poetry so fine that no folk could violate it. Ellison found the novels of Henry James too narrow in scope and too concerned with "stable areas" to express the fluidity and openness of American life. There were, and had to be, many varieties of modernism.[62]

Given the dynamic realities of American cultural diversity and social fluidity and the need to give form to our world in the transcendent experience of art, the dialogue of which Eliot and Botkin were part can still speak to contemporary needs. Perhaps on one level Eliot's *Waste Land* will continue to speak to us as a cautionary tale. His concern with transcendent and permanent values was admirable. Certainly, pluralism can become a form of relativism that offers neither guidance nor solace. And much that Eliot accomplished in his poetry has become the permanent inheritance of all later writers. In the end, however, Eliot offered no guidance for dealing with the American experience. Botkin thought that a belief in an inclusive, democratic, and egalitarian American community and attention to the folk and lore of today as well as yesterday could inspire the creation of an American literature that reflected and contributed to our democratic traditions. It has in the past. And it could again. For it to continue to do so, it helps to review the variations in the seemingly permanent dialogue on these matters among American writers—on one side, Nathaniel Hawthorne, Henry James, and T. S. Eliot, and on the other, Ralph Waldo Emerson, Walt Whitman, and B. A. Botkin.

■ NOTES

1. Jerrold Hirsch, "Folklore in the Making: B. A. Botkin," *Journal of American Folklore* 100 (1987): 3, 9.

2. Lyndall Gordon, *Eliot's Early Years* (Oxford: Oxford University Press, 1977), passim; "B. A. Botkin," in *Twentieth Century Authors: A Biographical Dictionary of Modern Literature*, ed. Stanley J. Kunitz (New York: H. W. Wilson, 1955), 101–102. For an overview of Botkin's career, see Hirsch, "Folklore in the Making, 3–38. See, e.g., Eliot's poems "Preludes," "Rhapsody on a Windy Night," "The Boston Evening Transcript," "Aunt Helen" and "Cousin Nancy," in T. S. Eliot, *The Complete Poems and Plays, 1909–1950* (New York: Harcourt, Brace and Company, 1950), 12–17; Gordon, *Eliot's Early Years*, 18–19; Eliot, "Burbank with a Baedeker, Bleistein with a Cigar" and "Sweeney among the Nightingales," in Eliot, *The Complete Poems*, 23–24, 35–36. On manners and modernism, see the discussion in John Murray Cuddihy, *The Ordeal of Civility: Freud, Marx, Lévi-Strauss, and the Jewish Struggle with Modernity* (New York: Basic Books, 1974), 4, 5, 220–221.

3. Geoffrey H. Hartman, *Criticism in the Wilderness: The Study of Literature Today* (New Haven: Yale University Press, 1980), 13–14.

4. Kunitz, "B. A. Botkin," 101; Botkin, "Autobiography of a Boy" (1918), unpublished manuscript in the author's possession.

5. See Niza Rosovsky, *The Jewish Experience at Harvard and Radcliffe* (Cambridge: Harvard University Press, 1986) and Marcia Synnott, *The Half-Open Door: Discrimination and*

Admissions at Harvard, Yale, and Princeton, 1900–1970 (Westport, Conn.: Greenwood Press, 1979). The words near the end of my paragraph paraphrase those of Harvard's dean of faculty, Henry Rosovsky, on the occasion of the dedication of the new Harvard-Radcliffe Hillel House in 1979. See Henry Rosovsky, "From Periphery to Center," in Rosovsky, *The Jewish Experience at Harvard and Radcliffe*, 57.

6. B. A. Botkin, "Applied Folklore: A Semantic-Dynamic Approach" (1967), 18, unpublished manuscript in the author's possession. The effort to reconcile provincialism and cosmopolitanism, and romantic nationalism and cultural pluralism, in an effort to redefine American nationality was at heart of the program national FWP officials developed. This is the central theme of Jerrold Hirsch, "Portrait of America: The Federal Writers' Project in an Intellectual and Cultural Context" (Ph.D. diss., University of North Carolina, 1984).

7. Marcus Klein, *Foreigners: The Making of American Literature, 1900–1940* (Chicago: University of Chicago Press, 1981), 4.

8. Ibid., 13, 18, 19, 20. Many of the points made by Klein and Hartman are part of a history of dissenting views regarding Eliot. However, when the New Criticism was at its apogee in the 1950s, Karl Schapiro recalls it was considered rudely ill mannered to criticize Eliot, who in the eyes of the dominant literary critics had achieved the stature of a saint. A summary of Eliot's poetry, Schapiro wrote, "seems a kind of blasphemy, or an act of unpardonable rudeness," for "Eliot is untouchable; he is Modern Literature incarnate and an institution unto himself." Nevertheless, Schapiro offered a critical view of Eliot that is worth noting in relation to the present discussion. According to Schapiro, Eliot's "fears of being taken for a provincial" explained the conspicuous erudition of his poetry. Furthermore, this fear tied him to the worst aspects of his New England heritage, the part that "leads the New Englander to become the Old Englander." Eliot was a "pseudo-American, the type which finally won New England from the immigrant and gave it back to 'history'." He was one of a long line of American writers who "was retracing the path back to Europe." Schapiro rejected Eliot's assumption "that the modern city is a degeneration of the Past." Eliot's prestige, according to Schapiro's analysis, was contrived: "Eliot created a literary situation deliberately; he and his 'situation' are fabrications." Schapiro attributed "Eliot's outlook to his provincial snobbery: The Historical Situation which Eliot exploits under the banner of Tradition was in the beginning the Educational Situation. It was local and Anglo-American, a defense of the Gentleman's Education. I put it vulgarly because that is the way it was." See Karl Schapiro, "T. S. Eliot: The Death of Literary Judgement," in Schapiro, *In Defense of Ignorance* (New York: Random House, 1960), 35 passim.

9. Ibid., 38.

10. Rita Dove, review of Arnold Rampersand, *The Life of Langston Hughes*, vol. 2, *New York Times Book Review*, 9 October 1988, 48.

11. Richard Dorson, afterword, *American Folklore Historiography* [special issue, *Journal of the Folklore Institute*] (June–August 1973): 110.

12. Henry James Jr., *Hawthorne* (London: Macmillan, 1879), 42–44.

13. Pound as quoted in Peter Ackroyd, *T. S. Eliot: A Life* (New York: Simon and Schuster, 1984), 56.

14. Kenneth Burke, *The Philosophy of Literary Form Studies in Symbolic Action* (Baton Rouge: Louisiana State University Press, 1941); T. S. Eliot, "Tradition and the Individual Talent," in *The Sacred Wood: Essays on Poetry and Criticism* (London: Methuen, 1920); Eliot, *The Waste Land* (New York: Boni and Liveright, 1922); B. A. Botkin, "Home Town," *Prairie Schooner* 4 (1930): 34–35; Botkin, "Old Man, What Are You Planting?" in *Folk-Say, A Regional Miscellany* (Norman: University of Oklahoma Press, 1931), 5; T. S. Eliot, *After*

Strange Gods: A Primer of Modern Heresy (New York: Harcourt, Brace, 1934); B. A. Botkin, "The Folk and the Individual: Their Creative Reciprocity," *English Journal* 27 (1938): 121–135.

15. Eliot, "Tradition and the Individual Talent," 52–53.

16. For an overview of Eliot's knowledge of anthropology, see Paul Vickery, *The Literary Impact of the Golden Bough* (Princeton, N.J.: Princeton University Press, 1973), 233–279. Eliot's dissociation myth is developed in "The Metaphysical Poets," in T. S. Eliot, *Selected Essays: 1917–1932* (New York: Harcourt, Brace, 1932), 247. For a critique of Eliot's concept of dissociation see Frank Kermode, *Romantic Image* (New York: Macmillan, 1957), 161, 166.

17. Vickery, *The Literary Impact of the Golden Bough*, 233–279. See also Alan Dundes, "The Devolutionary Premise in Folklore Theory," *Journal of the Folklore Institute* 6 (June 1969): 5–19.

18. B. A. Botkin, "Folk-Say and Space: Their Genesis and Exodus," *Southwest Review* 20 (1935): 322.

19. Ibid. For a complete listing of Botkin's book reviews in this period, see "Bibliography of the Writings of Benjamin A. Botkin," in *Folklore and Society: Essays in Honor of Benjamin A. Botkin*, ed. Bruce Jackson (Hatboro, Pa.: Folklore Associates, 1966), 169–192.

20. Botkin, reviews of *Destinations*, by Gorham B. Munson, *Daily Oklahoman*, 10 March 1929; *Phases of English Poetry*, by Herbert Read, *Daily Oklahoman*, 23 March 1930; *Poems*, by T. S. Eliot, *Daily Oklahoman*, 6 March 1927; *The American Caravan*, ed. Van Wyck Brooks, Alfred Kreymborg, Lewis Mumford, and Paul Rosenfeld, *Daily Oklahoman*, 4 December 1927.

21. Botkin, reviews of *Poems*, by T. S. Eliot, *Daily Oklahoman*, 6 March 1927; *Fandango*, by Stanley Vestal, *Daily Oklahoman*, 24 April 1927.

22. Botkin, reviews of *Cyclops' Eye*, by Joseph Auslander, *Daily Oklahoman*, 12 September 1925; *Destinations*, *American Caravan*, and *Cities and Men*, by Ludwig Lewisohn, *Daily Oklahoman*, 20 May 1928.

23. Botkin, reviews of *American Criticism: A Study in Literary Theory from Poe to the Present*, by Norman Foerster, *Daily Oklahoman*, 10 February 1929; *American Caravan* and *Phases of English Poetry*, by Herbert Read, *Daily Oklahoman*, 23 March 1930. T. S. Eliot, *The Uses of Poetry and the Uses of Criticism: Studies in the Relation of Criticism to Poetry in England* (London: Faber and Faber 1933), 154–155.

24. Botkin, review of *Color*, by Countee Cullen, *Daily Oklahoman*, 11 April 1926; Botkin, *The Folk and the Individual*; Botkin, review of *The Negro in American Fiction* and *Negro Poetry and Drama*, by Sterling Brown, *Opportunity: A Journal of Negro Life* 17 (June 1939): 184.

25. Botkin, review of *Color*.

26. B. A. Botkin, "Self-Portraiture and Social Criticism in Negro Folk Song," *Opportunity: A Journal of Negro Life* 5 (February 1927): 42.

27. Langston Hughes, "Ma Lawd" and "Wide River" in *Folk-Say: A Regional Miscellany, 1930*, ed. B. A. Botkin (Norman: University of Oklahoma Press, 1930), 283–284; Sterling Brown, "Dark of the Moon," "Ma Rainey," "Southern Road," in *Folk-Say: A Regional Miscellany, 1930*, 275–279; Sterling Brown, "Convict," "New St. Louis Blues," "Old King Cotton," "Pardners," "Revelations," "Slow Coon," in *Folk-Say: A Regional Miscellany, 1931* (Norman: University of Oklahoma, 1931), 113–123; Sterling Brown, "A Bad, Bad Man," "Call Boy," "Long Track Blues," "Puttin' On the Dog," "Slim in Hell," in *Folk-Say: The Land Is Ours* (Norman: University of Oklahoma, 1932), 249–256; Sterling Brown, "The

Blues as Folk Poetry," in *Folk-Say: Regional Miscellany, 1930*, 324–339. For critical analyses of Brown's work that further develops some of the points made here, see the Sterling Stuckey, introduction to *Collected Poems of Sterling A. Brown*, selected by Michael S. Harper (New York: Harper and Row, 1983), 3–15, and Joanne V. Gabbin, *Sterling A. Brown: Building the Black Aesthetic Tradition* (Westport, Conn.: Greenwood Press, 1985), esp. 87–184.

28. Botkin, review of *Rainbow Round My Shoulder*, by Howard Odum, *Daily Oklahoman*, 22 April 1928; Botkin, "Self-Portraiture and Social Criticism in Negro Folk Song," 43.

29. Botkin, "The Folk in Literature," 9–10, 12; Botkin, introduction to *Folk-Say: Regional Miscellany, 1930*, 16; B. A. Botkin, "'Folk-Say' and Folklore," *American Speech* 7 (1931): 404–406.

30. Botkin, "The Folk in Literature," 9–10, 16.

31. Ibid., 17. For an overview of changing trends in anthropology, see George Stocking, *Race, Culture, and Evolution: Essays in the History of Anthropology* (New York: Free Press, 1968), 64–90, 195–223.

32. Botkin, "Home Town," 34.

33. Ibid.

34. Ibid., 35.

35. These themes are foreshadowed in Botkin's master's thesis on the Manx dialect poet Thomas Brown; see B. A. Botkin, "The Early Life of Thomas Edward Brown, His Race, Family, Boyhood, School, and College Days: An Introduction to the Study of the Letters and Poems" (master's thesis, Columbia University, 1921).

36. Botkin, "Old Man, What Are You Planting?" 5.

37. B. A. Botkin, "Space: After Thirty Years," *Carleton Miscellany* 6 (Winter 1965): 26.

38. Ibid., 27.

39. Eliot, *After Strange Gods*, 15, 16–17, 20.

40. Ibid., 20; B. A. Botkin, "Regionalism and Culture," in *The Writer in a Changing World*, ed. Henry Hart (New York: Equinox Press, 1937), 151–152, 155.

41. Eliot, *After Strange Gods*, 19, 22, 31, 32.

42. Ibid., 24, 58; Botkin, "The Folk and the Individual."

43. T. S. Eliot, "Literature and the Modern World," *American Prefaces* 1 (November 1935): 19, 21.

44. T. S. Eliot, *The Use of Poetry and the Use of Criticism: Studies in the Relation of Criticism to Poetry in England* (London: Faber and Faber, 1933), 152–153.

45. B. A. Botkin, "Applied Folklore: Creating Understanding Through Folklore," *Southern Folklore Quarterly* 18 (September 1953): 199–206.

46. For an overview of Botkin's attitude toward the relationship between provincialism and cosmopolitanism, see especially his "We Talk About Regionalism: North, East, South, and West," *Frontier* 13 (1933): 286–296.

47. T. S. Eliot, "Ulysses, Order, and Myth," *Dial* 75 (November 1923): 482; B. A. Botkin, "The Folkness of the Folk," *English Journal* 26 (1937): 464.

48. Botkin, "The Folkness of the Folk," 465.

49. Botkin, "The Folk and the Individual," 132.

50. Ibid. 131, 130.

51. Eliot, "Tradition and the Individual Talent," 53, 58; Botkin, "The Folk and The Individual," 126.

52. Botkin, "The Folk and the Individual," 126; Paul Radin, *Primitive Man as Philosopher* (New York: D. Appleton, 1927), 79–82.

53. Botkin, "The Folk and the Individual," 126, 132.

54. Botkin, "The Folk and the Individual," 133. Carl Sandburg, *The People, Yes* (New York: Harcourt, Brace, 1936), 26.

55. Radin, *Primitive Man as Philosopher*, viii; Paul Radin, *Method and Theory of Ethnology: An Essay in Criticism* (1931; reprint, New York: Basic Books, 1966), 101, 120–121.

56. Botkin, "The Folk and the Individual," 126. See Jerrold Hirsch, foreword, and B. A. Botkin, introduction to *Lay My Burden Down: A Folk History of Slavery*, ed. B. A. Botkin (1945; reprint, Athens: University of Georgia Press, 1989), ix–xxx, xxxv–xl.

57. Roosevelt's letter to Green is quoted in Botkin, "We Called It 'Living Lore,'" *New York Folklore Quarterly* 14 (Fall 1956): 193.

58. Ralph Ellison, *Shadow and Act* (New York: Random House, 1964), 103–104.

59. Ibid., 160; Robert G. O'Meally, *The Craft of Ralph Ellison* (Cambridge: Harvard University Press, 1980), 20, 21, 163–165.

60. Ralph Ellison, *Invisible Man* (New York: Random House, 1952), 439.

61. Ellison, *Shadow and Act*, 103–104.

62. Botkin, "We Talk About Regionalism," 289. Eliot said Henry James had "a mind so fine no idea could violate it." Cuddihy, alluding to Eliot, writes, "the modernist idea of a novel bequeathed to Saul Bellow in the early forties by Hemingway, was of a genre so fine that no Jew could violate it"; *The Ordeal of Civility*, 217. Ellison, *Shadow and Act*, 103.

Four Types of Writing under Modern Conditions; or, Black Writers and "Populist Modernism"

When the Stranger says, "What is the meaning of this city?
Do you huddle together because you love each other?"
What will you answer? "We all dwell together
To make money from each other"? or "This is a community"?
And the Stranger will depart and return to the desert.
O my soul, be prepared for the coming of the Stranger,
Be prepared for whom who knows how to ask questions.

—T. S. ELIOT, *Choruses from "The Rock"*

The stranger is thus being discussed here, not in the sense often touched upon in the past, as the wanderer who comes today and goes tomorrow, but rather as the person who comes today and stays tomorrow. The unity of nearness and remoteness involved in every human relation is organized, in the phenomenon of the stranger, in a way which may be most briefly formulated by saying that in the relationship to him, distance means that he, who is close by, is far, and strangeness means that he, who also is far, is actually near.

—GEORG SIMMEL, *Das individuelle Gesetz: Philosophische Exkurse* (trans. Werner Sollors)

"What Is the Meaning of This City?" was a question raised by T. S. Eliot in "Choruses from 'The Rock.'" Modern urban civilization is looked at from the point of view of the Stranger (for Eliot that appears to be death), who questions human aims and the "meaning of this city." The answer Eliot proposes in the poem seems to be: The departure from a sacred purpose makes city dwellers empty pursuers of monetary gain, technological progress, secular happiness, and collective enthusiasm. Eliot's chorus continues in the following way right after the quotation excerpted in the epigraph:

O weariness of men who turn from GOD
To the grandeur of your mind and the glory of your action,
To arts and invention and daring enterprises,
To schemes of human greatness thoroughly discredited,
Binding the earth and the water to your service,
Exploiting the seas and developing the mountains,
Dividing the stars into common and preferred,
Engaged in devising the perfect refrigerator,
Engaged in working out rational morality,
Engaged in printing as many books as possible,
Plotting of happiness and flinging empty bottles,
Turning from your vacancy to fevered enthusiasm
For nation or race or what you call humanity;
Though you forget the way to the Temple,
There is one who remembers the way to your door:
Life you may evade, but Death you shall not.
You shall not deny the Stranger.[1]

Eliot may be drawing a particularly sharp opposition between the quest for the "perfect refrigerator"—for print culture, technological inventions, and nationalisms—on the one hand, and the "way to the Temple"—to wisdom, traditional religion, transcendental meaning, and acceptance of death—on the other. Yet Eliot was hardly alone in his juxtaposition of the secular and the sacred in the modern city. Modernization, industrialization, and urbanization have often been viewed as movements from the sacred to the secular. Listen, for example, to the description of this process offered by Richard Wright, the author of the famous novel *Native Son* (1940) who had migrated from rural Mississippi to Chicago: "Holy days became holidays; clocks replaced the sun as a symbolic measurement of time. As the authority of the family waned, the meaning of reality, emotions, experience, action, and God assumed the guise of teasing questions."[2] In this description Wright followed the terms of the anthropologist Robert Redfield; and again, urbanization, the movement of people to cities that has been at the center of modernity for the past century and a half, is understood as a process analogous to the loss of religious faith.

The ways in which individuals reacted to the modern world of cities and technology varied significantly, though there was often some ambivalence about the mixed blessings of modernity in their perceptions. The historian David Hollinger has made a very useful distinction between modernity (embodied by the processes of secularization on the one hand, and of urbanization and industrialization on the other) and modernism (the formally experimental ways in which many writers, composers, and artists chose to express themselves in the twentieth century).[3] Hollinger thus invites investigations that focus especially on the ways in which a given writer's views of modernity may be at variance with his or her attitudes toward modernism. This gives us four basic literary types of investing meaning in cities:

I. A writer may be critical of the modern city and use traditional, premodern (non-modern, or antimodern) literary forms in order to voice his criticism. The Ohio poet Paul Laurence Dunbar may serve as an example here.

BALLADE

a	By Mystic's banks I held my dream.
b	(I held my fishing rod as well,)
a	The vision was of dace and bream,
b	A fruitless vision, sooth to tell.
b	But round about the sylvan dell
c	Were other sweet Arcadian shrines,
b	Gone now, is all the rural spell,
c	Arcadia has trolley lines.
a	Oh, once loved, sluggish, darkling stream,
b	For me no more, thy waters swell,
a	Thy music now the engines' scream,
b	Thy fragrance now the factory's smell;
b	Too near for me the clanging bell;
c	A false light in the water shines
b	While solitude lists to her knell,—
c	Arcadia has trolley lines.
a	Thy wooded lanes with shade and gleam
b	Where bloomed the fragrant asphodel,
a	Now bleak commercially teem
b	With signs "To Let," "To Buy," "To Sell."
b	And Commerce holds them fierce and fell;
c	With vulgar sport she now combines
b	Sweet Nature's piping voice to quell.
c	Arcadia has trolley lines.

L'envoi

b	Oh, awful Power whose works repel
c	The marvel of the earth's designs,—
b	I'll hie me otherwise to dwell,
c	Arcadia has trolley lines.[4]

Dunbar views the intrusion of the trolley car as the vulgar extension of the din and noise of commercialism and industry into a pastoral landscape. This is truly a case of a machine spoiling a garden; and the Edenic dimensions of the garden scene at the banks of the Mystic (a river with a name that underlines the loss the poem describes) also support the interpretation of this process as a new fall from the sacred and natural environment of Arcadia to the secular world of factory work, monetary exchange, and trolley lines. Dunbar's streetcar might be called decline; the vision may also be one of death.

The regular form Dunbar chooses shows no influence from the free forms of Walt Whitman, but a traditional orientation toward a consistent rhyme scheme (*ababbcbc*) that stresses the last line of each stanza without making it formally disjointed from the rest: the intrusive "trolley lines" still rhyme peacefully with "Arcadian shrines" (and "water shines" as well as "now combines"). The poem's opposition to modernization is matched by its adherence to an old-fashioned form.

Claude McKay's "Subway Wind" is an unusually balanced poem: eight lines each articulate an urban and a rural ethos in traditional, regular *abab* verse:

a	Far down, down through the city's great gaunt gut
b	The gray train rushing bears the weary wind;
a	In the packed cars the fans the crowd's breath cut,
b	Leaving the sick and heavy air behind.
c	And pale-cheeked children seek the upper door
d	To give their summer jackets to the breeze;
c	Their laugh is swallowed in the deafening roar
d	Of captive wind that moans for fields and seas;
e	Seas cooling warm where native schooners drift
f	Through sleepy waters, while gulls wheel and sweep,
e	Waiting for windy waves the keels to lift
f	Lightly among the islands of the deep;
g	Islands of lofty palm trees blooming white
h	That lend their perfume to the tropic sea,
g	Where fields lie idle in the dew-drenched night,
h	And the Trades float above them fresh and free.[5]

The repetition of the word "seas" introduces the abrupt shift from a metropolitan to a down-home scene—McKay was born in Jamaica—without any alteration in the poetic form. Formally conservative, McKay's poem is less explicitly nostalgic than Dunbar's. The sentiment clearly veers toward the island and is critical of urbanization, but country and city get equal time. The formal consistency also suggests an inner continuity between the worlds that are here juxtaposed.

2. Literature may express love for urban modernity yet refrain from employing very modern forms. The following sonnet by James Weldon Johnson is a case in point:

MY CITY

a	When I come down to sleep death's endless night,
b	The threshold of the unknown dark to cross,
b	What to me then will be the keenest loss,
a	When this bright world blurs on my fading sight?
c	Will it be that no more I shall see the trees
d	Or smell the flowers or hear the singing birds
d	Or watch the flashing streams or patient herds?
c	No, I am sure it will be none of these.
e	But, ah! Manhattan's sights and sounds, her smells,
f	Her crowds, her throbbing force, the thrill that comes
e	From being of her a part, her subtle spells,
f	Her shining towers, he avenues, her slums—
g	O God! the stark, unutterable pity,
g	To be dead, and never again behold my city![6]

These lines express sentiments opposite to those of Dunbar's "Ballade." In "My City" a speaker claims Manhattan with the possessive pronoun and expresses love for his adopted city and the thrill of belonging to it. Many features of modernity—skyscrapers, noise, even the slums—are embraced by the speaker, who, again, is reviewing life from the point of view of death (Eliot's "Stranger"), only to find that, unlike Dunbar, he will hardly miss Arcadian scenes, while the thought that death will remove him from seeing his *city* seems unbearable. What matters to the speaker of this poem is precisely what seemed so vapid to Eliot's chorus: the throbbing force and thrill of being a part of the city. One senses a resacralization of the city not as a community but as a power, as a meaningful agglomeration of crowds and contrasts.

Yet the use of the sonnet form by a poet in the first third of the twentieth century indicates a traditional formal orientation; the rhyme scheme domesticates the word "slums" as it echoes "comes." The poem's concluding couplet adds weight to the prourban and promodern sentiment, yet the poem is not at all "modernist."

3. A writer may be deeply critical of modernity and prefer, for example, traditional religious beliefs, but say so in a modernist fashion. Much literature discussed under the modernist label falls into this category of experimentally expressed critiques of (or laments about) modernity. Eliot himself is a prime example, both in the lines in which death asks about the meaning of the city (implying that there is none that compares with old sacred meanings), and in such poems as:

THE BOSTON EVENING TRANSCRIPT

The readers of the *Boston Evening Transcript*
Sway in the wind like a field of ripe corn.

When evening quickens faintly in the street,
Wakening the appetites of life in some
And to others bringing the *Boston Evening Transcript*,
I mount the steps and ring the bell, turning
Wearily, as one would turn to nod good-bye to La Rochefoucauld,
If the street were time and he at the end of the street,
And I say, "Cousin Harriet, here is the *Boston Evening Transcript*."[7]

Eliot's open-verse technique shows the arrival of modernist writing. The sententious, yet mysterious beginning in which modern urban themes are represented with nature imagery ("ripe corn") resembles Ezra Pound's famous poem:

IN A STATION OF THE METRO

The apparition of these faces in the crowd;
Petals on a wet, black bough.[8]

Both poets focus on trivial scenes associated with modernity—the newspaper delivery and the subway station—in order to use modernist writing strategies (irregular lines, no rhymes, and somewhat enigmatic images, drawn surprisingly on nature).

Yet Eliot's poem hardly advocates the ascent of modernity: the arrival of the *Boston Evening Transcript*—after which the poem is entitled and which is fully mentioned no fewer than three times in the short poem—is hardly a new gospel or revelation, but rather appears to belong to the world of empty bottles and perfect refrigerators that was castigated in the chorus from "The Rock." The poetic principle of repetition has here come to resemble an advertisement. After all, the newspaper may not be, as Hegel thought, modern man's substitute for a morning prayer, but merely the best expression of the maximized desire to print as much as possible.

Eliot offered his most influential vision of modernist writing against modernity in *The Waste Land* (1922). Where (irregular) rhymes appear, they seem to be used ironically, as in the following lines from section III, again thematizing a tramway:

"Trams and dusty trees.
Highbury bore me. Richmond and Kew
Undid me. By Richmond I raised my knees
Supine on the floor of a narrow canoe."[9]

In the vignette titled "Becky" in his experimental book *Cane* (1923), Jean Toomer (who in his essay "The Flavor of Man" looked at the machine gun and the prophylactic as the twin symbols of modernity) includes the following description:

Six trains each day rumbled past and shook the ground under her cabin.
Fords, and horse- and mule-drawn buggies went back and forth along

the road. No one ever saw her. Trainmen, and passengers who'd heard about her, threw out papers and food. Threw out little crumpled slips of paper scribbled with prayers, as they passed her eye-shaped piece of sandy ground. Ground islandized between the road and railroad track. Pushed up where a blue-sheen God with listless eyes could look at it.[10]

Becky's world is framed by the tracks of modern transportation. "God" is qualified by an indefinite article and the strange adjective "blue-sheen" (in their combination interpreted by Darwin Turner as "locomotive"). Modernity has arrived, but whether this is a salutary development seems rather doubtful in a book that strikes a balance between the rural and the urban and in which the sacred may or may not appear in the shape of the modern secular. The image of an "eye-shaped piece of sandy ground" is eerie: based on an unusual association (similarity of shape), it is evocative of God's all-seeing eye, an effect enhanced by the prayers. The passage also implies a larger comment on the sacred and sacrificial spot that Becky takes in the community.

Toomer prefaced the section titled "Seventh Street" (a reference to urbanization in Washington, D.C., and a street that is described as "a bastard of Prohibition and the War") with the following poem:

Money burns the pocket, pocket hurts,
Bootleggers in silken shirts,
Ballooned, zooming Cadillacs,
Whizzing, whizzing down the streetcar tracks. (71)

Like Zora Neale Hurston, Toomer also deplored the ways in which phonographs altered folk culture. Toomer did sound the note of an elegy, of a swan song, and he mourned a loss that he clearly and deeply felt. Yet compared to Pound and Eliot, Toomer was less of a conservative in that his hope was not so much in conserving a religious past as in preparing a better spiritual future, which he saw in the coming of a new race, the rise of his newly imagined, all-inclusive, and no longer racially and sexually divided "American." Though he was certainly sharply critical of many facets of modernity, he could not advocate a "return" to an earlier historical and ideological phase such as Eliot's monarchism and Anglicanism as a cure against the ills of modernity.

4. Writing may be promodern and modernist at once. The first stanza of Langston Hughes's poem "Migrant" may serve as an illustration:

(CHICAGO)

Daddy-o
Buddy-o
Works at the foundry.
Daddy-o

Buddy-o
Rides the State Street street car,
Transfers to the West Side,
Polish, Bohunk, Irish,
Grabs a load of sunrise
As he rides out on the prairie,
Never knew DuSable,
Has a lunch to carry.[11]

The poem significantly begins with the name of the setting (as in stage directions), and the character after whom the poem is titled is given a misleadingly familial invocation. Yet the "father" and "friend" turns out to be defined by work and public transportation, which carries him across a polyethnic territory (rendered in a Whitmanian catalog in which the central term "Bohunk" may suggest ethnic friction) to street names that obscure the geography (the prairie turned into Prairie Avenue). Daddy-o knows nothing of Chicago's history; his history (the second stanza tells us) is in Southern cotton fields, from which even his urban, work-defined life-in-a-hurry may be an advance; the blues form, to which this poem vaguely alludes rather than to formal European poetic traditions, underscores this particularly black American urban-rural tension.

No matter how pro- or antimodern, how modernist or premodernist the different writers may be, literary images of modernity often draw on a set of objects—modern gadgetry (alarm clock, phonograph, or refrigerator), buildings (urban skyscrapers, monuments, bridges, and tunnels), means of communication (newspaper or advertisement), or public transportation (trains and trolleys, subways, buses, and automobiles). It is in such objects that the less tangible features of modernity are most fully visualized: the way in which the secular strangers in a mixed populace are thrown together into the same modern landscape, encounter each other briefly and haphazardly, read about each other, live in great proximity to each other, and follow the modern rhythms of work and leisure. These vehicles of modernity not only had thematic significance, they sometimes also had formal consequences in modernist art: one only has to think of such pairings as trains and blues, newspapers and collages, technology in general and futurism, or the incongruous experience of temporal or spatial dislocation and surrealism.

What this naturally simplified fourfold distinction reveals, however, is that what is often first associated with "high modernism" may be a particular Anglo-American blend of antimodernity and aesthetic modernism, whereas many African American writers may have been less inclined to condemn modernity—if only because conservative nostalgia is, as is occasionally noticeable in Dunbar's poetry, particularly inappropriate in a culture whose memory of a past has to confront the history of slavery. For this as well as other reasons, black (and some other ethnic) poets may have been drawn toward expressing at least a partially promodernity stance in often self-consciously nonmodernist forms (our case 2, illustrated also by some of Countee Cullen's work in the sonnet form), or, and perhaps even more frequently, toward writing in a pro-modernity and modernist mode (our model 4, which characterizes the best of Langston Hughes)—a mode that may also combine with expressions of "forward-looking" social criticism. This special location of "ethnic modernism"—its tendency to be just as experimental but not as "conservative"—had certain consequences: some ethnic writing veered toward a populist radicalism, at the expense of "down with the audience" modernisms; in other words, it tended to follow (as did Langston Hughes) the models of Carl Sandburg and Vachel Lindsay rather than those of Eliot and James Joyce. Fear of disloyalty to ethnic-group audiences (expressed by writing incomprehensibly or by siding with Anglo-Eliotic modernists) and of the charge of elitism may have strengthened this populist side. This populist tendency may have made some ethnic modernisms more "political" or politicized, on the one hand, in encouraging poets to take up politically volatile issues of ethnic constituencies; on the other hand, it may have also made such forms of modernism more compatible with commercial culture in so far as they were not excluded on ethnic grounds. From the vantage point of classic high modernism, this form of modernism, especially its populist side (the Sandburg-Lindsay tradition audible in the promodernity-modernism position) seems embarrassing and lacking in "detachment," hence "not really" modernist.[12]

A final example may further extend and, perhaps, complicate this scheme. Richard Wright and Langston Hughes coauthored the "Red Clay Blues," written in a modern blues form, which at first purports to be an urbanized speaker's nostalgic yearning for the rural South, embodied by Georgia's famous red earth, but then turns out to be a revolutionary protest poem against property arrangements in the South:

> I miss that red clay, Lawd. I
> Need to feel it on my shoes.
> Says miss that red clay, Lawd, I
> Need to feel it on my shoes.
> I want to see Georgia cause I
> Got them red clay blues.
>
> Pavement's hard on my feet, I'm
> Tired o' this concrete street.
> Pavement's hard on my feet, I'm
> Tired o' this city street.
> Goin' back to Georgia where
> That red clay can't be beat.
>
> I want to tramp in the red mud, Lawd, and
> Feel the red clay round my toes.
> I want to wade in that red mud,
> Feel that red clay suckin' at my toes.
> I want my little farm back and I
> Don't care where that landlord goes.

I want to be in Georgia, when the
Big storm starts to blow.
Yes, I want to be in Georgia when that
Big storm starts to blow.
I want to see the landlords runnin' cause I
Wonder where they gonna go!

I got them red clay blues.[13]

When the "landlord" is introduced in the third stanza, the poem's "nostal-gia" turns out not to be a backward glance to a rural arcadia, but a forward look to a socialist utopia, the "red" of the clay now endowed with a new political meaning. This poem raises the general issue of how apparent nostalgia may also function as an expression of modernity from the left.

LeRoi Jones (Amiri Baraka) may be most radical heir to this tradition. His poem, titled, after Thomas Hardy, "Return of the Native," no longer seems to offer any place for a native to return to. Instead, the poem opens with:

Harlem is vicious
modernism. BangClash.
Vicious the way it's made.
Can you stand such beauty?
So violent and transforming.[14]

The poetry is sharply modernist in form, and the expression veers toward an existential and somewhat enigmatic acceptance of city life. When Jones used the phrase "populist modernism" in his introduction to *The Moderns*, he was trying to connect his own aesthetic production with the tradition from William Carlos Williams to the beats, and he placed his own prose amid the writings of William Burroughs, Jack Kerouac, John Rechy, Hubert Selby, and others. His term may also give a name to a black branch of modernism whose legitimacy has often been questioned.[15]

■ NOTES

This essay was inspired by a discussion at the W. E. B. Du Bois Institute after a presentation by Josef Jařab. In a different version it forms part of the entry "Ethnic Modernism, 1910–1950," in the *Cambridge History of American Literature*, edited by Sacvan Bercovitch (forthcoming).

1. T. S. Eliot, *Collected Poems, 1909–1962* (London: Faber and Faber, 1963), 171.

2. Richard Wright, introduction to *Black Metropolis*, 2 vols. (1945; reprint, New York: Harper Torchbooks, 1962), 1:xxii.

3. David A. Hollinger, "The Knower and the Artificer," *American Quarterly* 39 (Spring 1987): 37–55. It should be stressed that I am offering an extremely shortened and

simplified account of Hollinger's marvelous essay in order to phrase my question more sharply.

4. Paul Laurence Dunbar, *Lyrics of Love and Laughter*, in *The Complete Poems of Paul Laurence Dunbar* (New York: Dodd, Mead, n.d.), 204.

5. Claude McKay, "Subway Wind," in *Selected Poems of Claude McKay* (New York: Harcourt, Brace, and World, 1953), 75.

6. James Weldon Johnson, "My City," in *The Book of American Negro Poetry* (New York: Harcourt, Brace, 1931), 125.

7. Eliot, "The Boston Evening Transcript," in *Collected Poems*, 30.

8. Ezra Pound, "In a Station of the Metro," in *Selected Poems*, ed. and introd. T. S. Eliot (London: Faber and Faber, n.d.), 113.

9. Eliot, "The Fire Sermon," section III of *The Waste Land*, in *Collected Poems*, 74.

10. Jean Toomer, *Cane* (1923; reprint, New York: Harper Perennial Classic, 1969), 9.

11. Langston Hughes, "Migrant," in *Selected Poems* (1959; reprint, New York: Vintage Books, 1974), 178–179, at 178. Another short Langston Hughes poem, "Subway Rush Hour," may further illustrate this tendency:

> Mingled
> breath and smell
> so close
> mingled
> black and white
> so near
> no room for fear.

An interesting discussion is offered by Gianfranca Balestra, "Poetry of the Subway," *Rivista di studi anglo-americani* 6, no. 8 (1990): 89–100. Balestra notes the presence of eight poems on the subway in one collection of 1923 alone: Dana Burnet, "Roses in the Subway"; Chester Firkins, "On a Subway Express"; Ruthe Shepard Phelps, "The Subway"; Ruth Comfort Mitchell, "The Subway"; Maxwell Bodenheim, "Summer Evening: New York Subway-Station"; Joseph Morris, " At a Subway Exit"; John Presland, " In the Tube"; and Malleville Haller, "In the Subway." In Eda Lou Walton's fascinating anthology of poems *The City Day* (New York: Ronald Press, 1929) are also Lawrence Lee, "Subway Builders"; Elinor Wylie, "A Crowded Trolley Car"; and Alan Tate, "The Subway."

Hughes's poem lends itself to a comparison with the Yiddish poem by A. Leyeles, "In the Subway," and its illustration, by Joseph Foshko. In A. Leyeles, *America and I* (1963), reprinted in Benjamin and Barbara Harshav, *American Yiddish Poetry: A Bilingual Anthology* (Berkeley: University of California Press, 1986), 103:

> Walled-in
> In the gray, moving wall,
> Close to each other,
> A white girl and a Negro.
> Smell of strong musk
> Hugs the flask of a girl,
> Her fearful flutter.
> The Negro squeezes tighter
> Against the girl.
> Black craving
> Blesses white crowding.

Compare also Charles Chesnutt, "Uncle Wellington's Wives"; Pietro Di Donato, *Christ in Concrete* (1939); Ralph Ellison, *Invisible Man*; and LeRoi Jones [Amiri Baraka], *Dutchman*, for streetcar or subway scenes in which proscribed sexual closeness is experienced, whether as liberation or as threat.

In Henry Roth's novel *Call It Sleep* (1934), a high modernist verbal explosion takes place when the young protagonist, David Schearl, attempts to stick a milk ladle on the electric rail of the trolley tracks on New York's Lower East Side. External descriptions alternate with the sounds of the streetcars: "Klang! Klang! Klang!" or "*Zwank! Zwank! Zwank!*" This is the onomatopoeia of modernity that Dunbar avoided but that appeared, for example, in Hugh Martin's and Ralph Blane's "Trolley Song" from *Meet Me in St. Louis* (1944); in Frank Loesser's song "Clang Dang the Bell" from *Greenwillow* (1960); and in Pat Rooney's "The Trolley Ride." David Schearl's vision (in which echoes of Paul's second letter to the Corinthians and of Isaiah's prophetic image of burning coal appear) has a modern sacred dimension—right in the middle of urban modernity, expressed in modernist ways. As in Johnson's poem, the city is resacralized here (though this process makes the city also a haunting and sinister force); and this is done in a thoroughly modern form.

12. For the characterization of "modernist" art as "detached," see, e.g., Maurice Beebe, "What Modernism Was," *Journal of Modern Literature* 3 (July 1974): 1065–1084, esp. 1073.

13. Richard Wright and Langston Hughes, "Red Clay Blues" (1939); reprinted in *The World of Richard Wright*, ed. Michel Fabre (Jackson: University of Mississippi Press, 1985), 248.

14. LeRoi Jones [Amiri Baraka], "Return of the Native," in *Black Magic: Sabotage— Target Study—Black Art: Collected Poetry, 1961–1967* (Indianapolis: Bobbs-Merrill, 1969), 108. James de Jongh, *Vicious Modernism: Black Harlem and the Literary Imagination* (Cambridge and New York: Cambridge University Press, 1990), 1, 111, takes its point of departure from Baraka's poem; de Jongh also appends a helpful "Checklist of Black Harlem in Poetry."

15. LeRoi Jones, ed., *The Moderns: An Anthology of New Writing in America* (New York: Corinth, 1963); see my discussion in *Amiri Baraka/LeRoi Jones: The Quest for a "Populist Modernism"* (New York: Columbia University Press, 1978), 77–78, 166.

Exploring "Something New"

The "Modernism" of Claude McKay's
Harlem Shadows

■

In a collection on race and modernism one might be surprised to find an article on the poetry of Claude McKay, who, as a writer perhaps best known for his use of the sonnet, is not typically considered a modernist. Although he is commonly associated with African American writing during the Harlem Renaissance, a period successfully argued by Houston Baker Jr., among others, as reflecting a uniquely African American form of modernism, in truth McKay had already passed through Harlem by the time the Renaissance was really under way.[1] Throughout his autobiography, significantly titled *A Long Way from Home* (1937) ("home" being Jamaica), he repeatedly asserts his lack of sympathy with both the movement's leaders and their aspirations. Furthermore, the modernist aspects of the Harlem Renaissance are usually attributed thematically to the movement's nationalist and collective impulses, most clearly reflected in its classic manifesto, *The New Negro*, and formally to its goals to "deform" the "mastery" (to modify Baker's terms) of traditional white literary structures by celebrating African American folk expression and cultural traditions through the use of the vernacular.[2]

But McKay's sonnets fit neither of these qualifiers. First, as an immigrant from Jamaica whose work (as I have argued at length elsewhere) signals his profound dissociation from African Americans, McKay actually resisted the nationalist impulses of the period.[3] He went out of his way, in fact, to define himself as an "internationalist," which, for him, meant "a bad nationalist."[4] Indeed, he preferred to identify his work as motivated by a desire for universal appeal rather than to express a distinct group affiliation. To illustrate this with just one representative example, consider McKay's response to the unofficial adoption by black Americans of his most famous piece, "If We Must Die," as a type of nationalist anthem following the race riots of 1919. McKay claims that, when composing the poem, he had no intention that it be understood as expressing the thoughts and feelings of anyone but himself. "I myself was amazed at the general sentiment for the poem," he claims in his autobiography. "For I am so intensely subjective as a poet that I was not aware, at the moment of writing, that I was transformed into a medium to express a mass sentiment."[5] Shortly before his death, he echoes this statement on a Folkways recording of African American writers. "'If We Must Die,'" he states, "is the poem that makes me a poet among colored Americans. Yet frankly I have never regarded myself as a Negro poet. I have always felt that my gift of song was bigger than the narrow confining limits of any one people and its problems."[6] Similar comments riddle McKay's autobiography, *A Long Way from Home*, indicating his strong sense of difference from native-born blacks in the United States.

Second, with respect to the Renaissance's formalist objective to divest traditional white literary structures of aesthetic authority and invest authority instead in African American vernacular, McKay ceased writing vernacular poetry altogether when he arrived in the United States. Although nearly all his earliest poems had been written in the idiom of Jamaican peasants, following his departure from the island in 1912 he completely rejected using the voice of "the folk" as a mode of poetic expression.[7] Indeed, McKay's extensive use of the traditional and highly structured sonnet form would, at first glance at least, seem to ally him much more closely to the formally conservative colonial sensibilities under which he was educated than to innovative forms of African American modernism.

And yet, one of African America's most committed modernists, Melvin Tolson, pays homage to McKay as a definitive source for his own aesthetic sensibilities. Tolson celebrates McKay, whom he dubs "*the* Negro poet of the 20's and 30's" (emphasis mine), for "breaking the mold of the Dialect School and the Booker T. Washington Compromise" by infusing political radicalism into his poetry. He commends McKay, the "poet-rebel," for traveling "*his* hypotenuse and not the right angle, toward *his* reality."[8] Not surprisingly, given his respect for McKay, Tolson invokes McKay generally and "If We Must Die" specifically in his 1965 modernist masterpiece *Harlem Gallery*.

The two settings of *Harlem Gallery*, the Zulu Club and the Harlem Gallery itself, in many ways represent the poles of McKay's own Harlem, at least insofar as it is parlayed through his fiction. The general atmosphere and patrons of the Zulu Club recall both the character types and social interactions depicted throughout McKay's first novel, *Home to Harlem*, while the setting of the gallery, in which discussions about the roles of the black artist and black bourgeoisie take place, provides the opportunity to revisit debates with which McKay himself was adamantly involved during the 1920s and 1930s. More specifically, Tolson's Jamaican bartender at the Zulu Club draws upon McKay's most popular sonnet explicitly:

> "God knows, Hideho, you got the low-down
> on the black turtle and the white shark
> in the Deep South."
> Then,
> describing a pectoral girdle,
> his lower lip curled,
> and he blurted—like an orgasm:
> "And perhaps in many a South of the Great White World!"
> He fumed, he sweated, he paced behind the bar.
> "I too hate Peeler's pig in the boa's coils!

> I was in the bomb-hell at Dunkirk. I was a British tar.
> In Parliament, *white* Churchill quoted one day,
> 'If we must die, let us not die like hogs . . .'
> The words of a poet, my compatriot—*black* Claude McKay."

Here, Tolson relies on McKay as a reference for his own commentary on race relations in the American South, on colonialist and imperialist oppression, on the "use" of black soldiers to fight in white wars—all issues to which McKay himself devoted considerable ink and attention. Finally, to emphasize this social critique, Tolson invokes the highly ironic image of Winston Churchill, representing the imperial rule of Great Britain, naively citing Claude McKay, who is in effect his colonial "subject," in an effort to boost morale for "the war to end all wars."[9]

Still, it is not clear what constitutes the link between McKay's Victorian verse and Tolson's modernist montage. Where should the formally backward looking and thematically forward looking Claude McKay be located in relation to modernist aesthetics? The answer must begin with a careful distinction between modern*ity* and modern*ism*, terms that are too frequently used interchangeably, as well as one between Anglo-American and African American modernist aesthetics.

While both modern*ity* and modern*ism*—and their "definitive" moments of inception and conclusion—have been hotly debated over the years, most scholars agree that whether or not a wholesale "change" in "human character" actually took place, as Virginia Woolf claimed, a distinct shift in sensibilities, cultural practices, assumptions, and propositions can be noted around the turn of the twentieth century that marked the latter period as conspicuously different from its Victorian predecessor. At its most basic, this shift was generally characterized by a rebellion against the mores and values dominating the late nineteenth century, ranging from a belief in a predictable universe and a coherent and fixed set of truths to a dichotomous worldview that ordered life around simplified oppositions such as animal/human, black/white, savage/civilized, inferior/superior.[10] This shift was caused, in large part, by the conditions of modernity: increasing urbanization, the growth of industry, technological advances, and so on—all of which threw into crisis the stability and certainty on which the Victorian *mentalité* depended. The aesthetic corollary of modernity can be described as modernism—the outcome of or response to this shift within the arts. Modernist art, whether exemplified in the rejection of realism demonstrated by impressionist or symbolist painting or the rejection of poetic convention typified in the writing of T. S. Eliot or Ezra Pound, experimented radically with aesthetic form as it sought new ways to express the themes of alienation, fragmentation, and uncertainty characteristic of this new era in which, as Yeats claimed, "the center would not hold," in which "things fell apart."

This distinction, though seemingly banal, is important to our understanding of McKay's significance to the emerging modernist aesthetic in black arts. Indeed, as Werner Sollors shows in his article in this volume, "Four Types of Writing under Modern Conditions; or, Black Writers and 'Populist Modernism,'" what has typically been considered "high modernism"—a blend of antimodern themes and aesthetically modernist forms—largely represents a particularly Anglo-American form of modernism. African American modernism necessarily had to develop along a different axis due to the different impact that the conditions of modernity had upon the black population in the United States. For most African Americans participating in the Great Migration (the movement of large numbers of black southerners to urban areas in the North that took place roughly between 1890 and 1930), for example, relocation to the modern city represented freedom, not fragmentation; it signified a coming together of community rather than a falling apart. As Sollors explains, while many white writers responded to modern conditions with a nostalgic longing for an arcadian past, that longing was generally absent among African American modernists, since it necessarily implied a confrontation with the history of slavery. This unique situation, Sollors states, gave rise in part to an alternative form of African American "populist modernism" that blended political and social critique with experimental aesthetics (as illustrated by the work of Langston Hughes, for instance).

But Claude McKay fits neither of these camps. His aesthetic patterns are neither stereotypically Anglo-American nor African American. (Indeed, I contend that McKay's assumed kinship with African American writers, and particularly those cited as foundational to the Harlem Renaissance, has led to misinterpretations of much of his work.) Rather, McKay's writings—rooted in his experiences as an immigrant from Jamaica—reflect a typically Anglo-modernist nostalgia for a rural past combined with a typically African American "populist" critique of urban America. This interesting hybridity stems from two important circumstances. First, as the son of a prosperous Jamaican farmer, McKay's recollection of the past was less scarred by a history of slavery than it was tinged with the sentimental hue of a pastoral tropical paradise, thus linking him thematically to the antimodern nostalgic strains of Anglo-American modernism. Second, as a somewhat privileged child in a nation in which blacks constituted the racial majority, McKay did not experience the full impact of institutionalized societal racism until he arrived in the United States. As a result, the conditions of modernity were, in his mind, inextricably bound with social inequities rooted in racial differences. His use of art to critique this injustice thus links him again to the "populist" strains of African American modernism. In short, the distinctive way in which the conditions of modernity affected McKay, as a black immigrant to the United States, provoked his somewhat unusual modernist aesthetic: the use of a traditional form to capture extremely nontraditional sentiments. In so doing, McKay at once recalled the formal conservatism of Paul Laurence Dunbar and foreshadowed the thematic radicalism of Melvin Tolson. His work thus represents a critical juncture on the journey from Victorian verse to the "vicious modernism" (to borrow from Amiri Baraka) of black arts.[11]

McKay first encountered Harlem in 1912 at the age of twenty-two, having finally arrived at his destination following a journey that began in his home village of Sunny Ville, progressed first to Booker T. Washington's Tuskegee Institute and then on to Kansas State College (both places in which McKay pursued degrees in agronomy), and finally ended, for a time at least, in Harlem. In the memoir of his youth, *My Green Hills of Jamaica*, McKay describes his expectations about the United States: "Going to America was the greatest event in the history of our hills. . . . It was the new land to which all people who had youth and a youthful mind turned. Surely there would be opportunity in this land even for a Negro."[12] McKay's association of the United States with youth and youthfulness links him to many early-twentieth-century immigrants as well as modernist immigrant authors who similarly viewed the act of migration as providing the potential for growth and maturation. (One need think only of Henry Roth's *Call It Sleep* [1934] or of Ralph Ellison's *Invisible Man* [1952], though postdating McKay, as among the most brilliant literary expressions of this view.) More interestingly, however, McKay's reference to the "newness" of the United States reflects a provocative conflation of typical immigrant visions of the "new world" with this particular immigrant's vision of the United States as a "new land" especially suited for generative poetic practice. He elaborates upon this in his autobiography:

> After a few years of study at the Kansas State College I was gripped by the lust to wander and wonder. The spirit of the vagabond, the daemon of some poets, had got hold of me. I quit college. I had no desire to return home. What I had previously done was done. But I still cherished the urge to creative expression. I desired to achieve something new, something in the spirit and accent of America. Against its mighty throbbing force, its grand energy and power and bigness, its bitterness burning in my black body, I would raise my voice to make a canticle of my reaction.[13]

The "canticle" of McKay's "reaction" to the United States, and particularly to the increasingly urban and racialized environs of New York City during the years leading up to the Harlem Renaissance, is most clearly expressed in his 1922 collection of verse, *Harlem Shadows*. Consisting of seventy-four poems written between his arrival in the United States and his departure for Russia in 1922 (a departure that would mark the beginning of a twelve-year exile), *Harlem Shadows* reveals how a confrontation with modernity thematically and structurally redirected the Jamaican "peasant/poet's" conception and articulation of his art from something rooted in nostalgic pastorals written in dialect to highly crafted sonnets embodying the tumultuous racial tensions of the era.[14] Especially when compared to the collections he published in Jamaica, McKay's "Harlem verse" conveyed an increasing awareness of the definitive impact that race had on every aspect of his life in the United States. Structurally, as he explored this new reality, McKay provided an alternative model of modernist writing during the period by addressing distinctly modern themes, particularly surrounding race and urbanization, in an antimodernist form. It is precisely this coupling of the old and the new—Baraka's "changing same," referring to the Eliotic relationship between tradition and individual talent in black music—that identifies McKay as the fulcrum for the turn from orthodox nineteenth-century to unorthodox modernist black American poetry.[15]

Prior to publishing *Harlem Shadows* in 1922, McKay had produced three other volumes of poetry: *Songs of Jamaica* (1912), *Constab Ballads* (1912), and *Spring in New Hampshire* (1920).[16] The first two collections consist primarily of dialect verse written by McKay while in Jamaica under the tutelage of his mentor, the folklorist and British expatriate Walter Jekyll.[17] Although McKay himself, as he states in *My Green Hills of Jamaica*, preferred conventional poetic forms even at this early stage of his career, Jekyll's patronage, personal views, and intellectual interest in folk culture persuaded McKay to confine himself to the vernacular in his effort to capture the voices of the peasant community.[18] He did so with varying degrees of success. For the most part, those poems that sing of nature and romance in *Songs of Jamaica* and *Constab Ballads* remain rather inconsistent in form and unconvincing in content. Others, however, such as "Two-An'-Six," "Quashie to Buccra," "Hard Times," and "Dat Dirty Rum" are underscored by a political fervor, usually involving social disparities rooted in class differences, that infuses them with considerable force. When McKay writes about the poverty of the peasants, the frustration of toiling in the hot sun for the benefit of a white landowner, the evils of tourism, alcoholism, or the brutal effect of urban poverty on prostitutes and police alike, his poetry gains an authenticity lacking in the poems not engaged with issues of social injustice.[19]

Because of a social structure in Jamaica in which one's economic and family backgrounds were as important determinants of social standing as color, however, the majority of McKay's early "protest" poetry revolves more around issues of class and colonialism than around race.[20] Importantly, however, the focus of his writing shifts dramatically upon his immigration to the essentially (and essentialized) "black" and "white" climate of the United States. Indeed, many of the verses contained in *Harlem Shadows*, published ten years after he initially arrived in the United States, reflect McKay's increasing preoccupation with the personal, political, and even poetic ramifications of racism.[21]

Upon McKay's arrival in the United States, he was shocked by the general American preoccupation with racial distinctions and the denial of fundamental human rights to African Americans. Although he had been forewarned about this by both Jekyll and Tom Redcam, the prominent Jamaican journalist who told McKay that he would "be changed, terribly changed" by the United States' harsh and segregating social structure, McKay's youthful optimism, combined with his supreme self-confidence, seemingly prevented the young artist from recognizing the impact that racism would have upon his professional and personal career.[22] In an article published in *Pearson's Magazine* in 1918 titled "A Negro Poet Writes," McKay conveys his surprise about the rigidity of segregation in the United States: "I had heard of prejudice in America, but never dreamed of it being so intensely bitter; for at home there is also prejudice of the English sort, subtle and dignified, rooted in class distinction—color and race being hardly taken into account. . . . At first I was horrified, my spirit revolted against the ignoble cruelty and blindness of it all."[23] McKay expressed this revulsion in his poetry.

Numerous sonnets in the collection, including most notably "The Lynching," "Outcast," and "Enslaved," record the frustration and anger as well as the determination with which McKay responded to the denial of his civil rights. "In Bondage," however, perhaps most dramatically suggests the contrast he felt between his naive and somewhat blissful youth in Jamaica and his increasing maturation—and implicit contact with racism—in the United States. A traditional English sonnet, "In Bondage" is composed of three quatrains and a closing couplet. The first quatrain and opening couplet of the second quatrain depict a world free of racial distinctions where "man," "bird," and "beast" live "leisurely." "Life is fairer" here, it is "less demanding," and children "have time and space for play": in short, the world McKay describes resembles strongly the vision of Jamaica that can be found in many of the purely nostalgic poetic recollections in *Harlem Shadows* (see, for example, "Home Thoughts," "The Plateau," or "Homing Swallows"). But at line seven, McKay introduces a slight turn that signals an actual turning point in the lives of the children at play: it marks the moment when they, having "come to years of understanding," realize the world is ruled by people motivated by "insatiate lust" who will wage "wars" to ensure their dominance over others. The position of line seven at the center of the first stanza and its closing punctuation of a dash suggest a hesitancy and sense of continuing realization as well as dread about what those "years of understanding" imply. The remaining quatrain then reverts to describing the speaker's ability to transcend earthly greed by remembering that "life is greater than the thousand wars" and that it will "remain like the eternal stars / When all that shines to-day is drift and dust."[24]

The closing couplet of "In Bondage," however, abruptly undermines the transcendent tone of the first twelve lines of the poem. In keeping with the conventional form of the Shakespearean sonnet, McKay crafts the *volta* to fall between lines twelve and thirteen. But whereas the closing couplet of a traditional sonnet usually provides some type of resolution for the conflicts or issues described by the first three quatrains, the "resolution" offered by "In Bondage" is one of utter despair as the speaker acknowledges, "But I am bound with you in your mean graves / O black men, simple slaves of ruthless slaves." This final couplet and its separation from the first part of the poem convey poignantly the speaker's sense of entrapment by race. Reluctantly, the speaker admits that despite his origins in a land that he conceives to be "fairer, lighter, less demanding," he is irrevocably bound with those who must toil under the shackles of bigotry.

McKay's allusion in this poem (as well as in "Subway Wind" or "When Dawn Comes to the City") to a Jamaican childhood relatively unscarred by the burdens of industrialization, urbanization, and racism again recalls a tradition of immigrant writing in which the move to the "new land" is as linked to "Americanization" as it is to modernization and maturation. But for McKay, becoming "Americanized" does not follow the stereotypical patterns of assimilation and upward mobility; rather, for McKay, to become "Americanized" is to become racialized—and in the context of the United States, along with racialization comes racism.[25] Whereas "In Bondage" responds to this process pessimistically, however, another of McKay's sonnets, "The White City," suggests the potential to convert the affronts of racism into defiant energy.

A modification of a Shakespearean sonnet, "The White City" begins with a strikingly declarative refusal by the speaker to accommodate in any way the demands of "the white city." The first quatrain asserts the speaker's willingness to bear "nobly" the condition of ostracism that feeds his "life-long hate," while the second then elaborates upon this, arguing that indeed, without this "dark Passion" feeding his soul, the speaker would literally die—he would be reduced to a mere "skeleton, a shell." The third quatrain and first line of the end couplet shift slightly to delineate how this passion transforms the speaker's vision (and perhaps the artist's as well) of "the white world's hell" into a personal "heaven," and the closing line concludes the poem forcefully by insisting that the very symbols of power and modernity that surround him (mechanized trains carrying "goaded" masses, "poles" and "spires" evoking religious authority, and the "fortressed port" that allows or prevents entry into "the white city" by outsiders) prove to be "wanton loves" because they kindle his "hate." Like McKay, whose rage fed his poetic production, the speaker of "The White City" is at once burdened and yet also somehow strengthened by the intolerance he must confront daily in a "white" urban world.

The race sonnets in *Harlem Shadows* are coupled with another group of poems that focus on the dehumanizing aspects of the modern "waste land." In "The Castaways," for instance, McKay disrupts the bucolic image of a park with the presence of homeless and "withered women"—the "castaways of life"—who, "desolate and mean," serve as continuing reminders of the abuse one can willfully allow to be inflicted on others in an environment characterized by isolation and anonymity. As the narrator of the poem laments, however, he himself, "moaning," still "turn[s] away," having "the strength to bear but not to see" the "shadows" of life, "dark and deep," that dominate these women's lives. "On the Road" and "The Tired Worker" comment upon the drudgery of laboring in the type of menial positions commonly designated for the poor during the period, while "Alfonso, Dressing to Wait at Table" and "Dawn in New York" explore this theme using explicitly racial references. "Harlem Shadows" and "Harlem Dancer" address inequities of race and gender as they describe the commodification of African American women who are forced to sell their bodies in order to survive. In all cases, the poetry stemming from McKay's experiences in the United States between 1912 and 1922 displays the profound impact that the conditions of modernity had upon the "peasant/poet's" aesthetic vision.

Thus, somewhat ironically, McKay's move to a more modern environment freed him to write in the most antimodernist of forms, the sonnet and to make that form his own by imbuing it with insurgence. This coupling is nowhere more poignantly demonstrated than in McKay's most famous sonnet, "If We Must Die." Written in response to the increasing racial violence of the Red Summer of 1919, "If We Must Die" first appeared in the July 1919 edition of Max Eastman's radical journal the *Liberator*. In this masterpiece, McKay endowed the restrictive form of a Shakespearean sonnet with the defiance and determination of people literally fighting for their lives during a period of race riots, lynchings, and escalating violence by the Ku Klux Klan. Not surprisingly, the poem has resonated far beyond that place and time. Despite McKay's own claims later in life that he never intended to encourage any sort of unified action, "If We Must Die" has been put to many different uses over the years. Henry Cabot Lodge submitted it as evidence in the *Congressional Record* of the dangers of black radicalism. During World War II, according to McKay, it was requested by an English anthologist for use in a collection intended to stir up esprit de corps.[26] Later, it was found on the body of a white soldier from the United States who had been killed in battle. More recently, during the Attica prison riot in 1971, inmates reportedly circulated it among themselves as a means of sustaining support for the uprising, although *Time* magazine did not recognize it as having been written by McKay and instead attributed it to one of the inmates.[27] In the realm of popular opinion, at least, "If We Must Die" represents the zenith of McKay's efforts to harmonize political content with poetic form.

But his success at this endeavor has not gone undebated by scholars. Indeed, ever since *Harlem Shadows* was first published, critics have been divided over whether the form McKay chose liberates or limits his message. Robert Littel, in a contemporary review of the collection in the *New Republic*, in some ways diminished McKay's aesthetic efforts by stating that "a hospitality to echoes of poetry [McKay] has read has time and again obscured a direct sense of life and made rarer those lines of singular intensity which . . . reveal [his] naked force of character." Littel praises, nevertheless, the content of McKay's work. In comparing him with other poets represented in James Weldon Johnson's *Book of American Negro Poetry* (1922), Littel notes that "if McKay and the other poets don't stir me unusually when they travel over the poetic roads so many others have traveled . . . they make me sit up and take notice when they write about their race and ours. They strike hard and pierce deep. It is not merely poetic emotions they express, but something fierce and constant, and icy cold, and white hot." In the *Negro World*, the main organ of Marcus Garvey's United Negro Improvement Association, Hodge Kirnon praised McKay's ability to capture urban life, extolling McKay's poetic "revelation of the spiritual isolation and loneliness which many of us—rich and poor, white and black—have felt quite often in the heart of the noise and bustle of this great city." Particularly appealing to Kirnon, himself an immigrant, was McKay's sonnet "America." He believed it conveyed "in a most satisfactory manner what I have always felt and thought to be the main redeeming feature of America. And I daresay many other aliens like myself have felt and thought in like manner without ever giving [it] expression." Finally, Clement Wood reviewed *Harlem Shadows* for the *New York Evening Post* and acknowledged that while McKay's form was traditional, his message was distinctly "modern in its directness and simplicity, its vigor and variety."[28]

McKay himself clearly wrestled with the relationship between the form and content of his work. In the "Author's Word" that precedes *Harlem Shadows*, he insists upon his "allegiance to no master," stating that "in putting ideas and feelings into poetry," he merely "tried in each case to use the medium most adaptable to the specific purpose."[29] On one hand, seemingly justifying his preference for the sonnet over dialect poetry, McKay argues that the "native songs" of Jamaica are "all singularly punctuated by meter and rhyme," and thus "nearly all my poetic thought has always run naturally into . . . regular forms." On the other, he defends himself against the charges of literary modernists: "although very conscious of the new criticisms and trends in poetry, to which I am keenly responsive and receptive, I have adhered to such of the older traditions as I find adequate for my most lawless and revolutionary passions and moods." In what reads as a defensive attempt on McKay's part to reconcile the themes and structures of his poetry, he concludes that the forms he used, however confining, actually enable him to work "with the highest degree of spontaneity and freedom."[30]

But a poem in the collection itself casts doubt upon this assertion. In "O Word I Love to Sing," McKay confronts directly the very tension for which his work has been criticized:

> O word I love to sing! thou art too tender
> For all the passions agitating me;
> For all my bitterness thou art too tender,
> I cannot pour my red soul into thee.

McKay likens his poetry to fragile glass that cannot contain his "stormy thoughts" and as a result prevents relief from the "burden" of his heart. The final stanza most dramatically brings into stark clarity the struggles McKay faced in creating art:

> O tender word! O melody so slender!
> O tears of passions saturate with brine,
> O words, unwilling words, ye cannot render
> My hatred for the foe of me and mine.

In his landmark study of the period, *Harlem Renaissance* (1971), Nathan Huggins, my teacher and friend to whom this volume is dedicated, agrees with the implications of "O Word I Love to Sing." He concurs that the formal artistic conventions McKay preferred could not fully embody the militancy of his message. In a stinging reading of McKay's lyrics, Huggins asserts that "formal matters as well as personal attitudes inhibited McKay from transforming bitterness and disillusionment—which no doubt many Negroes felt—into memorable or powerful art." He goes on to say that McKay's sonnets, "failing in the poetic demand—to reduce to crystalline purity the emotional center of experience— . . . are strangled by the arbitrary restraints of form which McKay could not master. What emerges," in Huggins's view, "is a tone of personal defiance—echoing late Victorian attitudes; too often a braggadocio—depending almost wholly on rhetorical and argumentative style." While Huggins concludes that "it may be too precious to say, 'a poem should not mean but be,'" he does insist that "a poem should be its own validity." In his opinion, "none of these 'sonnet-tragedies' achieve that."[31]

I take issue with Huggins's statement that McKay could not "master" the form of the sonnet and argue instead that his attempt to wed modern content with antimodernist form importantly paves the way for the more extreme challenges to black poetic tradition later expressed in the work of African American poets such as Tolson, Baraka, Gwendolyn Brooks, Bob Kaufman, Lucille Clifton, and Ishmael Reed. In his 1954 review of McKay's posthumously published *Selected Poems*, Tolson praises several of McKay's poems as illustrations of his ability to "explore the axis of day and night" by holding "the looking glass to his ego, his race, his moment, his milieu." Highlighting McKay's sonnet "I Know My Soul," Tolson lauds McKay's ability "to etch with a Dantean simplicity terrifying in detail, a picture of himself as a surgeon in the grotto of the self." Discussing "Africa," another sonnet, Tolson extols McKay's skill in transforming that which most shocks and disturbs him—the decimation of the continent into a "harlot" of colonialism—into poetic expression. Finally, citing McKay's almost elegiac "O Word I Love to Sing," Tolson commiserates with his fellow artist's continual "urge" and "drive . . . toward the rain of fluid rock," with his ceaseless attempt to create meaning through poetry.[32]

It is important to acknowledge, however, that McKay's contributions to the modernist canon were not necessarily intentional. Tolson admits that McKay was relatively "unaffected by . . . New Poetry and Criticism," in Tolson's view largely because of race, and he argues that this did inhibit McKay's artistry: "The logic of facts proves Mr. Tate's observation that this literary ghetto-ism 'too often limited the Negro poet to a provincial mediocrity,' from which he is just now escaping."[33] Believing this, Tolson has no choice but to conclude "that in an era of ethnic mutation, McKay's radicalism was in content—not in form."[34]

While critics are likely to debate forever whether McKay was successful at harmonizing his themes with his structures, his most important collection of poems, *Harlem Shadows*, demonstrates clearly that this artist's encounter with modernity in the United States, on the eve of modernism in the arts, liberated him to write his most socially scathing, if also formally antimodernist, verse. In so doing, he provides the vital link between the thematically more subtle and formally conventional critiques of racism offered by Phillis Wheatley, Frances E. W. Harper, James Corrothers, and Paul Laurence Dunbar and the radically thematic and experimental affronts articulated by those who came after him. Linking the past with the present, the old with the new, McKay's Harlem poetry provides a valuable illustration of an important transitional moment in African American poetic expression. In so doing, it adds another dimension to our understanding of the complicated ways in which race, modernity, and modernism intersect.

■ NOTES

1. See Houston A. Baker Jr., *Modernism and the Harlem Renaissance* (Chicago: University of Chicago Press, 1987), for a persuasive account of how the Harlem Renaissance, and *The New Negro* in particular, are characterized by a "mastery of form" and "deformation of mastery" that signal a discursive African American modernist praxis. For McKay's own comments about the Renaissance and his relationship to it, and more specifically about the conflicts he experienced with both Alain Locke and W. E. B. Du Bois due to his differing views about the relationship between art and politics, see his autobiography, *A Long Way from Home* (1937; reprint, New York: Harcourt, 1970), 95–115; 307–323.

2. Baker makes this argument throughout the text but he makes it explicit in his discussion of the vernacular as the primary fruit of Renaissancism in the 1930s. See Baker, *Modernism and the Harlem Renaissance*, 91–98.

3. For a discussion of the effects of McKay's status as an immigrant on his relationship to African Americans, see Heather Hathaway, *Caribbean Waves: Relocating Claude McKay and Paule Marshall* (Bloomington: Indiana University Press, 1999).

4. McKay, *A Long Way from Home*, 300.

5. Ibid., 227–228. It is impossible, of course, to prove McKay's intentions when writing "If We Must Die." Mark Helbling, however, in his article "Claude McKay: Art and Politics," *Negro American Literature Forum* 7 (Summer 1973): 49–52, argues that whatever the authorial intention, the effect of the publication of "If We Must Die" was nearly ideal in McKay's mind because out of the expression of an individual creative artist came the makings of a consequent political reaction.

6. Claude McKay, *Anthology of Negro Poets in the USA: Two Hundred Years* (Folkways, n.d.); this is a recording of poems from *The Poetry of the Negro, 1746–1949*, ed. Langston Hughes and Arna Bontemps (Garden City, N.Y.: Doubleday, 1949).

7. McKay does employ the vernacular in his fiction, however, and his use of it in his novels conforms more readily to the rubric of African American modernism as it was expressed in *The New Negro*.

8. Tolson, "Claude McKay's Art," 289.

9. Numerous scholars claim that Churchill did indeed quote McKay to the British Commons during World War II, but McKay's biographer Wayne Cooper refers to this as apocryphal. See Wayne Cooper, review of *Claude McKay: A Black Poet's Struggle for Identity*, by Tyrone Tillery, *Journal of American History* 79, no. 4 (1993): 1656–1657.

10. For a thorough and thoughtful analysis of modernism in America, see Daniel Joseph Singal, "Towards a Definition of American Modernism," *American Quarterly* 39 (Spring, 1987): 7–26. Singal provides one of the most detailed and interdisciplinary investigations of the issue in print; the far too reductive differences I have sketched here are explained in full in his excellent essay.

11. Amiri Baraka, in his poem "Return of the Native" describes Harlem as "vicious modernism": "Harlem is vicious / modernism. BangClash. / Vicious the way its made. / Can you stand such Beauty? / So violent and transforming?" For a study that gives particular attention to this concept, see James De Jongh, *Vicious Modernism: Black Harlem and the Literary Imagination* (Cambridge: Cambridge University Press, 1990).

12. Claude McKay, *My Green Hills of Jamaica and Five Jamaican Short Stories*, intro. and ed. Mervyn Morris (Kingston, Jamaica: Heinemann, 1979), 84–85.

13. McKay, *A Long Way from Home*, 4.

14. It should be noted that McKay's residence in the United States during this period was broken by a two-year period (1919–1921) during which he lived in England and worked for Sylvia Pankhurst on the *Worker's Dreadnought*. McKay first lived in Harlem between 1914 and 1919, again in 1921 and 1922, and intermittently between 1934 and 1943. Between 1922 and 1934 McKay traveled extensively throughout Europe and North Africa. In 1943 he moved to Chicago, where he remained until his death in 1948. See Wayne Cooper, *Claude McKay: Rebel Sojourner in the Harlem Renaissance* (New York: Schocken, 1987), for the most detailed account of McKay's biographical history. For a useful chronology, see James Giles, *Claude McKay* (Boston: Twayne, 1976).

15. I borrow here Baraka's characterization of the "changing same" as related to Eliot's famous theorization about the relationship between tradition and innovation (or in Baraka's terms, improvisation) in modernist writing. See Amiri Baraka, *Black Music* (New York: William Morrow, 1967).

16. The title of *Constab Ballads* warrants explanation. In 1911, testing out possible careers, McKay joined the constabulary in Spanish Town, Jamaica. He was not well suited to the brutality or the regimentation often required by the position and as a result served less than one year of his five-year enlistment. The collection of verse *Constab Ballads*, while dedicated to his superiors at the constabulary, contains numerous poems critiquing the relationship between the police and the community. For a more detailed account of McKay's experiences in the police force, see Cooper, *Claude McKay: Rebel Sojourner*, 33–34.

17. Walter Jekyll was born into a wealthy family in Surrey, England in 1849, graduated with honors from Cambridge in 1872, and spent the majority of his life before moving to Jamaica both teaching and studying music (in 1884 he translated and published Francesco Lamperti's *The Art of Singing According to Ancient Tradition and Personal Experiences*). In 1895 Jekyll moved to the island permanently and began studying the folk music and tales of the peasants; this culminated with his publication in 1907 of *Jamaican Song and Story: Annancy Stories, Digging Sings, Ring Tunes, and Dancing Tunes*. McKay met Jekyll by chance in 1907, and the two immediately became close friends; Jekyll financially sponsored and arranged for the publication of McKay's first two books of poems and paid for McKay's education in the United States. For a more detailed account of Walter Jekyll's life and his relationship with McKay, see Cooper, *Claude McKay: Rebel Sojourner*, 22–33.

18. In *My Green Hills of Jamaica*, McKay acknowledges that he was never "very enthusiastic" about writing in dialect partly because he had been taught under the colonial educational system that peasant vernacular was a "vulgar tongue." Although he consented to Jekyll's guidance while in Jamaica, McKay claims that he always desired to write in "straight English": "I had read my poems before many of [the literary] societies and the members used to say: 'Well, he's very nice and pretty you know, but he's not a real poet as Browning and Byron and Tennyson are poets.' I used to think I would show them something. Someday I would write poetry in straight English and amaze and confound them." *My Green Hills of Jamaica*, 86–87.

19. In "Two-An'-Six," for example, McKay captures the powerlessness of the peasants over the economy and the tragedies that can strike them when, as in the poem, "Sugar sell fe two-an'-six." In "Quashie to Buccra" and "Hard Times," he expresses the anger felt by laborers working for a sedentary, aristocratic landowner who knows nothing of the crops, their cultivation, or the exertion that was put into their production—and yet who benefits grandly from their harvest while the peasants themselves gain nothing. In "Fetchin' Water" McKay condemns white tourists who, like "Buccra," find the daily chores of peasant children in the hot sun to be quaint and "sweet" while the tourists themselves, by their very

presence, reinforce the imperialism that keeps the children chained to lives of poverty and oppression. In "Dat Dirty Rum" he describes the debilitating effects of liquor on those who give in to the temporary escape it offers from the trials of impoverishment. Interestingly presaging some of the poetry in *Harlem Shadows* that comments upon the potentially negative consequences of urbanization, in "A Midnight Woman to the Bobby" McKay explores the tension that emerges between a peasant-turned-prostitute and a peasant-turned-constable under the corrupting influence of the city. In all these poems McKay's dialect is powered by a social consciousness and conviction that dramatically increase its impact. That said, many of the poems commenting upon the poverty of the peasants end in a conciliatory manner. In almost all cases, McKay adopts a noble-martyr motif that enables the peasant to feel the "hardship melt away," to "try an' live as any man, / An' fight de wul' de best we can," or to "trust on in me Gahd" (see "Quashie to Buccra," "Whe' Fe Do?" and "Hard Times"). "Whe' Fe Do?" epitomizes this tendency and reflects to some degree McKay's youth, but it also foreshadows his increasingly romantic vision of the peasants themselves. As he moves further from Jamaica literally and figuratively, this romantic vision appears more frequently in his work.

20. Put most simply, Jamaican legal structure theoretically extended civil equality to all, regardless of race. Blacks could join whites and mulattoes as part of the ruling gentry if they possessed the intellectual skills or financial standing required. Among this group, class associations were emphasized while racial distinctions were downplayed in an effort to maintain a hegemony of the elite of all colors. See Rupert and Maureen Lewis, "Claude McKay's Jamaica," *Caribbean Quarterly* 23, no. 2–3 (1977): 38–53, for a more detailed explanation of the socioeconomic structure of Jamaica during the late nineteenth century and of McKay's position within it, as well as an analysis of his attitudes toward class and color conflicts on the island.

21. McKay's third volume of poetry, *Spring in New Hampshire*, was reprinted in full in *Harlem Shadows*, with the exception of five poems: "Flowers of Passion," "To Work," "Reminiscences," "Love Song," and "Sukee River." The poem originally titled "The Choice" in *Spring in New Hampshire* was reprinted in *Harlem Shadows* under the title "The Wild Goat." Additionally, McKay had used the title "Sukee River" for a different poem on the same subject in *Constab Ballads*. He states repeatedly in his autobiographical writings that one of the main reasons for producing *Harlem Shadows* was the omission of "If We Must Die" from *Spring in New Hampshire*. See in particular McKay, *A Long Way from Home*, 98–99.

22. McKay, *My Green Hills of Jamaica* 86.

23. Claude McKay, "A Negro Poet Writes," *Pearson's Magazine* 39 (September 1918): 275–276, as quoted in Cooper, *Claude McKay: Rebel Sojourner*, 65.

24. This line is quoted from the version of "In Bondage" that is in *Harlem Shadows*. It represents a revision of the version published in *Spring in New Hampshire*, which reads, "When all that is to-day is ashes and dust."

25. Werner Sollors makes a similar point about the various ethnic narrators of the immigrant autobiographies collected by the editor of the *Independent*, Hamilton Holt, in 1909 and republished in 1990 with a new introduction by Sollors. For many of these speakers, Sollors notes, "ethnic identification seems to intensify with the modernization experience." See Sollors, "From the Bottom Up," in *The Life Stories of (Undistinguished) Americans*, ed. Hamilton Holt (New York: Routledge, 1990), xxv.

26. McKay, *Anthology of Negro Poets*.

27. Cooper, *Claude McKay: Rebel Sojourner*, 101.

28. Robert Littel, Hodge Kirnon, and Clement Wood, as quoted in Cooper, *Claude McKay: Rebel Sojourner*, 164–166.

29. McKay, *Harlem Shadows*, xix.

30. Ibid., xx.

31. Huggins, *Harlem Renaissance*, 220.

32. Melvin Tolson, "Claude McKay's Art," *Poetry* 83 (February 1954): 287–288.

33. Tolson is referring to Allen Tate (1899–1979), the Tennessee poet, critic, and editor of the *Fugitive*, the bimonthly magazine published by the Agrarians at Vanderbilt University.

34. Tolson, "Claude McKay's Art," 289.

■ JAMES E. SMETHURST

The Strong Men Gittin' Stronger

Sterling Brown's *Southern Road* and the Representation and Re-Creation of the Southern Folk Voice

■

Sterling Brown's own critical distinction between the term "Harlem Renaissance," which he dismisses as strictly box office, and the term "New Negro Renaissance," which describes a literary moment with which Brown identifies, is not just a question of semantics or geographical accuracy. It is in fact a distinction between the values derived from a nationalism embodied in his 1932 collection of poetry *Southern Road* and similar to that which produced the Irish language Gaelic League and those of the allegedly transnational values of modernism.[1] In making this distinction, Brown accepts the premise of Eliot and Pound—and of the Comintern for that matter, at least so far as life under modern capitalism was concerned—that modern urban life is afflicted by a sickness of the spirit caused to a large extent by rampant individualism and the breakup of social and moral consensus; in fact, this spiritual malaise is in Brown's view perhaps more intense for African Americans in the northern urban centers than for other Americans.

Brown rejects the notion, however, that such a sickness was universal in "the West" and instead posits an essential African American culture in the South that is able to resist the sickness of modern society if only black Americans are willing to hold on to their history and the cultural forms of expression and resistance that developed in the intense racial oppression of the South. Though African American writers and intellectuals in the North do not directly figure in *Southern Road*, the book, then, is a direct challenge to a "Harlem Renaissance." *Southern Road* is consciously antimodernist in its explicitly thematized opposition to Jazz Age primitivist fantasies, which Brown connected to a feminized mass consumer culture. Yet *Southern Road* could be termed modernist in its use of that gendered construct of mass culture and in its implicit attempt to solve the crisis of identity posed by "high" modernism. Of course, Brown's particular engagement with history, race, nationality, and place was quite at odds, and quite consciously at odds, with "high" modernism insofar as his solution of the particular crisis of the African American intellectual, and of the folk, involved not the embracing of a vision of the Holy Roman Empire or modernity itself as embodied, say, by the Brooklyn Bridge, but the embracing of the African American folk, whose consciousness of itself and its needs is in turn raised by the "returning" intellectual. The terms of engagement of *Southern Road* with society and with aesthetics, however, is very closely bound up with those of the "high" modernists.

The very title *Southern Road* is a declaration of independence from the "Harlem Renaissance," specifically set in opposition to the poem "Bound No'th Blues" by Langston Hughes, a writer who is often connected to Brown because of Hughes's exploration of African American vernacular English and expressive culture as the basis of literature that went beyond the humor and sentimentality of nineteenth century "dialect" and "regional" poetry. In "Bound No'th Blues," from the 1927 collection *Fine Clothes to the Jew*, Hughes creates a black narrator who rejects his former life in the South and surrenders himself to the uncertainty and cultural dislocation of the immigrant on the "northern road":

> Road's in front o' me,
> Nothin' to do but walk.
> Road's in front o' me,
> Walk . . . and walk . . . and walk.
> I'd like to meet a good friend
> To come along an' talk.[2]

Here is a rendering of the most common type of "folk blues," wherein the first line of a stanza is repeated in the second line (sometimes with a slight variation or "worrying"), setting a scene and/or identifying a conflict, followed by a third rhyming line that is generally a resolution of, and conclusion to, the first two lines. Hughes splits each of the usual three lines in this type of blues stanza to create six-line stanzas, with the break between Hughes's lines corresponding to the caesura characteristic of lines as they are actually performed in the "folk blues."[3] Thus, in what Hughes himself saw as a traditional southern rural blues form, the narrator clearly articulates a rejection of the South and the narrator's past life there.[4] It is clear that the narrator is not simply rejecting southern racism and poverty, but also the black communities of the rural and small-town South, in which not a single sympathetic or supportive person can be found.

This alienation contrasts with *Southern Road*, where, even in Brown's road poems and poems of individual portraiture set in the South, the protagonists' generally positive connections to other members of the southern African American community are emphasized. If the narrators and characters of *Southern Road* move around, it is not the linear and unidirectional movement of the emigrant, but rather a circular movement that generally terminates back home in the South— sometimes after trial and disillusionment in the North, as in the poem "Tin Roof Blues." Ironically, Hughes's use of a folk blues form and rhetoric as the vehicle for this declaration of alienation from the South and of a search for a new community—"to find somebody / To help me carry this load"—by a southern emigrant suggests a certain continuity of culture between North and South—a continuity that Brown would basically deny in *Southern Road*. Thus the emigrant narrator of "Bound No'th Blues," who has detached himself practically and psychologically from his former community in the South, seeks another, more nurturing community in the North while remaining emphatically and even traditionally "Negro" in culture.[5]

Brown's choice of *Southern Road*, as opposed to Hughes's "Northern Road," as a title indicates that he is following a different path in writing. Brown focuses on the endurance of African Americans in the rural South, which occasionally flashes into anger and heroic, and fatal, self-defense, but more often finds expression in more oblique forms of cultural resistance. The opposition to Hughes's poem suggested by the collection's title is further emphasized in the form of the title poem. "Southern Road" is unusual in that it, as Joanne Gabbin and Henry Louis Gates Jr. point out, is a work song with its stanzas cast in the form of a blues—the first published instance of Brown's use of the blues form. As in the Hughes poem, the lines of the basic three-line blues stanza are split to create six-line stanzas: [6]

Swing dat hammer—hunh—
Steady, bo';
Swing dat hammer—hunh—
Steady, bo';
Ain't no rush, bebby,
Long ways to go.[7]

Though the form of Brown's stanzas here resembles that of Hughes's, the implications of the work song–blues hybrid are far different. The "hunh" that punctuates the first and third lines of each stanza is a reminder that the narrator is a member of a community engaged in a common effort, albeit against its will. (The focus on the coercive power of the state operating on a group of people, as opposed to individual acts of racism or "unofficial" social attitudes, also distinguishes this poem from most of the poetry of the Harlem Renaissance concerning racism and racist violence (e.g., Cullen's "The Black Christ" or Hughes's "Song for a Black Gal"), though it does link the poem to much poetry of the 1930s, such as Hughes's verse play *Scottsboro Limited*.[8] The "hunh," of course, marks the moment when all the men on the chain gang swing their hammers together. The injunction "Steady bo'" of the first stanza is directed by the narrator not to himself but to the rest of the crew he is presumably leading, as is "Ain't no rush, bebby, / Long ways to go." This injunction is a call to communal self-preservation, endurance, and a type of resistance that attempts to negotiate the terms of the community's exploitation by setting a limit to the work pace. Thus the voice of the narrator is speaking a communal story in which the narrator's individual story (or what might be considered the blues aspect of the poem) is inextricably bound up with the group's common experience and activity, signified by elements drawn from the work song.[9] While the dominant sentiment of the poem seems to be that of personal despair, the hybrid of blues and work song, and of individual and community, emphasizes communal resistance and survival in the face of crushing oppression from which there is no immediate escape.[10]

However, that there is no immediate escape does not imply, as Jean Wagner and Alain Locke have suggested, that there is no hope or that resistance is futile.[11] The narrator does not accept his situation stoically, as Wagner puts it; his condition weighs "on his min'." Rather, when read with the other poems of the "Road So Rocky" section of *Southern Road* grouped under the epigraph from this old spiritual ("Road may be rocky / Won't be rocky long"), "Southern Road" implies that the survival of community and a communal expression that authorizes and frames the individual narrative, even on the chain gang, is a form of resistance.[12] Unlike Hughes's poem, wherein the narrator denies the possibility of community in the South and leaves for the North seeking a new type of community, Brown's speaker in "Southern Road" recounts in much more detail than Hughes's the disruption of community through the loss of family and freedom while at the same time affirming his relationship to other black men in the South. He could not sunder this relationship even if he wished to do so, since it is not merely a matter of a common culture or shared past but is actually enforced by the power of the state, as embodied in the shackles and guards of the chain gang. What obtains is a masculinist reconstruction of the African American family in which the folk becomes totally male. Such a recasting of the folk as male appears again and again in Brown's work, from "Strong Men" to "Side by Side."

This notion of survival of African Americans as a community as the main form of resistance to racism becomes more obvious when "Southern Road" is seen in conjunction with "Strong Men," which ends the first section of Brown's collection:

> What, from the slums
> Where they have hemmed you,
> What, from the tiny huts
> They could not keep from you—
> What reaches them
> Making them ill at ease, fearful?
> Today they shout prohibitions at you
> "Thou shalt not this"
> "Thou shalt not that"
> "Reserved for whites only"
> You laugh (*SR*, 53)

Interestingly, the rhetorical opposition demonstrated by these concluding stanzas of "Strong Men" is not "They" and "We," but "They" and "You." There is a certain distance, not only between black and white, but also between the folk and the sympathetic narrator, who is presumably the persona of the black poet-intellectual coming to grips with the folk. This distinction between the poet's persona and the folk is seen in many of the poems in *Southern Road* where an unnamed narrator observes the folk. This narrator speaks in essentially "standard" English. At certain moments he adopts a "folk" voice, usually to render indirectly the speech or thoughts of "folk" characters. As in "Strong Men," the relationship between the observer and the observed is often uneasy, if sympathetic. In "When De Saints Go Ma'ching Home," the speaker's statement about the singer "Big Boy" Davis,

> he'd go where we
> could never follow him
> to Sophie probably
> or his dances in old Tinbridge Flat (*SR*, 18)

does not indicate, as Kimberly Benston suggests, the alienation of the singer from the folk community, but rather the distance between his immediate audience of black intellectuals and the blues culture from which the singer comes.[13] Thus the project of *Southern Road* is not simply a portrayal of southern black folk and a northern falling away from the folk, but also a representation of the difficult process of an urban intellectual's attempt to reconnect with the folk community.

The clearest expression of the distinction between the narratorial consciousness of *Southern Road* and the folk that is represented and re-created is the frequent anticlericalism or discomfort with religion on the part of the persona of the narrating poet-intellectual, as seen in "Maumee Ruth":

> Preach her lies about
> Jordan, and then
> Might as well drop her
> Deep in the ground,
> Might as well pray for her,
> That she sleep sound. . . . (*SR*, 11)

This antireligious sentiment can also be found in the parodies of spirituals, as in the second section of "The Memphis Blues," where the traditional "Sinner man, where you gonna run to" is transformed into a series of humorous stanzas involving such figures as "Mistah Lovin' Man" and "Mistah Gamblin' Man" ("Gonna pick up my dice fo' one las' pass"). While there are some nonparodic invocations of spirituals, notably "Sister Lou" and "New Steps," these always occur in the first-person vernacular of a sympathetic folk persona rather than in the voice of the more detached narrator of, say, "Maumee Ruth"—and even the protagonist of "New Steps" has a certain pathos about her. When Brown does draw on African American sacred music, he draws on the spiritual rather than the more contemporary urban and commercial gospel music, possibly as part of some antagonism toward mass culture that causes him, as we shall see, to avoid or criticize the more commercialized and urbanized forms of blues and jazz. This antireligious sentiment, which relies more on irony, is perhaps less overtly antagonistic to folk religion than the militant denunciations of religion in Hughes's "Good Bye Christ" or

"God to a Hungry Child." But it is clear that there is a distinction not only of voice, but also of attitude and certain social values, between the narratorial consciousness of the collection and the embodied folk.

If it is true that, as Jean Wagner suggests, the black folk characters of *Southern Road* inhabit what they see as a tragic universe without hope, this is not the view of the explicitly or implicitly narrating poet-intellectual, who recognizes in the African American folk characters the ability to endure and ultimately to outlast their oppressors as long as the former are able to resist the pull of mass culture and hold on to the "authentic" values of the folk community, particularly as embodied in the forms of folk expressive culture. The poet-intellectual's contributions are consciousness of the dimensions of this struggle and awareness of the weaknesses of the folk, particularly in the face of the challenge posed by the great migration to the North and the potential penetration of mass culture as represented by the North into the "authentic" culture of the South.[14]

Brown characterizes life in the cities of the North, especially New York City, in the "Tin Roof Blues" section of *Southern Road* as fraudulent, pretentious, and downright delusionary, and the black immigrants there as similarly pretentious and deluded, if not immoral:

Maggie came up from Spartanburg,
Tom from Martinique,
They met at a Harlem house-rent stomp,
And were steadies in a week.

Tom bought him a derby and pearl gray spats,
When his first week's work was done,
Mag bought herself a sealskin coat,
Hot in more ways than one. (*SR*, 109)

If these new black city dwellers in the North are tragic, they are tragic only in their pettiness and self-deceit and their integration into the mass commercial culture that dominates the North, at least on the level of induced consumer desires, if not in terms of social equality. Here the sympathetic tone of the poems in the "Road So Rocky" and "On Restless River" sections, which are set in the South and often narrated in a first-person vernacular voice, is missing. Instead, the narrative voice of the poem speaks in the singsong stanzas of the comic song's 4/3/4/3 ballad meter using what might thought of as a "standard" colloquial diction, which ironically interpolates words and phrases such as "house-rent stomp," "hot," and "O milk and honey of the promised land!" that derive from sacred and secular African American rhetoric without being particularly identifiable as African American. The tone of the poem is distant and contemptuously satiric, without any sympathy for the poem's protagonists—a sympathy that had been accorded to murderers, thieves, and prostitutes in the first two sections of *Southern Road*. Similarly, Brown's use of the word "hot" here, invoking a complicity, at least, with crime and a shallow mass consumer culture—like his portrayal of sexual infidelity in other poems in the "Tin Roof Blues" section—connects the poem with a sense of immorality that is missing in the poems of the "Road So Rocky" and "On Restless River" sections, despite works such as "Georgie Grimes" and "Johnny Thomas," which describe what would appear to be far greater social transgressions than those of Maggie and Tom. Interestingly, Brown ignores or dismisses the participation of Maggie and Tom in a communal and distinctly African American vernacular culture, as signified by the "house-rent stomp," possibly because the "house-rent stomp" is, as its name suggests, essentially a commercial venture. Thus the "stomp" is part of the contaminating consumer culture, since it exists only, in Brown's account, as a financial relationship, emphasizing the couple's discarding of old "authentic" racial and ethnic identities while literally assuming the "bargain" costume of a ludicrous consumer fantasy.

This dichotomy of the real and the unreal, or of the "authentic" folk culture and the embodiment of mass culture, is not simply an opposition of town and country. There are two sorts of cities in *Southern Road*. One sort is the cities of the South and the border states—Atlanta, New Orleans, St. Louis, Memphis, even Washington, D.C.—though Washington is somewhat liminal between North and South. In Brown's poetry these cities have a dual character for their black residents. As centers of the "sporting life," they are home to brothels, gutbucket saloons, gambling houses, and a whole gamut of institutionalized vices. African Americans in these cities are also exposed to much the same raw oppression as are black people in the rural South. Brown's poems claim that the southern and border-state cities have a long-standing relationship to the mass of African Americans still living on the land. These poems affirm a cultural and social continuity between black communities in the country and in the city in the South. Musicians, for example, particularly rural male blues singers and guitarists—such as the protagonist of "The Odyssey of Big Boy" and "When de Saints Go Ma'ching Home," Calvin "Big Boy" Davis—after the manner of better-known musicians such as Blind Lemon Jefferson, Huddie Ledbetter, and Robert Johnson, would move from the country to the city and back again.

Thus even the most degraded African American residents of the urban South are presented with a sympathetic seriousness that acknowledges these subjects as members of an authentic African American community, as in the "Market Street Woman" portion of "New St. Louis Blues":

Market Street woman have her hard times, oh my Lawd,
Market Street woman have her hard times, oh my Lawd,
Let her git what she can git, 'fo dey lays her on de coolin' board.
(*SR*, 70)

This portrait of the Market Street Woman, an aging prostitute, can be directly opposed to the ironic portrait of a northern ghetto "easy" woman in "Effie" in the "Tin Roof Blues" section:

She who would veer with any passing wind
Like a rusty vane with rickety ways,
She is aloof now, and seems—oh, so determined;
And that is the Paradise crowning her days. (*SR*, 106)

In "Effie," the satiric and detached tone, the "standard" diction, and the "standard" quatrains filled with alliteration and assonance skillfully create a ponderous and decorous formal permanence that mirrors that of Effie in death and contrasts with her lack of identity in life. Each line that begins with the construction "She who" functions as an indictment of Effie. In fact, the poem resembles an ironic and idealized courtroom speech in which the reader's condemnation of Effie is demanded by the speaker, acting as prosecuting attorney. What Effie is indicted for is an absence of an authentic self, opting instead for a sort of "supply and demand" selfhood according to what she gauges the emotional market to be.

This ironic and condescending indictment contrasts sharply with the sympathetic vernacular voice of "Market Street Woman." A telling moment of comparison is the "oh" of "oh my Lawd" in "Market Street Woman," as seen against the "oh" of "oh, so determined" in "Effie." The former is an apostrophe, which conveys an overflow of empathic compassion connecting the poem's speaker and the Market Street Woman emotionally within an African American rhetorical tradition. The phrase itself is interjection of a communal sacred song or rhetoric within the more individual rhetoric of the blues, creating a hybrid that functions much like the work song–blues form of "Southern Road." The "oh" here is a mark of empathy and community. The "oh" in "Effie," tellingly separated from "so determined" by a comma, archly emphasizes this break—the distance between the speaker and Effie—and undermines any sense of communal identification with Effie. The reader might ask why was it all right for the Market Street Woman to "git what she can git," while Effie was condemned because she was "easy with any chance lover" and veered "with any wind." But this would to be to miss the point suggested by the formal aspects of the poem as well as by the denotative sense of the poems: the Market Street Woman is sympathetic, despite the fact that she literally makes her body a commodity, because she is connected to the African American culture of the South and makes no attempt to shed that connection—at least in the mind of the implicit authorial consciousness ventriloquizing the speaking folk subject who insists on the connection; Effie has abandoned that culture—or so judges the speaker, now speaking in an openly "high" authorial (and authoritative) voice—and has no true identity, only a series of disposable poses that are the emotional and spiritual analogs of the northern consumer culture.

At times the condition of the southern urban black poor is presented in a deceptively lighthearted manner, drawing on the trickster tall tale and the "badman" story. An example is the Slim Greer poems, which lampoon Jim Crow in rollicking short lines with two stresses each in a literary two-step that re-creates and thematizes African American folk dance as well as music:

An' he started a-tinklin'
Some mo'nful blues,
An' a-pattin' the time
With No. Fourteen shoes.
The cracker listened
An' then he spat
An' said, "No white man
Could play like that . . ." (*SR*, 84)

Once again the humor here differs from poems set in the North with a similarly light tone, such as "Mecca" and "Sporting Beasley," in that in the Slim Greer poems it is Jim Crow that is satirized, while in "Mecca" and "Sporting Beasley" it is the black immigrants to the North who are lampooned. As Joanne Gabbin notes, while the Slim Greer poems draw on the popular tradition of minstrelsy and vaudeville, they turn these jokes back on themselves, critiquing mass culture's use and misuse of African Americans. Poems such as "Mecca" and "Sporting Beasley" represent the northern migrants as essentially reducing themselves to a sort of vaudeville or minstrel show without even ironic self-knowledge of their acts.

The other sort of city in *Southern Road* besides the southern and border-state cities is the northern city, to which African Americans were moving in larger and larger numbers by the beginning of the twentieth century. A dozen poems in *Southern Road* are set in or mention northern cities. The bulk of these poems are found in the "Tin Roof Blues" section of the collection. Of the dozen, four are explicitly set in or refer to New York City and Harlem. In fact, Harlem is only black community mentioned in the poems dealing with African American life in the North, even though some of ghettos growing in other cities of the North at the same time as Harlem's transformation into a black neighborhood were as old or older and, in the case of Chicago's South Side, nearly as large. One of the poems, "Cabaret," is set in Chicago, though Chicago never appears by name in the body of the poem. The other poems in the dozen mention no particular city, but are located in generic northern urban setting. This singling out of Harlem again suggests that it is not merely the life of the immigrant to the North, who could live in any number of ghettoes from Omaha to Boston, that is under satiric scrutiny, but also the northern African American intellectuals and artists who were associated almost exclusively, if inaccurately, with Harlem. Harlem is singled out because Brown associates it with a system of patronage in which the artists and writers who participate in the system are essentially a form of exotic entertainment, like the "primitive" costumes of Cotton Club dancers, purchased by the rich patrons. And, by extension, this critique also applied to various modernist appropriations and distortions of African American and African culture, from Vachel Lindsay to Picasso, which removed various folk elements from their "authentic" context.

The tone of the "Tin Roof Blues" section is in sharp contrast to "Vestiges," the other section of *Southern Road* that is rendered exclusively in some kind of "standard" "literary English." In "Vestiges," the narrators' restrained and gloomy diction, derived from Frost and Robinson, seldom mocks, except where the narrator mocks himself, and is nearly always sympathetic. Thus there is greater distance between the narrative voice and the subject of the poems in the "Tin Roof Blues" section than in any other section of the book, underscoring the satire on the subjects of the poems in the section without the sympathy for and emotional identification with the subjects that characterize the narrator in the other sections of *Southern Road.*

Interestingly, with the exception of the title poem, formally a standard blues lyric, where the narrator is about to leave the North to return to the South, none of narrators in the poems in the "Tin Roof Blues" section of *Southern Road* (or any of the poems that deal with Harlem in the "Harlem Stopover" section of Brown's later unpublished collection *No Hiding Place,* for that matter) attempts to represent African American vernacular speech. Instead the narrator(s) of these poems speak(s) in a sardonic "standard" English, generally employing a "literary" diction with an occasional colloquial touch. African American vernacular diction and forms are invoked, though not exactly re-created, as in "Chillen Get Shoes," which draws on the spiritual "All God's Chillen Got Wings," and the lullaby "All the Pretty Little Horses," which portrays a prostitute and her envious younger sister who will follow her older sister "bye and bye":

Envying bitterly
Moll's fine clothes,
And her plump legs clad
In openwork hose.

Don't worry Lily,
Don't you cry;
You'll be like Moll, too.
Bye and bye. (*SR,* 110)

The ironic invocation here of the lullaby and the hymn serve to emphasize the corruption of Moll and, in thought if not deed, Lily, who have abandoned the folk community for the crassest mass consumer culture. (And once again, the lack of sympathy by the speaker for their condition stands in marked contrast to that for the Market Street Woman.)

In "Sportin' Beasley," as in "Chillen Get Shoes," the vernacular is invoked in a parody of African American religious and secular song and anaphoric rhetoric that makes the black subject of the poem the butt of the parody rather than the vernacular itself:

Tophat cocked one side of his bulldog head
Striped four-in-hand, and in his buttonhole
A red carnation; Prince Albert coat

Form-fitting, corset like; vest snugly filled
Gray mourning trousers, spotless and full-flowing,
White spats and cane. (*SR*, 113)

The poem's parodic nature is emphasized by the fact that the speaker seems to be someone who has adopted a hyperbolic vernacular for the purpose of mocking Beasley, but whose natural speech appears to be a rather "high" standard English. Rather than connecting Beasley to a larger community, this parodic use of the vernacular emphasizes his distance from authentic community. Instead of using the minstrel tradition against itself, as does Slim Greer, Beasley has essentially transformed himself into a version of the stock minstrel character "Zip Coon," who makes himself ridiculous through his inept aping of upper-class whites.[15] As in "Effie" and "Mecca," the poem's protagonist is engaged in a willful delusion and self-forgetting. The self-forgetting is emphasized by the anaphoric "forget":

Forget the snippy clerks you wait upon,
Tread clouds of glory above the heads of pointing children,
Oh, Mr. Peacock, before the drab barnfowl of the world.

Forget the laughter when at the concert
You pace down the aisle, your majesty,
Down to Row A, where you pulled out your opera glasses.

Unlike the people on the black circuit between city and country in the South, few of these migrants to the North in *Southern Road* are coming back. In Brown's view, they are radically separated from the folk and are engaged in self-delusion on a massive scale. Perhaps the most succinct exposition of this is in "Tin Roof Blues" where the speaker prepares to return to the rural South:

I'm got de tin roof blues, got dese sidewalks on my mind,
De tin roof blues, dese lonesome sidewalks on my mind,
I'm goin' where de shingles cover people mo' my kind. (*SR*, 105)

Like the speaker of Hughes's "Bound No'th Blues," the isolated and alienated speaker here is emigrating in search of community, only for Brown's speaker it is a return to the rural South rather than a flight to the urban North. It is significant that this poem of return is the only first-person poem in the section and the only poem that re-creates the vernacular in an allegedly unmediated form as, well as the only poem that uses a vernacular form, the blues, without parody or irony.

This practical and ideological separation of African Americans in the North from the folk Brown sees as particularly true for many of the African American artists and intellectuals of the period associated with the Harlem Renaissance. He engages in a polemic with poets such as Hughes, Cullen, and McKay, who write about the South on occasion in the early and middle 1920s but poetically locate the central drama of modern African American culture in the urban North, especially Harlem. For example, Brown mocks what he considers the pretensions of these writers who endow the Harlem landscape with an overwrought literariness in his "Harlem Street Walkers":

> Why do they walk so tragical
> Oh, never mind, when they are in
> The grateful grave, each whitened skull
> will grin. . . . (*SR*, 112)

Here the diction of this brief poem combines the "literary" ("grateful grave"), the pseudo-archaic ("tragical") and the colloquial ("Oh, never mind") to undermine the notion of such a landscape as the scene for anything as profound as tragedy. In addition to its general mockery of northern social and intellectual pretension, "Harlem Street Walkers" particularly satirizes Claude McKay's 1917 "Harlem Shadows," the first poem to establish Harlem as *the* literary landscape of the modern era.[16]

In contrast to the poetry of Langston Hughes in the 1920's and many of the novels of the Harlem Renaissance, and despite the association of *Southern Road* with vernacular African American musics, jazz and gospel music figure in *Southern Road* only in the poem "Cabaret," except for a mention in passing in "New Steps"— unless one considers the "classic" blues singer Ma Rainey to be a jazz singer.

"Cabaret" is the most extreme example of cultural co-optation and hucksterism, of the fraudulent exhibitionism and primitivism that Brown associates with the northern cities and with Harlem in particular—though the scene in this case is in Chicago:

> The jazzband unleashes its frenzy.
> Now, now
> To it, Roger; that's a nice doggie,
> Show your tricks to the gentleman. (*SR*, 115)

This empty and degrading show of supposedly joyous and carefree black life, where African Americans have been reduced again to commodities as they were during slavery, is contrasted with the real drama and tragedy of African Americans in the South:

> I've been away a year today
> To wander and roam
> I don't care if it's muddy there
>
> *(Now that the floods recede,*
> *What is there left the miserable folk?*

> *Oh time in abundance to count their losses,*
> There is so little left to count.) (*SR*, 116)

As Jean Wagner points out, the formal arrangement of the poem presents a counterpoint of three psychological levels: that of the white customers in a Chicago jazz club; that of the performers in the club; and that of the common black people of the rural South. Perhaps it is more accurate to say that the counterpoint is not so much between what Wagner calls "the customers, the performers, and the people" as it is between the supply-and-demand cultural production of the club (where black performers transform African American vernacular music—and themselves—into a product both exotic and reassuring to rich white audiences) and the actual conditions of "the people" in South as seen through the mediating consciousness of the poem's speaker.[17] The three levels of the poem are not so much the three psychological levels of audience, performers, and people as they are the narrator's attitude toward those three groups. Thus the nonitalicized sections set in the club are descriptive and bitterly satiric, while the bracketed and italicized sections set in the South are descriptive and sympathetic and, and one occasion, ventriloquize the voice of the folk:

> (*In Mississippi*
> *The black folk huddle, mute, uncomprehending,*
> *Wondering "how the good Lord*
> *Could treat them this a way")* (*SR*, 117)

There are also two unbracketed italicized stanzas that seem to be the speaker's direct comments to the band and the dancers. Here the speaker compares the performers to domesticated animals, suggesting that they are participating in a double erasure: of their own identity as human beings and of the true identity of the black communities of the rural South. Again, Brown's concern here is the abandonment of true identity to a commercialized delusion and the destruction of communal expression. Brown not only critiques the studied "primitivism" of the shows at such whites-only (so far as the audience was concerned) clubs as the Cotton Club, but also the patronage system of the Harlem Renaissance, in which artists and intellectuals willingly become performing animals for their patrons.

What links the different sections of the poem together is the music the band plays, represented by song lyrics and onomatopoeic imitations of instrumental riffs. For the speaker the music represents the greatest crime, since it is appropriated from "the people" and transformed and falsified into a vehicle for the erasure of both the musicians as full humans and the southern black communities from which the music was ultimately drawn. Brown's attitude here toward jazz and African American participation in mass culture is remarkably like many communist cultural critics in Europe and the United States for whom jazz is at best a plaything of the bourgeoisie and at worst a means of disseminating a false consciousness in the working class, or in Brown's case, African Americans—especially in the

North.[18] Thus this poem could be seen in opposition to Langston Hughes's "Negro Dancers" from *The Weary Blues*, which uses a similar onomatopoeic representation of jazz to proclaim a sort of African American difference and resistance to white appropriation by remaining one step ahead, in trickster fashion.[19]

Brown also uses popular music, especially jazz, in *Southern Road*, not only to critique a commodified exoticism designed to retail black "primitivism" and "natural" joy to the prurient tastes of jaded white people, but also to figure a corrupting commercialization of African American culture. This commercialization causes African Americans in the urban North to lose touch with the folk to such an extent that they no longer know what they are missing. Though jazz is not specifically identified, "Children's Children" extols the blues, hollers, work songs, and spirituals of the rural South at the expense of what appears to be jazz, which becomes the cultural embodiment of the foolish and self-destructive forgetting of the southern past and present of African Americans by the intellectuals and "strivers" associated with Harlem:

> They have forgotten, they have never known,
> Long days beneath the torrid Dixie sun
> In miasma'd riceswamps;
> The chopping of dried grass, on the third go round
> In strangling cotton;
> Wintry nights in mud-daubed makeshift huts,
> With these songs, sole comfort. (*SR*, 107)

The rhymes here, when they do occur, are almost never exact. The anaphoric phrases "When they hear" and "They have forgotten" beginning the poem's stanzas give the poem a certain regularity. But even this regularity breaks down after the twenty-first line—a regularity that was none too regular in the first place, given the varying length of the poem's lines and stanzas. As a result there is a sense of slackness, particularly in stanzas describing the "children' children," where the alliteration of liquids and sibilants dominates, corresponding to the self-willed forgetfulness that again erases both the southern folk and African American subjects themselves as African Americans ("With their paled faces, coppered lips, / And sleek hair cajoled to Caucasian straightness.").

In many respects, the final "Vestiges" section is the most crucial to Brown's vision of African American community, even if the poems there are also the most conventional. "Vestiges" shares with the other sections of *Southern Road* a sense of orality, where a narrative voice actually speaking is strongly present in every poem. However, even more than in the "Tin Roof Blues" section, the voice heard here is the naked voice of the poet's persona, without the ventriloquisms or re-creation of the folk that mark the earlier sections. "Vestiges" represents an intellectual's return to the folk in which the folk's values and ability to endure are wedded to a vision of the future and an understanding of the present that the returning intellectual-artist can provide.

This section is prefaced by the graphic of the well-known African American cartoonist E. Simms Campbell, which shows the homecoming of a well-dressed male, presumably the returning African American intellectual or artist, to a cabin outside which an older couple in homespun clothes, presumably his parents, wait. Campbell's illustration serves as a visual gloss on Brown's poetry, providing a coherence to the section that might otherwise escape the reader. (The progression of Campbell's graphics throughout *Southern Road* from images of hard and often forced labor preceding the first section, to scenes of disaster and displacement before the second section, to figures of commercialism, ostentation, and northern Jim Crow before the third, to the scene described above function as a gloss on the movement of the collection and reinforce the unity of the sections and the logic of their sequence.)

This intellectual prodigal's return is most clearly seen in the sonnet "Salutamus," which begins the section:

> And yet we know relief will come some day
> For these seared breasts; and lads as brave again
> Will plant and find a fairer crop than ours.
> It must be due our hearts, our minds, our powers;
> These are the beacons to blaze out the way.
> *We must plunge onward; onward, gentlemen . . . (SR,* 123)

The poem is more or less an Italian sonnet with a slightly variant sestet (*cdeecd* instead of *cdecde* or *cdcdcd*) in a fairly uniform iambic pentameter using equally "high" and formal "poetic" diction. While Joanne Gabbin is no doubt correct in pointing the resemblance of this poem to "high" works by James Weldon Johnson and Countee Cullen as well as to the spirituals, it worth noting that it also re-creates the images of agriculture and journey found in many of the vernacular poems of the first two sections within the framework of a very "high" and conventional literary practice.[20] It is also a counternarrative of the Cain and Abel story, which was of tremendous importance in both the justification of slavery (Africans were seen as the children of Ham, whose lineage was traced to the tiller Cain) and of African American folk religion, where the branded tillers of the soil will, through the tilling of their intellectual capacities, escape the irrational curse placed upon them. Thus the formal aspects of "Salutamus" can be seen to embody the hybrid consciousness of the returning intellectual and his revisioning of the folk.

However, the section itself is not as neat or schematic as "Salutamus" and Campbell's graphic would seem to indicate. In practice, the section appears to be a catch-all for a number of Brown's "high" lyrics—sonnets, elegies, praise poems, and so on—so that the section would seem to be at odds with the rest of the collection. Of course, the notion of a "high"-culture tour de force to demonstrate that the African American artist speaks in a distinctly African American lexicon because he or she chooses to speak that way, the *tour de force* becoming a mark of the artfulness of his or her vernacular achievement rather than his or her intellectual or artistic limitations, has a long tradition in African American expressive culture.[21] While Brown may be drawing on this tradition, it is telling that he chooses to end his book with this section, so that it is the "high" poems that leave the final impression on the reader, rather than the vernacular ones.

The question of why Brown chooses to do this is further compounded by the enigmatic title of the section itself. Vestiges of what? the reader asks. African American rural culture? (After all, two of Brown's most important predecessors in representations of the folk, Jean Toomer with *Cane* and James Weldon Johnson with *God's Trombones*, were convinced that the southern rural African American expressive culture they were representing and re-creating was vanishing.)[22] "High" Euro-American culture? Bourgeois individualism? Romanticism? Given the "high" form of the poems in this section and the thematic concerns that dominate this section—loss, decay, death, uncertainty, and romantic disappointment—and that can be characterized as those of an individual experiencing or imagining extreme isolation, it is the poet-intellectual's consciousness that we are left with at the end whose subjectivity is embodied in the "high," bourgeois individualistic, romantic voice of the section. There we see that though the poet-intellectual may be necessary to the folk in order that they may envision a future beyond one of simple endurance, he also needs the folk to end his isolation, which even connections of family and romantic love are not enough to overcome (because such individual connections are mortal, while the folk is not). However, while *Southern Road* formally and thematically projects a guarded optimism, it does not suggest that the sort of synthesis of a new type of intellectual and the folk will be an easy one and that vestiges of individualism and romanticism with be not so easily left behind insofar as they exert an often morbid appeal that is as strong as, perhaps even a part of, the consumer culture that lures other classes of African Americans.

While Brown does reject the idea of a "Harlem Renaissance," he did subscribe to the notion of a "New Negro Renaissance," which implies that he shares Alain Locke's sense of a quasi-nationalist movement, or at least a wish for such a movement, similar to that of a "New Ireland" or "New Czechoslovakia."[23] Brown and Locke, like many European nationalists of the nineteenth and early twentieth centuries, saw a true national identity arising from somewhat static peasant culture whose essence was basically ahistorical. Or perhaps it is more accurate to say that Brown was not so much antimodernist as against any sort of African American modernism that abandoned the experience and culture of the southern folk. Thus even writers such as Toomer and Johnson, who invoked and represented the vernacular in their works, become problematic for Brown in that they saw the culture represented in *Cane* and *God's Trombones* as fading and their works as in part elegies for that culture.

Of course, unlike Locke, Johnson, and other promoters of a "Harlem" Renaissance, Brown clearly puts no stock in the notion of Harlem as the new cultural capital that will synthesize the various folk strains of Afro-America into new "high" art forms. In general, Brown is far more dubious than Locke and Johnson about the effect of the new urban concentrations of black people on African American culture. It is also unclear to what degree Brown is interested in "elevating" the folk utterance or whether in fact he thinks it already as "high" as it needs to be. What Brown seems to be interested in is closer to the slogan of the CPUSA-led League of Struggle for Negro Rights, "Promote Negro Culture in Its Original Form with Proletarian Content."[24] In other words, rather than attempting to transmogrify the form of the folk expression into something "higher," Brown proposed to approach this expression on something like its own formal terms, but with a different, and presumably higher, consciousness. (Again, this approach can be compared to that of Hughes in *Fine Clothes to the Jew*, where the poet for the most part attempts to re-create and document the folk voice without comment or any sense that the narratorial consciousness is significantly different from that of the folk. In this sense, Brown makes the problem of representing and re-creating the folk subject and the folk utterance overt, whereas in Hughes it is covert.)

This positing of rural southern African American folk culture as the mythic foundation of African American identity stands also in contradistinction to Marcus Garvey's use of a mythic Africa for a similar purpose. As Jean Wagner points out, Africa never appears directly or indirectly in *Southern Road*; this absence distinguishes Brown's work from that of even those black writers of the period such as Hughes, Waring Cuney, Helene Johnson, and Zora Neale Hurston, who did do significant work in the vernacular.[25] The intellectual nineteenth-century European nationalism that influenced Locke and Brown was quite different than the distinctly twentieth-century mixture of utopian nationalism and black capitalism of Garvey, whose literary followers in the United States almost always employed an extremely "high" poetic diction. What Brown did share with the literary Garveyites of the *Negro World* was a masculinist rhetoric in which the voice of the poetry was definitely gendered and definitely male.[26] While women often appear in *Southern Road* as subjects of tragic or pathetic portraits, only one of the many first-person poems of *Southern Road*, "Sister Lou," is in the voice of a woman. Even in the one poem that portrays the expressiveness of a female subject, "Ma Rainey," the actual voice of the singer Ma Rainey appears only briefly in the fourth section of the poem and even there is filtered through the voice of a secondary male narrator rendered by the poem's primary narrator, whose gender is not specified but who is, given gendered nature of so many of the book's poems, almost certainly male.

There is an academic feel, a curatorial sense, to the work of both Locke and Brown. Locke proposes rural African American folk culture as a basis for "high" culture that would place the African American artist and intellectual within the arena of international art and scholarship, but that would not change that scholarship much, only add to it in a manner that is not unlike T. S. Eliot's notion that literary tradition is something that is added to incrementally and changed slowly and nearly imperceptibly.[27] Brown, on the other hand, proposes a whole new type of academy. The poems of *Southern Road*, written near the beginning of Brown's literary and academic career, are consonant with Brown's lifelong work as a poet, anthologist, critic, teacher, and promoter and preserver of African American literature, music—including jazz—and folklore. *Southern Road* is a radical redefinition of what has come to be known as the canon to include a far wider variety of cultural forms, specifically African American folk forms, than had been accepted before. His project in *Southern Road* is not, however, the academization of the folk, but rather the representation of a process whereby an urban intellectual is able to rejoin the folk without glossing over the difficulties of such a process. At the same time this process is not simply a sentimental return to the folk or a new primitivism on the part of the intellectual, but also involves the intellectual-poet's giving a new consciousness to the folk that allows to see its power and destiny more clearly while recognizing its weaknesses. As Kimberly Benston notes:

> Indeed, the "tradition," reconstructed anew with every Brown poem, is very much the poet's subject—but, as Brown incessantly examines it, tradition must be understood in its etymologically contradictory aspects of "betrayal" and "inheritance." How, Brown's poems ask, can the transaction between individual and communal voice preserve the *continuous* integrity of each and thereby enlarge rather merely reify a vital image of the Afro-American self.[28]

Thus Brown is authorized to create new "folk" forms such as the blues work song in "Southern Road" and feels free to ridicule black folk religion and even black sacred rhetoric and music while recognizing a secular value in the religion and its rhetoric and music. In this sense Alain Locke is certainly correct that Brown does establish "a sort of common denominator between the old and new Negro," however critical Brown may have been of those aspects of the New Negro movement associated with Harlem by such black intellectuals as Locke and Johnson.[29] If it can be said that Brown's work is in a sense curatorial, in that it seem to valorize older rural "folk" cultural forms while rejecting newer more urban and commercial forms, Brown does not have the feel of the "moldy fig" about him. He is not claiming that there has not been a good song since 1898. Rather, he is attempting to promote what he sees as a vital oppositional culture rather than a residual one—one that is largely, though not entirely outside the orbit of the supply-and-demand commercial culture. For Brown, commercialized blues and jazz are both alienating and a mark of the alienation of the black individual from community and from history, while folk forms are signs of communal resistance and in fact perhaps the most important community-building activity.[30]

Southern Road is also a rejection of what Brown perceives as the cosmopolitan values of the Harlem Renaissance. His collection contains criticism and commentary on specific African American writers as well as what he perceived as the general values of the scene associated with Harlem. Brown examines Harlem and the writers around it in view of his newly defined canon and finds it, and them, wanting. However, unlike Wallace Thurman and the critical descendants of his views on the period expressed in *Infants of the Spring*—Nathan Huggins, for example, in his seminal work on the Harlem Renaissance—who found the New Negro writers too parochial in their material and their standards, Brown found them insufficiently grounded in the struggles, traditions, and aesthetics of the masses of their own people in the rural South, as well as far too pretentious.[31] From this perspective, Brown in *Southern Road* could be said to have much in common with eighteenth-century English neoclassical satire in that his bitter attacks on various sorts of economic and intellectual "strivers" are measured against an idealized past, though in Brown's case it is not a neoclassical idealization of Greece and Rome, but that of the rural folk, that is the measuring stick. Thus, again, Brown's enterprise can be said to be both deeply radical and deeply conservative. His location of the locus of authentic African American culture in the South, his emphasis on authenticity itself, his opposition to mass culture (and the modernism that is an agent of mass culture) set against a residual folk culture, his radical yet curatorial approach to folklore and his notion of the vanguard intellectual who rejoins the folk remain a pole of attraction for African American writers, even the neomodernist writers of the late 1940s and early 1950s such as Melvin Tolson, Robert Hayden, and Gwendolyn Brooks, whose works would seem as far from the spirit of *Southern Road* as one could imagine.

■ NOTES

This essay is an earlier version of part of the second chapter of my *The New Red Negro: The Literary Left and African American Poetry, 1930–1946* (New York: Oxford University Press, 1999).

1. See Brown, "The Negro in Literature, 1925–1955," in *The New Negro Thirty Years Afterward*, ed. Rayford Logan, Eugene C. Holmes, and G. Franklin Edwards (Washington, D.C.: Howard University Press, 1955) for Brown's clearest written statement on the Harlem Renaissance.

2. Langston Hughes, *Fine Clothes to the Jew* (New York: Knopf, 1927), 87.

3. While what distinguishes a "folk" blues from other more commercial or more urban forms of blues is ambiguous, folk blues is generally considered to be marked by the use of a common stock of traditional themes, images, phrases, and rhetorical devices. One aspect of the folk blues, and other forms for that matter, that makes blues poetry both difficult and distinctive is that while the typical twelve-bar blues is for the most part regularly stressed— four stresses to a line—these stresses are unrelated to line length. Thus in Brown's blues poetry and other vernacular poetry, lines usually contain the same number of stresses but they often come at irregular intervals. For a good discussion of this subject, see the Steven Tracy, "Defining the Blues," in *Langston Hughes and the Blues* (Urbana: University of Illinois Press, 1988), 59–140.

4. See Hughes's comments in the liner notes to the record *Langston Hughes Reads and Talks about His Poetry*.

5. Of course, *Fine Clothes to the Jews* as whole represents the experience of the migrant North far more problematically, especially in the "Railroad Avenue" section of the collection, which, I would argue, is an important influence on the poems in the "Tin Roof Blues" section of *Southern Road*—with the difference that Hughes is far more sympathetic to the northern migrants than Brown. In this regard, the whole notion of Hughes as strictly a northern city poet is problematic here if one is referring to the locale in which the poems are

set rather than where the poet is from; by this standard Brown, who grew up in Washington, D.C., and whose father was a minister and a professor at the Howard University School of Religion, might be considered alien to the Deep South, since the bulk of the poems in *Fine Clothes to the Jew* that have an identifiable location are set in the South.

6. Joanne V. Gabbin, *Sterling A. Brown: Building the Black Aesthetic Tradition* (Westport, Conn.: Greenwood Press, 1985), 122; Henry Louis Gates Jr., *Figures in Black* (Oxford: Oxford University Press, 1987), 231–232. See also Vera Kutzinski, "The Distant Closeness of Dancing Doubles: Sterling Brown and William Carlos Williams," *Black American Literature Forum* 16, no. 1 (Spring 1982): 19–25.

7. Sterling A. Brown, *Southern Road* (New York: Harcourt, Brace, 1932), 46; hereafter cited as *SR*. All quotations in this essay will be cited from this edition of the text and cited parenthetically.

8. Countee Cullen, *The Black Christ and Other Poems* (New York: Harper, 1929); Langston Hughes, *Scottsboro Limited* (New York: Golden Stair, 1932).

9. Jean Wagner, *Black Poets of the United States: From Paul Laurence Dunbar to Langston Hughes* (Urbana: University of Illinois Press, 1973), 489–490; Gabbin, *Sterling A. Brown*, 121–123.

10. In this respect it is interesting to compare Brown's poem to Waring Cuney's "Chain Gang Chant," which also appeared in the 1930 issue of B. A. Botkin's *Folk-Say*, in which "Southern Road" was first published. Cuney's poem reads:

> How long, how long,
> Oh, tell me how long?
> I call ma mother,
> But she don't answer me.
> No, Lawd.

Cuney's poem presents a very similar list of disruptions of the speaker's connection to community. However, unlike Brown's poem, it makes no mention of the new black community in which the convict is located except in the title. While the "No Lawd" at the end of the first three stanzas of the Cuney poem may be the response of the work gang to the leader, there is no clear address by the poem's speaker to his fellow convicts framing the poem in the way there is in the first stanza of Brown's poem. Thus the narrative consciousness of Cuney's poem is more akin to that Hughes's "Bound No'th Blues" than it is to "Southern Road," despite their ostensible similarity of subject and proximity in *Folk-Say*, which invites the reader to consider them together. See Waring Cuney, "Chain Gang Chant," in *Folk-Say: A Regional Miscellany, 1930*, ed. Benjamin A. Botkin (Norman: University of Oklahoma Press, 1930), 280.

11. Wagner, *Black Poets of the United States*, 496–503; Alain Locke, "Sterling Brown: The New Negro Folk-Poet," in *Negro*, ed. Nancy Cunard (London: Wishart, 1934), 90. Hughes's poetry in the early 1930s would change with respect to the possibility of African American community in the South, though his vision, as in *Scottsboro Limited*, where the "boys" unite with white workers, is far more interracial that of Brown during the same period.

12. It is also worth noting that even when direct resistance is represented as essentially futile in any practical sense, that does not prevent such resistance from occurring, as in "Sam Smiley" and "Johnny Thomas," where the protagonists resist violently at the cost of their lives. It also does not prevent more successful and less direct rebellion, as in "Ruminations of Luke Johnson," where the character Mandy Jane steals from the plantation owner's kitchen as partial restitution for the enslavement of her grandfather and her own exploitation.

13. Kimberly Benston, "Sterling Brown's After-Song: 'When de Saints Go Ma'ching Home' and the Performances of Afro-American Voice," Callaloo 14/15 (1982): 33–42, cited material on 40–42; for Brown's description of Davis's audience, see Gabbin, *Sterling A. Brown*, 34–35.

14. The notion of the corrupting influence of the northern commercial spirit in the South and the importance of the intellectual in resisting that corruption was not original with Brown, as the "Of the Wings of Atalanta" chapter of W. E. B. Du Bois, *The Souls of Black Folk* (1903; reprint, New York: Signet, 1969), attests. Of course, in Brown the task of the intellectual is to allow the folk to know itself, whereas in Du Bois the task is to allow the folk, or some portion of it, to transcend itself. In this *Southern Road* is closer to much of the work of Claude McKay, where a similar split between the black intellectual and the folk is represented. The difference is that the narrative consciousness of Brown's poetry has a sort of vanguard consciousness, missing or much less emphasized in McKay, which the folk needs if it is ultimately going to free itself. McKay's poetry and novels as well as Brown's poetry posit a narratorial persona that is not "rooted in the soil" but alienated from the folk and "the soil," so that their works become a process of return for the intellectual-artist, both figuratively and literally. While both writers indicate that such a return will be salutary for the alienated intellectual and the folk alike, Brown's sense of the importance of the intellectual for the folk is far greater than McKay. Thus the narratorial consciousness of many of Brown's poems does not simply defend the "purity" of the "racial heritage" but feels free to pointedly criticize it, albeit from a sympathetic point of view. In an example Wagner himself notes (*Black Poets of the United States*, 490–496), it clearly attacks what is seen as an accommodationist tradition of African American folk religion, as in "Maumee Ruth" in *Southern Road* and "The Young Ones" in *No Hidin' Place*. Brown's sympathetic yet critical attitude toward the folk, particularly with respect to religion, is quite consonant with the construction of the African American folk by the Communist Party of the United States of America (CPUSA) during the era of the "Third Period." (It is not hard to see how this implicit intellectual vanguardism would be appealing to critics of the communist Left, to which such a move would be in keeping with the general sense of the CPUSA's own political mission.) At the same time it is quite different from the work of Hughes in the 1930s in that the narrative consciousness is dialogic and the poet's voice is—sometimes quite explicitly, as in the 1936 "Air Raid Over Harlem"—simply another voice among many.

15. For a discussion of minstrelsy and its importance in American culture, see Eric Lott, *Love and Theft: Blackface Minstrelsy and the American Working Class* (New York: Oxford University Press, 1993).

16. Claude McKay, *Harlem Shadows* (New York: Harcourt, Brace, 1922), 60. The poem reads:

> I hear the halting footsteps of a lass
> In Negro Harlem when the night lets fall
> Its veil. I see the shapes of girls who pass
> To bend and barter at desire's call.
> Ah, little dark girls who in slippered feet
> Go prowling through the night from street to street!

17. Wagner, *Black Poets of the United States*, 479–480.

18. For an example of this criticism, see Maxim Gorky, "Fat People's Music," in *Articles and Pamphlets* (Moscow: Foreign Languages Publishing House, 1951).

19. Langston Hughes, *The Weary Blues* (New York: Knopf, 1926).

20. Gabbin, *Sterling A. Brown*, 171–172.

21. An example of this tradition would the stride pianist Willie "the Lion" Smith's claim that he could "play Chopin faster than any man alive." See A. B. Spellman, *Black Music: Four Lives* (New York: Schocken, 1970), 5.

22. James Weldon Johnson, *God's Trombones* (New York: Viking, 1927); Jean Toomer, *Cane* (New York: Liveright, 1923).

23. Alain Locke, ed., *The New Negro: An Interpretation* (New York: Boni, 1925.), 7.

24. The vision of the folk promoted in *Southern Road* became problematic during the Popular Front era of the middle and late 1930s, though such notions of the folk still had currency with respect to the reception of African American authors—for example, Brown was the African American poet most enthusiastically and consistently admired by the communist Left through the Popular Front and beyond. The attachment to earlier constructions of the rural folk as the authentic representatives of oppositional African American culture uncontaminated by mass culture remained and even flourished in the leftist folk music and folklore boom that began during the Popular Front. Nonetheless, the more dynamic political and artistic activities of the communist Left with respect to African Americans concentrated on the urban and the industrial, so that the jazz of the Count Basie Orchestra and other urban African American musics such as boogie-woogie piano, the urban blues, and gospel, not the singing of work songs, were the focus of the famous 1938 and 1939 concerts organized in New York by John Hammond under the auspices of various CPUSA-led organizations. Even those leftist African American writers, notably Richard Wright, who remained engaged with the pre–Popular Front Comintern analysis of the "National Question," became increasingly concerned with the African American urban experience—and urban vernacular culture—and the migration to the North in a way that Brown seemed unwilling or unable to consider.

For discussions of African American culture and the communist Left during the 1930s, see Robin G. Kelley, "'Afric's Sons with Banner Red," in *Race Rebels* (New York: Free Press, 1994); William J. Maxwell, *New Negro, Old Left: African-American Writing and Communism between the Wars* (New York: Columbia University Press, 1999), 125–178; Mark Naison, *Communists in Harlem During the Depression* (Urbana: University of Illinois Press, 1983), 193–226; James E. Smethurst, *The New Red Negro: The Literary Left and African-American Poetry, 1930-1946* (New York: Oxford University Press, 1999), 16–59. For examples of the communist enthusiasm for Brown from the early 1930s to the late 1940s, see Eugene Clay, "The Negro in Recent American Literature," in *American Writers' Congress*, ed. Henry Hart (New York: International, 1935), 149–151; Eugene Clay, "Sterling Brown: American People's Poet," *International Literature* 2 (June 1934): 117–122; James W. Ford, *The Negro and the Democratic Front* (New York: International, 1938), 192; Harry Haywood, *Negro Liberation* (New York: International, 1948), 149.

25. Wagner, *Black Poets of the United States*, 490.

26. For a discussion of the conjunction of nationalism and masculinity in the poetry of the *Negro World* and the Communist Party journal the *Negro Liberator*, see Kelley, "'Afric's Sons with Banner Red." For broader examinations of gender, African American political and artistic activism, and the communist Left, see Maxwell, *New Negro, Old Left*, 125–152, and Smethurst, *The New Red Negro*, 55–59. For a broader consideration of gender and the literary Left, see Paula Rabinowitz, *Labor and Desire: Women's Revolutionary Fiction in Depression America* (Chapel Hill: University of North Carolina Press, 1991). For examinations of gender and the literary construction of mass culture, see Sandra M. Gilbert and Susan Gubar, *No Man's Land: The Place of the Woman Writer in the Twentieth Century*, vol. 1, *War of the Words* (New Haven: Yale University Press, 1988), and Andreas Huyssen, *After the*

Great Divide: Modernism, Mass Culture, Postmodernism (Bloomington: Indiana University Press, 1986).

27. T. S. Eliot, *Selected Essays* (New York: Harcourt, Brace, 1950), 3–11.

28. Benston, "Sterling Brown's After-Song," 34.

29. Locke, "Sterling Brown: The New Negro Folk Poet," 92.

30. While Brown, "The Blues as Folk Poetry," in *Folk-Say: A Regional Miscellany, 1930,* ed. Benjamin A. Botkin (Norman: University of Oklahoma Press, 1930), 324–339, sets up a rigid theoretical binary of the "authentic" folk and the commercial, he admits that the practical situation is more complex: owing to the market situation, recording companies recorded the most "primitive" folk utterances, and eminently commercial performers such as Bessie Smith and Ma Rainey frequently captured the "authentic" folk spirit in their recordings and performances.

31. Nathan I. Huggins, *Harlem Renaissance* (New York: Oxford University Press, 1971), 190–243; Wallace Thurman, *Infants of the Spring* (New York: Macauley, 1932).

Waldo Frank, Jean Toomer, and the Critique of Racial Voyeurism

In the summer of 1922, Waldo Frank dropped a note to Jean Toomer proposing a journey together into the American South. Frank had first met Toomer more than two years before at a Greenwich Village party, but their friendship had developed, mostly by mail, only in the previous six months. Frank was living in New York, Toomer in Washington, D.C. Toomer was a struggling writer a few years younger than Frank. He had published a few poems and sketches, and he was elated to be in the company of an established, if controversial, literary figure. Frank, for his part, was delighted to find a young writer who took him seriously and could second his animosity toward the critics who had been tough on *The Dark Mother* and *Rahab*. They shared an intense spirituality, a sense of alienation from the literary mainstream, and a commitment to experimentation with literary form. Now Frank wanted to refresh his sense of the southern locale in which he planned to set his new book: "a short novel that sprang into being one night in the pinewoods of an Alabama village, full of the songs and calls of the black folk, and that has been germinating, forming ever since."[1] Toomer was partly of African American ancestry, he had recently spent time in Georgia, and he had family in the South: he volunteered to make the arrangements.

In September the two men spent three weeks in the Carolinas, and on their return from the South both writers went right to work. Toomer finished up work on a collection of his writings that Frank had encouraged him to gather into a book. Frank spent two feverish months in the fall of 1922 completing the first draft of his novel. Toomer's *Cane* and Frank's *Holiday* were accepted by Boni and Liveright, and both were published in 1923.[2]

These two works shared a great deal. Both shunned the tradition of fictional realism, stressing instead a "lyrical" treatment of environment and character. Both experimented with language using an admixture of prose and poetry, stream of consciousness, and expressionistic prose. Both treated the South as a land of exoticism, emphasizing the interplay of sensuousness and violence. Both books directly addressed the question of race relations (both contained apocalyptic lynchings), yet both also suggested that in some ways the issue of race was symbolic as well as sociological. And both books, after mixed reviews, passed swiftly into literary oblivion.

Cane was "rediscovered" in the 1960s as an African American classic—indeed, as one of the finest artistic achievements of the Harlem Renaissance, even though its author never lived in Harlem and after 1925 refused to consider himself a Negro. *Holiday*, on the other hand, has never been revived: when it is remembered at all, it is lumped together with the "Negrotarian" novels of the period, works such as Sherwood Anderson's *Dark Laughter* and Carl Van Vechten's *Nigger Heaven*, in which, it is charged, "black American culture became a kind of Africa for whites, an inaccessible homeland where all the passion and vitality kept in check by 'Puritanism' were expressed."[3]

There is no denying that Waldo Frank's discovery of black America included an exploitation of the Negro folk spirit. Yet it also included a searing indictment of that exploitation. *Holiday* and *Cane* are best examined together. Jean Toomer and Waldo Frank, while they were not collaborators in a formal sense, shared ideas, commented on each other's manuscripts, and together forged a literary "invention" of the meaning of the black experience that permeated both books.[4] This was not, in fact, a simple "primitivism," nor was it just a call for the absorption of the African American past into the consciousness of the present, although both these elements were present. It was, instead, an attempt to make the condition of blackness a metaphor for a kind of spiritual incompleteness, a way of transcending the condition of race without losing sight of the day-to-day realities of American life. Both felt intensely the note of personal and spiritual failure in their effort, and a haunting note of self-criticism permeates both *Cane* and *Holiday*. Together, Frank and Toomer challenged overconfident generalizations about race, art, and the relationship between them.[5]

Ever since *Cane* was resurrected following the publication of the paperback edition in 1969, critics have been arguing over the extent of Waldo Frank's "influence" on Jean Toomer. There is no doubt that Toomer responded eagerly to Frank's aesthetic and philosophical concerns. He read *Our America* with intense interest before the men's friendship flourished; thereafter he immersed himself in the older writer's work to the point that he confessed to Gorham Munson in 1923, "I cannot *will* myself out of Waldo. With the exception of Sherwood Anderson some years ago (and to a less extent Frost and Sandburg) Waldo is the only modern writer who has immediately influenced me."[6] This homage, along with *Cane*'s evident formal and structural debt to Frank's earlier work, has convinced critics such as Robert Bone that "it would be difficult to overstate the influence of Waldo Frank on Jean Toomer. The younger was quite simply a disciple of the older man."[7]

This assessment overstates the case. Toomer, after all, had already written significant portions of the work that would become *Cane* before the two men became friends and before he had read Frank's fiction. While Frank did indeed come to play an enormous part in Toomer's life from 1922 to 1924, their relationship was more one of mutual enrichment than of mentoring. They needed each other, they used each other, they profited from each other, and, to a certain extent, they harmed each other.

Waldo Frank first met Jean Toomer in the summer of 1920 at a Greenwich Village party hosted by the poet and editor Lola Ridge. A chance meeting in Central

Park the next day gave them an opportunity to explore further their mutual interests in art, religion, and literature. Toomer was struggling to establish himself as a writer after a decade of spiritual and intellectual wandering, but he was also interested in music, and Frank offered to put him in touch with the composer Ernest Bloch. Shortly thereafter, however, Toomer returned for a year to his native Washington, D.C., and the two men fell out of touch.[8]

During that time the writers were working on parallel tracks. Just as Frank was awakening to the aesthetic potential of black life, so too was Toomer. His mixed ancestry, his light skin, and his childhood shifts between white and black communities had made racial identification a matter of choice. In 1920 and 1921, Toomer explained in a later letter to Frank, he had spent a "disproportionate" amount of time on the Negro side of his heritage because "what facts are known [about blacks] have too often been perverted for purposes of propaganda."[9] Toomer's concern was with an explicitly aesthetic and self-conscious appropriation of black life. He valued his own detachment from its confines. Hence, during 1921 he worked principally on his play *Natalie Mann*, a withering indictment of Washington's middle-class black community.

While both writers were excited about mining black life for their art, they also showed signs of anxiety about the inherent dangers in this process. Perceptions of whiteness and blackness, so tempting as literary symbols, could degenerate into dehumanizing abstractions. A rediscovery of the black "folk spirit" could become an exercise in sentimentality or condescension. Toomer explored these dangers in one segment of *Natalie Mann*, Frank in a *City Block* segment ironically titled "Hope."

Natalie Mann contrasts the conventionality of the black community of Washington with the "inclusive philosophy" of Nathan Merilh, a nonconformist and an artist. Nathan Merilh has been interpreted as a "partly autobiographical, partly idealized portrait of Jean Toomer as savior."[10] Certainly Merilh embodies a certain kind of ideal: in contrast to the "scrupulously clean and neat" parlors of the Washington matrons, Merilh's eclectic study features a triptych with a portrait of Leo Tolstoy on the left, an "etching of a powerful black man" on the right, and in the center "a remarkable idealization which might easily be a composite of the other two" (*WS*, 296). He embodies not only a willingness to transcend race, but also an ability to give himself to the passionate frenzy that characterizes the Negro "low-life" scorned by middle-class Washington. It is his ecstasy on the dance floor, ultimately, that jolts Natalie Mann into a wholehearted rejection of convention. Not only does Merilh challenge the Washington establishment, but he also argues vociferously with the "part-philosophies" of his radical New York friends, represented schematically by an aesthete, a black racialist, a socialist, and a Freudian. When they challenge him to offer an example of the "inclusive" point of view that he advocates, he gives them "Karintha" (*WS*, 310–312).

A sketch in poetry and prose, "Karintha" was eventually extracted from *Natalie Mann* and left to stand alone as the first piece in *Cane*. Its origins in the play are instructive. An attempt to capture the beauty and the tragedy of rural black woman's life, the portrait appears in the play as a self-conscious response to the overintellectualized, ultimately sterile part-philosophies of Merilh's friends. As Merilh reads the sketch, the others in the room gradually join in humming the spiritual Natalie is strumming on the guitar in the background. The story's rhythm and color make possible a kind of union that their philosophical differences had obstructed.

"Karintha" tells the story of a girl, "perfect as dusk when the sun goes down," whose beauty is exploited by "the interest of the male, that wishes to ripen a growing thing too soon." The secret of Karintha's beauty is its remoteness: her "skin is like dusk on the eastern horizon"; her "running was a whir." Toomer juxtaposes the language of serenity with the tragic story of Karintha's seduction by young men and old, her lapse into cynicism, and the apparent abandonment of her child on "a bed of pine-needles in the forest." In the background lingers the neighborhood sawmill, its black smoke "so heavy you tasted it in water" representing the corrupting presence of machinery that, in part, makes possible the corruption of this southern woman.

The sketch serves the purpose of reuniting these overintellectual city folk with the simple, if tragic, rhythms of folk life. Repetition, the language of call-and-response, the echoes of spirituals—through these tropes Merilh gropes toward a mood that will encompass both the strength of the African American spirit and the circumstances of its extinguishing.[11]

Yet, at the same time "Karintha" sows seeds of doubt about that very process of cultural recovery. Nellie McKay has pointed out that the sketch is a paradigm for a series of intersecting issues: Karintha stands not only for exploited women but also as a metaphor for the exploitation of blacks in white society and the exploitation of the poor amidst the abundance of American life.[12] To these I would add that Karintha's story can be read as a paradigm of the exploitation of black folk culture by those who have left it behind. Her "perfect" beauty, her serenity, her childish energy, her elusiveness, her bright contrast to the blurring influence of the sawmill, that she cannot successfully conceive a child, even the fact that she is slowly dying: these qualities describe the woman, but they also reflect the very attributes of black folk culture Nathan Merilh is offering to his friends. Because they find her vulnerable to exploitation, the men around Karintha misread her: although as a child of twelve she was wild enough to stone cows, beat her dog, and fight with other children, the local preacher "told himself that she was as innocently lovely as a November flower." The men succeed in extracting vitality from her—"Karintha indulges them when she is in the mood for it"—but they fail to penetrate her essence. "Men do not know that the soul of her was a growing thing ripened too soon. They will bring their money; they will die not having found it out." They see in this woman of the soil the attributes they wish to see; they participate in a willful misreading that leaves them complacent but unknowingly incomplete. So, too, Toomer suggests, can black folk culture be misread and exploited by those who purport to save it.

While Nathan Merilh emerges finally as a liberating hero for Natalie Mann, Toomer emphasizes the potential for exploitation in his celebration of the pastoral spirit. The scene of harmony is undercut a moment later by the news of the tragedy of two minor characters whom Washington society has succeeded in destroying (*WS*, 312–313). Toomer may have imagined himself as a demigod through the figure of Nathan Merilh, but in "Karintha" he delivers a startling self-criticism. He allows his reader to see that just as Karintha (the character) is misunderstood and exploited, so too can Karintha (as a symbol of folk culture) be misunderstood by artists and their public. She is inevitably a creation of those around her; this is her promise, and her peril.

"Hope" describes briefly the encounter between a nameless white man and a nameless black prostitute. The story is scarcely more than a sketch, mostly the man's interior meditation on his whiteness and loneliness: "He was walking a long time [the story begins]. It seemed to him he was walking always . . . walking toward no thing . . . walking away. He had the sense of himself very white, very dim yet sharp: white thin throat weary with pressing through black air, white feet weary with walking away. He had the sense of himself a white thing walking forever from the dark, through dark" (*CB*, 169). The man's past is "beingless and thoughtless"; his whiteness suggests a hollowness accentuated by the fact that he has recently left his lover and is now face to face with an essential loneliness he had never before confronted squarely. As he walks along the block, whiteness and blackness guide his responses, even all his sensations: an "empty whiteness" overtakes his stomach; "black fumes of people" brush against him; the children on the street are "black all about their whiteness" (*CB*, 170). The black body of a prostitute he encounters on the block seems to promise him some escape from his own sense of emptiness. In the woman's body he detects what he thinks is a combination, a "white mist running through . . . making it alive." If he can only touch that combination of whiteness and blackness, that physical breakdown of the arbitrary distinctions of the visual world, perhaps he can escape: "He . . . separate white, living through black . . . felt the need and felt the power to be merged in her, to join the white mist that made her black alive" (*CB*, 173). After he "took her," after he played his part and "made her alive," after he "was impress of life upon her substance," the man reaches a kind of contentment:

> He lay smiling with shut eyes on his back.
> She left the bed and knelt on the floor beside him.
> She kissed his feet. She kissed his knees. She took his fingers, pressed each finger one by one, on her eyes. His fingers were cold.
> She beat her brow, dashed her brow and her breast against the iron bed. (*CB*, 174)

It is only in these last sentences of the story that we leave the man's consciousness and his obsession with black and white, and we catch a glimpse of the human situation.

In "Hope," the perception of race is not simply a metaphor for the chaotic human condition. Instead, Frank is groping toward a deeper stance that both depends on and transcends the categories of race and sex as he makes use of them. The story as a whole, especially its devastating final line, opens up for question the very perceptions and obsessiveness of the white man himself. By seeing the world in black and white, he sees it only in pieces, not as a whole; he cannot see himself as a part of the natural process. By imagining that he will find in the prostitute some artificial harmony of whiteness and blackness, he heaps upon her the indignity of his own dysfunctional perspective. He satisfies himself, he finds a source of "hope" in their merging, but he leaves the woman (and perhaps the world) more stranded and isolated than ever.

Frank, of course, makes no pretense to the familiarity with black life and language that Toomer demonstrates in "Karintha." The characters in *Natalie Mann*, unlike those in *City Block*, have at least some historical and cultural connection with the scene Nathan Merilh evokes. Yet even before their friendship developed, both writers saw the uses and the dangers of the racial metaphor. Their friendship modified and elaborated upon this theme.

In the spring of 1922, when Jean Toomer broke the year-long silence, the two men needed each other. Toomer was writing a great deal, especially after his abortive but stimulating stint as a teacher in Sparta, Georgia, but he had published little and felt cut off from the center of the literary world. He wrote Frank in March, reminding him of their earlier meeting, and asked whether he could send along some of his work. Toomer slipped in a few words of praise for the older writer's work, though he also complained that Frank had left the Negro out of *Our America*.[13]

A warm letter of praise from a potential acolyte could hardly have arrived at a better time. The first negative reviews of *Rahab* were just beginning to appear. In his first letter to Toomer, Frank admitted that Toomer's overture "has helped enormously" to alleviate the "bile-venting of ugly journalists who hate me with a hate I can never understand." The idiocy of the nation's critics became a recurring theme of their early correspondence, with Toomer eagerly joining in the chorus: "Our reviewers are covered with their sin," he intoned. "Verily, they are of the species Unfrocked Churchmen." They imagined themselves as heralds of light who would banish the critical darkness: "The so-called literary and artistic milieus are indeed strewn with excrement and decay," Frank assured his new friend, "but so are the fallow fields."[14]

Frank also responded at length to the work Toomer sent him, which included *Natalie Mann*, an early version of "Kabnis," and a number of the poems and prose poems that would later appear in *Cane*. He was most impressed by "Kabnis," which he found "an embryon of an expression which America has not had even the faintest inkling of." He responded most enthusiastically to the more intense, spiritual aspects of Toomer's writing: he preferred the "gorgeous symbolism" of the relationship between Nathan and Natalie to the "the talk of the incidental" that Toomer satirized in the Washington tea parties. He embraced Toomer as a comrade in literary arms and unabashedly predicted for him a glorious future as a writer.[15]

What is most striking in Frank's early response to Toomer's writing is the absolute absence of commentary on race. Even in examining such pieces as "Kabnis," where it would be thought that race could scarcely be avoided, Frank emphasizes instead the sense that the parts of the narrative are "the harmonics of a unit." He complains that the "the speech of the Ancient at the end was a sudden drop into particulars failing to take along and light with itself the general atmosphere you had built about his relationship with Kabnis," but he shows no understanding of why Toomer has had the former slave intone his mysterious words. Frank seems determined to meet Toomer on the level of art, even though Toomer himself introduced the subject of race in his first letter.

Frank's tentativeness continued even after he proposed in July that the two writers travel together through the South that autumn. For the first time he confessed his interest in adding a chapter (apparently never completed) on the Negro to a revised edition of *Our America*, and he hinted that he was interested in writing a novel. Toomer wrote back enthusiastically about the idea, but Frank still felt that "I am probably presumptuous to write about the negro, and particularly since I know you who are creating a new phase of American literature (O there's no doubt of that my friend)." Toomer hastened to assure Frank that he was not at all troubled by the fact that they would be exploring similar terrain: "There is no poaching in the domain of pure art. I think that we (postulating my own maturity) could take the identical subject and create works similar only in such broad things as impulse and purpose. Each would have its own individual identity, each its own organic life. My profit from Holiday will be greater than anyone's save your own." Toomer intimated that such a book would, in fact, pose a significant challenge to white literary appropriations of the African American experience. "That novel should be a wonder," he wrote. "Those unspeakable pale-faces who have been championing Birthright, and who have been clamoring for the black folk in our literature, will hate you for it."[16]

Although Toomer was in Harpers Ferry, he urged that they travel deeper into the South: West Virginia was too tame. "Oppression and ugly emotions seem nowhere in evidence. And there are no folk-songs. A more stringent grip, I guess, is necessary to force them through." Louisville, he suggested a week later, might be one substitute: "The actual Kentuckians whom I have seen seem to carry to vividity and color, the dash and love and waywardness conjured to the art mind by 'nigger.' I'd love to go there." Perhaps Toomer was simply casting about, catering to what he thought the white writer was looking for, but he wrote with great conviction about the elements of black life that had never deeply touched his own life: "Have you ever been in a Negro church?" he asked.

> Not the white-washed article of respectable colored folks; but the shanty
> of the peasant Negro. God, but they feel the thing. Sometimes too vio-
> lently for sensitive nerves; always sincerely, powerfully, deeply. And
> when they overflow in song, there is no singing that has so touched me.
> Their theology is a farce (Christ is so immediate); their religious emo-
> tion, elemental, and for that reason, very near sublime.

He was also attracted to the immersion in the experience of oppression: he would have to travel as a Negro, he explained, because "only by experiencing white pressure can the venture bear its fullest fruit for me."[17]

The trip was clearly a powerful experience for both men. They decided in the end to spend some time in Spartanburg, South Carolina, where Toomer's grandmother lived. Frank's Semitic looks were dark enough to allow him to "pass" in the reverse of the usual direction. He was welcomed as another "professor from the North," and the two of them were treated royally both in town and in the country:

> Wherever we went, to welcome and honor us, turkeys and hogs were slaughtered, and the richest yams were smothered in brown sugar. The farther away from town, the more complete the Negro plasm, the more free the sweetness of this people. Of course, the two young guests were entertained by those economically placed to bring them the most comfort. But humbler neighbors dropped in, and I soon got a sense of the community. Those that worked at home or on a farm, the least touched by the white world, were the happiest; those who went to Spartanburg each day to make their living—lifters of heavy loads, barbers, servants, et cetera—were the most confused, resentful and neurotic. I felt shame, as if I must confess the sins of my own fathers; I felt *with* the Negro. This empathy was startling.[18]

From one angle, the trip confirmed Frank's "primitivism." The "Negro plasm," preserved in greatest purity in the countryside, suggests that there is a fundamental simplicity and goodness among African people that allows them to live more happily and harmoniously than others if they are uncorrupted by modern life. That this sentiment remained strong for Frank when he recalled the experience from the vantage point of the early 1960s testifies to its enduring power.

Yet when Frank came to feel "empathy" himself for the blacks, his connection was to their sense of "shame." Following the "confused, resentful and neurotic" qualities of those blacks who work in town, Frank's sense of shame bridged the white and black worlds. He felt both oppressed by the white world (his "empathy" with the Negro's resentment) and responsible for it (his guilt about the "sins of my own fathers"). He was not altogether eager to make the connection—he needed to reassure himself of his whiteness in the night when the "startling" empathy entered his dream life—but the lives of blacks became for him a metaphor less for innate vitality than for the condition of being surrounded by the "grinding" ugliness of white society. Frank's attitudes toward blacks and whites were woven together. In a manner that is paradoxical but not uncommon, his racial prejudices and his powerful critique of mainstream American life were inextricably linked. He wrote to Toomer as soon as he returned to New York to let him know that what he had really taken from the trip was a *loosened* consciousness of race: "Spartanburg gave me what I knew I needed: liberation: the possibility of writing about a negro without seeing and saying negro all the time. Anymore than when I write about a white man, I say white skin, white skin, all the time."[19]

It is more difficult to measure the impact that the trip had on Jean Toomer. Although his autobiographical fragments devote considerable discussion to Waldo Frank, they are curiously circumspect on the details of this trip. "We went South. We came back," he wrote in "On Being an American." This reticence may, of course, be due in part to the later falling-out between the men, but Toomer seems to suggest that the trip reinforced some of his nervousness about the depth of his friend's understanding. He began to fret that Frank did not comprehend his ideas about transcending the concept of race, the ways that the United States made possible a genuine unity through diversity. Frank spoke approvingly of this "vision," but on their return Toomer "was concerned with whether or not he understood that it was not a vision, but an actuality." He was unsure that the trip had sufficiently convinced Frank of his own belief that "a new type of man was arising in this country—not European, not African, not Asiatic—but American." The elements of African American life were to be treasured and preserved—not for the sake of shoring up black identity, but for the sake of enriching this "united people existing in the *United* States."[20]

Both men, then, returned from the South pulled in two directions. On the one hand, they both continued to steep themselves in the salvific potential of rural black life; yet both found reason to continue the battle against the overconsciousness about race they had sketched earlier in *Natalie Mann* and *City Block*. "I cannot think of myself as separated from you in the dual task of creating an American literature," Toomer had written to Frank shortly before their departure. The trip made that "dual task" concrete. Among its most important functions would be the creation of a literary African American spirit that would serve as a metaphor both for freedom and for suffering and ultimately lead the way toward a cosmic whole that transcended race altogether.

Waldo Frank wrote *Holiday* in eight intense weeks of work in the autumn of 1922. "These are not letter writing days," he wrote to Toomer in October, for now he was "in medias res! Hard . . . but fun. I find color falls off and quality comes forward. I am inside my folks, white and black, and when occasionally I see the glint of their skin it rather shocks me that so little should mean so much."[21] Shocked though he might have been, Frank himself eagerly participated in the process of making meaning out of the symbol of skin color.

Holiday is the story of an unconsummated spark of attraction between a black man and a white woman in a small southern town that ends in an apocalyptic lynching. The narrative is swift and elliptical, the characters sketched rather than filled in; Frank makes much of mood and atmosphere, and he makes few concessions to the novel's historical obligation to a complex social setting.

What he is left with, then, is a schematic community portrait. The black man's name is John Cloud. He is somehow detached from earthly concerns; his presence casts a deep shadow; and he is more than faintly reminiscent of another figure with the same initials. The white woman is Virginia Hade: she combines the purest innocence with the cruelest impulses from the ancient underworld. They live in the southern town of Nazareth, on the Gulf of Mexico. The bay between the town and the shimmering city is traversed by a ferryboat called the *Psyche*. John and Virginia are both embedded in and alienated from their own communities. He is emotionally bound to the land, but he chafes at his mother's bland acceptance of Negro suffering. She works for her father, a prominent judge, but she feels stifled by his puritanical values.

Much of the book's power derives from the sensuality of Frank's writing, his indulgence in the rich though staccato evocations of human interaction with the landscape, and even his use of whiteness and blackness as (shifting) symbols of repression and spontaneity. This is dangerous ground, but Frank saves the book from self-indulgence and condescension by constantly keeping the reader's attention focused on the question of perception. The crudeness of the novel is also part of its power, as Frank rejects fineness and subtlety in favor of an overstatement that calls attention to its own design. It is as though he concedes that misunderstandings, even racism, are inevitable in literary representation, and he challenges the reader to examine closely the ways in which such perceptions are created.

The setting for *Holiday*, the town of Nazareth, is in the throes of simultaneous religious revivals: under the big tent in "White Town," in a wooden church in "Nigger Town." Tensions simmer like the weather in this unseasonably hot "fall" when a black man drowns by the pier as the ferry is coming in; no white will take the plunge to save him. Virginia Hade is outraged by the inaction of her brother (a champion swimmer) and the other whites; she refuses to join her family in the revival and strikes out for a walk through Nigger Town. Hidden in the bushes, she watches John Cloud swim naked in an isolated pond; when he emerges, the two face each other, talk, and acknowledge obliquely their attraction for one another. But John pulls away: he neither understands nor trusts Virginia's advances. She persuades him, however, to exchange knives with her.

Once this symbolic sexual act is performed, she returns to town, the murmurings of White Town and Nigger Town echoing in her mind, and she cuts herself about the abdomen with John's knife. The white community is emerging from the revival tent. They are restless, unsatisfied; the church that seemed to promise them release has merely repressed them further. They see bloody Virginia coming down Main Street, they see Cloud's knife, and the mob rumbles toward its inevitable destiny. John Cloud burns, while Virginia returns to the cool of her room.

If this is primitivism, however, it is primitivism of a very sober sort. *Holiday* does not show the blacks of Nazareth as carefree celebrants of a primal life force. Sensuality can be expressed only within the narrowest of confines. Humor, spontaneity, free-flowing sexuality, an uninhibited moral sense, and a happy-go-lucky response to life's travails: these essential antidotes to overcivilization are virtually absent from the novel. For all the power and beauty Virginia Hade sees in him, John Cloud is hardly the "child-primitive" portrayed in the manner of E. E. Cummings's "Jean Le Negre."[22] Far from carefree, the man is deadly serious; he responds to the restrictions of white society not with subversive humor but with unmitigated bitterness. When John protests that the life in the swamp is "chokin'" him, his mother answers harshly, "Chokin's our life" (*H*, 21). The extent to which John Cloud is a child of nature, then, is less important in Frank's scheme than the extent to which he is hampered by the general social distrust—among both whites and blacks—of genuine feeling. If he is a Christ figure, he is a far cry from the submissiveness of an Uncle Tom; he bears his burdens impatiently.

As the novel progresses, Frank draws his reader's attention increasingly toward the subtly evil nature of his observer/heroine. The ominousness of observation suggested in John Cloud's entrance into town is followed immediately by a description of Virginia in her father's office, who, "within the rigid pine frame of the door, [watches] dark women flow and undulate" (*H*, 92). Frank has introduced Virginia to us as something of a sympathetic rebel: she is outraged that her brother and other whites have let the black man drown at the pier; she despises the revival tent and its hypocrisies; and she is unintimidated by the stares of Nigger Town. She is a resentful victim of White Town's repressiveness, but by the end of the book, we see that she is also its chief instrument of rage.

Virginia strides out of Nazareth, away from the "furnace" of the revival tent, and into the forest. She thinks of the tent as a "mucilaginous sack holding a spider's eggs . . . myriad black live spots that will crawl, that will spread" (*H*, 121). She passes through the black community, a curiosity, an untouchable apparition. Her quest is for "feeling," and she envies the blacks she sees their connection to the soil, completely unconscious of the irony in her thought: "My feet wander in pain, toward you they wander. Pity for me. *Low down*. . . . Pity for me! I'll not feel sorry for you blazing niggers. You grow out of the soil. Your flesh stays sweet in the dank flames of the South. We wage a pallid fight, an ugly—there you are, blazing in ease, in truth, against our lies. Pity for me!" (*H*, 143). Here the underside of Virginia's romanticism of African American life is exposed—for Frank shows us how the language of "primitivism" is entangled in the language of lynching. Virginia's identification with blacks, her hope that by pitying them she herself is more deserving of sympathy, is scarcely distinguishable from anger. Virginia may find the metaphorical "dank flames of the South" exciting; but when the mob finally seizes John Cloud at the end of the book, the black man is hardly "blazing in ease."

Virginia emerges by the shore of the bay, where she "longs to cast off her clothes, to lie naked, to run naked in the world" (*H*, 155). She lurks in the shadows and, like the nameless watcher in Walt Whitman's "Song of Myself," she observes John Cloud, naked, plunging into the water. As she watches coolly from the bank, her mind swirls with incoherent fantasy: she is immersed in the water with him; she is "dancing on his groin"; he is sucking the udder of a cow. Sex and violence, activity and passivity, light and dark are mingled in her mind, and her thoughts penetrate those of John Cloud as he swims innocently in the bay "like a speared fish," belly up (H, 157–159). The sequence is a daring experiment in shared stream of consciousness, rendered powerful by Frank's relentless reminders of the pressures of the social situation on Virginia's passion.

Frank originally planned for *Holiday* to revolve around an actual rape, rather than a metaphorical sexual encounter. The more restrained treatment in the novel as published calls the reader's attention more dramatically to the menacing aspects of Virginia's innocence, her unconscious search for a scapegoat for her own sexual impotence. The drama erodes our confidence in the very categories of whiteness and blackness that the beginning of the novel seemed to erect.

Frank's depiction of the perception of race in Nazareth is cross-cut by the question of gender. Virginia Hade stands in a long line of repressed, manipulative women in Frank's fiction extending as far back as Julia Deering in *The Unwelcome Man*. While the depiction of the community is indeed laced with self-critical rage at white abuse of power, the portrait of Virginia is also tinged with anger at feminine manipulation. In this sense, Frank's novel has its parallel in Eugene O'Neill's *All God's Chillun Got Wings* (1925), in which the white heroine, psychologically destroyed by her own family and community, takes out her rage on the upright and upwardly mobile black man whom she has daringly married. Virginia Hade and Ella effectively destroy the black men by whom they are simultaneously attracted and repulsed. It is crucial to Frank's scheme, of course, that the repression of women's more sensual and passionate nature should cause a correspondingly powerful reaction of rage, but his fearful combativeness toward his heroine inevitably undermines his examination of power relations.

Early critics of *Holiday* assumed that Frank was most invested in the character of John Cloud—that the black man represented the epitome of the mystic spirit Frank was beginning to champion in the early 1920s. Clearly the man who dreamed he was a Negro on his trip to Spartanburg did indeed identify with his black protagonist, but this "mystic spirit" was less a matter of immersion in nature than a confrontation with suffering. Yet the strength of the novel lies in Frank's refusal to separate the experiences of John and Virginia and his identification with both the victim and the perpetrator. Frank's principal motivation in *Holiday* is not to advance a political or social message, nor to raise public consciousness about the horrors of lynching, nor to epitomize the nature of American race relations, but to jolt his readers into an understanding of the interconnections between the individual and the cosmic, the social and the religious.[23] A novel whose language depends fundamentally on racial stereotypes, *Holiday* also delivers a scathing criticism of the very exploitation in which Frank himself indulged.

In the months while Waldo Frank was dashing through the first draft of *Holiday*, Jean Toomer was putting the finishing touches on *Cane*. Over the summer Toomer had told his friend of his idea to collect his poems, sketches, and stories into a single volume, and Frank had been encouraging. At the very start of their relationship the older writer had been impressed by "the power and fulness and fineness of your Say." It did not take a lot to convince him that a collection of Toomer's work would be a significant literary event.

Although they were completed and published at around the same time, *Cane* is a very different sort of book from *Holiday*. Frank's book had simmered in his consciousness for more than two years, but it was essentially the product of several months of intense work. *Cane* represented (with the significant exception of *Natalie Mann*) virtually the entire body of Toomer's work as a mature writer. Despite its brevity, it is in many ways an extremely ambitious book: in its interweaving of poetry, prose, and drama; in its broad geographical focus; and in its implicit claim to serve as the preserving agent of an authentic Negro voice and culture. Toomer has much more command of his setting than Frank ever pretended to. The variety of the locales in *Cane*—the sun-soaked Georgia fields, the middle-class houses and the red-light district in Washington, the schoolteacher's shabby shack—is one of the book's principal strengths. The variety of characters is another, and these elements have focused readers' attention on *Cane*'s value as a portrait of the complexity of the African American community.

Yet, like Frank, Toomer is preoccupied not only with what he sees, but with the dangers of the process of seeing. *Cane*, like *Holiday*, is in part a book about voyeurism, about exploiting blackness as a metaphor, and about the dangers of that literary appropriation. "Karintha" introduces this theme, and it is no coincidence that Toomer plucked Nathan Merilh's soliloquy out of *Natalie Mann* as the first piece in *Cane*. Outside of its context in the play, the theme of appropriation is less evident, since the reader neither sees a narrator for the sketch nor is exposed to the impact of its recounting. But the sketches that follow in the first section of the book do introduce a nameless narrator whose relationship to the stories he tells is at the crux of the overall design.

The "I" of "Becky," "Carma," and "Fern," as well as of the poems "Reapers" and "Song of the Son," is not an active presence, but he is constantly calling attention to the nature of his formulations. In "Becky," he is the sympathetic narrator of the story, but he is also a member of the community that ostracizes the white woman for bearing two illegitimate Negro sons. He directs our suspicions to the act of narration in "Carma" by calling that story (of a wife who is killed by her husband after he wrongly suspects her of adultery) "the crudest melodrama"; as one critic has pointed out, however, the story "is made melodrama as much by the way the narrator tells it as by the way the characters in it act." The narrator in "Fern" warns that "men are apt to idolize or fear that which they cannot understand, especially if it be a woman." His account of this part Negro, part Jewish woman is much more about his own efforts to penetrate Fern's mystery than an evocation of the woman herself. This "spectatorial artist" calls his reader's attention to his own difficulty in presenting the lives of black women in the South and echoes aspects of the self-consciousness that Frank exemplified and explored in *Holiday*.[24]

In a letter to Frank written around the time he was finishing work on *Cane*, Toomer remarked that "if anything comes up now, pure Negro, it will be a swansong." He continued:

> Dont let us fool ourselves, brother: the Negro of the folk-song has all but passed away: the Negro of the emotional church is fading. A hundred years from now these Negroes, if they exist at all will live in art.

And I believe that a vague sense of this fact is the driving force behind the art movements direct towards them today. (Likewise the Indian.) America needs these elements. They are passing. Let us grab and hold them while there is still time.[25]

Toomer represents his project in *Cane* as an effort to preserve "the Negro of the folk-song," even as he suggests in this letter and implicitly in the structure of the book that the essence of black life cannot simply be distilled to simple, agricultural folk culture. "Seventh Street [in Washington, D.C.] is the song of a crude new life," he insists, an area of Negro life that Sherwood Anderson, for one, would not appreciate or understand. The life of the "emotional church" is losing out to a more complex, more cosmopolitan, and less innocent form of ethnicity.

Toomer makes clear that he is not engaged in a project of cultural reconstruction, a futile effort to make sure that the folk spirit has a continuing day-to-day life among African Americans. To the contrary, he explicitly concedes defeat; there is nothing he or anyone else can do to prevent the folk culture from passing away. "In those pieces that come nearest to the old Negro," he wrote to Frank, "in the spirit saturate with folk-song: Karintha and Fern, the dominant emotion is sadness, from a knowledge of my futility to check solution. There is nothing about these pieces of the buoyant expression of a new race." The folk culture will survive, ultimately, only as art. Under the rubric of art, the folk spirit will be vulnerable to the misapprehensions and personal whims of the artist—this is the source of the self-critical portrait of the narrator in the pieces in the first part of *Cane*. But, equally important, once in the realm of art, Negro folk culture will no longer belong exclusively to Negroes. It becomes a universal property, an idea forged partly (and distantly) from the realities of the African American experience and partly from the whims and needs of the artists who will absorb it into mainstream culture.[26]

In *Cane*, Toomer explores the artificiality of the construction of "the Negro." But rather than insisting on some more genuine means of capturing the black folk spirit, Toomer insists that the concept is inevitably invented, that its artificiality must be constantly acknowledged and confronted. He is unwilling to give up the idea of blacks (or women) as metaphors for various aspects of human experience: innocence, ties to nature, suffering, and religiosity. This exploitation of a group's experience is too powerful not to be an inevitable aspect of an artist's encounter. But self-consciousness is crucial to a successful rendering: this was why Toomer ultimately preferred *Holiday* to Sherwood Anderson's less ironic appropriation of blackness as a metaphor for vitality.

After their return from Spartanburg in September, Frank and Toomer stayed in close contact through the rest of 1922 and 1923. The trip had cemented a bond between the men that both inspired their work and aroused their sense of mission. "Never forget," Frank wrote that fall, "we are the intimately sanctified priests of the new Vision, and of the eternal God. We must have pride, we must have the humility of pride in our secret work. We must have courage. We must go on, wheresoever: and we must not be downcast. For a deep joy in our consecration in one of the heralds of its truth."[27] Although they worked independently on their manuscripts—Frank in New York and Darien, Connecticut; Toomer in Washington, D.C.—they clearly saw the production of their two books as an enactment of their collaborative task in creating a new American literature. Frank helped persuade his own publisher, Horace Liveright, to publish *Cane*. For a time, the two writers entertained the hope that their books might appear on the same day. Both before and after the books were accepted, the two men shared their manuscripts, commenting liberally, testing ideas, and bolstering each other's confidence.

These critical suggestions were, by and large, minor. Toomer had already polished many parts of *Cane*; Frank appears to have had the most significant impact on the Washington, D.C., sketches in part 2, especially "Theatre" and "Box-Seat." These stories, with their syncopated urban rhythms, their harsh commentary on middle-class values, and their abstract aesthetic, most clearly echo the experimentation in Frank's early novels and *City Block*. *Holiday*, too, went through relatively few changes following Frank's rapid composition of the first draft in the fall, but the white writer appealed to his friend's greater expertise when he sent him the manuscript in January: "May I ask you, aside from giving your general aesthetic impressions, to go into details with me? as to language, 'business,' anything else that occurs to you. You know, the spirit of this world is nearer to me than its body. If you can help me, where I may have gone off as regards the body, I shall be indeed obliged."[28] Toomer responded enthusiastically to the novel as a whole, and he acceded to Frank's request by providing suggestions about the use of dialect: "John would never say, 'May I kiss you, Mary?' Better: 'Ken I kiss you, Mary?' or, if beneath his conflicts he really loves her, then it would probably be, 'Ken I kiss you, hon?' Negroes are lyrical and fulsome about love, feined [*sic*] or real. 'I sho do love you, Mary.' They are emphatic. Etc."[29] Appealed to as an expert, Toomer had little hesitation about holding forth on the general qualities of the Negro. Nevertheless, the African American writer did not fully grasp the subtleties of Frank's portrait of John Cloud. Frank was eager to challenge the generalization of the Negro as "lyrical and fulsome." John Cloud was passionate but awkward, trapped between two foreign worlds. Some stiffness in his language was necessary to convey his unease with a world of pure sensuality. Still, Frank continued to appreciate Toomer's suggestions to the extent that "I greedily ask for all that come to you."[30]

More than the specific suggestions, however, it was the intensity of feeling between the men that charged their sense of collaboration during this period. An unavoidably erotic undercurrent runs through their correspondence, especially after their return from the South. "Most of all, Spartanburg brought me You," Frank wrote Toomer that fall. "It is true," the latter replied. "Spartanburg . . . gave us each other as perhaps no other place could. A bond that is sealed in suffering endures."[31] Although there is no evidence to suggest that they explicitly thought of each other as lovers, the intensity with which they approached their shared writing suggests a form of displacement.[32] When writing to Toomer, Frank's letters consciously or unconsciously scrambled the language of creativity, friendship, and sexuality. To Toomer's invitation to visit him in Washington in the spring, Frank responded, "I know that a week's visit with you, and at least two nights of Bacchanale would oil me up, put gasoline in my tank and grease my ballbearings something fine."[33] At nearly every critical point in his life, Frank's writing was buttressed by such passionate friendships, but his relationship with Jean Toomer was invested with unusual intensity.

Despite their protestations of fellowship, the friendship first foundered on the rock of race. At first, superficially the men seemed to agree on an ideal of a transethnic America. When Toomer complained that Sherwood Anderson "limits me to Negro," he won a rapid response from Frank: "The day you write as a Negro, or as an American, or as anything but a human part of *life*, your work will lose a dimension."[34]

Only gradually did they come to see a significant underlying difference. Frank's conception of wholeness depended on a continuous recognition of individuality and distinctiveness: a reckoning, as in *Holiday*, with the inevitable consequences of fragmentation. But Toomer was moving toward a more ethereal stance: his personal history of nebulous racial identity had convinced him that racial harmony was an "actuality" that could be achieved by the nation, as well as by the individual, through a simple act of will. Regarded in the proper light, racial and ethnic differences could simply vanish; indeed, the process was already well underway:

> There is one thing about the Negro in America which most thoughtful persons seem to ignore: the Negro is in solution, in the process of solution. As an entity, the race is loosing [*sic*] its body, and its soul is approaching a common soul. If one holds his eyes to individuals and sections, race is starkly evident, and racial continuity seems assured. One is even led to believe that the thing we call Negro beauty will always be attributable to a clearly defined physical source. But the fact is, that if anything comes up now, pure Negro, it will be a swan-song.[35]

This letter has sometimes been taken to affirm Toomer's commitment to preserving and expressing the African American side of his identity. *Cane*, in this light, becomes an affirmation of his cultural heritage. But what stands out most clearly here is Toomer's *detachment* from that ancestry: the Negro whom he regards as passing away is something outside himself. Having personally embodied the process of "solution," Toomer imagines cultural preservation as a wholly aesthetic process. American blacks, he makes it clear, have no genuine resources with which to combat "mechanical civilization." It is the *artist*—the Toomer of "Theatre" and "Box Seat," the Frank of *Holiday*—whose evocation of the process of solution might have the power to heal.

Again, much of this is close to Waldo Frank's sentiments. Toomer's pessimism about the durability of marginalized cultures echoes Frank's thoughts on

Native American and Mexican peoples in *Our America*. Yet Toomer's rigorous insistence on the detachment of the artist from these fading ethnic ties subtly divided him from his friend. Frank, after all, kept making self-conscious attempts to return to his Jewish heritage, not from any faith in institutionalized religion, but from a continuing conviction that ethnicity was a living power to be harnessed and not fought. Like Toomer, he believed that the hope for preservation of alternative cultures lay in the work of artists, but he refused to take the further cynical step of asserting that therefore the persistence of those cultures was entirely illusory. Frank did not realize how firmly Toomer drew the line with those who would "limit" him "to Negro."

After he had helped persuade Boni and Liveright to publish *Cane*, Frank volunteered to write an introduction for the book. Toomer was enthusiastic, even after Frank warned him that this essay would inevitably involve artistic compromises. Frank doubtless realized that Liveright's excitement about *Cane* was in part stimulated by the idea of bringing a undiscovered black writer into print. In a sense the older writer had misled his protégé. Frank's constant ranting about the inanities valued by publishers, critics, and readers concealed his savvy about making the necessary arrangements and compromises to get his work into print.

Yet in the foreword, Frank specifically undertook to emphasize Toomer's artistry, his liberation from the narrow categorization forced upon most Negro writers:

> The gifted Negro has been too often thwarted from becoming a poet because his world was forever forcing him to recollect that he was a Negro. The artist must lose such lesser identities in the great well of life. The English poet is not forever protesting that recalling that he is English. It is so natural and easy for him to be English that he can sing as a man. The French novelist is not forever noting: "This is French." It is so atmospheric for him to be French, that he can devote himself to saying: "This is human." This is an imperative condition for the creating of deep art. The whole will and mind of the creator must go below the surfaces of race. And this has been an almost impossible condition for the American Negro to achieve, forced every moment of his life into a specific and superficial plane of consciousness.[36]

This is close to Toomer's own sentiments—but not exactly the same. For while Frank emphasizes the need to go "below the surfaces of race," he also makes it clear that this process rests on a confident and self-developed sense of cultural identity. The English and French writers can write universally because their Englishness and Frenchness are ingrained. American blacks, on the other hand, are forced into "a specific and superficial plane of consciousness" about race because their particularity has been thrust upon them. Negro art will flourish not when blacks abandon their heritage altogether, but when they embrace it closely enough on their own terms that they need no longer insist upon it. This, Frank believed, was Toomer's achievement. Rather than giving portraits of "a downtrodden soul to be uplifted" or a sociological discussion of Washington's "brown belt," Toomer gives his reader "that absolute and abstract thing called Art."

At first Toomer appreciated the foreword. "The more I read it the better I like it," he enthused. "Everything considered, I think you did a splendid piece of work." He was especially grateful for Frank's refusal to overemphasize race: "The one thing I was uneasy about in a foreword was this: that in doing the necessary cataloging and naming etc. the very elements which the book does not possess would get plastered across its first pages. I was sure of you. I knew you could do the thing. You have."[37]

Toomer's feelings changed, however, as he began to realize that Boni and Liveright were eager to make race a marketing tool. The first warning came from Frank: "I did see Liveright yesterday and he says he is going to enlist your help in reaching a possible Negro public for HOLIDAY. I know you'll do what you can in this. Unfortunately, I have to think of sales . . . more and more. . . . There's such an ironic abyss between honors and receipts." Liveright himself approached Toomer soon after, when he returned the writer's autobiographical sketch for revisions: "I feel that right at the very start there should be a definite note sounded about your colored blood. To my mind this is the real human interest value of your story and I don't see why you should dodge it."[38]

At this Toomer bristled. "My racial composition and my position in the world are realities which I alone may determine," he replied to Liveright.

> As a unit in the social milieu, I expect and demand acceptance of myself on their basis. I do not expect to be told what I should consider myself to be. Nor do I expect you as my publisher, and I hope as my friend, to either directly or indirectly state that this basis contains any element of dodging. In fact, if my relationship with you is what I'd like it to be, I must insist that you never use such a word, such a thought, again. As a Boni and Liveright author, I make the distinction between my fundamental position and the position which your publicity department may wish to establish for me in order that *Cane* reach as large a public as possible. In this connection I have told you . . . to make use of whatever racial factors you wish. Feature Negro if you wish, but do not expect me to feature it in advertisements for you. I have sufficiently featured Negro in *Cane*.[39]

Toomer's resentment at the publisher's exploitation of his background was intensified, perhaps, by his ambivalence about his own artistic exploitation of the black folk spirit. His bitterness carried over to his friend and collaborator. In the light of Liveright's marketing aspirations, Frank's foreword, circumspect though it was, now seemed subtly to underscore the question of Toomer's race. By dwelling at such length upon Toomer's transcendence of his Negro background, Frank had effectively highlighted that very ancestry. "Why should any such thing be incorporated in a foreword to *this* book?" he wondered later. "Why should Waldo Frank or any other be my spokesman in this matter? . . . My suspicions as to Waldo Frank's lack of understanding of, or failure to accept, my actuality, became active again."[40]

In fact, Frank's foreword was probably motivated as much by ego as by racism. Frank's insecurities, however, even when they exploited the concept of race, should not overshadow the sincerity of his effort to meet Toomer on mutually defined ground. But he could not share Toomer's nebulous faith that racial division and difference could or should simply vanish. Whatever his shortcomings in his understandings of blacks as individuals, Frank understood the confining nature of America's obsession with racial identification. His foreword's faith in "that abstract and absolute thing called Art" was his defense against evils of distinction and prejudice that he understood to be inevitable.

Underlying the tensions over the foreword was an explosive personal situation. Frank's marriage to Margaret Naumburg had always been tempestuous, but a period of relative tranquility had followed the birth of the couple's son Thomas in the spring of 1922. Waldo had spent most of 1922 and 1923 (with the exception of the trip to Spartanburg) at home, finding the presence of the child both exhilarating and confining.

Yet in the middle of 1923 the marriage struck its fatal shoals. At Waldo's invitation, Jean Toomer came to spend some time with the family in Darien, Connecticut, and there, for the first time, he met his friend's wife. The spark of attraction between them seems to have been almost immediate. "I . . . felt the whole world revolve," Toomer later wrote. "My birth, and it was truly a birth, came from my experiences with Margaret Naumburg."[41]

It is not clear how quickly the lovers acknowledged their passion for each other or consummated their affair, but it was certainly well under way by the fall of 1923. Frank was apparently in the dark, although something about Toomer's summer visit touched off tensions between the friends. In early September, Toomer wrote Frank a letter acknowledging that "ever since I came to you that day at Darien there has been a most cruel silence on the sheer life-plane, on the plane where we have had such deep and sustaining contacts."[42] Recriminations about evasions replaced statements of their joint artistic purpose.

For a brief time, the near-simultaneous release of *Cane* and *Holiday* reaffirmed the writers' shared sense of purpose. "Well old soldier," Toomer wrote at the end of September, "it looks as if Holiday and Cane are going over. Not best sellers—hell no—but the sort of selling and notice that really count."[43] Frank's foreword and the timing of the publications called attention to the affinity between the books, and they were frequently reviewed together. One reviewer was even convinced that the writers of both books were one and the same.[44]

Frank made sure that the writers did their best to back their own cause. He convinced Toomer to repay the favor of the foreword to *Cane* by reviewing *Holiday* for the *Dial*. But even here the tensions between the men became apparent.

Toomer was a clumsy if supportive critic, and Frank particularly resented the opening statement that "the primary approach" to *Holiday* "should not be sectional."[45] "Practically all the critics are jumping on me for not knowing the South, and you are one man who knows I do, who was in a position to state so with some authority."[46]

In November 1923 Frank left the United States for an extended stay in France and Spain, with both his marriage and his friendship under strain. In his absence, Toomer and Naumburg's affair developed with passionate intensity. In the summer of 1924 Toomer secretly accompanied Naumburg when she went to Reno to secure her divorce. Once the divorce was final, the affair became public, and the lovers left for Fontainebleau, France, together to immerse themselves in the teachings of George Ivanovitch Gurdjieff. "As a means to life as I desire to live it, as an end-in-itself, I have given up art—as we have practiced it," Toomer wrote to Gorham Munson (who would later join him in Fontainebleau). "And I am about (have already imperfectly commenced) to undertake the Gurdjieff discipline. I have no evidence from Waldo of any similar elimination and intention."[47]

Thereafter Toomer ambled from one religious identity to another, the phases linked by his continued rejection of an African American identity and by a consistent quest for the annihilation of the self in a larger cosmic plan. This quest for annihilation had always been anathema to Waldo Frank: he had dedicated much of his work to trying to explicate a version of mysticism that adamantly preserved selfhood. The two men's subtle difference on the question of race had blossomed into a full-blown metaphysical and spiritual divide. Toomer's insistence on transethnic identity as an "actuality" led him toward a cosmic consciousness that obliterated individuality. Frank continued to struggle with the actuality that racial differences were an inevitable source of conflict and a potential source of strength.

Curiously enough, Frank never again wrote as compellingly about blacks in the United States.[48] His later occasional observations lapsed into a sentimental and condescending mode that he had managed to avoid in *Holiday*. The saving grace of southern blacks became once again their healthy detachment from the modern world, from the neuroticism of the industrial or intellectual life. In *The Rediscovery of America* (1929), his reworking a decade later of the themes of *Our America*, African Americans were scarcely more visible than they had been in the earlier work of cultural criticism. A lengthy footnote applauded the "rudimentary" wholeness of southern blacks: "They are attached to the soil; attached to each other: and their instinctive harmony of worship, work and play produces the sweetest human material of which I am aware in our land."[49] Such shallowness, along with Toomer's equally vapid rejection of the concept of race, reiterates how much the two writers profited from each other during the short period of their friendship. They shored up each other's confidence, they pruned each other's excesses, and they sharpened each other's writing. More important, however, their collaboration constantly kept them focused on the question not of inherent racial differences but of how those differences were perceived.

Their friendship also raises larger questions about the ambivalence with which American writers have addressed the subject of African American life in the United States. While there can be no doubt that white artists have often appropriated and dehumanized the "black experience" in the service of self-aggrandizement or sentimentality, the more thoughtful among them have recognized that their very ignorance of black life is itself a compelling and unsettling phenomenon. If we read such writers for their insights into, say, the lives of black sharecroppers or Harlem numbers runners, we are bound to be sorely disappointed, if not outraged. But if, on the other hand, we understand that many writers themselves saw the tension between knowledgeable evocation and exploitative appropriation as the *subject* of their work, these writings remain lively and provocative. They are powerful reminders that the divisions of race cannot simply be willed away.

■ NOTES

1. Waldo Frank to Jean Toomer, 22 July 1922, Jean Toomer Collection, Beinecke Library, Yale University; hereafter cited as JTC.

2. Jean Toomer, *Cane* (New York: Boni and Liveright, 1923); hereafter cited as *C.* Waldo Frank, *Holiday* (New York: Boni and Liveright, 1923); hereafter cited as *H.*

3. Wendy Steiner, "The Diversity of American Fiction," in *Columbia Literary History of the United States,* ed. Emory Elliott (New York: Columbia University Press, 1988), 854.

4. Werner Sollors, ed., *The Invention of Ethnicity* (New York: Oxford University Press, 1989).

5. Several accounts have addressed the friendship between Toomer and Frank, though always from the perspective of its impact on Toomer and *Cane.* See Mark Helbling, "Jean Toomer and Waldo Frank: A Creative Friendship," in *Jean Toomer: A Critical Evaluation,* ed. Therman B. O'Daniel (Washington, D.C.: Howard University Press, 1988); and Robert Bone, *Down Home: A History of Afro-American Short Fiction from Its Beginnings to the End of the Harlem Renaissance* (New York: Putnam's, 1975), 204–222. The Norton critical edition of *Cane,* edited by Darwin Turner (New York: W. W. Norton, 1988), includes some important excerpts from the Frank-Toomer correspondence.

6. Toomer to Munson, 21 October 1922; quoted in Cynthia Earl Kerman and Richard Eldridge, *The Lives of Jean Toomer: A Hunger for Wholeness* (Baton Rouge: Louisiana State University Press, 1987), 102.

7. Bone, *Down Home,* 212.

8. Kerman and Eldridge, *The Lives of Jean Toomer,* 72–73.

9. Toomer to Frank, 24 March 1922, Waldo Frank Collection, University of Pennsylvania (hereafter WFC).

10. Darwin T. Turner, ed., *The Wayward and the Seeking: A Collection of Writings by Jean Toomer* (Washington, D.C.: Howard University Press, 1982), 237; hereafter cited as *WS. Natalie Mann* is included in its entirety in this collection, and page numbers in this article refer to this edition.

11. See Barbara E. Bowen, "Untroubled Voice: Call and Response in *Cane,*" in *Black Literature and Literary Theory,* ed. Henry Louis Gates Jr. (New York: Methuen, 1984), 187–204.

12. Nellie Y. McKay, *Jean Toomer, Artist: A Study of His Literary Life and Work, 1894–1936* (Chapel Hill: University of North Carolina Press, 1984), 94–96.

13. Toomer to Frank, 24 March 1922, box 23, WFC.

14. Frank To Toomer, 2 April 1922, JTC; Toomer to Frank, 24 April 1922, box 23, WFC; Frank to Toomer, 11 April 1922, JTC.

15. Frank to Toomer, n.d, JTC.

16. Frank to Toomer, 17 July 1922; n.d.; 26 July 1922. Toomer to Frank, 27 July 1922; 25 July 1922; box 23, WFC.

17. Toomer to Frank, 17 July 1922; 25 July 1922; 15 August 1922; 21 August 1922; box 23, WFC.

18. Waldo Frank, *Memoirs of Waldo Frank*, ed. Alan Trachtenberg (Amherst: University of Massachusetts Press, 1973), 105.

19. Frank to Toomer, n.d., JTC.

20. Turner, *The Wayward and the Seeking*, 125, 121.

21. Frank to Toomer, n.d., JTC.

22. Nathan Huggins compares the two in *Harlem Renaissance*, 116. See E. E. Cummings, *The Enormous Room* (New York: Modern Library, 1934).

23. In 1932, however, Frank noted proudly that one review in the Negro press had called *Holiday* the modern *Uncle Tom's Cabin*, though he went on to say that this judgment "did not flatter the artist in me" ("How I Came to Communism," *New Masses* 8 (1932): 7). I have not located the review to which Frank refers.

24. This theme is treated by Susan L. Blake in "The Spectatorial Artist and the Structure of *Cane*," in *Jean Toomer: A Critical Evaluation*, ed. Therman B. O'Daniel (Washington, D.C.: Howard University Press, 1988), xx.

25. Toomer to Frank, n.d., box 23, WFC.

26. Toomer to Frank, n.d., box 23, WFC.

27. Frank to Toomer, n.d., JTC.

28. Frank to Toomer, 1 January 1923, JTC.

29. Toomer to Frank, n.d., box 23, WFC.

30. Frank to Toomer, n.d., JTC.

31. Frank to Toomer, n.d., JTC.

32. For a relevant discussion, see Wayne Koestenbaum, *Double Talk: The Erotics of Male Literary Collaboration* (New York: Routledge, Chapman and Hall, 1989).

33. Frank to Toomer, n.d., JTC.

34. Frank to Toomer, n.d., JTC.

35. Toomer to Frank, n.d., box 23, WFC.

36. Turner, ed., *Cane*, 139.

37. Toomer to Frank, n.d., box 23, WFC.

38. Liveright to Toomer, 29 August 1923, JTC.

39. Toomer to Liveright, 27 February 1923; in Turner, ed., *Cane*, 156–157.

40. Turner, ed., *Cane*, 143–144.

41. Turner, ed., *Cane*, 144.

42. Toomer to Frank, 9 September 1923, box 23, WFC.

43. Toomer to Frank, n.d., box 23, WFC.

44. Bruno Lasker, "Doors Opened Southward," *Survey* 51 (1 November 1923): 190–191.

45. Jean Toomer, "Waldo Frank's Holiday," *Dial* 75 (October 1923): 383.

46. Frank to Toomer, n.d., JTC.

47. Toomer to Munson, 17 July 1924, JTC.

48. Frank did, however, write compellingly about the admixture of African, native, and European elements in South America. See *America Hispana: A Portrait and a Prospect* (New York and London: Scribner's, 1931).

49. Waldo Frank, *The Re-Discovery of America: An Introduction to a Philosophy of American Life* (New York: Charles Scribner's Sons, 1929), 239–240.

"Among Negroes"

Gertrude Stein and African America

■

In the 1988 foreword to John Kouwenhoven's classic study of American culture, *The Beer Can by the Highway*, Ralph Ellison recalls Gertrude Stein in the sentence, "A can is a can is a can. . . ."[1] Ellison's playful riff invokes the underexplored relationship between Gertrude Stein and African America. From her earliest writings, the black voice, body, and experience had an intriguing role in her creative life. Hortense Sänger, Stein's "dark-skinned" alter ego of the Radcliffe themes, later emerged as Melanctha in *Three Lives* (1909).[2] After Paul Robeson's visit to 27 rue de Fleurus in 1925, Stein wrote "Among Negroes," collected in *Useful Knowledge* (1928). In *Everybody's Autobiography* (1937), the narrative of her journey back to the United States after a thirty-year absence, Stein included conversations with several black Americans, including one of the actors to appear in her opera, *Four Saints in Three Acts* (1934). And in *Brewsie and Willie* (1946), the last work published in her lifetime (and reviewed by Richard Wright), African Americans became the exemplars of "pioneering" the nation's best hope for the future. But the focus of Gertrude Stein's relationship to African Americans remains the short story "Melanctha." "Melanctha," composed in 1905 and published in *Three Lives*, is a retelling, with an all-black cast, of a failed love affair of Stein's. "Melanctha" steals the spotlight because it marks the beginning of radically experimental modernist writing and paradoxically employs offensive, reactionary stereotypes of black Americans.

Until very recently, the scholarship on "Melanctha" has tended to either ignore the racial aspects of the text and focus exclusively on its innovative form or to dismiss Stein and the story as racist.[3] More recently, scholars have argued the need to explore the relationship between the narrative's poetics and its use of racial stereotypes to understand the ways in which race and modernism are linked.[4] Laura Doyle's discussion examines modernism's twin and conflicting desires to transgress and recuperate racial boundaries. Michael North contends that like many of the creators of literary modernism, Gertrude Stein's use of a "black" enabled her to break with constraining social and literary conventions. Carla Peterson discusses the ways Gertrude Stein employed features of the African American musical tradition in the making of "Melanctha." These discussions bring much-needed insight and new contextual evidence to bear on the previous and partial interpretations of "Melanctha." It is, however, Stein's appropriation of black American musical forms in the making of "Melanctha" that fills an enormous gap in our understanding of the text and of her ongoing interest in African Americans and their art.

In the criticism of the racial stereotypes in "Melanctha" (on and off the record), little is ever made of the fact that since its publication in 1909, many black American writers have credited "Melanctha" with inaugurating a new era in the representation of black Americans by white writers. James Weldon Johnson stated that Gertrude Stein was the first white writer to treat African American characters as "normal members of the human family."[5] Eric Walrond reportedly told Leo Stein: "Gertrude was the only white person who had given real Negro psychology."[6] And Nella Larsen wrote in a letter to Stein, "I never cease to wonder how you came to write it and just why you and not some one of us should so accurately have caught the spirit of this race of mine."[7] Richard Wright adored "Melanctha" because it enabled him to hear English, "as Negroes spoke it: . . . melodious, tolling, rough, infectious . . . laughing, cutting. . . . And not only the words, but the winding psychological patterns that lay behind them!"[8] Clarence Major has argued that earlier black characters created by both black and white writers possess "none of the humanity that Jeff and Melanctha obviously possess. In this sense Stein broke the white American literary tradition of portraying black characters as subhuman or as fools."[9] Given the story's frankly crude racial stereotypes, such appreciative remarks from African American writers are surprising. But the ways in which Gertrude Stein synthesized material from her personal experience, European and American literary forms, and features of popular black American music may account for this high praise.

Most discussions of "Melanctha" note that it is another telling of Gertrude Stein's failed love affair with May Bookstaver; the original narrative, *Q.E.D.: Things as They Are*, had been written a few years earlier.[10] As Bridgman has observed, Stein also drew on her childhood and early adult experiences of sexuality to create the internal and familial conflicts expressed through these stereotypical characters.[11] For this retelling, Gertrude Stein moved the setting of the story from the all-white Anglo-Saxon Protestant upper middle class to the comparatively marginalized African American community of Baltimore. Relocating the story from the "pure" white center to the "muddier" margins of society is suggestive. Using the black voice made it easier for Gertrude Stein to see "the senses, even the body itself, as ruled by convention."[12] But the African American context also suggests the distance at which Gertrude Stein may have felt her sexual identity placed her vis-à-vis her middle-class Jewish origins. This point is underscored in her choice of residence during her medical school years. Rather than live in Baltimore's middle-class German Jewish neighborhood in the northwestern part of the city, where her family resided, Stein chose to make her home east of it in a neighborhood peopled by immigrants and the black middle class. It was a "geographic and linguistic borderland culture of the American metropolis."[13] In "Melanctha," Gertrude Stein was writing literally and figuratively from the borderland; it yielded new insights and encouraged formal (and social) innovation. The borderland of Gertrude Stein's "Melanctha" parallels the mixed race and class of her characters just as it recalls the mixed origins of the narrative itself.

"Melanctha's" European origins in Gustave Flaubert's *Trois Contes* and in the paintings of Paul Cézanne are well known.[14] On the other side of the Atlantic, *Three Lives* had its origins in several forms of American popular culture. "The Good Anna" and "The Gentle Lena" came out of the genre of immigrant narratives, very popular at the turn of the century, such as Jacob Riis's *How the Other Half Lives* (1890) and Abraham Cahan's *Yekl: A Tale of the Ghetto* (1896) and the brief immigrant narratives ("lifelets") that appeared in Hamilton Holt's *Independent*.[15] *Three Lives* is also rooted in Gertrude Stein's study of psychology with William James at Harvard. Stein's use of repetition, circularity, and imprecision grew out of her sense that everyday, ordinary human speech revealed character. Related to this interest in the vernacular, Carla Peterson's well-documented essay locates "Melanctha"'s origins in the African American musical forms so popular during the 1890s, when Gertrude Stein was a medical student at Johns Hopkins.[16]

According to Peterson, Stein borrowed the stereotypes for "Melanctha" from the "coon" song tradition popular at the end of the nineteenth century. These songs, sung by whites and blacks alike, were, like Melanctha and Gertrude Stein's neighborhood, also of mixed origins. The tradition had its roots in the earlier minstrel show, itself a hodgepodge of various Euro-American art forms such as Scottish and Irish folk songs and dances; songs and stories of the American frontier; and African American dance step, folk expressions, and instruments such as the banjo and jawbone.[17] The story's frame characters, James Herbert, Jem Richards, and Rose Johnson, are mirrored in the songs "My Coal Black Lady," or "May Irwin's 'Bully' Song." The racial stereotypes in "Melanctha" emerge from the lyrics of coon songs, but its sensibility and innovative narrative style are more closely linked to early blues.

Thematically, early blues typically addressed problems of betrayal, loneliness, bad luck, and hard times. Jane Harden and Melanctha do their "wandering" in blues sites such as railroads and roundhouses. They are blues women who "flout social convention to insist on their geographic mobility and freedom to express their sexuality as they please. And if Stein inscribes the racial color hierarchy, "it is because in the world of the blues it is the light-skinned women who are most self-sufficient and unpredictable."[18] Coon" songs provided Stein with the stereotypes, but the poetics of early blues, its open treatment of female sexuality, and particularly its use of repetition lent much to the narrative's innovative form.

Throughout "Melanctha" Stein employs repetition to destabilize meaning, anticipating much-later deconstructionist theorists. Far from firmly establishing his certainty, when Jeff Campbell uses "certainly" eighteen times in a single paragraph, he is in fact certain of very little.[19] Or when Rose Johnson is described as "black," "real black," "a real black negress," "black childish Rose," and "black girl" in the space of fifteen paragraphs, the impact of the word "black" is diminished and its meaning becomes uncertain. In another instance, repetition is used to ridicule stereotypes. Consider, for example, how and when the obnoxious phrase "the wide abandoned laughter that makes the warm broad glow of negro [*sic*] sunshine" is applied. It is first used to characterize what Rose Johnson is *not* (*TL*, 59). Nor did James Herbert, Melanctha's overbearing father, ever have "the wide abandoned laughter that gives the broad glow to negro sunshine" (*TL*, 64). The sole "negro" to possess this defining quality is Jeff Campbell, the "whitest" and least stereotypical of all the characters (*TL*, 77, 96). Repetition of the stereotypes also contributes to their "bumptious" quality, drawing an even greater distinction between reality and representation.[20] But the way in which early blues used repetition catalyzed Gertrude Stein's use of it in the development of her narrative style.

"Melanctha" revels in sounds and patterns of speech-become-song that wonderfully illustrate Sherley Anne Williams's description of repetition in blues. According to Williams, "Repetition in blues is seldom word for word and the definition of worrying the line includes changes in stress and pitch[,] . . . changes in word order, repetitions in phrases within the line itself."[21] This excerpt from "Melanctha" illustrates Williams's description:

> "I don't see Melanctha why you should
> talk like you would kill yourself just
> because you're blue. I'd never kill myself
> Melanctha just 'cause I was blue. I'd maybe
> kill somebody else Melanctha 'cause I was
> blue, but I'd never kill myself. If I ever
> killed myself Melanctha it'd be by accident
> and if I ever killed myself by accident
> Melanctha, I'd be awful sorry" (*TL*, 60)

This blues lyric–like passage includes four sentences that contain versions of each other. The first sentence establishes the pattern (and states the problem); the following three disrupt or "worry" that pattern through changes in stress and word order (and make fun of the problem). By the end of the riff, suicide becomes part of the punch line. The repetitions work to "worry" or to stretch, push, or dislocate fixed meaning. Repetition in blues does not simply destabilize meaning, but through the use of musical and verbal irony, it provides an atmosphere in which analysis can take place and another meaning can be provided.[22] In the excerpt, the way the words and phrases are repeated changes the tone from tragic to comic, rendering the suggestion of suicide absurd. Related to this blues strategy, Henry Louis Gates argues that in African American vernacular, repetition with difference, one aspect of "signifyin'," responds to and revises conventional and dominant meanings.[23] Echoing blues music, Stein placed repetition at the center of her efforts to create twentieth-century American literature.

When she wrote *Lectures in America*, the six lectures she composed for her American tour (1934–1935), Stein explicated her understanding and use of repetition. In "Portraits and Repetition," Stein recalls that she became fascinated with repetition in colloquial speech when she moved from a solitary life in California to Baltimore. There she lived with "a whole group of very lively little aunts who had to know anything."[24] In hearing a story repeated over and over, Stein realized, "there can be no repetition because the essence of that expression is insistence, and if you insist you must each time use emphasis and if you use emphasis it is not possible while anybody is alive that they should use exactly the same emphasis" (*LA*, 167). Here Stein's emphasis of "emphasis" locates the origins of this discursive strategy in oral and aural cultural forms, that is in phrases, sentences, and stories that are repeatedly spoken or sung, each time with a difference. Again, in "Poetry and Grammar" Stein insists that "poetry is concerned with using with abusing, with losing with wanting, with denying with avoiding with adoring and replacing the noun" (*LA*, 231). Repetition is again the weapon of choice: "When I said. A rose is a rose is a rose is a rose . . . I caressed and completely caressed and addressed a noun" (*LA*, 231). In this instance word-for-word repetition puts pressure on the noun, "worrying" it, in such a way, that, in Stein's view, restores the original relationship between sign and signified: the rose is once again red. Stein's "lively little aunts" made her attentive to repetition in the patterns of colloquial speech. But the early blues inspired, if not instructed, her use of repetition to simultaneously write and revise, to construct and critique "Melanctha." This lesson left a lasting impression on Stein and accounts for her lifelong interest in African America. And just as she took inspiration from their cultural forms, Stein formulated, through the African American experience of marginality, her ideas on creativity.

In *Paris France*, Stein insists, "Everybody who writes is interested in living inside themselves in order to tell what is inside themselves. That is why writers have to have two countries, the one where they belong and the one in which they live really."[25] Stein's claim is an effort to come to terms with a nagging paradox: Gertrude Stein, the mother of twentieth-century American literature, lived all of her creative life in France. "Melanctha," Stein's step "away from the nineteenth century and into the twentieth century in literature," was effected through a figurative expatriation. Stein came to appreciate the insight and originality generated by being in but not of a place. She claimed this position for herself (and Pablo Picasso), but she also attributed the special genius of black American artists to this same inside-outsider perspective. Stein realized the validity of this insight at least as early as 1925, when, in letters to Carl Van Vechten, she ascribed such a perspective to Paul Robeson and Taylor Gordon.[26]

After meeting Paul and Essie Robeson in November 1925, Stein wrote a portrait entitled "Among Negroes."[27] The piece featured Robeson and the three African American women who starred in the Revue Nègre (all of whom Stein had met): Josephine Baker, Maud de Forrest, and Ida Lewelyn. What intrigued Stein about Robeson was that he "knew american [*sic*] values and american life as only one in it but not of it could know them."[28] A few years later Stein echoed this observation in her enthusiasm for the entertainer Taylor Gordon's autobiography, *Born to Be*. Again in a letter to Van Vechten, Stein wrote: "Thanks a thousand times for the Born to Be of Taylor Gordon, I have enjoyed it immensely. . . . Already I have been impressed with Robeson who made me realize middle class America as no one else had made me see it . . . and now Gordon makes clear a way of seeing it from the inside and the outside . . . the way a white can't do it, it is not realism it is reality and that's what interests me most in the world."[29]

For Stein, who had fled "to the kindly comfort of an older world accustomed to take all manner of strange forms into its bosom," the feeling of being in but not of one's place had a deeply felt familiarity.[30] In *Everybody's Autobiography*, Stein makes clear that this inside-outsider position is the source of her own originality. At the College of William and Mary, Stein badgered the students for placidly accepting the ideas and opinions of their elders. "Somebody has to have an individual feeling and it might be a Californian or a Virginian. It was a Californian. I can call myself a Californian because I was there from six to seventeen and a Virginian might have an individual feeling. California and Virginia have at one time had a feeling that they were not part just being American."[31] As Virginians they were in an excellent position to question, doubt, disagree, or to have an "original feeling." Although Stein spoke almost exclusively at colleges and universities such as William and Mary, in her "homecoming narrative" the African American artists and "everybody" are a part of the national portrait.

The African Americans Stein met in the thirty-year interval between 1904, when she left the United States, and 1934, when she returned, were artists. Even during World War I Stein, as a supply driver for the American Fund for the French Wounded, reveled in the company of the doughboys but never mentions having encountered African Americans. So once back in the United States for the seven-month lecture tour, Stein seemed eager to talk to black Americans wherever she went. These exchanges include a meeting with the all-black cast of her opera (music by Virgil Thomson) *Four Saints in Three Acts* and a reception organized by Carl Van Vechten, at which James Weldon Johnson and Walter White were among the many intellectuals and artists Stein encountered.[32] In Texas she discussed the criminal justice system with a chauffeur and met the cast of *Porgy and Bess*. In Chicago she toured the ghetto in a squad car and visited one of the overcrowded houses. That Stein's homecoming narrative included any mention of African America may have seemed odd to her contemporary readers and critics. But as if to underscore the significance of African Americans for this narrative, among the eight photos in the text (all by Carl Van Vechten) Stein included one of Beatrice Wayne-Robinson and Edward Matthews, the stars of *Four Saints in Three Acts*. These photos and the cameo appearances of African Americans throughout the text make the larger point: the portrait of Gertrude Stein's America—that is, *Everybody's Autobiography*—would be incomplete without the presence of black folk. Indeed, the beginning and end of Stein's American tour were punctuated by two encounters she had with black American women.

Portraits and Prayers was released to coincide with Stein's arrival in New York in October 1934. On that day she was out walking when a young black woman, recognizing her from the photograph on the cover of the book displayed in a store window, pointed to it and then smiled at her (*EA*, 8). At the end of her seven-month journey, Stein recalls a brief telephone conversation with Beatrice Robinson-Wayne.[33] On the eve of their departure the phone rang, and "when I said who is it, a voice answered Saint Theresa, and that was my farewell to America, it was she . . . and she was Saint Theresa for herself and for us" (*EA*, 195). In these encounters the African American reader and performer confirm Gertrude Stein's identity as an artist. That Stein frames her journey with these exchanges bespeaks their significance to her.

Stein's treatment of black Americans in this text may seem condescending and naive to many readers. Still, her portrait of African America includes "everybody" from music teacher to actor to waiter to educator to head of the National Association for the Advancement of Colored People. But she also included the grimmer side of the black American experience. One evening Stein and Alice B. Toklas rode around Chicago with a homicide detective. In the black neighborhood they "went into one of the houses and it might have been a Southern one it might have been one of those in Baltimore . . . there were ten or twelve there and others in other rooms men and women . . . one in a corner cooking, some in bed doing nothing . . . and they told me where they came from each one of them mostly from . . . the South . . . now they were here . . . and they had no plans about anything" (*EA*, 214). Stein's description echoes Wright's portrait of the crowded room in which the Thomas family lives and captures Bigger's sense that he will have no opportunity and no future. The parallel Stein draws between the living conditions in Chicago and that of the more southern city of Baltimore argues that life for black Americans had not changed in her thirty-year absence. Stein enlarges this dismal portrait by prompting the detective to make a confession. He admits that the Chicago Police Department failed to investigate the murder of an elderly black man; "he was of no importance and so nobody was put on the job of finding out about him. . . . I said it worried him and he said yes it did, it did come back to him" (*EA*, 215). *Everybody's Autobiography* illustrates Stein's attentiveness to the black American experience and by extension to racial oppression; it was a subject to which she returned with greater intensity after World War II.

Stein and Toklas refused to leave France during the war and lived precariously in two small villages near the Swiss and Italian borders. When the first American GIs appeared in their village in August of 1944, the two women greeted them as if they were long-lost children.[34] After her return to Paris in December 1944, Stein continued to converse, lecture, badger, cajole, and comfort her "boys" with the devotion of a grandmother. *Brewsie and Willie* grew out of her conversations with the American GIs, black and white. Stein also wrote two articles for *Life* and the *New York Times Magazine* and gave an interview to the soldier and journalist Vincent Tubbs for the *Baltimore Afro-American*.[35] In *Brewsie and Willie*, the articles, and her interview, Stein addresses the many fears the GIs have shared with her, as well as America's social and economic challenges in the postwar period. Chief among these concerns was American racism.

Thematically, *Brewsie and Willie* interrogates the ethnic and racial prejudices that fueled World War II. Indeed it is an early example of the way American racism would be viewed in light of the Holocaust. In the *Times* article, Stein recalls a conversation with a southern solider as they watched the arrival of former prisoners of war: "There were a number of Negroes and the French populace who were standing around to greet them and to help them[,] put up their hands to help them down the tired men and to take their bundles and help, and the white and black hands were all equally happy to be helped and to be helping all mingled together . . . and the Southerner said, could you see that in any city in the United States. Well I said you see to the French any soldier of France is as good as any other soldier."[36] In a parallel scene from *Brewsie and Willie*, one of the soldiers reports having just seen a black man sharing a park bench with three white women. Brewsie, "the outfit's thinker," wonders, "when we get home will we get mad and all excited up about something that really didn't amount to anything to us like we did before this war."[37] The African American officer speaks most eloquently to the legacy of slavery, Jim Crow, and the ghetto. When asked why, after nine years of marriage, he has no children, he replies, "is this America any place to make born a Negro child" (*BW*, 12).

Unlike the white soldiers, the black soldiers are the only GIs who can speak French; indeed, they share their superior status with the Red Cross nurses, Janet and Pauline, admirers of the feminist and political activist who was the subject of Stein's last play, "The Mother of Us All"—Susan B. Anthony. After much animated and difficult discussion, the only answer to America's social ills is to "pioneer," and African Americans are the models. As one soldier reluctantly admits: "Yeah it's funny . . . the only real pioneering there is in America these days is done by Negroes. They're pioneering, they find new places, new homes, new lives, new ways and they more and more own something" (*BW*, 65). In the hostile clime of American racism, black Americans have always had to pioneer, to find "new lives" and "new ways."

Even though her letters to Richard Wright have been missing since 1967, it is reported that Stein's first letter began: "Dear Richard, It is obvious that you and I are the only two geniuses of this era." Wright's life and work spoke eloquently for Stein's notion that a culture's most original work begins with that "individual feeling" from the perspective of the insider-outsider. In his reply (three pages single-spaced), Wright gracefully acknowledged her praise and then addressed her concerns: "I can well understand why the American soldiers are worried about Negroes. And why you wonder about them."[38] White people, Wright continues, frequently ask him how Negroes feel and often confess that if they felt that way, they would commit suicide. Wright concludes, "To most of them I say, if . . . I ever killed myself, it would be by accident, and if I ever killed myself by accident, I'd be awful sorry. I expect them to laugh with me, but . . . they don't; so far no one has laughed."[39] Wright concludes the serious discussion of black American life and art by returning Stein to her blues lyric from "Melanctha."

Stein never explicitly acknowledged her debt to African American musical forms in the composition of "Melanctha." As Peterson has argued, Stein may have feared "being assimilated to blackness of actually being identified as a 'nigger.'"[40]

But in the forty years following the composition of *Three Lives*, she came to appreciate the centrality of the African American experience for American life and art. In a 1945 interview for *Transition* magazine, Stein said of *Uncle Tom's Children*, "I do not think there has been anything done like it since I wrote *Three Lives*."[41] It was the most generous compliment Stein had ever paid another writer. It is difficult to imagine higher praise.

■ NOTES

1. Ralph Ellison, introduction to John Kouwenhoven, *The Beer Can by the Highway* (Baltimore: Johns Hopkins University Press, 1988).

2. Richard Bridgman, *Gertrude Stein in Pieces* (New York: Oxford University Press, 1970), 28. Gertrude Stein, *Three Lives* (1909; reprint, New York: Penguin, 1990); hereafter cited parenthetically in text as *TL*.

3. Representative of the first group are Maryann DeKoven, *A Different Language: Gertrude Stein's Experimental Writing* (Madison: University of Wisconsin Press, 1983), and Lisa Ruddick, *Gertrude Stein: Body, Text, Gnosis* (Ithaca, N.Y.: Cornell University Press, 1990); of the latter, Milton Cohen, "Black Brutes and Mulatto Saints: The Racial Hierarchy of Stein's 'Melanctha,'" *Black American Literature Forum* 26 (1986): 112–121, and Sonia Saldivar-Hull, "Wrestling Your Ally: Stein, Racism, and Feminist Critical Practice," in *Women's Writing in Exile*, ed. Mary Lynn Broe (Chapel Hill: University of North Carolina Press, 1989), 182–195.

4. Laura Doyle, "The Flat, the Round, and Gertrude Stein: Race and the Shape of Modern(ist) History," *Modernism/Modernity* 7, no. 2 (2000): 249–271; Michael North, *The Dialect of Modernism: Race, Language, and Twentieth-Century Literature* (New York: Oxford University Press, 1994), 59–76; Carla Peterson, "The Remaking of Americans: Gertrude Stein's 'Melanctha' and African American Musical Traditions," in *Criticism and the Color Line: Desegregating American Literary Studies*, ed. Henry Wontham (New Brunswick, N.J.: Rutgers University Press, 1996), 140–157.

5. John Malcolm Brinin, *The Third Rose: Gertrude Stein and Her World* (London: Weidenfeld and Nicolson, 1960), 121.

6. Edmund Fuller, ed., *Journey into the Self: Being the Letters, Papers, and Journals of Leo Stein* (New York: Crown, 1950), 137.

7. Donald Gallup, ed., *The Flowers of Friendship: Letters Written to Gertrude Stein* (New York: Knopf, 1953), 216; Corinne Blackmer, "African Masks and the Arts of Passing in Gertrude Stein's 'Melanctha' and Nella Larsen's 'Passing,'" *Journal of the History of Sexuality* 4, no. 2 (1993): 230–263.

8. Richard Wright, "Memories of My Grandmother," TMs (photocopy), p. 20. Beinecke Library, Yale University.

9. Clarence Major, "*Three Lives* and Gertrude Stein," *Par Rapport: A Journal of the Humanities* 2 (1979): 58.

10. Gertrude Stein, *Fernhurst, Q.E.D., and Other Early Writings* (New York: Liveright, 1971).

11. Bridgman, *Gertrude Stein in Pieces*, 48–58.

12. North, *Dialect of Modernism*, 70.

13. Peterson, "The Remaking of Americans," 142, 144.

14. Bridgman, *Gertrude Stein in Pieces*, 46–48.

15. Werner Sollors, introduction to *The Life Stories of Undistinguished Americans*, ed. Hamilton Holt (New York: Routledge, 1990), xv.

16. Peterson, "The Remaking of Americans," 146–149.

17. Ibid., 146.

18. Ibid., 151.

19. Stein, *Three Lives*, 94–98.

20. Blackmer, "African Masks and the Arts of Passing," 232.

21. Sherley Anne Williams, "The Blues Roots of Contemporary Afro-American Poetry," *Massachusetts Review* 18 (1977): 544.

22. Ibid.

23. Henry Louis Gates Jr., *The Signifying Monkey: A Theory of African American Literary Criticism* (New York: Oxford University Press, 1988), 62–64.

24. Gertrude Stein, *Lectures in America* (New York: Random House, 1935), 168; hereafter cited parenthetically in text as *LA*.

25. Gertrude Stein, *Paris France* (1940; reprint, New York: Liveright, 1970), 2.

26. In a letter to Carl Van Vechten of 9 November 1925, she wrote of this meeting, "[Paul] Robeson is a dear and he sang for us and I had a nice long talk with him and everybody liked him." In Edward Burns, ed., *The Letters of Carl Van Vechten and Gertrude Stein, 1913–1946* (New York: Columbia University Press, 1986), 123. Stein was critical of Robeson's singing spirituals; she felt they were not part of his experience. See Martin Duberman, *Paul Robeson* (New York: Knopf, 1988), 92.

27. Gertrude Stein, *Useful Knowledge* (London: Bodley Head, 1928), 60–62; hereafter cited parenthetically in text as *UK*.

28. Quoted in Duberman, *Paul Robeson*, 92.

29. Burns, 202–203.

30. Gertrude Stein, *The Making of Americans* (1925; reprint, New York: Something Else Press, 1966), 21.

31. Gertrude Stein, *Everybody's Autobiography* (New York: Random House, 1937; reprint, Cambridge: Exact Change, 1993), 256–257; hereafter cited parenthetically in text as *EA*.

32. Linda Wagner-Martin, *Favored Strangers: Gertrude Stein and Her Family* (New Jersey: Rutgers, 1995), 210.

33. Although Stein does not mention her name in the narrative, it is included on the reverse side of her photograph, which is among eight others included in the text. These photos were taken by Carl Van Vechten for *Everybody's Autobiography*. With the exception of three, one of Stein and the dogs, one of Alice, and one of Lucy Church in Bilignin, these photos underscore the important features of the American tour. One pictures William Rogers, the GI that Gertrude and Alice adopted during World War I and who later became instrumental in their decision to make the trip. There is another photo of Stein surrounded by students at William and Mary, and a portrait of her wearing the dress in which she delivered her lectures. Finally, there is a photograph of Edward Matthews who played the role of Saint Ignatius from the opera, *Four Saints in Three Acts*. Interestingly, there are no photographs of her name in lights or of her shaking hands with the first lady.

34. Gertrude Stein, *Wars I Have Seen* (New York: Random House, 1945).

35. Gertrude Stein, "Off We All Went to See Germany," *Life*, 6 August 1945, 54–58; "This New Hope Is 'Our Sad Young Man,'" *New York Times Magazine*, 3 June 1945, 15, 38. Vincent Tubbs, "Gertrude Stein Talks for Afro," *Baltimore Afro-American*, 28 July 1945, 5.

36. Stein, *New York Times Magazine*, 38.

37. Gertrude Stein, *Brewsie and Willie* (New York: Random House, 1946), 43; hereafter cited parenthetically in text as *BW*.

38. Gallup, *The Flowers of Friendship*, 379.

39. Ibid.

40. Peterson, "The Remaking of Americans," 153.

41. Robert Haas, ed., "A Transatlantic Interview," in *A Primer for the Gradual Understanding of Gertrude Stein* (Los Angeles: Black Sparrow Press, 1971), 31–32.

A Black Man in Jewface

■

In his printed autobiography, the African American stride pianist Willie the Lion Smith outlines unflinchingly how musical materials circulated in New York during the 1910s and 1920s. Throughout this "as-told-to" memoir Smith relates how non–African Americans (usually Jews) appropriated musical styles developed by African Americans. Smith offers one anecdote in particular that provides a sharp accounting of the complex interactions between Jewish and African American musicians in the age of ragtime and jazz. He tells of a party he attended in 1924 (along with fellow piano players Fats Waller and James P. Johnson) that celebrated the debut of George Gershwin's *Rhapsody in Blue* at Paul Whiteman's famous Aeolian Hall concert.

> We all knew Gershwin because he used to come up to Harlem to listen to us and he was the one who got us invited. It looked for a while as though he was going to stay seated at the piano all night himself and hog all the playing. We three were standing at the bar getting up our courage and the more we imbibed the more anxious we became to get at those keys.
>
> I finally went over and said to Gershwin, "Get up off that piano stool and let the real players take over, you tomato." He was a good-natured fellow and from then on the three of us took over the entertainment. (225–226)

The power relations described in this vignette offer a penetrating view into the musical world of New York in the 1920s. First we see Gershwin as pupil coming "up to Harlem" to learn about African American culture—much as he would go to the South Carolina Sea Islands ten years later to prepare for writing *Porgy and Bess*—with the aim of appropriating these "raw" materials and interpreting them to audiences that had no direct access to them. In this one moment, then, Smith describes Gershwin as both student and privileged initiate. Next, Smith, Waller, and Johnson are in the position of supplicants, nervously hoping for a chance at the keys. Gershwin occupies a position of entitlement: it's his party and he'll play if he wants to. But as with the entire event of the *Rhapsody* debut, Gershwin gains musical sanction through his already firm social status. Gershwin is obviously more at home in the social world of this party than Smith and his friends are. More significant yet, by 1924 it was an article of faith for many audiences that Jews made the most of this sort of music.

In the final twist of this episode, Smith insults Gershwin with a display of mock jocularity and takes over the keyboard. Put crudely, we might say that while Smith, Waller, and Johnson are recognized here as the authentic creators of music—they are the "real players"—Gershwin seems to control (or at least have greatest access to) the means of production.

Smith outlines this situation even more starkly when he reminisces about parties he played that were attended by white musicians (Gershwin and Harold Arlen included) who "would study our work and try to get our music-arranging ideas."[1] Most pernicious, as Smith recalls, was the practice of plying his friend and protégé Fats Waller with wine in order to encourage his continued playing and singing. Even earlier in his autobiography, Smith makes a more pointed reference to Jews capitalizing on African American materials, telling of "the phony Mike Bernard, the Jewish ragtime kid," who made a career out of copying the "great Negro ragtime originator, Ben Harney's style" (54). Smith goes on to claim that Bernard "got more money out of ragtime than did all the colored stars put together" (54).

I cite these examples in detail to call attention to an overlooked but central fact of African American–Jewish relations: some of the most significant interactions between these two groups have been enacted in social spaces marked by the higher status of Jews. Discomfort with this condition has led to a few significant results. First, commercial relationships have generally been ignored by interested observers, who have instead established civil rights work as the primary terrain for contact between the two groups. Secondly, in a sort of collective reaction formation, both groups have—with varying degrees of consciousness and explicitness—created a space for representatives to discuss intergroup contact in language characterized by metaphors of sacred and mystical attachment.

However we understand the place of Jews in "black" music, no simple narrative of colonial exploitation can possibly do justice to the dynamic interplay of African Americans and Jews in the age of ragtime and jazz; Jewish involvement in the business of promoting, adapting, and creating music popularly recognized as "Negro" was too multivalent for such a one-dimensional explanation. Jewish men and women in large numbers made careers that depended on African American music—as performers, songwriters, music publishers, agents, club owners, critics, publicists, and fiction writers. To obtain a satisfactory understanding of the meanings of this musical affiliation, we must consider a variety of sources, including musicians' claims about themselves and their careers; novels, poems, and plays; and contemporary and later accounts of the interactions.

I want to introduce this difficult subject with a detailed reading of one relatively overlooked resource: the life and career of Willie the Lion Smith as presented in his printed and recorded memoirs (*Music on My Mind: The Memoirs of an American Pianist* [1964]; *The Memoirs of Willie the Lion Smith* [1968]). These autobiographical acts, both of which are in "as-told-to" form, are complicated performances whose most significant implications have been almost entirely neglected. In them Smith makes a variety of declarations about his natural affinity for religious Judaism and Jewish culture. While some serious attention has been paid to the various meanings of Jews in blackface, what can we make of this black man in "Jewface"? "Passing"—the only readily available interpretative category that attempts to explain African American adoption of or merging with a "white" identity—is simply inadequate to explain this phenomenon. Smith's invocation of his Jewish heritage does not explicitly coincide with any attempt to claim the corresponding privileges of living as "white."

My investigation will take relevant portions of Smith's autobiographies as "performances" of black-Jewish relations. First I will first discuss how Smith's description of his personal attachment to Judaism (as well as Jews and Jewishness) participates in the construction of musical activity as a natural site for black-Jewish sympathy. After establishing the content—the "what"—of Smith's approach to Jewishness, I then move on to the "how." Here I suggest four major ways that Smith's particular narratives summarize general tendencies in the discourses of black-Jewish sympathy. In doing this I hope to reveal how Smith's autobiographies stand as a variation on some major themes of black-Jewish relations. The organizing principle here is that "black-Jewish relations" is best understood as a rhetorical tendency (and not a concrete set of events); this rhetorical practice always retains a threshold level of intelligibility due to its (allegedly) conspicuous historicity. It may prove useful, then, to examine the words of a major practitioner of this rhetorical activity.

Willie the Lion Smith was one of the most influential of the Harlem school of pianists, a loose aggregation of players who rose to prominence in the 1910s and 1920s. Along with James P. Johnson and Fats Waller, Smith has come to be an emblem for a style of jazz piano playing that derived from ragtime but placed much greater emphasis on left-hand innovations on the keyboard. Smith explicitly positioned stride as the fulfillment of the unmet promise of ragtime, suggesting that ragtime held sway "when they didn't have good left hands" and was dominated by players who simply did not "know the keyboard."[2] Stride piano is remembered today as much for its overall performing milieu as for its musical content: the style summons images of cutting contests, rent parties, and basement clubs.

Smith has much to offer to musicological studies of jazz, but he also makes major contributions with his appropriately confusing accounts of the cultural context of jazz. Smith's memoirs speak particularly to the status of jazz as a site where people of various racial and ethnic backgrounds met and shared their musical materials, although he also reserves the right to characterize jazz in terms of its unmediated African American purity. Smith's scripts range widely from optimistic reports of cross-ethnic collaboration to rueful chronicles of the antagonisms caused by the outright theft of African American music.

The ethnic encounter most pertinent to Willie Smith was that between Jews and African Americans. In the course of his printed and recorded autobiographies

Smith offers three different grounds (which often become conflated) for his own connection to Jews, Judaism, and Jewishness. I denote the three as genealogical, commercial (including other intergroup exchanges based on urban contiguity), and mystical/sacred. Willie Smith's chosen terms of comparison do not exhaust the ways in which African Americans and Jews were drawn together in popular music. For instance, he rarely takes part in the popular practice of discerning perceived similarities in the historical determinants that shaped each group; nor does he ever render the intergroup affiliation in the explicitly sexualized terminology that often entered these discussions. But Smith does provide a valuable introduction to the identity politics of African American–Jewish relatedness in music, and he serves the particular function of reminding us of how a generalized discourse (which at times seems free-floating and without agency) can have meaning for, and find unique expression in, an individual life.

Smith introduces the genealogical theme in the very first paragraph of his autobiography: "The Lion is here. Full name: William Henry Joseph Bonaparte Bertholoff Smith. Quite a name. Takes in French and Jewish. What I'm going to tell you is all the true facts. . . . First, the Lion has always had music on his mind" (1). While it is unnecessary for Smith to cite his most identifying heritage—his "Negro" blood—in this introduction, he does inform us early on that his mother was of Spanish, Negro, and Mohawk Indian descent (5).

Genealogy looms large at numerous points in his written autobiography. Smith reports, among other things, that his heritage granted him special access to various cultural traditions. In the opening moment of the autobiography, quoted above, Smith draws a direct line from the "true facts" of his lineage to his obsession with music. A few pages later the connection between birth and music is made even more explicit, as Smith recounts how "the first sound, the first musical sound, that inspired me was the cry of a newborn baby" (7).

Smith never does make very clear how he comes by his Jewish blood. His natural father, Frank Bertholoff, died when Smith was a young boy ("Smith" came from a stepfather). Willie Smith describes Frank Bertholoff as a "light-skinned playboy," but he offers no direct information about Bertholoff's having Jewish ancestry. The missing father holds the key to Jewishness, but his very absence problematizes simple descent-based definitions of self because it places too heavy a burden on the physical properties of blood.

Genealogical explanations for the relationship between African Americans and Jews have rarely had widespread effectiveness—particularly in the United States. In Smith's particular instance, his actual Jewish heritage is shadowy and hard to trace concretely, existing on the level more of metaphor than of established fact. Because Smith is interested in presenting his own mixedness as organic, he couples it with various assertions about the fusions that led to jazz. Occasionally Smith explains that jazz is the fruit of an exclusively black diasporic tradition; more often he contributes to the long-dominant understanding of "jazz"—broadly conceived—as a meeting-place of many cultures, most notably Jewish and African American.

Even so, genealogy is shaky ground for comparisons of Jews and African Americans; it could never have supported the multifarious discursive formations that have developed over time. As a result, Smith proposes two other "clusters" around which his attraction to Jewishness might be related, one based in a spiritual/mstical similarity of African Americans and Jews, the other in commercial relations (and other deeply ambivalent interactions) in a shared urban space. I separate these two units only for organizational purposes. Smith usually presents them as being complexly related.

Smith's descriptions of concrete exchanges between Jews and African Americans—whether of cultural materials or of labor and capital—are uncommon, if not unprecedented. In this era generally, and in the realm of discourses around music more particularly, it was customary to overlook, ignore, or actively repress the contemporary (nonmetaphorical and nonhistorical) ways in which African Americans and Jews were related. While Jews and African Americans might be linked through a number of shaky anthropological or pseudohistorical premises, little attention fixed on the urban sites of physical contact between the two groups. The musical discussions of the period carried a similar resistance to imagining that Jews and African Americans communicated, collaborated, and negotiated in a common social world. Instead, a powerful narrative developed that argued that the attraction of Jews for African American music derived from a connection these musicians (many of whom were sons of cantors) had to a sacred Old World music which shared many traits with secular "Negro" music. In fact, a conflation of cantorial singing and jazz playing forms the secret heart of the discourse of musical similarity linking African Americans and Jews: while much of the rhetoric surrounding George Gershwin, Irving Berlin, and others suggested that Jews were especially good at "improving" African American materials, the sacralizing tendency made it possible to understand African American music as a product of the Jews' Jewishness.

Because of this tendency to underplay material exchanges, it became possible, as both Michael Rogin and Lawrence Levine have pointed out, to construct overly metaphorical versions of the origins of jazz that left African Americans out of the picture altogether.[3] Smith's account of urban and commercial transactions during the 1910s and 1920s recuperates an important basis of African American–Jewish relations that would not begin to be articulated until events such as the Harlem riot of 1935 made it impossible to neglect the centrality of *propinquity*—geographical and/or commercial—as an explanatory category. Even so, Smith too reproduces and augments sacred myths of intergroup unity.

Smith relates a great deal of information in his memoirs that helps to demystify the aura of organic inevitability surrounding the musical "miscegenation" that not only fascinated his contemporaries but also continues to infuse most critical discussion. In his autobiographies, Smith insists on multiethnic participation as constitutive of jazz performance, although he does make a case early on for exclusive African American origins. But even as he stakes his claim in the first few pages of *Music on My Mind* for his own privileged (African American) position, he also highlights the interracial makeup of northern riverboat bands (4). One of the treasured narratives of jazz history details the vanguard role mixed bands played in fostering racial understanding; the focus is usually on the 1930s and the rise of the Big Band, and not surprisingly Jews (Benny Goodman and Artie Shaw, for instance) figure importantly in these stories.[4] Perhaps no one articulated this approach as completely as did Marshall Stearns, a jazz scholar convinced of the utopian thrust of jazz. Writing of the swing era, Stearns suggested that a "mutual feeling of personal identity arose amid the teamwork that big-band arrangements made necessary."[5] Most notable here is Stearns's ascription of social instrumentality to musical form. Dissenters from this optimistic mode have been many (Amiri Baraka [LeRoi Jones], for one) but the most evenhanded is Burton Peretti, who concludes that the influence of jazz on "cultural integration and biracial understanding" was ambiguous.[6]

Smith spends some time in his memoirs describing how the urban space shared by Jews and African Americans led to some stressful transactions; I will soon turn to the question of how Smith finessed the commercial relationships between Jews and African Americans so as to incorporate them—via a rhetoric of sacralization—into a safer framework of group likeness. In doing so Smith defuses the potentially explosive narratives that lurk in the margins of his autobiography of exploitation of African Americans by Jews.

Smith domesticates this risky material through appeals to the persona of his mother, who is a shadowy but central figure in the construction of his personal vision of a link between African Americans and Jews. Smith's family lived in Newark, New Jersey, where his father drove a hog wagon, making deliveries even to "several well-to-do Jewish families . . . who could eat pork" (11). Through these contacts Smith's mother was able to contract washing and ironing work, enlisting young Willie's help in delivering finished bundles and making collections. In the written memoir Smith moves on almost immediately from describing this labor relationship—a central site for interactions between African American and Jewish women—into a description of how contact with Jewish families led him to a "discovery" of his own Jewishness. Smith has already set up for us what sort of Jewish families he is describing—the wealthy kind who eat pork. These Jews are likely of German descent, not eastern European, and they live outside the initial sites of immigrant settlement. Secular and assimilated as these families are, Smith nonetheless locates his "conversion" narrative in one such home:

> Our best customer was a prosperous Jewish family named Rothschild out on South Orange Avenue. They were in the wallpaper-hanging business. On Saturdays when I made my deliveries there, a rabbi was at Mrs. Rothschild's home to teach her children their Hebrew lessons.
>
> The chanting sounds coming out of the parlor during the lessons fascinated me from the beginning, and Mrs. Rothschild soon noticed. She permitted me to go into the study and sit and listen. It didn't take much time before I began to learn the meanings of the Hebraic words. When

the rabbi saw how well I was doing, he took special pains to teach me, and it wasn't long before I was talking Hebrew as well as the Rothschild kids. (11–12)

Smith has already made clear before this that his deepest affiliations were organized around aural experiences; he notes that while his mother encouraged him to visit "any church where God was in attendance," he seeks out and is moved by those places where he can hear "emotional music"—and as such finds inspiration in the "singing, the rhythmic singing at the Baptist services." But it is the sounds of Jewish chanting that lead Smith to make his most extended commitment:

As it turned out, I favored the Jewish religion all my life and at one time served as a Hebrew cantor in a Harlem synagogue. You could say I am Jewish partly by origin and partly by association. When I was thirteen years old, I had my bar mitzvah in a Newark synagogue. A lot of people are unable to understand my wanting to be Jewish. One said, "Lion, you stepped up to the plate with one strike against you—and now you take a second one right down the middle." They can't seem to realize I have a Jewish soul and belong in that faith. (12)

A remarkable claim—to have a Jewish soul—for an African American man to narrate in 1964 about his youth in the early decades of the twentieth century.

Smith's rendering of his acquisition of Jewishness includes many of the major themes of African American–Jewish relatedness as it played out on the field of popular music. I want to move out from this consideration of what Smith construes as his individual attachment to Jewishness—the genealogical, commercial, and sacred modes I have noted—to a summary of the ways in which Smith's reminiscences represent a detailed articulation of some key elements of the rhetoric of African American–Jewish relatedness.

For all the attention Smith pays to his own postulated Jewish "origins," his most significant constructions of likeness remain generally on the level of metaphor; this dovetails with the commonly held belief that Jews and African Americans somehow ended up resembling each other—in physiognomy, a shared penchant for expressive melancholy, and so on—even though the two groups evolved from distinct gene pools. (Only in the hands of a few crackpot, if influential, "anthropologists" has a claim for actual shared heritage been made, usually in the interest of a racialist agenda.) For Smith, the assertion of Jewish origins appears finally as a post hoc explanation of behaviors that might otherwise seem to lack rational grounding. As he admitted himself, it did not make a lot of sense to take "a second one down the middle."

Because it seems to be metaphorical construction that most interests Smith, we need to be wary of taking Smith's account of his Jewish origins too literally, mostly because of the sleight of hand he performs when it comes to pinning down how he comes by his Jewish roots. Very early on in the autobiography, Smith hints that he is Jewish by way of his light-skinned father, whose last name is Bertholoff, not through his mother, with her identified Spanish, Mohawk, and Negro blood-lines. But Smith's father drops out of the picture quickly, and it is through his mother (and her bloodlines) that Smith finds the source for the most significant aspects of his character, his musicality and spirituality above all; for Smith, we soon realize, blood is a metaphor that connects a vague genealogy to a significant body of sentiment. In short, "blood" equals "spirit" for Smith. It follows that as Smith limns his strong attractions to Jews and Judaism, he will subtly shift focus and accent a symbolic genealogy of "Jewishness" inspired by his mother, rather than the positivistic demonstration of patrilinear descent implied initially.

This substitution manifests itself fully in Smith's chronicle of his mother's final illness and death. After suffering a stroke, Smith's mother is hospitalized in Newark's City Hospital, where she receives sub-par care. After her release and a second stroke, Smith has her admitted to Beth Israel, a "Jewish hospital on the outskirts of Newark" where Smith feels sure they will "take good care of her" (245). Smith's rededication to Judaism comes with his mother's eventual death:

> The people at Beth Israel were very considerate and I began to think more about religion. I had always thought about the possibility of becoming a rabbi, but the opportunity to get the right education didn't come up. After my mother's death I became a member of a congregation of Jewish Negroes in Harlem and started studying religion. I got as far as becoming a cantor. Because of my devotion to Judaism, I was called The Lion of Judea. (245–246)

Here, through the alchemy of his mother's death and the kindness of a Jewish hospital's staff, Smith is able to rediscover his own "Jewish soul."

Why, after hinting at a concrete blood connection to Jewishness, would Smith reconstruct this relationship as a metaphorical one derived mysteriously from his mother? In addition to the great emphasis Smith put on his mother's influence in most of the important areas of his personal development, he also would have known from his Jewish studies that for Jews, the condition of the child follows that of the mother. This is a detail that might have had a certain poignancy for Smith, given that African Americans had a parallel social construction foisted upon them in American slavery.

The organizational unity granted to Smith through his use of metaphorical constructions (usually expressed in mystical and sacred terms) provides us with a helpful first clue to why discussions of African American and Jewish musical relatedness so often embraced—or resorted to—figurative expression. Smith, like so many of his contemporaries, was more comfortable with drawing hazy analogies between African Americans and Jews than with focusing attention on the geographic and social contiguity of the two groups in American cities. To understand the complexities of these intergroup exchanges in music and the rhetorics describing them, we must first acknowledge the constitutive performative aspect of this discourse: the creation, repetition, and revision of metaphor has always defined the field of images now received as a positivistic tale of "black-Jewish relations."

As a result, it is not surprising that along with directing our attention to the centrality of various functional metaphors in constructing a vision of African American–Jewish likeness, Willie the Lion Smith's memoirs purposefully avoid specificity: a clear-cut vagueness is required for his (and virtually all such) productions of resemblance. I have related how blurry Smith's appeals to genealogical Jewishness are; his descriptions of how (and why) he became attracted to Jewish religious life and secular culture are similarly inexact. Once past his early ruminations on an inherited Jewishness, Smith next focuses on a "natural" interest in Hebrew prayer that he picks up at the Rothschild home. For the bulk of his memoirs, however, Smith leaves behind the explicitly religious allure of Jewishness. Instead, he calls attention to a Jewishness defined by such nebulous concepts as "soul" or to his own skills at the languages of Jewishness, described variously as Hebrew, Yiddish, or Jewish, but at times revealed to be simply the language of commerce. In the first case we have the example of Smith's encounter with an Irish woman who sings the Yiddish song "Eli, Eli" with Duke Ellington's band:

> I've forgotten her name, but she was Irish and I could never figure the tongue she was singing the number in, because it sure wasn't Hebrew. She would sing "Eli, Eli" (O Lord, why hast thou forsaken me?), but I got in a fight with her because I told her she shouldn't be singing the song if she didn't know what the words meant. I talked Jewish to her but she didn't understand a thing. But being Irish, she had a soul. (173–174)

The language difficulties plaguing this "Irish" singer are ultimately excused because even with the established distance from the material she is interpreting— which Smith holds sacred—she has the requisite "soul" to ratify her performance. Such vexed concepts as "soul" help define a field of metaphor best demarcated by the litmus-test tautology embedded in the jazz dictum "if you gotta ask, you'll never know." The unspoken reverse of this—something like, "if you don't ask, you must already know"—is central to the oft-repeated, rarely questioned assumptions that linked African Americans and Jews in the musical worlds of the early twentieth century. The very absence of strong challenges to the rhetoric of "natural" similarity goes a long way toward confirming its naturalness.

Smith's remarks on his linguistic facility and his attraction to "Jewish" languages are even more purposeful than his insistence on the centrality of "soul." His looseness in defining the parameters of Hebrew and Yiddish (or "Jewish," as he and many others often termed it) inserts both into a public sphere that removes from them, respectively, sacred character and historical specificity. The effect is to remove "chosenness" as a key category for understanding Jewishness, and to make the boundaries between Jews and others more porous than previously understood.

Smith is taught Hebrew during his childhood after he exhibits a marked and mysterious attraction for it, but he rarely repeats this claim on the sacred language of the Jews.

The only other reference to Hebrew appears in a markedly performative context. Smith describes having a calling card (reproduced on the inside of the jacket of his recorded memoirs) on which he billed himself not only as an instructor in piano, swing, voice, and microphone use, but also as a "Hebrew Cantor." We should note first that on the business card, there is writing in Yiddish that should be transliterated as "Der Yiddischer Chazan" and most appropriately translated as either "The Yiddish Cantor" or "The Jewish Cantor." His translation marks the unfixedness of the categories Yiddish, Jewish, and Hebrew. Smith then goes on to note that "at that time I was cantoring at the synagogue located at 122nd Street and Lenox Avenue, where I was as fast as the rabbi with singing and chanting. This work was enjoyable but I still had to make a living by playing the piano all night" (246). Remarkable here is Smith's equation of "cantoring" with the sort of pianistic cutting contests that are recounted throughout his autobiography (32–33, 54). This is a radical (and hilarious) reversal of the central authenticating strategy used by supporters of Jewish appropriation of African American musical materials and styles: in those instances, the secular and commercial musical creations Jews built upon African American foundations were imbued with higher meaning through appeals to the perceived connections these artists had to a sacred Jewish past. In Smith's revision his Hebrew "cantoring" (sounding now like it is a kind of horse race) is validated through comparison with his well-known skill as a stride pianist—thus equating the sacred language of the Jews with the "low" sounds of Harlem jazz.

I have located use of metaphors and overall vagueness as the first two major ways in which Smith's memoirs embody broad tendencies in the rhetoric of African American–Jewish relatedness. The third major summary aspect of Smith's narrative is that he, like many of the architects of this discourse, willfully downplays the commercial transactions that played such a large part in bringing African Americans and Jews together in music.

"Vagueness" alone cannot do justice to this rhetorical activity, and the language issue provides the best example. Somewhere along the line Smith attains at least a passing knowledge of Yiddish: one contemporary observer was moved to note that Smith, "Harlem's only genuine colored Jew[,] . . . cheerfully speaks a fluent Yiddish on no provocation whatever."[7] Why does Smith never pause to invest this linguistic acquisition with the same drama as his earlier encounter with Hebrew?

This elision is best understood if we approach Smith's autobiographical acts of cross-ethnic sympathy not as parallel to stage blackface—the title of this essay notwithstanding—but as akin to the invention of Jewish white Negroism. The key figures of Jewish white Negroism—Mezz Mezzrow, above all—had no direct access to the visual repertory of theatrical blackface and so relied in large part on verbal fluency to ratify their authenticity. The "descent" into (and claim of descent from) blackness by the Jewish white Negroes is most effectively communicated through the authoritative reproduction of the "black" vernacular—whether spoken, sung, or played. While such moves might be authenticating and liberatory for the Jewish white Negro, embedded in them is a hierarchical assumption about the direction the Jewish subject must travel in order to arrive at this "vernacular."

With this in mind, we might consider Smith's (absent) narrative of how he came to learn Yiddish to be a wickedly apt reversal of the Jewish white Negro's appropriation of "low" black talk. Yiddish—Hebrew's Other in Jewish culture—is the language of the street; according to Fats Waller's son, Smith indeed "learned to speak Yiddish on the streets of Newark."[8] But Yiddish is also the language of the kitchen, and this gives us another clue to Smith's telling vagueness on how he acquired Yiddish. Smith's portrayal of his relationship to this "domestic" language (the *mama-loshen*) as somehow innate, rather than learned, supplements the development of the spiritual "Jewish" genealogy he roots in his relationship to his own mother.

Smith also reveals that Yiddish is a language of urban commerce, even as he tries to draw attention away from this feature of it. Immediately after describing his success at cantoring, Smith writes that "[d]uring this time, the Lion collaborated with Cantor Goldman on several Yiddish compositions" (246). For this brief moment Smith acknowledges the real financial benefit that could accrue to him through his closeness to Jews and Jewish culture, but just as immediately he reinvests these cultural productions with spiritual meaning: one of the songs written with Goldman, according to Smith, "was entitled 'Wus Geven Is Geven,' when translated it means 'Gone—Never to Return,' and it was written as a memorial to my mother" (246). In effect, Smith removes (at least rhetorically) the commercial taint from his association with Jewishness with another brilliant revision of the prevailing discourse: he writes a "mammy" song! To reduce this to a scheme, we might say that in order to draw attention away from the fact that he profits from a carefully cultivated closeness to Jewish culture, Smith adapts the symbolically noncommercial apparatus of the Jewish songwriters and performers who created and put across nostalgic "mother" songs as a way to divert notice from their own acts of formal appropriation and thematic colonization. In this moment Smith effectively responds to the ideological violence done by mammy songs, which—from minstrelsy to Tin Pan Alley—proposed that fissures in the African American family were benignly normative, the product of the usual (non–race specific) intergenerational dramas that trouble all families. In a postscript to this passage, Smith recounts that although he continues to investigate many "different religious beliefs," he remains "loyal to Judaism and won't answer [the] telephone on Yom Kippur" (246). With this Smith marks himself off from Jakie Rabinowitz—the "Jazz Singer"—another icon of his day who split his time between cantoring and secular song.

A final example gives further credence to the notion that Smith understood the benefits to be derived from his access to concrete forms of Jewishness, even though he never explicitly connects his jazz career to his Jewishness. In his oral autobiography Smith more or less claims to have "discovered" Duke Ellington when the great bandleader was suffering through some lean times in New York (*Memoir*, side 3). Smith describes two major ways he helped Ellington, both involving food. First, because Smith is "well-known" at kosher places in Harlem, he and Ellington can always obtain satisfying meals. Smith's other mode of assisting Ellington is less direct: he teaches him a Yiddish song that revolves around the phrase *nokh a bisl* ("give a little," "a little slice," or "a little more").

Why would Smith teach this to Ellington? For much of the mid-1920s (1923–27) Ellington's band, the Washingtonians, made their New York headquarters at the Hollywood, known after the spring of 1925 as the Kentucky Club.[9] This venue, located in a basement on West Forty-ninth Street (between Broadway and Seventh Avenue), was run by Leo Bernstein, a Jewish man alleged to have gangland connections.[10] Although this club provided excellent exposure for Ellington and his band, putting them in contact with significant musical and business players in New York, salaries were low. To augment the regular pay, Ellington and his drummer, Sonny Greer, would continue to play for tips (sometimes a hundred dollars each) deep into the morning, after the rest of the band had gone home. Ellington writes of this time:

> I had one of those little studio upright pianos on wheels that you could push around from table to table, and Sonny would carry his sticks and sing. Answering requests, we sang anything and everything—pop songs, jazz songs, dirty songs, torch songs, Jewish songs. Sometimes, the customer would respond by throwing twenty-dollar bills away from him as though they were on fire. When business was slow, we'd sing "My Buddy." That was the favorite song of the boss, Leo Bernstein, and when we laid that on him he was expected to throw down some bills too.[11]

For Smith to pass along to Ellington not only a Yiddish song, but also one explicitly about sharing the wealth, appears in this light eminently practical, if complex in its valences. The song Willie the Lion Smith sings is really simple in its message: if you have a little, give a little. If the performance of a Yiddish song by an African American man bears more than a hint of cutting capers, it is also significant that Smith is offering a revised picture of the urban landscape, where materials with the ostensible aspect of ethnic exclusivity are revealed to be flowing in various directions. Of course, the small benefit that might have accrued to Ellington or Smith through appropriation of Jewish songs should not be compared to the systematic use of African American resources by Jewish songwriters and performers claiming special access. But Smith's deletion of any explicit reference to the multifarious financial aspects of the relationship between Jews and African Americans in music is typical of the larger discourse of black-Jewish relations. In constructing his personal narrative of natural attraction to Jews and Jewishness, Smith calls our attention to the urban closeness of African Americans and Jews, but he quickly incorporates (and hides) any hint of commerce into a larger tale of musical sympathy. The governing version of musical and racial likeness which Smith represents always relies heavily on directing attention away from its grounding in business exchanges.

The fourth and final sense in which Willie the Lion Smith's configuration of "relatedness" typifies the broader discourse of black-Jewish relations is its overly masculinist cast. Narratives of a natural alliance between African Americans and Jews have been limited, with remarkably few exceptions, to interpretations of contact between men; utopian visions of the musical mergers of the two groups (Smith's is one) have followed this lead and almost entirely excluded women.

In Willie the Lion Smith's case, the masculinist bias is revealed starkly as he blots out the most significant interactions of African American and Jewish women—particularly in describing his first contact with Judaism via the rabbi in the Rothschild home. While dwelling in detail on his mystical attraction to the sounds of chanted Hebrew—and his resulting lifelong association with the Jewish religion—Smith draws attention away from the work relationship that directly led to this first contact: Smith's mother did domestic labor for Jewish families. But Smith introduces his brief remarks on this subject by writing, "We took in washing to help ourselves out with money" (11), moving on in short order to his own religious awakening. To construct a retrospective "naturalness" for his own Jewishness, Smith detaches its development from the unromantic milieu of domestic labor. Urban relations—especially those of a commercial nature and involving women—are thus suppressed in the interest of creating a more organic and optimistic sense of group relations. But then "black-Jewish relations"—organized around a vision of male affiliation—have always relied on evocations of feminine subject positions that call attention to actual women only in order to enact their erasure and thus maintain the safe workings of interracial activity.

The evidence of historical "links" uniting Jews and African Americans has never been in short supply—but it is exactly those presumably "natural" links that have to be studied with the most care. Historical congruence has become a part of the given landscape of the black-Jewish question. The pressing concern is to explore why and how various actors have manipulated these "given" conditions. For Willie the Lion Smith, it became especially compelling to explore the porous boundaries between African Americans and Jews in order to develop powerful arguments about the diverse kinds of fusion dominating the contemporary city—as expressed in his own music and in his own complex self.

■ NOTES

1. Willie the Lion Smith, with George Hoefer, *Music on My Mind: The Memoirs of an American Pianist* (New York: Da Capo Press, 1978), 227. Further references to this memoir will be made parenthetically.

2. Willie the Lion Smith, *The Memoirs of Willie the Lion Smith*, side 1 (RCA, 1968). Further references to this recorded memoir will be noted in the text as "Memoir." After

completing an early draft of this section, I came upon Robert Dawidoff's essay on Sophie Tucker, in which he coins the word "Jewface." See Dawidoff, "Some of Those Days," *Western Humanities Review* 41, no. 3 (1987): 263–286.

3. See Michael Rogin "Blackface, White Noise: The Jewish Jazz Singer Finds His Voice," *Critical Inquiry* 18, no. 3 (1992): 449; and Lawrence Levine, "Jazz and American Culture," *Journal of American Folklore* 102, no. 403 (1989): 16.

4. For a good summary of this tendency, see Burton Peretti, *The Creation of Jazz: Music, Race, and Culture in Urban America* (Chicago: University of Illinois Press, 1992), 187–210.

5. Marshall Stearns, *The Story of Jazz* (New York: Oxford University Press, 1956), 320.

6. Peretti, *The Creation of Jazz*, 209.

7. Rian James, quoted in Barry Singer, *Black and Blue: The Life and Lyrics of Andy Razaf* (New York: Schirmer, 1992), 72.

8. Maurice Waller and Anthony Calabrese, *Fats Waller* (New York: Schirmer, 1977), 32.

9. Mark Tucker, *Ellington: The Early Years* (Chicago: University of Illinois Press, 1991), 98–118. What I refer to here as Ellington's band was originally Elmer Snowden's Washington Black Sox Orchestra. Ellington took over sometime in 1924. See Tucker's excellent book for a full accounting of chronologies, name changes, and so on.

10. Tucker, *Ellington*, 116.

11. Edward Kennedy [Duke] Ellington, *Music Is My Mistress* (1973; New York: Da Capo Press, 1985), 72.

Incognito Ergo Sum

"Ex" Marks the Spot in Cahan, Johnson, Larsen, and Yezierska

■

> What points of contact existed between these languages [Gaelic and He-
> brew] and between the people who spoke them? . . . their antiquity,
> both having been taught on the plain of Shinar 242 years after the del-
> uge in the seminary instituted by Fenius Farsaigh, descendant of Noah,
> progenitor of Israel, and ascendant of Heber and Heremon, progenitors
> of Ireland: their . . . literatures comprising the works of rabbis and
> culdees, Torah, Talmud, Massor, Pentateuch, Book of the Dun Cow,
> Book of Ballymote, garland of Howth, Book of Kells: their dispersal,
> persecution, survival, and revival . . . the proscription of their national
> costumes in penal laws and jewish [sic] dress acts: the restoration in
> Chanan David of Zion and the possibility of Irish political autonomy or
> devolution.
>
> —JAMES JOYCE, Ulysses

The epigraph to this essay traces parallel lines from lineage to culture to exile to desire (for redemption), but the vantage point in Joyce's most modernist of texts is
purposely retrospect. With modernity added as a fifth element to Joyce's cultural
itinerary, and with American blacks and American Jews standing in for Hebrews
and Gaels,[1] the trajectories marked out by the five texts I discuss in this essay become visible. *The Rise of David Levinsky*, by Abraham Cahan; *The Autobiography of
an Ex-Colored Man*, by James Weldon Johnson; *Passing*, by Nella Larsen; and
"Soap and Water" and "Children of Loneliness," by Anzia Yezierska:[2] each of these
fictions offers a study in ethnic erasure and self-fashioning. In each, what classical
poetics calls *recognition*—albeit amplified from plot lineaments to the thematic
and the political[3]—takes the form of that small mark either linking (hyphen) or
subtracting (minus sign) "American" to and from ethnoracial identity—the sign
that one's people is inflected by modernity. Though the mark itself is actually visible only in the case of the Ex-Colored Man—it hyphenates his very name—it
plays no less a constitutive role for the protagonists of the other fictions inasmuch
as they ride or pass under its sign.

Sociologically configured, cultural difference can be represented by the same mark, the hyphen or the minus sign of double consciousness that evinces both a split self and a particularist culture. The hyphen marks, as well, the encompassing cleavage between that cultural margin and the ambient mainstream taxonomizing it as such. Although "twoness" and "how it feels to be a problem" were phrases coined by W. E. B. Du Bois to define racial difference specifically, it is fair, I think, to apply the modernist burden they assert to minority cultures more broadly conceived.

The readings in this essay will focalize certain parallels in order to pivot them as allegories of entanglement, or as constructed hyphens of their own—that is, "black-Jew." I emphasize this point to distinguish between my purposes here, as reflected in my occasional allusions to Levinas and Bakhtin, and an alternate genealogy of culture studies–based interventions such as that of Walter Benn Michaels, for example, as well as to reserve another sense altogether of the hyphen and the space of "hybridity" it locates.[4]

■ Riding the Hyphen or Passing under Its Sign

The "burden" of double consciousness as represented within modernist fiction tended to keep pace with a burgeoning sociological literature in the first half of this century that had evolved beyond more racist notions of cultural difference rooted in Herder, Gobineau, and their nineteenth-century legatees in science and *Geisteswissenschaft*.[5] In contrast to such models of rapprochement befitting a consolidated First World at midcentury, more recent literary theory about ethnicity has selected out the ethnic writer's duty to exploit gap and division, to pit minor against (while within) major. The margin has now been reconfigured as possessed of its own distinct locational advantages. "The issue," writes William Boelhower, for example, "is not ethnicity *per se* but the *uses* of ethnicity in a post-industrial society."[6]

According to this view, "ethnicity" becomes a displaced persons camp always on the move (or road).[7] Ethnic semiosis, Boelhower's model, collapses positionality into movement and celebrates the *perpetuum mobile* that results as a triumph over the face of topography. Hence, Boelhower correlates (and validates) "facework" (or ethnic legerdemain) with homelessness, and of "being a foreigner in one's own country" with minority discourse, the record of perpetual dispossession and exile. As one masks the face, so one throws the voice, forever *manipulating* ethnicity to be an always unstable and destabilizing property. Citing John Cournos's extremely vexing novel *The Mask* (1931) as exemplary (Cournos was both a converted Jew and a Christian apologist), Boelhower entertains the following dialogue:

> *Cournos*: " . . . a tall, well-built man, dressed like other men except for a large sombrero hat . . . paused in front of the boy. . . . 'I'm a circus cowboy and broncobusting is more in my line. Now you wouldn't take me

for one of God's own chosen people, would you? Well I am. But one day
I got tired of it. Now I'm everything under the sun. . . . And so, my boy,
I say to you: Chuck it! . . . Straighten your face out! . . . If you must say
Shema Israel [*sic*], say it on the q.t. all to yourself. . . ."

Boelhower. Cournos' Jewish cowboy has created a new ethnic space
that, in reality, is a hermeneutical non-space in the culture of the national
map. Simply put, he cannot be located ethnically, and there is now no
way of telling when his Jewishness will surface. As such he is a figure of
eruption, a catastrophic subject. His ethnic appearances are spontaneous,
aleatory, shifting, his "identity" ambiguous, cryptic and allotropic.[8]

But in the case of the protagonists created by James Weldon Johnson, Abraham Cahan, Nella Larsen, and Anzia Yezierska, such a prescription for ethnic identity seems diagnostically inopportune. A certain linguistic indiscretion turns
"exile" and "catastrophic subject" into discursive properties, as though the play of
difference on a linguistic plane of language naturally transposes itself onto the
plane of ethnic identity and experience themselves. The texts I wish to focus upon
this essay all work in the opposite direction, finding in language another rehearsal
of transcendental homelessness rather than a respite of or solution to it.

Boelhower's worrisome characterization of ethnicity as "a mute and virtual
language"[9] suggests more than a passing affinity with Deleuze and Guattari's concept of minority discourse as *deterritorialization,* or as the authors put it, "how to
become a nomad and an immigrant and a gypsy in relation to one's own language."[10] According to this model (founded on a reading of Kafka's entire oeuvre,
though Kafka himself propounds a fairly restrictive concept of a "literature of small
peoples" as opposed to "minority "discourse"),[11] one speaks *against* the major
grain. Ethnicity produces purposeful estrangement or defamiliarization. Communicative speech is made abstinent, and expression becomes a kind of hunger art:
"To speak and above all to write, is to fast": "Language always implies a deterritorialization of the mouth, the tongue, and the teeth. . . . There is a certain disjunction between eating and speaking, and even more, between eating and writing.
Undoubtedly, one can write while eating more easily than one can speak while eating, but writing goes further in transforming words into things capable of compet-
ing with food."[12]

In practice, this defamiliarization means a disjunction between content and
expression and thus mimes the ethnic subject's existential predicament (itself emblematic) of being a stranger to oneself and of discovering, in Michel de Certeau's
words, the "impossibility of one's own place." Thus, as expression cuts off alimen-
tation, so sound cuts off sense, and in what Cahan's Levinsky himself would call a
marvelous transformation, the ethnic tongue is now set free to wander in Babel,
calling attention to the precariousness of place *in the first place.* This is the revolutionary potential of ethnic discourse: "To bring language slowly and progressively
to the desert . . . to find points of nonculture or underdevelopment, linguistic
Third World zones by which a language can escape."[13]

With its constant recourse to animal imagery and Freudian primary process, Deleuze and Guattari's manifesto rides minority discourse, in all its anarchic orality, like the postmodern suckerfish to modernity's foraging predation (if ethnicity were any kind of a genuine threat, that is).[14] Such deterritorializing freedom of the word becomes the chief privilege accruing to the modern ethnic subject.[15] But even prior to the question of how serviceable such a schema is for different minority discourses in different sociocultural conditions, before we rush to superimpose territory on territory and ethnic writer on ethnic writer, if we pause and turn this model around to reveal the trauma behind the tableau—the common burden shared by the literary blacks and Jews assembled here—we discover another sense altogether of disjunction and nomadic, gypsy citizenship.[16]

A moment late in *The Rise of David Levinsky* captures what I have in mind here. Levinsky finds himself in a railroad dining car in the company of three bourgeois whose "easy urbanity" gives him "a sense of uncanny gentility and bliss" (*RDL*, 331). Suddenly *chez sois*, he relaxes sufficiently while eating to talk and proceeds to demonstrate Deleuze and Guattari's equation with a vengeance: "I was so absorbed in the topic and in the success I was apparently scoring that I was utterly oblivious to the taste of the food in my mouth. But I was aware that it was 'aristocratic American' food, that I was in the company of well-dressed American Gentiles, eating and conversing with them, a nobleman among noblemen" (*RDL*, 329).[17] Levinsky continues in this rhapsodic, enchanted vein—"Can it be that I am I?" (*RDL*, 330),[18] much as Boelhower lauds in *Through a Glass Darkly*—until such self-questioning brings him catastrophically back to himself: "After dinner, when we were in the smoking room again, it seemed to me that the three Gentiles were tired of me. Had I talked too much? Had I made a nuisance of myself? I was wretched" (*RDL*, 330). That last observation puts a period to Levinsky's wonder at "still discovering America" and his doubt about any piloting skills he may have demonstrated: the face of topography reasserts itself as Levinsky, sufficiently deterritorialized as to be almost in steerage again, loses his cultural sea legs.

James Weldon Johnson's *The Autobiography of an Ex-Colored Man* contains a similar scene, also staged in a railway car (a classic diasporic emblem in and for American culture, along with its interurban counterpart, the streetcar—the site, one recalls, of Homer Plessy's staged arrest in 1896).[19] Quietly observing a conversation on "the Negro question" in the company of a Texan, an old Union soldier, a Ohio professor, and "a fat Jewish looking man," the narrator notes of the last that "[his] diplomacy was something to be admired; he had the faculty of agreeing with everybody without losing his allegiance to any side" (*AECM*, 158). Indeed, such capacity for ethnic shape-shifting had previously been claimed by the narrator for "the Negro," not "the Jew": "It is remarkable, after all, what an adaptable creature the Negro is. . . . I have no doubt that the Negro would make a perfect Chinaman, with exception of the pigtail" (*AECM*, 153). More interesting perhaps is the admiration (despite sentiments he hears that fall upon him "like a chill") the narrator afterward expresses for a Texas racist, "the [kind of] man who could not be swayed from what he held as his principles" (*AECM*, 165).

Throughout, we are meant to infer the hollowness of the perception here, and the fact that it gravitates (self-consciously or not) to what is already so troubling in the narrator's own compromised identity formation: the self as allegory of itself, as Emmanuel Levinas analyzed it in an early essay, "Reality and Its Shadow." There Levinas speaks briefly but suggestively about allegory and, by implication, its relevance for ethics and criticism when he delineates the meaning of an image as uniquely predicated on resemblance—a doubling between original and copy, *already* allegorized from within.

> But then to understand an image as such is to see the anomaly it locates in being *itself.* Being is not only itself, it escapes itself. . . . Reality would not be only what it is, what it is disclosed to be in truth, but would be also its double, its shadow, its image. . . . Every image is already a caricature. Thus a person bears on his own face, alongside of its being with which he coincides its own caricature, its own picturesqueness. . . .
> There is then a duality in this person, a duality in its being. It is what it is and it is a stranger to itself.[20]

This other name Levinas gives to the problem of self-resemblance is *allegory*, "an ambiguous commerce with reality in which reality does not refer to itself but to its reflection. An allegory thus represents what in the object itself doubles it up." Art, as Levinas puts it further on in the essay, lets go of the prey for the shadow. But reality, one realizes, is shadowed too.

Besides the phenomenon of such *dedoublement*, the salient connection to be made with *Levinsky* here is the fact that the narrator merely observes: he is not included nor does he involve himself in the conversation. His becomes a "mute and virtual language" in the plainest sense. This irony cuts most deeply when the narrator puts a period to this (mis)recognition scene by saying, "When I reached Macon, I decided to leave my trunk and all my surplus belongings, to pack my back, and *strike out into the interior*" (*AECM*, 167). And indeed, the interior is precisely where he remains in exodus and in dispossession, shadowed from within, just as his surplus belongings, in Levinas's sense, are the gear of selfhood, not suitcase. The subsequent ritual culture journey "behind the veil" finds the Ex-Colored Man with the identical *exterior* vantage point in the company of black people that he sustains with whites. He takes refuge under the sign of the hyphen and is minused by it. At the end of the novel, he wonders aloud whether all he has ever been is "a privileged spectator of [Negroes'] inner life" (*AECM*, 210), including, presumably, his own.

It is not, therefore, chiefly their status as postmodern manifestos that impairs the relevance of approaches like Boelhower's and Deleuze and Guattari's for novels like Cahan's and Johnson's, or for Larsen's and Yezierska's fiction. Rather, I would say it is their intentionally untragic sense in comprehending ex-colored men and self-riven Levinskys alike, personifications of the modernist vicissitudes besetting group identity.[21] Postmodern ethnic semiosis may trade on the same emblematic capital but purchases it, I would suggest, at too cheap a price.

The estrangement within liberal society that produces identity crises such as these is better captured perhaps by John Murray Cuddihy as the "ordeal of civility" in his book of that title, where riding the hyphen gives way to more awkward negotiations with or behind it. For Cuddihy, the misfire characterizing Jewish and Gentile rapprochement against the backdrop of modernity involves a swift escalation of "ritually unconsummated social courtship" into a *Kulturkampf* between *Yiddishkayt* and the Protestant aesthetic.[22] Or, as the narrator says of the father in Yezierska's "Children of Loneliness," "his daughter's insistence upon the use of a knife and fork spelled apostasy, anti-Semitism, and the aping of the Gentiles" ("CL," 141).[23]

Cuddihy's courtship is really an eroticized way of talking about that defining framework for intersubjectivity Levinas and the sociologist Erving Goffman alike call "the face-to-face." Indeed, Cuddihy himself refers in this very context to Goffman[24] and—probably much more soundly—analyzes the barely sublimated component of *desire* in a minority culture's libidinal relationship to Americanness than Deleuze and Guattari's or Boelhower's models. In explaining the friction between particularist and universalizing claims on identity, an integrated self (or culture) riven by perpetually subdividing twoness, Cuddihy rehearses the by now commonplace view of modernity as an inexorable drive toward differentiation.[25] "Refinement" is the term Cuddihy favors to capture differentiation's double edge here: the well-brushed uniform of civility that facilitates entry at civilization's checkpoint—the passing that accompanies any passage from home.

Although the phenomenon of passing does not lie at the absolute core of Cuddihy's analysis, it does manage to compress into one word both the wish to submerge and be assimilated and the hope of making the grade, getting by, that the ordeal of civility is really all about. Walter Benn Michaels calls this the project of racial identity; it can be created as well as embodied, having a capacity for mobility that at the same time ensures a certain existential anomie. Of the Ex-Colored Man, Michaels writes, "It is precisely because he doesn't seem to be black that the ex-colored man can imagine the need to make himself black." And later, "The possibility of concealing one's racial identity—of looking and behaving in ways that do not reflect one's race—makes available the desire to reveal it."[26]

Beyond even this double utility, "passing" is uncannily rich in multiple semantic possibilities as placed at issue by the sign of the hyphen. As one colloquial use of it makes plain, for instance, the term can also signify departure or death. "And so," writes the Ex-Colored Man, "I have often lived through that hour, that day, that week, in that was wrought the miracle of my transition from one world into another; for I did indeed pass into another world" (*AECM*, 20). Across the allegory of narrative experience signified by the phrase, "ex-colored"—from "ex" to "-" to "colored"—we can track a compressed allegory of passing on, of death, modernity's sanction for everything the storyteller can tell. At this broad level, "passing" betokens simply the phenomenon of modern ethnicity itself, which at its worst can spell world alienation for the genuinely catastrophized subject, making out of himself a Negro (in James Weldon Johnson's piquant phrase), permanently uneasy at home.

"This hazardous business," as Irene Redfield describes passing in Larsen's novel of that name, entails "breaking away from all that was familiar and friendly to take one's chances in another environment, not entirely strange perhaps, but certainly not entirely friendly" (*P*, 157); the text later on frames the reverse operation in similar terms: "It's always a dangerous business, this *coming back*" (*P*, 195). Neither strange nor friendly, passing over and coming back, escapes from, and returns to, home—the Uncanny, by another name.[27] If to pass means to bypass the hyphen, it nevertheless cannot elude the logic of differentiation, and just as necessarily, the hyphen-as-mark merely places on graphic display the ambivalence around identity living an underground life in the clandestine operations of passing.

And yet such ambivalence need not be explained by ethnicity per se, since it is so often linked as well with the class-specific demands of refinement and distinction. As a rite of passage on many fronts, it is fair to say that the ordeal of civility is never entirely passed through. The more *re*fined the appearance, the more inescapably *de*fined becomes one's essential identity; the more distinction as taste, the more distinction as stigma. The correlation of mouth and minority status here, whether we want to recall Deleuze and Guattari or not, is probably not entirely fortuitous: both, to echo Goffman, incur parallel kinds of spoliation as conduits for differentiated expression.[28]

Maurice Samuel's memorable bon mot about Jews up against the tribulations of modernity—"the only people in the world to whom it has ever been proposed that their historic destiny is . . . to be nice"[29]—describes a continuous ordeal undergone not only by Abraham Cahan's and Anzia Yezierska's hyphenate American-Jews, but just as palpably (and tragically) by the implicitly hyphenate New Negroes in the fiction of Nella Larsen and James Weldon Johnson.[30] Indeed, without attempting to efface crucial differences, I have purposely set the blacks and Jews in this essay in self-unknowingly hyphenate relation with *each other*—that is, American black–American Jew—as their own uncanny double helix.

Cahan's *Rise of David Levinsky*, Johnson's *Autobiography of an Ex-Colored Man*, and Yezierska's short story "Soap and Water" all add another dimension to the problem of the hyphen because they are (or purport to be) autobiographies, a genre whose authorial subject is already split into two, a narrating and a narrated self.[31] (*Levinsky*, incidentally, was first published under the title *The Autobiography of an American Jew*, and Cahan, echoing Henry Adams this time and not William Dean Howells, titled his own autobiography *The Education of Abraham Cahan*.) In much ethnic autobiography, of course, these two selves become four: *the self I wish to be* (American, present or future tense, plural, sometimes postethnic as in, for instance, ex-colored) and *the self that cannot pass*, or for that matter entirely *pass on* (black, Jew, past tense, single, ethnic).

In addition to the complications of such identity multiples, a kind of belatedness hangs over the whole first-person enterprise anyway, for the confessional "I" and its apologia represent pieces of heavily circulated discursive currency.[32] Deleuze and Guattari's problematic of becoming a gypsy in relation to one's own language and Boelhower's nonlocatable, virtual ethnic subject give way, in Levinsky's and the Ex-Colored Man's cases, before the more immediate question of *residence*; how to choose a language in the first place, to mint new words from worn linguistic currency, to speak on a full stomach, to pass successfully from one world to another.

What I have so far called the feat of riding the hyphen, or the consequences of being thrown by it, can also be configured as a certain pressure on recognition. And the stakes riding on it increase proportionately when the hyphen specifies a twoness as already perceived from without, in addition to any such cleavage experienced by and within the interior self. Not simply the naked predicate, *to speak*, but a thornier syntactic dilemma: whom exactly to speak *to*? Several audiences? In whose company, and with whose permission, *to pass*? If modernity is the curse of differentiation, then ethnicity lives under a particularly baleful hex—something "stamped with a die," as the Ex-Colored Man puts it.

Moreover, as I will suggest below, a certain spectral quality gets superadded to the acts of inscription, as revealed by the five texts in this essay. In Mikhail Bakhtin's words, "a peculiar *emptiness, ghostliness*, and an eerie, frightening solitariness" haunts them, or to recall Levinas's image, a shadow falls on their various doubled selves[33]—as for Irene Redfield when, caught passing in an encounter scene late in Larsen's novel, "in the first glance of recognition, her face had become a mask" (*P*, 227). Or for Rachel Ravinsky when she laments, "One alone is a shadow, an echo of reality" ("SW," 155). It is to them I turn first.

■ Between Worlds: Rachel Ravinsky and Irene Redfield

Anzia Yezierska

Yezierska's short story "Soap and Water" imagines hyphenate ethnic identity and the vagaries of (mis)recognition as a function of cultural border patrol. The story begins with a evocatively rendered ordeal of civility that, in addition to introducing us to yet one more sense of passing, divides the ethnic self at skin level.

> What I so greatly feared, happened! Miss Whiteside, the dean of our college, withheld my diploma. When I came to her office, and asked her why she did not pass me, she said that she could not recommend me as a teacher because of my personal appearance. She told me that my skin looked oily, my hair unkempt, and my finger-nails sadly neglected. . . . And she ended with: "Soap and water are cheap. Any one can be clean." ("SW," 163)

True, according to a model of sanitized pluralism *any one* can be clean, but then dishabille is not really the issue here. A rite of passage into one of modernity's defining institutions is held up because the narrator's non-White side remains exposed; trapped in ethnic tautology, the narrator can pass only if she *passes*.[34] "Gentility" holds Jews at linguistic bay anyway (as Shakespeare has Shylock inopportunely discover when words will not conform to bonds). The question posed by this story's class lesson is whether the hyphen will add or subtract. And as becomes obvious, "Soap and Water" is as much a construct of class difference as cultural difference, a doubling exploited by all four writers I discuss here.

Passing now means upward as well as transverse mobility—in short, once you are over, then you stand above. At intercultural and intersubjective levels alike, a politics of recognition decides who looks and who will be looked at, and moreover, which kind of looking will finally count. The diploma serves merely as a token of an institutionalized twoness that screens off consent rituals from the stigma of descent. Civility serves as modernity's prophylaxis, or, as the narrator herself puts it, "I came against the solid wall of the well-fed, well-dressed world— the frigid whitewashed world of cleanliness" ("SW," 169).[35] In her fiction Yezierska will repeatedly portray such failures of acculturation in terms of invisibility and willful blindness: "She never looked into my eyes . . . She could see nothing in people like me, except the dirt and the stains on the outside . . . One glance at my shabby clothes, the desperate anguish that glazed and dulled my eyes and I felt myself condemned by them before I opened my lips to speak" ("SW," 164, 171). Here, as I have noted above, the hyphen can be understood as bridging inner and outer worlds since it is the *anticipation* of withheld recognition that reciprocally dulls and glazes the very eyes looking out in fear of encountering it.

The story, however, poses a countervailing influence that, rather than withholding recognition, bestows it as a gift. In the person of Miss Van Ness, a sort of pedagogical good angel, civility becomes not ordeal but ordination, an entry pass into the promised land. After meeting with Miss Van Ness in her office, the narrator extravagantly proclaims, Levinskylike, "America! I found America." Miss Van Ness, the narrator writes, "not only recognized me, but stopped to ask how I was, and what I was doing. . . . Just as contact with Miss Whiteside had tied and bound all my thinking processes, so Miss Van Ness unbound and freed me, and suffused me with light" ("SW," 176–177).

The rhetoric of emancipation is unmistakable (earlier the narrator speaks of "visions of America . . . like songs of freedom of an oppressed people." In *Bread Givers*, to become American is to be transmogrified at the root, "changed into a person."[36] And yet, it bespeaks precisely the sort of recognitive asymmetry Frantz Fanon, for instance, critiques in *Black Skin, White Masks* as unacceptable for a rapprochement between *cultures*.[37] Ethnic self and nationalist other must not assume the hyphenate dynamic of bondage-lordship that so often underpins the I-you.

If the suggestion of Hegel seems too grandiose (or simply unhelpfully dialectical), one might prefer instead the more immediately apposite culture heroism of John Dewey, with whom Yezierska had more than simply an intellectual and pedagogic relationship.[38] And yet Dewey's organicist theory of democratic culture—his greatest debt to Ralph Waldo Emerson's philosophy of self-creation and plurality—arguably finds its most pragmatic expression in his programmatic ideas about education and the varieties of pedagogic experience. Dewey writes in *The Child and the Curriculum*,

> Action is response; it is adaptation, adjustment. There is no such thing as sheer self-activity possible—because all activity takes place in a medium, in a situation, and with reference to its conditions. But again, no such thing as imposition of truth from without, as insertion of truth from without, is possible. All depends upon the activity that the mind itself undergoes in responding to what is presented from without. . . . The case is of the child. It is his present powers that are to assert themselves; his present capacities that are to be exercised. But save as the teacher knows, knows wisely and thoroughly, the race expression that is embodied in that thing we call the Curriculum, the teacher knows neither what the present power, capacity, or attitude is, nor yet how it is to be asserted, exercised, and realized.[39]

But if Dewey's thought had a great failing, it was his limited vision of social relatedness in the largest sense, as reflecting the contours of small and nondiversified communities. Cornel West expands the scope of that critique to include what we might call Dewey's romance of communication, since "his emphasis on culture leads him to principally pedagogical and dialogical means of social change." Hence, Dewey "falls back on 'communication' as the major way in that 'the great community' comes into existence."[40]

What does this have to so with "Soap and Water?" For one thing, I think it is possible to read Yezierska's thematic of recognition as the sentimental correlate to Dewey's simultaneous bias for utopian individualism and homogeneous democratic loyalties *minus* the pressure of ethnic, cultural, and even gender difference. In other words, the way characters express longing by looking, or carelessness by looking through someone or away, ultimately aims at the soft and ultimately assimilative ideal of Deweyan "communication." Students looking at teachers and Jews looking at Gentiles—that is how people literally commune in these stories.

But that whole machinery of looking and being granted or denied recognition in return betrays the basic tensions of consent desires and descent loyalties, the territorial sway of the ethnic as it hyphenates one culture and another—features simply alien to Dewey's antiseptic cultural vision (it was Dewey, inconsistently or not, who gave the phrase "hyphenated American" its original currency in 1916). Moreover, the teacher-student relationship in Yezierska's story here substitutes friendship and Deweyan communal goodwill for—in the best sense—a political engagement with difference. And although Emmanuel Levinas will speak the face-to-face as a relation with the one who teaches, who approaches from a height, any ethical reckoning with difference in "Soap and Water" is similarly vitiated because the thrust of the desire for recognition here involves so much libidinal melodrama.

When, in his "Individualism Old and New," Dewey writes of lost individuals amid the conformity and technocracy of modern corporate life, he propounds (in direct relation to Yezierska's prevailing trope of orality) the most ethnologically undernourished analysis of impoverished individual life: no mention of urban displacement, of generational friction on the material planes of language, clothing, bodies (Yezierska's unscrubbed skin of the Other). There is little sense of the hyphenate ethnoracial self, self-divided, self-multiplied, Other-obsessed. "The unrest, impatience, irritation, and hurry which are so marked in American life are inevitable accompaniments of a situation in which individuals do not find support and contentment in the fact that they are sustaining and sustained members of the a social whole."[41] While in an abstract sense inarguable, Dewey's cultural judgments here merely underscore the pathos of Yezierska's heroines in the face of the Frank Bakers, the Miss Whitesides, and the Miss Van Nesses to desire culturally, as it were, to come clean. (Dewey mentions nationalism and the role of religion later in the same essay, but his discussion remains anthropological in the most general sense, and ethnographically empty.)[42] Ironic or percipient, Yezierska's soap and water captures the bland whiteness of such facile social prescription. No hyphen has intervened for Dewey. But it leaves the protagonist stranded, whether or not she has scrubbed her face. She cannot pass over or under.

At the end of "Children of Loneliness," the heroine writes, "But am I alone in my seeking? I'm one of the millions of immigrant children, children of loneliness wandering between worlds that are at once too old and too new to live in" ("CL," 161). The loneliness she speaks of (which, unbeknownst to her, just as plausibly applies to that other set of children, her culturally infantile parents), the loneliness of the hyphen deeply complicates—both impeding and potentially enriching—Dewey's "type of individual whose pattern of thought and desire is enduringly marked by consensus."[43] In Yezierska's fiction, then—despite what I think we can specify as their arcing toward Dewey's brand of pragmatism—we find characters whose pattern of thought and desire is marked not by the solutions of consensus, but instead by contingencies of ethnic loneliness, the hunger that is not-hunger. America's stepchildren remain unconsoled by the statue of Lady Liberty, in the face of enduring mother loss and a persistent ethnic taste in the mouth.

What in "Soap and Water" is benign ethnic cleansing Yezierska transposes to the context of intraethnic and familial strife in "Children of Loneliness." Here, Rachel Ravinsky's "uncivil" *Ostjudische* parents represent to her the foul contact preventing her from making fresh contact with the whitewashed Gentile world of cleanliness.[44] Not surprisingly, this is depicted in terms not only of dirt, but also of food.

> *Ach!* what sickening disorder! In the sink were the dirty dishes stacked high, untouched, it looked for days. The table still held the remains of the last meal. Clothes were strewn about the chairs . . . I couldn't endure it, this terrible dirt! . . . It would mean giving up order, cleanliness, sanity, everything I've striven all these years to attain. . . . To think that I was born of these creatures! It's an insult to my soul. What kinship have

I with these two lumps of ignorance and superstition. . . . They want to wallow in dirt. . . . Beauty and cleanliness are as natural to me as if I'd been born on Fifth Avenue instead of the dirt of Essex street. ("CL," 154–155, 148–149)[45]

"Oh mother, can't you use a fork?" is the story's first sentence, and our initiation into its particular ordeal of civility. Rachel is repulsed not only by her parents' lack of manners but also by the very sort of food they eat: "I can't stand your fried, greasy stuff," Rachel tells her mother. The father, himself divided between eating and tirades against his daughter's apostasy—"To speak is to fast"—at one point remarks, "The old Jewish eating is poison to her; she must have *treyfa* ham—only forbidden food" ("CL," 150).

Reterritorialization at midtown, however, is not to be; Rachel's bid for consent over descent founders upon the merely touristic attentions paid her by the Gentile man of her dreams, or as the narrator aptly puts it, "the sightseer's surface interest in curious 'social types'" ("CL," 161). The story ends with Rachel's overheated testament to diasporic identity (she is not a character, really, but a poster child), the lament for "children of loneliness" quoted earlier.

If literariness be a matter of what Vladimir Nabokov's Humbert Humbert calls a fancy prose style, both of these stories are unremarkable. Yet their value for me lies in how transparently a thematics of recognition shows at the textual skin, how naked is the pure exigency assigned to the drama of "differentiated modernity" as faces yearning to be seen or repulsed by what they see. Intentionally or not, texts such as these serve as manuals, kit bags (even if left at home, as it were) for negotiating the perils of the hyphen. They are all cautionary tales, all versions of the same story: how to ride the hyphen, when to get off, how to fall when thrown off. And as they attest, the hyphen communicates, septically as it were, its burden through and across concentric arenas of recognition. It is not confined to just the ethnic self alone, or to interchanges between ethnic self and nonethnic Other, but ramifies within that very dimension that is—appropriately enough for the Miss Whitesides of the world—*beyond the pale*: that is, among members of the same stigmatized social group.

Consider, for example, the deficiencies in Rachel's own perceptual apparatus through which her father alternately appears negatively typified (another "social type") and transcendentalized, in each case rendered either less human or idealized:

To think that I was born of these creatures! It's an insult to my soul. What kinship have I with these two lumps of ignorance and superstition? They're ugly and gross and stupid. I'm all sensitive nerves. They want to wallow in dirt. ("CL," 150)

The skull-cap, the side-locks, and the long grey beard made him seem like some mystic stranger from a far-off world and not a father. The father of the daylight who ate with a knife, spat on the floor, and who was forever denouncing America and Americans was different from this mystic spirit stranger who could thrill with such impassioned rapture. ("CL," 154)

Of course, Rachel's question about kinship is meet. She begins as a kind of teacher to her intractable parents, a vengefully Deweyan pedagogue to be sure, insofar as she carelessly projects a consent axis onto her parent's stubborn adhesion to descent. "You think you can put our necks in a chain and learn us new tricks?" her father asks. "You think you can make us over as Americans?" It becomes evident that the only way in that Rachel can visualize the kinship she laments is in fact as a vision, an imaginative substitute for the Real—a vantage taken, not unimportantly, from within "the dark hallway of tenement": "There flashed before her a vivid picture of him. . . . Thousands of years of exile, thousands of years of hunger, loneliness, and want swept over her as she listened to her father's voice" ("CL," 154). The outcome? A flaccid sentimentality: "Love, love—nothing is true between us but love," a spilled emotionalism that easily gives way to contempt when forced against visible proof: "She stationed herself at the air shaft opposite their kitchen window, where for the first time since she had left in a rage she could see her old home. '*Ach!* What sickening disorder.'"[46]

Rachel is not oblivious to her ambivalence. "My greatest tragedy is life is that I always see the two opposite sides at the same time" ("CL," 156), she confesses, something we might attribute to a certain surplus of "ethnic seeing" that forces her onto the hither side of catastrophe and keeps her straddled uncomfortably on the hyphen. And yet she misrecognizes over and over again, romanticizing her Gentile white knight, Frank Baker, for example, an occasion always worded by Yezierska as a visionary experience: "A vision of Frank Baker passed before her" ("CL," 149); "with a vision of herself and Frank Baker marching side by side to the conquest of her heart's desire" ("CL," 159). Or else, in similarly selective valuational terms, she becomes emulsion paper whenever she photonegatively glimpses her parents— "their sorrowful eyes, the wrung-dry weariness on their faces, the whole black picture of her ruined, desolate home, burned into her flesh" ("CL," 157).

This last melodramatic flourish resonates as more than mere melodrama when one recalls how threatened Rachel feels at the level of the flesh—and stomach: just as Reb Ravinsky assails his daughter, "You think you got a different skin from us because you went to college" ("CL," 145), just as Mrs. Ravinsky laments her husband and daughter's antipathy, "*Gottuniu*! my flesh is torn to pieces" ("CL," 151), so Rachel responds in kind (but in another sense, more kin than kind) by referring to her parents as the consanguineous ghouls of foul contact: "Vampires, bloodsuckers fastened on my flesh" ("CL," 151). Later she guiltily confesses to having "a fastidious soul that can't stomach their table manners" ("CL," 158), one more variation on the theme of eating your heart out. Ellen Golub nicely captures such flesh-based angst: "Those who hunger for beauty in Yezierska's world are twice as hungry as those who hunger for mere food. . . . So America is still a place to be hungered for and not fully digested. . . . Food is not food. Hunger is not hunger. They are the libidinal language of the Jews which gives voice to the double-edged knife of immigration."[47]

For Rachel, kinship gets thematized as the prison of the body, in line with the prison of tenement life and the prison of stifled or, better, stillborn American-ness. Her parents are "superfluous" ("CL," 153), "frozen, each-shut-in-himself Americans" ("CL," 152), "stand[ing] between me and the new America that I'm to conquer." Yezierska here, like Cahan's *Levinsky* and other Jewish-American fiction before hers, is playing the familiar card of the ethnic subject as neo-Columbus. Whereas Cahan and later Henry Roth will temporarily resolve the problem of exile through the home that is the mother tongue,[48] Yezierska will replay the double bind of in-the-body and out-of-the-body experiences as counterpointed failures to negotiate America.

"One's supreme relation," wrote Henry James in *The American Scene*, "was one's relation to one's country—a conception of one's countrymen and one's coun-trywomen." Finding himself on Ellis Island and in the Lower East Side at the turn of the century, James gives vent to the pathos of "*un*settled possession": the disrup-tion, by immigrants, of the *American's* supreme relation, the "free assault on it, this adjustment of it in *their* monstrous, presumptuous interest [that] the aliens, in New York, seemed perpetually to insist." A further excerpt concerning the "sensi-tive citizen" who happens to "look in" on the immigrant American scene will, I think, illustrate an instructive correspondence with the aspects of Yezierska's fic-tion I have been teasing out, a simultaneous consonance and dissonance with the ethnic Columbus. Both near and far—on the figural plane of sense metaphor—James's nativist anxiety uncannily suspends itself relative to Yezierska's heroines' own, very alien but oddly comparable despondency:

> He comes back from his visit not at all the same person that he went.
> He has eaten of the tree of knowledge, and the taste will be forever in his
> mouth. He had thought he knew before, thought he had the sense of
> the degree in that it is his American fate to share the sanctity of his
> American consciousness, the intimacy of his American patriotism, with
> the inconceivable alien; but the truth had never come home to him with
> such force. In the lurid light projected upon it by those courts of dismay
> it shakes him . . . to the depths of his being; I like to think of him, I pos-
> itively *have* to think of him, as going about ever afterwards with a new
> look, for those who can see it, in his face, the outward sign of the new
> chill in his heart. So is stamped, for detection, the questionably privi-
> leged person who has had an apparition, seen a ghost in his supposedly
> safe old house. Let not the unwary, therefore, visit Ellis Island.[49]

Certainly more proximate to the recognitive traits of a Miss Whiteside than of a Miss Van Ness, but, more important, closer to the disdainful looks of Rachel Ravinsky than to Frank Baker as either vision or autonomous sightseer, I think, is how we must imagine the pained and troubled mien of James's sensitive citizen.

Later James rhapsodizes—almost on the model of the sublime—about the immensity of the "American spectacle" and its consequent refractoriness to convenient conclusions or reductive solutions—"the *il*legible word, accordingly, the great inscrutable answer to the question, hangs in the vast American sky, to his imagination as something fantastic and *abracadabrant*, belonging to no known language."[50] And yet he remains positively—and stubbornly—"unsettled" (his word) by what he calls "the ethnic question" as posed by the "vast, Yiddish world with its deeps and complexities," and above all, in his capacity as author, as man of letters—one who very likely knew the spurious etymology of the word "abracadabra" as cabalistic and quasi-Judaic: "For it was in the light of letters, which is in the light of our language as literature has hitherto know it, that one stared at this all-unconscious impudence of the agency of future ravage . . . That was where one's 'lettered' anguish came in—in the turn of one's eye from *face to face* for some prehensile hook for the linguistic tradition as one has known it"(my italics).[51] Such literary nativism holds profound implications for the Jewish-American writer, for Cahan as well as Yezierska, let alone the characters whose unlettered voices they ventriloquize (not to mention James himself, who, one remembers, has merely returned temporarily to America from his adopted English homeland in order to sightsee and survey).

What I would emphasize here is how luxurious, in a way, can be the in-betweenness, as well as the very loneliness, of Yezierska's "children of loneliness." While Rachel Ravinsky takes lettered umbrage at her parents' untutored Americanness, the only margin of legible *Yiddishkayt* she can grant them is a religiosity that remains numinous probably because it now functions as a foreign tongue to her. That is to say, only as a chanter of liturgical "mystic" (abracadabrant?) Hebrew can her father instill admiration or even devotion, not as a speaker of Yiddish or of broken English. Rachel becomes almost Jamesian in her critical distance and contempt.

Recognition—for these American stepchildren—can be as tellingly defective as that manifested by a Great New England White Father such as Henry James when he gazes uncomprehendingly across a cultural chasm at inscrutable aliens. Indeed, James is only slightly less obtuse in the face of black America, when he acknowledges in a later chapter, "One understood at a glance how [the Negro] must loom, how he must count, in a community in which, in spite of the ground it might cover, there were comparably so few other things." But here at least, in the South, he restrains the impulse to pronounce judgment and lament the loss of footing: "The observer from without had always, as a tribute to this truth [the Negro's omnipresence] to tread on the scene on tiptoe."[52]

Let me, then, use James's tentative figure as both foil and hinge, as I now turn from Yezierska's stories to Nella Larsen's novel, *Passing*. The segue from Jewish American text to African American may seem questionable only inasmuch as the semantic and functional values attaching to the hyphen in each case weigh out *differently*. As literature, one must also grant that Larsen's and Yezierska's fiction do not comfortably align given the former's subtlety and the latter's comparative triteness. Additionally, Larsen possesses a much keener class consciousness than Yezierska and is careful in both *Quicksand* and *Passing* to delineate a complexity of class relations within the ethnoracial group Yezierska tends to flatten.

As I have already noted, however, race has no monopoly on twoness, nor does more-highbrow art necessarily perform more valuable cultural work. Despite phenomenological differences in race, ethnicity, and religion, the experience of cultural difference within modernity per se can function as a ligature binding "black" and "Jew." Moreover, the staged presence of a "fat Jewish looking man" in the railway car scene in Johnson's *Ex-Colored Man* and the very name "Whiteside" and allusion to American slavery in "Soap and Water" themselves bespeak a level of allegorical entanglement anterior to the parallels between literary traditions drawn here.

Nella Larsen

In the following scene from *Passing,* Irene Redfield and her husband Brian discuss together the novel's own topic—the passing for white of light-skinned blacks. Irene herself, we are told, could pass but does not. Her friend Clare is the novel's Other, a Negro passing for white, a sublimated object of conceivably sexual desire. Yet the bourgeois complacency Irene indulges in makes for its own kind of passing, the bad faith that routinely translates obliquity into pseudo-self-awareness: "It's funny about 'passing.' We disapprove of it and at the same time condone it. It excites our contempt and yet we rather admire it. We shy away from it with an odd kind of revulsion, but we protect it" (*P,* 184–185). Her husband, if not as fascinated with the phenomenon of racial undecidability as his wife, is not entirely a stranger himself to a hypocrisy of class interest when it needs to differentiate old from "new" Negroes: "'Uplifting the brother's no easy job. I'm as busy as a cat with fleas, myself.' And over his face there came a shadow. 'Lord how I hate sick people, and their stupid meddling families, and smelly, dirty rooms, and climbing filthy steps in dark hallways'" (186).

If the first passage sounds a sort of false note—as if the novel's narrator were "throwing her voice"[53]—the second carries its irony adroitly; the shadow falling upon Brian's face suggests to me both the dubious fantasy (which Brian has forsworn) of emigrating to "darker" Brazil (a nation hardly exempt from its own politics of the color line), and an echo of Melville's marvel of ambiguity, *Benito Cereno*: "You are saved," says Captain Delano; "what has cast such a shadow upon you?" "The negro," replies Benito Cereno. It also recalls Levinas and the pathos and cruelty of allegorized self-identity—racial being and its shadow.

But the insight at text level incriminating both its speakers' blindnesses speaks over their heads. It calls attention to the urgency of recognition as the novel's correlate to its own theme of passing, something to which ultimately only readers can be privy, and even then ambiguously, since the text remains so stubbornly tacit and elusive. The story ends with its main character falling into unconsciousness, though not before the text has its ironic last word: "Through the great heaviness that submerged and drowned her she was dimly conscious of strong arms *lifting her up.* Then everything was *dark*" (*P*, 242; my italics). Even here, however, one notes a momentary parallax, as the pronoun reference is ever so briefly shared by Clare and Irene.[54]

In the domestic scene at the Redfields' apartment described earlier, a moment I wish to highlight comes surreptitiously into view. A thin and syncopated narrative line tracks the movements of the Redfields' black servant, mimetically reproducing the shadow life she is asked to conduct in life:

> With his long, nervous fingers [Brian] picked up the morning paper from his own chair and sat down.
> Zulena, a small, mahogany-coloured creature, brought in the grapefruit.
> They took up their spoons. . . .
> Zulena came in bringing more toast. Brian took a slice and bit into it with that audible crunching sound that Irene disliked so intensely, and turned back to his paper. (*P*, 184–185)

It is precisely at this point that Irene provides the disquisition on passing quoted earlier, the text having discreetly registered this couple's selective race consciousness. In ensuring the hyphen in "mahogany-colored" remains a minus sign, the Redfields' capacity for recognition does not extend beyond the veil shadowing their eyes and making them, as Yezierska phrases it, "glazed and dulled," strangers to themselves.

Zulena, moreover, is subtracted by the text itself. While perhaps the novel's most "colored" character at skin level, she is its most monochromatic in plot function, merely functional, an indistinct patch of white (though mahogany-colored) noise. In her article "How It Feels to Be Colored Me," Zora Neale Hurston wrote of a certain studied unselfconsciousness she could deploy in the presence of white people: "No brown specter pulls up a chair beside me when I sit down to eat. No dark ghost thrusts its leg against mine in bed. The game of keeping what one has is never so exciting as the game of getting."[55]

Now, although it is Irene who disparages Clare Kendry for her "having way," a domestic scene such as the one above shows how Irene herself can have her cake and get it too, successfully limiting her own self-consciousness as well as her awareness of proximate, and in this case browner and lower classed, "specter" others. Levinas's observation on the caricature or allegory that reality bears on its own face is apposite here: "The characters of a novel are beings shut up, prisoners. Their history is never finished, it still goes one, but makes no headway."[56]

I have chosen this admittedly minor element in Larsen's text because it so tellingly refracts the novel's large-scale grammatical burden: the conjugation, if you will, of *passing* through its several moods and degrees of *recognition*. To pass is to deterritorialize, to dissemble (or to "slip," as Wentworth, the text's Van Vechten–like character puts it), to succeed, to tell, not to tell, to extinguish, to subtract, to differentiate.[57] Among its various object complements are miscegenation, class envy, fresh contact, and the severance of family ties. All of these are resolutely spec-ular entities in Larsen's text: Clare's "How I want to see Negroes . . ."(*P,* 200) alongside Wentworth's amateur eye for detecting passers (*P,* 206); Irene's mirrored self-contemplation (*P,* 217) alongside her ambivalent ocular obsession with Clare ("the look she gave Irene . . . was like an image of her futile searching and the firm resolution in Irene's own soul" [*P,* 200]; "[Irene] had only to turn away her eyes, to refuse her recognition" [*P,* 178]).

The very structure of Larsen's novel keys itself to a syntax of recognition, its two main sections—"Encounter" and "Re-encounter"—narratively motivated by that dependable novelistic figure for damaged intimacy and substitute communi-cation, a letter. The description of the letter makes it the very emblem of passing: "Out of place and slightly alien . . . a thin sly thing that bore no return address to betray the sender . . . furtive but in some peculiar, determined way a little flaunt-ing" (*P,* 143). The first section's letter (chronologically its second) prompts a flash-back to Irene's unexpected encounter with her childhood friend Clare Kendry, who now passes for white (the action framing the first section being thus, strictly speaking, a re-encounter). The women's encounter is modernist anagnorisis, a recognition scene keyed far more to character than plot, a complex cross-hatching of sight lines and face planes:

> her unseeing eyes far away on the lake . . . by some sixth sense she was
> acutely aware that someone was watching her. Very slowly she looked
> around and into the dark eyes of the woman. . . . But she evidently
> failed to realize that such intense interest as she was showing might be
> embarrassing, and continued to stare. . . . Feeling her color heighten
> under the continued inspection, slid her eyes down. . . . Again she
> looked up, and for a moment her brown eyes politely returned the stare
> of the other's black ones, that never for an instant fell or wavered. . . .
> She stole another glance. Still looking! What strange languorous eyes
> she had. (*P,* 149–150)

The face imagery continues throughout the novel, together with the general structure of encounter as recognition, either granted or withheld. A classic mirror scene late in the text, for example, finds Irene beholding her reflection as her hus-band looks on; makeup—"she dusted a little powder on her dark-white face and again examined it carefully" (*P,* 218)—functions here as a token for knowing re-pression. (It recalls the moment in *Ex-Colored Man* when the protagonist scans his own mirrored face and then his mother's in order to dis-cover himself, another scene of recognition mingled with repression, narcissism mixed with self-difference.)

Several pages later, another passage again correlates the face-to-face with what one does or does not recognize, what one knows or does not care to know:

> Clare's ivory face was what it always was, beautiful and caressing. Or
> maybe today a little masked. Unrevealing. Unaltered and undisturbed

by any emotion within or without. Brian's seemed to Irene to be pitiably bare. Or was it too as it always was? That *half-effaced look*, did he always have that? Queer, that she didn't know, couldn't recall. Then she saw him smile, and the smile made his face all eager and shining. Impelled by some inner urge of loyalty to herself, she glanced away. But only for a moment. And when she turned towards them again, she thought that the look on his face was the most melancholy and the yet the *most scoffing that she had ever seen on it.* (*P*, 220; my italics)

Half-effaced, of course, is the very sense of hyphenate identity in this text, as indeed the rhythm of looks sent and/or received calls us back to Yezierska's short stories. But whereas in "Soap and Water" the hyphen articulates both a gap between ethnic self and comprehending or uncomprehending Other, as well as a sentimental wish fulfillment, in *Passing* it more complexly reveals the way a minority culture can be "othered" from within, the way it transposes the defining culture's terms of difference into terms of its own.[58] "She was caught between two allegiances," the text says of Irene, "different, yet the same. Herself. Her race. Race! The thing that bound and suffocated her" (*P*, 225). And as Michaels says, astutely capturing the paradox of double allegiance, "Passing is thus understood first as a failure of affection and second as the occasion of its success . . . ; it is just because she has been able to disguise the fact that she belongs to her race that Clare has learned to care for it."[59]

Perhaps the uncanniest moment in this most uncanny of texts is the greeting Clare Kendry's white husband gives her in the company of Irene and another black woman who can pass: "Hello, Nig." This glib and facetious reference to Clare's olive complexion perfectly conveys the pure uncanniness of passing: a recognition expressed despite (or rather, through) not-seeing.[60] And its obscenity is precisely what extends answerability for such recognition from within the text outward.

Passing becomes, in short, a hermeneutic burden not to be passed on, in the sense of refused, as opposed to the meaning conveyed by the repeated tag line in Morrison's *Beloved*, which speaks of not passing on a story as being careful about its transmission. "Nor could [Irene] write it, or telephone it, or tell it to someone else": the referent here is the duplicity of racial masking, of self-allegory, not the naked "being" of race in the first place, and the violence inflicted on it from without when it cannot, by passing, dissemble, and conceal itself. For Larsen's novel, as for Yezierska's stories, the mental operation of *incognito ergo sum* may be abetted by a whiter pigment or ninety-nine and forty-four one-hundredths percent pure Ivory soap. But much like the Cartesian subject it echoes, it leaves its ethnic subjects solitary and ensconced. They are unmoored by the hyphen rather than anchored, cleansed ambiguously as so many whiter shades of pale, and finally, as American "untouchables" who lack the Brahmin status of a Henry James (and reversing Emerson's notion), still approaching an America that keeps itself at a distance.

The novel's self-consciousness that is at work here may be sharper than that of Yezierska's stories. But in reading faces and shadows of recognition, Larsen's and

Yezierska's fiction alike plays party to such allegoresis, and at the same time, as James said of the novel in general, publicizes what it cannot *not* tell. Especially, they tell us what they cannot name, flaunting the furtive—like the initial communicative token of Clare's letter or the guilty chattiness of the discourse as a whole in *Passing*, or like the tenement airshaft in "Children of Loneliness" reminding us that these are *poor* people, not simply Jews—these texts force themselves and their readers into public space. And in that space, the hyphen is not simply punctuation. It is brand and die.

■ Between Veils: The Ex-Colored Man

If we think of ethnicity as itself a kind of hyphen in the broad sense; if we think of the resulting intersubjective pressures as defining a thematics of recognition; and if such recognition is seen as keyed to a whole range of differentiated movement (something evident in the semantic migrations of a term like "passing"); then the "rise" of David Levinsky and the alternating journeys "*below* Washington" and "*up* into New York Harbour" rehearsed by *The Autobiography of an Ex-Colored Man* comprise the densest of the itineraries tracked by this essay.[61]

"My own last word about myself is in principle incapable of being the last word, the word that consummates myself," writes Bakhtin.[62] Indeed, confessional self-accounting (Bakhtin's phrase) produces potentially infinite discourse, since neither can its author, by definition, coincide with himself, nor can any alternative vantage points disclose themselves ("the axiological position of the *other* is absent").[63]

But the thrust of these texts, the test of their respective narrators' *Bildung*, does not therefore become something as trite as reliability. The confessional "I" always has at its disposal as much to withhold as to divulge (though at a basic pragmatic level these texts need to be reliable if they are to justify themselves as insiders' accounts of ethnic freemasonry).[64] For beyond Levinsky's and the Ex-Colored Man's autonomous narratives of self (mis)understanding lie the surplus dramas of recognition each transacts with others: both the set of multiple figures encountered within each tale, and the readers outside it through whose eyes its telling is refracted, to whom each text is, as confessional fiction, implicitly addressed.

The Ex-Colored Man, for instance, positions himself in both these camps as a criminal of sorts (we are reminded of the role played by gossip in *Passing* and the Yezierska stories' penchant for defamatory speech). On the discourse level, he invites his readers' collusion in what seems at first only to involve the witnessing of his confession, but that shortly bespeaks something a little less benign.

> I know that in writing the following pages I am divulging the great secret of my life. . . . I feel that I am led by the same impulse that forces the un-found-out criminal to take somebody into his confidence, although he knows that the act is likely, even almost certain, to lead to

his undoing. I know that I am playing with fire, and I feel the thrill that accompanies that most fascinating pastime; and, back of it all, I think I find a sort of savage and diabolical desire to gather up all the little tragedies of my life, and turn them into a practical joke on society. (*AECM*, 3)

In fact, the Ex-Colored Man confronts the consequences of his double life *within* the text when he determines to reveal his true colors, so to speak, to the woman he finally succeeds in marrying. Not surprisingly, she is described as a woman who "was white as a lily, and . . . dressed in white[: I]ndeed, she seemed to me the most dazzling white thing I had ever seen" (*AECM*, 198). He assures his readers that after meeting her he no longer had any investment in passing as "a sort of practical joke," yet it is only to this woman that he is prepared to divulge his secret.[65] And presumably it is this revelation we are to counterpose to all the previous ordeals of civility on both sides of the color line that Ex-Colored and Colored Man alike have had to endure.

The fetishistic tone the Ex-Colored Man employs here recapitulates several other scenes of discovery in the text this far: the mirror scene, where we find the narrator contemplating his ivory complexion (*AECM*, 17), his meeting with his absent white father who does not publicly acknowledge his paternity (*AECM*, 32–38), the loss of his necktie and his subsequent marking of it on someone else's person (*AECM*, 63, 84), and the grand recognition scene in a theater where he espies his estranged father and sister but elects to remain hidden (*AECM*, 134–135).[66] All of these disparate scenes are unified in their common concern with deception and at best partial, might we say hyphenate, revelation.

A dilemma remains, however. The text is defectively framed. If the narrator does return at the end of his story to his initial gambit of taking readers into his confidence, he does not allude to the context in which he first speaks of playing "a practical joke on society." As we do not occupy the same position as his wife, so for us it is not his passing but rather the entire apologia which divulges it that may in fact be motivating the narrator's "savage and diabolical" *ressentiment*. The joke—the gathering up of all the little tragedies of his life, as the narrator puts it—the burden of the hyphen, may be on us his readers, as passing (in its capacity as deception) in this text may involve crossing more than the color line.

Invisible Man's very similar double-voiced confession in *his* prologue to Ralph Ellison's novel only etches the recognitive stakes here more sharply: "Irresponsibility is part of my invisibility; any way you face it, it is a denial. But to whom can I be responsible, and why should I be, when you refuse to see me? And wait until I reveal how truly irresponsible I am. Responsibility rests on recognition, and recognition is a form of agreement."[67] It is certainly true that the inculpating rhetoric in the Ex-Colored Man's preliminary remarks serves to mark a cleavage between author and narratorial persona, or fictional antiself.[68] But what also becomes unmistakable (for my purposes) is the price exacted by modernity such loophole language attests to, the pure pathos of recognition and plangency of the ordinary (in Henry Louis Gates's words from his introduction to Johnson's text), that situates even the project of recounting a life under the sign of the hyphen. (Incidentally, "Invisible Man" is itself the name of Ellison's protagonist, whereas Johnson retains the indefinite article for his: "*an* Ex-Colored Man." But "Ex-Colored Man" minus the article might be a truer sobriquet, on the order not of comic-book superhero, such as "Negative Man" or "Deadman," but rather of subhero.)

In a famous early scene recounting a boyhood trauma, the Ex-Colored Man rushes up to the safety of his bedroom, having just been called "nigger" for the first time in his life. He stares at himself in a mirror:

> I was accustomed to hear remarks about my beauty; but now, for the
> first time, I became conscious of it and recognized it. I noticed the ivory
> whiteness of my skin, the beauty of my mouth, the size and liquid dark-
> ness of my eyes, and how the long, black lashes that fringed and shaded
> them produced and effect that was strangely fascinating even to me. I
> noticed the softness and glossiness of my dark hair that fell in waves
> over my temples, making my forehead appear whiter than it really was.
> (*AECM*, 17)

This recognition scene, however, produces only anxiety (the Ex-Colored Man routinely notes the presence of looking-glasses in successive interior scenes in the novel), and burying his head in his mother's lap, he blurts out, "'Mother, mother, tell me, am I a nigger?" . . . And then it was I looked at her critically for the first time . . . searching for defects. I could see that her skin was almost brown" (*AECM*, 18). A loophole seems to lie at the core of the narrator's perceptual faculty here as much it does for his diegesis. He founders on solipsism, unable to purify the expression of the reflected face. Bakhtin writes on the vicissitudes of such mirrored self-contemplation: "What occurs here is something in the nature of an optical forgery: a soul without a place of its own is created, a participant without a name and without a role—something absolutely extrahistorical. It should be clear that through the eyes of this fictitious other one cannot see one's true face, but only one's mask face."[69] Indeed, this sort of "soul slave" (the racial legatee of less fortunate body slaves) who "introduces a certain spurious element absolutely alien to the ethical event of being" corresponds exactly to the Ex-Colored Man in this axiologically empty sense, as the *ex-colored man*, a man under erasure, more integer than person.

In Johnson's novel, we discern the pained evidence for the caution to which I lay claim above in regard to the virtues of deterritorialization: to bring language slowly and progressively to the desert, to find linguistic Third World zones by which a language can escape—precisely on the expressive level where an accounting means a hearing—can amount to real disjunction, catastrophe, and exile. This is hardly to deny the Ex-Colored Man his agency but rather to put his tragic mulattohood into its proper *differentiated* context—cloven by the empty, the ghostly, the solitary. As the narrator tells us, "My words [were] dictated, my actions limited," and most tellingly (pun likely not intended), "my thoughts were *colored*" (*AECM*, 21; my italics). As how could they not be, when selfhood at the level of the body drains the color from itself? Where else could race be for the Ex-Colored Man but on the brain?

In a broader sociohistorical sense, the transition from use value to exchange value recorded by *The Autobiography of an Ex-Colored Man*—from "birthright" to "pottage," or as Walter Benn Michaels will argue, from race to culture[70]—follows the contours of a shift already mapped by modernity itself. Dewey's account of the "lost individual," for example, or William James's disequilibriated sensibility, offers signposts, but in this instance the far more materially grounded concept of the self *as* problem—class specific as well as historically so—specified by Du Bois in *The Souls of Black Folk* really points the way.[71]

It is in such a light I think the Ex-Colored Man's sense of aesthetic mission at the end of his narrative should be understood, similar to and yet significantly different from what Du Bois means when he speaks of the "doubled-aimed struggle of the black artisan." Though he remains unsure whether his motive to "catch the spirit of the Negro" in song derives from altruism or something more familiarly selfish (fittingly crystallized for him in Europe while in tow with his "millionaire," his white benefactor), he decides his future will lie with "voicing" the black folk's soul through the medium of "classical musical form."[72] That luxury of ambivalence between two types of authenticity (we could call them "primitive" and "elevated"; Zora Neale Hurston more pungently differentiates between "Negro" and "Nigger")[73] never leaves him, whether he plays peripatetic ethnomusicologist in the black South or salon pianist while wooing his white intended in his benefactor's apartment.

Indeed, the admission the Ex-Colored Man makes while playing voyeur at a lynching—"I was fixed to the spot where I stood, powerless to take my eyes from what I did not want to see" (*AECM*, 187)—goes a long way toward explaining how ultimately determinate and subservient his freedom of self-creation remains. At the end of his narrative, he famously confesses to have been "only a privileged spectator of [Negroes'] inner life," or else "a coward, a deserter . . . possessed by a strange longing for my mother's people" (*AECM*, 210).

More revealing by far than such calculated discursive set pieces, I think, is the late recognition scene with his boyhood friend, "Shiny" (who was an early catalyst for the Ex-Colored Man's recognition of his own double consciousness). He introduces his friend to his fiancée, and on the point of introducing him as "Shiny" stammers a second or two before recalling his real name (*AECM*, 203). It is a name—"Shiny" being at this point a refined and cultured adult—never disclosed to us by the text, one secret our confessional narrator elects not to divulge. Or perhaps he deems it unnecessary, therefore consigning Shiny to the permanent fate of quotation-mark artifice—the "incognito ergo es" of the applied nickname.

Has bestriding the hyphen, we wonder, yielded the Ex-Colored Man any "true self-consciousness," in Du Bois's phrase, when he so blithely colludes in the bondage of orthography? Can a dualism at the heart of modernity really get him off the hook so long as "Shiny" remains "Shiny?" Have any of his narrative's recognition scenes forced into consciousness the problematic of recognition for an Ex-Colored Man, "x"-ed out and unnamed? After all, to be sure, he withholds his own proper name from us too. He styles himself "an Ex-Colored Man," the hyphen in the middle of that syntactic unit occupying the dead center of pseudonymity. Unlike the women who flirt with passing in Larsen and Yezierska, Johnson's man passes right out of public knowledge and public space.

In his book on autobiography, Philippe Lejeune speaks of the several persons "federated" in any speaking "I" as grounded and legitimated by the Proper Name," that is why, to take a relevant example, slave narratives make such a point of their authors' identity right up front in their titles. Lejeune calls this the "pact" of autobiography.[74] Johnson's narrator, by contrast, has passed on his contractual obligations and in so doing all the more forcefully stations himself not only under the hyphen but behind it as the objectively "picturesque" element—the allegory—he bears on his own personhood, "stamped there," to borrow from the Ex-Colored Man himself, "with a die."

Between Home and Exile: David Levinsky

A similar legacy of, and perhaps skepticism about, the modernist ordeal sheds light on the peculiar temporal inversion recorded by Abraham Cahan's *The Rise of David Levinsky*, my final text of passing under the hyphen. Conversion narratives traditionally chart a phenomenological trajectory by which a new self supplants the old: "Thousands of things reminded me of my promotion in the world. I could not go to bed in a Pullman car, walk over the springy 'runner' of a hotel corridor, unfold the immense napkin of a hotel dining-room, or shake down my trousers upon alighting from a boot-black's chair, without being conscious of the difference between my present life and my life in Antomir" (*RDL*, 325). Levinsky, however, reverses the terms: beneath the overlay of a new *Gesellschaft* self, a *Gemeinschaft* self remains intact, indeed gives the lie to the marvelousness of any transformation that has taken place.

> Sometimes, when I think of my past in a superficial, casual way, the metamorphosis I have gone through strikes me as nothing short of a miracle. . . . And yet when I take a look at my inner identity it impresses me as being precisely the same as it was thirty or forty years ago. My present station, power, the amount of worldly happiness at my command, and the rest of it, seem to be devoid of significance. (*RDL*, 3)

And, again at novel's end, precisely framing it: "I cannot escape from my old self. My past and present do not comport well. David, the poor lad swinging over a Talmud volume at the Preacher's Synagogue, seems to have more in common with my inner identity than David Levinsky, the well-known cloak-manufacturer"

(*RDL*, 530). To the extent that Levinsky never entirely passes his ordeal of civility, he remains deterritorialized in the negative sense, an Ishmaelite, giving the lie to postmodern celebrations of expressive and ethnic nomadism; indeed, I think it fair to read his apologia as the modernist, hyphenate American's plea for recognition, or at least setting the scene for a possible response: "Call me Ishmael."

Like the Ex-Colored Man, Levinsky retains an Oedipal, almost fetishistic attachment to his childhood. He fondles his childhood and makes the maternal implications explicit: "I love to brood over my youth . . . My wretched boyhood appeals to me as a sick child does to its mother" (*RDL*, 4).[75] In contradistinction to such regression, however, the other side of Levinsky's double consciousness is devoted to ceaseless *becoming*: a perpetual leave-taking of "my native place" in order to "seek my fortune in the weird, distant world."

We are given cues early on Cahan's as well as Johnson's text to the protagonist children's respective adult métiers: Levinsky plays with buttons, anticipating the hoarding of capital, as the gold piece around the Ex-Colored Man's neck and the gift of a gold watch prefigure his subsequent devotion to Mammon. The orphan status of each becomes public knowledge, something to be left behind as quickly as possible. Both Cahan's and Johnson's narrators have absent fathers (dead or selected out); both have doting mothers who die; most important, both respond to those passings-on with passings of their own.

Levinsky writes, for example, "My surroundings had somehow lost their meaning. Life was devoid of savor, and I was thirsting for an appetizer, as it were, for some violent change, for piquant sensations. Then it was that word America first caught my fancy" (*RDL*, 59). And later, "It seemed as though [my mother] had died so that I might arouse sympathy and make a good start in America" (*RDL*, 103), similar perhaps to the way the Ex-Colored Man confesses to the "peculiar fascination that the South held over my imagination" as he bids farewell to "the friends and scenes of my boyhood" (*RDL*, 51).

Even more than Johnson's novel, the structure of Cahan's depends on an axial tension between the vertical world of rise-and-fall and the horizontal one of substitution, with Levinsky's self-division a constant engine for displacement (often in the shape of erotic attachments):[76]

> "O Master of the World! Master of the Universe! I love you so!" I would sigh. . . . I loved Him as one does a woman. (*RDL*, 38)

> My unhappy love never ceased to harrow me. The stern image of Matilda blended with the hostile glamour of America. (*RDL*, 87)

> I thought of [my mother] and of all Antomir, and my pangs of yearning for her were tinged with pangs of my unrequited love for Matilda. (*RDL*, 103)

> It was as though I were two men at once, one being in the toils of hopeless love and the other filled with the joy of loving, all injunctions and barriers notwithstanding. (*RDL*, 312)

The radical break *Levinsky* signals with earlier immigrant Jewish fiction here is the cautionary tale speaking through the fabulist, metamorphic trappings. A nonmarvelous, ultimately failed transformation awaits Levinsky at the end of all his *Bildung*. "Becoming" means material gain but substantive loss—of identity, of roots, of love. The hyphen in this text functions as both minus sign and deficient equals sign, as shown by the novel's series of multiple oppositions.

The prevailing distinction separates "greenhorn" from "American" selves, between "I read Talmud" (his initial self-description in Yiddish) and "All right" (his first words in English). It also lends a double-voiced quality to the retort Levinsky, the Talmudist-turned-tailor, makes to a fellow Talmudist-turned-socialist—"I haven't made the world, nor can I mend it" (*RDL*, 174) —where the mystical trope of *tikkun olam* gets overcoded by the language of cloak manufacturing. David's mirror scene is the reverse of the Ex-Colored Man; shorn of *peyes* and shtetl clothes, he stands transformed as an "American": "when I took a look at the mirror . . . I scarcely recognized myself" (*RDL*, 101), negatively purified, one suspects.[77] He contrasts "real American" English with deficient English tainted by accent (*RDL*, 176), and "genteel [read Gentile] American" dress with anything conspicuously vulgar (*RDL*, 260). Perhaps this hyphen-as-minus explains why a text about the most densely populated place on earth at the time—the Lower East Side—feels so conspicuously empty and desolate despite the many interpersonal exchanges that Levinsky situates within it.

But even outside of face or voice (indeed, we could well say, in place of them), Cahan's novel tracks the paradox of gain as loss in other ways. We should note, for instance, the differential chain of substitute texts passing through Levinsky's hands, and which he passes through himself: The Talmud, Charles Dickens's *Dombey and Son*, William Makepeace Thackeray's *Pendennis*, Herbert Spencer, and the Hebrew poems of the father-in-law he fails to secure, the last all the more piquant for their irrelevancy in conventional Lower East Side culture. Of them, Levinsky remarks:

> The dailies of the Ghetto, the newspapers that can afford to pay, are published, not in the language of Isaiah and Job, but in Yiddish. . . . I asked the librarian whether Tevkin wrote for these papers. . . . It appeared, however, that the articles that he wrote in his living mother-tongue lacked the spirit and charm that distinguished his style when he used the language of the prophets. Altogether, Tevkin seemed to be accounted one of the "has-beens" of the Ghetto. (*RDL*, 453–454)

Levinsky transcribes the following compositions of Tevkin's, almost as applicable to Levinsky himself as a surrogated self as they are to Tevkin:

> "Since the destruction of the Temple instrumental music has been forbidden in the synagogues. The children of Israel are in mourning. They are in exile and in mourning. Silent is their harp. So is mine. I am in

exile I am in a strange land. My harp is silent." And, "Most song-birds do not sing in captivity. I was once a song bird but America is my cage. It is not my home. My song is gone." (*RDL*, 458–459)

To speak—as speech itself—is to fast.[78]

We can also follow a logic of substitution through the series of erotic attachments to surrogate mother figures and of adoptive mentors through whose hands Levinsky himself passes—Reb Sender, Matilda, Mr. Even, Mr. Margolis, his landladies, and Mr. Tevkin. Or we can mark substitution working as repetition through an odd predilection the text seems to have for differentially linked names: there are two Levinskys, two Maxes (Maximum Max and Minimum Max), and two surrogate fathers and teachers—the first Sender, and the second Bender. We can also trace it in the form of a continuously self-revising symbolic capital, always resting on an internal split in Levinsky between some form of materiality and its opposite, the economies of love, money, and nationalism ever converging and interpenetrating.[79]

But not surprisingly, the most obsessively deployed motif in the novel although the text does not foreground it) is the recognition scene. A whole set of these ties Levinsky to the minor players in his life, all of whom make cameo reappearances both during and subsequent to his rise. A brief inventory of such scenes will serve as a vehicle for knitting together and facing[80] this chapter's entire battery of texts to emphasize by way of the conclusion what the hyphen forces into recognition (ours or the text's) and what remains incognito.

Although a stock device in dual-self narratives such as Levinsky's (we find it also in the Ex-Colored Man's recognition scenes with father, sister, and childhood friends), it has a pivotal role to play, I would argue, in ethnic American fiction and stories of rise and fall generally. It is not only in Hollywood that one greets on the way down those one has passed on the way up. The significance of such recognitions later in the novel is made plain by Levinsky on the very first page of his memoir: "I have a good memory for faces, but am apt to recognize people I have not seen for a quarter of a century more readily than I do some I used to know only a few years ago." As Levinsky observes of a rival student in yeshiva, "Memory alone is nothing" (*RDL*, 47). And thus like Irene Redfield and the Ex-Colored Man, David Levinsky is made to re-encounter the past he had thought to have left behind.

In contrast to a rabbinic text David reads in yeshiva at the beginning of his narrative that tells how R. Mathia miraculously regained his eyesight after gouging out his own eyes in order to avoid temptation, the chain of recognition scenes befalling Levinsky toward his story's end critiques and effectively cancels his marvelous transformation and marks him as born under the bad sign of the hyphen. To the extent that he does not, as is perhaps conventional, "recall [his] youth as something seen through a haze," Levinsky does not see through a glass darkly, but rather (though to negative effect), face to face.

He first reencounters Gitelson, "the tailor who clung to my side when I made my entry into the New World, sixteen months before" (*RDL*, 148).[81] At first failing to recognize him, Levinsky perceives him—as indeed Gitelson experiences himself—as "magic[ally] transform[ed]." In this instance the face-to-face encounter cedes in importance to the comprehensive glance *we* have of the two figures as they stand together in front of a mirror, as we note the juxtaposition along with Levinsky: "The contrast between his flashy clothes and my frowzy, wretched-looking appearance, as I saw ourselves in the mirrors *on either side of me*, made me sorely ill at ease" (*RDL*, 149; my italics).

This scene is itself mirrored and answered after David has left behind his hopes for religious as well as secular education[82] and begun his financial ascent.

> —Good evening, Mr. Even. Do you know me? I began.
> He scanned me closely, but failed to recognize me.
> —I am David Levinsky, the "green one" you befriended four and a half years ago. Don't you remember me, Mr. Even? It was in this very place where I had the good fortune to make your acquaintance. I'm the son of the woman who was killed by Gentiles in Antomir, I added, mournfully.
> —. . . Lord of the World! You are that young man! Why, I confess I scarcely recognize you . . .
>
> —After you provided me with a complete outfit, like a father fixing up his son for his wedding-day, and you gave me five dollars into the bargain, you told me not to call on you again until I was well established in life. Do you remember that? (*RDL*, 213–214)

Here, too, however, Levinsky feels rebuked: "I soon realized, however, that he did not care for me now. My Americanized self did not make the favorable impression that I had made four and a half years before, when he gave me my first American haircut." We might call this an ordeal of civility of a very different suit.

In Levinsky's next small recognition scene, with his former English teacher, the dynamic changes once again. After the customary exchange of surveying glances, Mr. Bender informs Levinsky that his ambition is merely to be teacher at a public day school. "Can't you think of something better?" Levinsky responds, "with mild contempt" (*RDL*, 313). Unlike the previous encounters, this one actually produces a change in relations, or in Levinsky's words, "a world of difference." For Levinsky makes his former tutor a business offer: "[Bender] had met me with a patronizing, 'Hello Levinsky.' When we parted there was a note of gratitude and of something like obsequiousness in his voice." Shortly thereafter Levinsky experiences a similar confab with Chaikin, a former partner, and the identical consequences ensue.

Proceeding from instrumental to recognitive power, Levinsky's subsequent meeting with a former college friend, Jake Mindels, assures him of his capacity for modernist ethnic facework, as William Boelhower would describe it: "I complimented myself upon the possession of all sorts of talents, but my keenest ambition was to be recognized as an unerring judge of men. . . . I was convinced that now at last my insight was a thoroughly reliable instrument, only a year later to look back upon my opinions of 1894 with contempt. I was everlastingly revising my views of people, including my own self" (*RDL*, 349–350). But the last two crucial re-encounters in the novel impress upon us (if not upon Levinsky) in serial anagnorisis that facework and ethnic shape-shifting can only superficially transcend, the catastrophic subject and his exile and his hyphen-as-minus-sign. He can conceal but he cannot really hide. Indeed, it is here that Levinsky confesses to a difficulty in looking such people "in the face" (*RDL*, 507).

The first apparition belongs to Shmerl the Pincher, a schoolmaster of David's back in Antomir, now a disheveled peddler. Levinsky rushes to make good on a promise he made himself to have his vengeance on such culturally sanctioned child abuse (though he also admits a "keen desire to help him").

> A tangle of wagons and trolley-cars caused me some delay. I stood gazing at him restively as he picked his weary way. . . . As I was thus waiting impatiently for the cars to start so that I could cross the street and greet him, a cold, practical voice whispered to me: "Why court trouble? Leave him alone."
>
> My exaltation was gone. The spell was broken. . . .
>
> Instead of crossing the street and accosting the old man, I stood still, following him with my eyes until he vanished from view. (*RDL*, 504–505)

"My heart was heavy with distaste and sadness" (*RDL*, 516) is how Levinsky similarly describes his final recognition scene, this one, with Gitelson the tailor, the counterstroke to the first such scene in Cahan's novel. Though Gitelson is described as neatly dressed, "at close range, however, his appearance [breaks Levinsky's] heart" (*RDL*, 514). For Gitelson personifies *Yiddishkayt*'s failed courtship with bourgeois Gentile culture. Yet it is an embarrassment that Levinsky feels in his own person as the two ethnocultural freemasons sit across from one another in an expensive restaurant that he makes sure to emphasize. "The French waiter, who was silently officious, seemed to be inwardly laughing at both of us. . . . There was something forced, studied in the way I uttered [my] words. I was disgusted with my own voice" (*RDL*, 515). The rise of David Levinsky has been all vertical; and yet he remains straddling the hyphen laterally, not fully able to pass . . . over: "At the bottom of my heart I cow before waiters to this day. Their white shirt-fronts, reticence, and pompous bows make me feel as if they saw through me and ridiculed my ways. They make me feel as if my expensive clothes and ways ill became me."

How different it had seemed before! Although worried about his ethnically marked speech and hands—"I [spoke] with exaggerated apathy, my hands so strenuously still that they fairly tingled with the effort" (*RDL*, 329)—Levinsky tries to rise above such restaurant-shame on that previous and memorable railroad trip west. After all, as he says, "the United States was still full of surprises for me. I was still discovering America" (*RDL*, 330). And discovery never anticipates ordeal, although it almost always promises it.

And so he ends his rueful narrative with sentences obsessively turning on the first-person I, an extended erotic litany (the "spell of morbid amativeness," he calls it), a rehearsal of equally hyphenate ethnic loyalties (German-Jewish, Portuguese-Jewish, Gentile-American), and finally, like his counterpart in some respects, the Ex-Colored Man, a sort of musical *envoi* lamenting his being David Levinsky— "the well-known cloak-manufacturer"—instead of the "Russian Jew who holds the foremost place among American songwriters and whose soulful compositions are sung in almost every English-speaking house in the world" (*RDL*, 529).

Interestingly enough, as in the case with Johnson's Shiny, Cahan prefers Irving Berlin—the ex–"Israel Balin"—to remain anonymous. And yet, would a marvelous transformation into "Irving Berlin" redress the fact that this narrator speaks in hide-and-seek, through what Bakhtin terms a mask-face? (The last words in the novel, one notices, are "cloak-manufacturer.") For Levinsky to ride the hyphen (comfortably or not), must Gitelson the tailor must remain "Gitelson the tailor" as opposed to "David Levinsky"? Cahan's novel marks a feat of recall that redounds to Levinsky's credit as perhaps his greatest luxury; but again, as Levinsky himself says while still a young man in Antomir, "Memory alone is nothing" (*RDL*, 47).

◼ In Exile from Diaspora

With the luxury of his own sightseer's perspective, like his sometime peer Henry James, all the better positioned to circle the wagons against the onslaught of modernity, D. H. Lawrence observed the following about the phenomenon of "discovering America": "Men are free when they belong to a living, organic, believing community . . . not when they are escaping to some wild west."[83] And in Lawrence, the West, more specifically the Indian West, locates a cultureless, aboriginal America, where the boundaries of local groupings such as nation and race can be transcended.

No skilled ethnic hand on the order of Boelhower's Jewish cowboy, David Levinsky comes to recognize the futility of such escape—but as only an immigrant can. He remains a perpetual foreigner, forever suspended between home and exile (or, in terms the text innocently sketches at the beginning, between meaning and melody: "It is with a peculiar sense of duality one reads [the Talmud]. While your mind is absorbed in the meaning of the words you utter, the melody in which you utter them tells your heart a tale of its own. You live in two distinct worlds at once" [*RDL*, 35]). If, in the double edge assigned to freedom, "America has never been easy" (as Lawrence goes on to observe), it is especially so for American ethnicities, and certainly at the point where ethnic marginality intersects with the romance of class mobility, where the hyphen, as it were, wants to look up instead of just sideways.

This has differentially been the case for American blacks and American Jews, "blacks" still "colored" by the word we use conventionally to identify them, and thus perhaps indelibly stigmatized in this country's history and its self-understanding. The gnomic utterance from *Invisible Man*'s introductory sermon—"Black will make you. . . . Black will unmake you"[84]—is as pithy an encapsulation of the black American experience as one can find. Jews, by contrast, can much more easily pass. But despite considerable material success, the ancient screw of *iz schwer tzu zayn a Yid* ("It is hard being Jewish") still has one more turn to undergo in America. Both peoples struggle with negotiations between what precedes the hyphen mark and what follows it, and for the purposes of this essay exist in a kind of hyphenate relation to each other.

Whatever potential benefits might be derived from and valorized in modernist ethnicity—"mobility" or "deterritorialization," "hybridity and intermixture" (Paul Gilroy), "cultural impersonation" (Henry Louis Gates Jr.), "identitarianism" or "the project of racial identity" (Walter Benn Michaels)—all owe a yet unpaid debt to the multiple ordeals of *modernity* passed or unpassed by Levinsky, the Ex-Colored Man, Clare Kendry, and Rachel Ravinsky alike.[85] Twoness, double consciousness, a cleft self, passing in its several vices: such burdens effectively hinder any easy escape to some Wild West, let alone linguistic Third World zones where one can throw the voice and mask the face.

To recall a previous image, let us think of the hyphen finally as a brand. Whether in Chicago for Clare Kendry, further west to St. Louis for David Levinsky, north, south, and across the Atlantic for the Ex-Colored Man, on the Lower East Side of Manhattan or midtown and further north, "-" remains notoriously difficult to efface. Indeed, in these cases it almost becomes a face—or takes the place of one. If only it were merely an exterior mark, the hyphen might be less of a problem. But, as the Ex-Colored Man attests so well, it is also written upon the memory, "stamped" there.

Having quoted early on from an essay by Emmanuel Levinas, I thought it symmetrical at least to conclude similarly, with a passage from a short, confessional piece on cultural politics titled "Means of Identification." It begins with the following declaration of qualified essentialism for a people dispersed, variously acculturated, and transnationalized:

> What identity does [Western Judaism] cling to? One that refers only to itself and ignores all attributes: one is not a Jew by being this or that. Ideas, characters, and things can be identified insofar as they differ from other ideas, characters, and things. But people do not produce evidence in order to identify themselves. A person is not who he is because he was born here rather than there, and on such and such a day, or because he has blond hair, a sharp tongue, or a big heart. Before he starts comparing himself to anyone else, he just is who he is. In the same way, one just is a Jew. It is not even something one adheres to, for that already sug-

gests the possibility of estrangement. It is not something one is possessed by, for adherence to a doctrine soon turns into fatalism . . ."You
are born a Jew; you don't become one." This half-truth bears out the ultimate feeling of intimacy. It is not a racist remark, thank God. For one
can indeed become a Jew, but it is as if there had been no conversion.
Can one subscribe to whatever is human? Certain Jews have a way of
saying "Jew" instead of the word "mankind", as if they took Judaism to
be the subject and humanity the predicate.[86]

The boldly essentialist claims here are restricted by Levinas himself as the
essay proceeds, since his burden is to underscore a sense of election deriving from
ethical responsibility—particularism originating as a vigilance to the universal, an
adherence to a preexisting allegiance that "listens and obeys like a guard who never
expects to be relieved."[87]

In *Our America*, on the other hand, a work to which I have made reference
several times in this essay, Walter Benn Michaels suggests a reverse operation at
work in nativist modernism that produced "a new model not only of American
identity but of other identities that would now be available in America"—not exactly Levinas's "West," but close enough.

Promoting a conception of identity as both description and responsibility, it made Americanness into a racial inheritance and culture into a set
of beliefs and practices dependent on race—without race, culture could
be nothing more than one's actual practices and therefore could never be
lost or recovered, defended or betrayed—but not reducible to race—if it
were nothing but race it could also not be lost or recovered, it could
only be a fact, never a project.[88]

Michaels's point here is the paradox of pluralism as a benign form of racism,
reversing a substitution of culture for race and preserving race as a baseline criterion for identity: as he puts it, deriving performative criteria (what we do) from essentialist criteria (who we are).[89]

The two positions, Levinas's and Michaels's, exhibit certain affinities as well
as discrepancies, but the most salient thing differentiating them, it seems to me, is
the split between a metaphysics and a politics of identity. In the context of the fic-
tive hyphenates assembled here, however, such differentiation appears more like
complementarity, a metaphysics *joined to* a politics—as if by hyphen. And to be in
exile from diaspora, the shared condition of the select blacks and Jews I have drawn
from American literary modernism, means to ride such a hyphen, to be (in Levinas's words) suspended on a tightrope: not between an identity "already lost" and
an identity one "still hangs on to" (of concern to both philosopher and literary
critic here), but rather between a reality saturated by the local and one answerable
to a different sort of density or weight. All this the tightrope-hyphen linking

adherence and allegiance. It is where the two David Levinskys keep company with Claire Kendry on either side of the color line, and where the Ex-Colored Man and Rachel Ravinsky continue to look in and out while treading on tiptoe.

■ NOTES

This essay, written in 1993, was the chronologically earliest chapter for my then–book in progress, *Facing Black and Jew: Literature as Public Space*. Appearing now belatedly but freely standing, it prompts me to repeat an observation by Elias Canetti about writing that is fated to undergo salubrious hibernation: "Such a book had to be with one for a long time; it had to travel; it had to occupy space; it had to be a burden; and now it has reached the goal of its voyage, now it reveals itself. . . . It could not say so much if it had not been there mutely the whole time, and what idiot would dare to assert that the same things had always been in it."

1. Joyce's archaic perspective may serve to explain why he is not invoked by John Murray Cuddihy in his juxtaposition of Jews and the Irish in *The Ordeal of Civility: Freud, Marx, Lévi-Strauss, and the Jewish Struggle with Modernity* (New York: Basic Books, 1974). See Rael Meyerowitz, *Transferring to America: Jewish Interpretations of American Dreams* (Albany: State University of New York Press, 1995), for a brief but incisive discussion of Cuddihy's very provocative thesis about Jewish intellectuals' compensation for Jewish civic impoliteness.

2. Abraham Cahan, *The Rise of David Levinsky* (1917; New York: Harper and Bros., 1960), hereafter cited in text as *RDL*; James Weldon Johnson, *Autobiography of an Ex-Colored Man*, hereafter cited in text as *AECM*; Nella Larsen, *Passing* (New Brunswick, N.J.: Rutgers University Press, 1993), hereafter cited in text as *P*; Anzia Yezierska, "Soap and Water," in *Hungry Hearts*, hereafter cited in text as "SW"; and Anzia Yezierska, "Children of Loneliness," in *The Open Cage* (New York: Persea, 1979), hereafter cited in text as "CL."

3. In the wake of Charles Taylor's analysis of "recognition" and the responses generated by it in *Multiculturalism: Examining the Politics of Recognition*, ed. Amy Gutmann (Princeton: Princeton University Press, 1994), the humanities has lit upon a new critical term for cross-disciplinary study. Along lines similar to my own in this essay, for instance, the anthropologist Jonathan Boyarin contributes a superb essay on the implications of recognition for identity politics entitled "Before the Law There Stands a Woman: In Re: *Taylor v. Butler* (with Court-Appointed Yiddish Translator)," in *Thinking in Jewish* (Chicago: University of Chicago Press, 1996), 87–107. In another discursive direction entirely, see Nancy Fraser, "Recognition without Ethics?" in *The Turn to Ethics*, ed. Marjorie Garber, Beatrice Hanssen, and Rebecca L. Walkowitz (New York: Routledge Press, 2000).

4. Robert J. C. Young, *Colonial Desire: Hybridity in Theory, Culture, and Race* (New York: Routledge, 1995); Aijaz Ahmad, *In Theory: Classes, Nations, Literatures* (London: Verso, 1992); Homi K. Bhabha, *The Location of Culture* (London: Routledge, 1994); and Homi K. Bhabha, ed., *Nation and Narration* (London: Routledge, 1990), all deploy "hybridity" as the overarching rubric for the vagaries of racial, ethnic, and cultural difference. The "hyphen" (with at least two letters in common together with certain theoretical implications) has become the focus of recent cultural studies as well, including Jean François Lyotard and Eberhard Gruber, *The Hyphen: Between Judaism and Christianity*, trans. Pascale-Anne Brault and Michael Naas (Amherst, N.Y.: Humanity Books, 1999); and Gustavo Pérez Firmat, *Life on the Hyphen: The Cuban-American Way* (Austin: University of Texas

Press, 1994). See also the introduction to Adam Zachary Newton, *Facing Black and Jew: Literature as Public Space in Twentieth-Century America* (Cambridge: Cambridge University Press, 1999), 1–23.

5. On the role of mediation see, Daniel Aaron, "The Hyphenate Writer and American Letters," *Smith Alumnae Quarterly* (July 1964): 17–28; Jules Chametzky, *Our Decentralized Literature: Cultural Mediations in Selected Jewish and Southern Writers* (Amherst: University of Massachusetts Press, 1986), esp. chaps. 1 and 3; Werner Sollors, *Beyond Ethnicity: Consent and Descent in American Culture* (New York: Oxford University Press, 1982), and "Ethnicity," in *Critical Terms for Literary Study*, ed. Frank Lentricchia and Thomas McLaughlin (Chicago: University of Chicago Press, 1990), 288–305.

6. William Q. Boelhower, *Through a Glass Darkly: Ethnic Semiosis in American Literature* (New York: Oxford University Press, 1986), 120.

7. Happily perhaps for a theory of ethnic semiosis, one of the book divisions comprising *The Rise of David Levinsky* is titled "On the Road."

8. Boelhower, *Through a Glass Darkly*, 137.

9. Ibid.

10. Gilles Deleuze and Félix Guattari, *Kafka: Toward a Minor Literature*, trans. Dana Polan (Minneapolis: University of Minnesota Press, 1988), 19–20. See also Gilles Deleuze and Felix Guattari, *Anti-Oedipus: Capitalism and Schizophrenia*, trans. Robert Hurley, Mark Seem, and Helen Lane (New York: Viking, 1977), and the companion volume, *A Thousand Plateaus: Capitalism and Schizophrenia*, trans. Brian Massumi (London: Athlone, 1988), which analyze cultural territorialism, broadly defined.

11. Kafka, entry for 25 December 1911, *Diaries*, ed. Max Brod (New York: Schocken Books, 1976), 149.

12. Deleuze and Guattari, *Kafka*, 19–20.

13. Ibid., 26–27. Renato Rosaldo, "Politics, Patriarchs, and Laughter," in *The Nature and Context of Minority Discourse*, ed. Abdul R. JanMohamed and David Lloyd (New York: Oxford University Press, 1990), 65–85, nicely critiques the applicability of Deleuze and Guattari's model. See also Angelika Bammer, "Mother Tongues and Other Strangers: Writing 'Family' across Cultural Divides," in *Displacements: Cultural Identities in Question*, ed. Bammer (Bloomington: Indiana University Press, 1994), 90–109.

14. In what is still probably the best single piece on *Levinsky*, Isaac Rosenfeld describes a prelinguistic orality—hunger as such—as the quintessence of the diasporic Jewish identity, a self-reflexive desire, which by feeding on itself, remains endlessly yearning, insatiable. Rosenfeld, "David Levinsky: The Jew as American Millionaire" (273–281) and "Adam and Eve on Delancey Street" (182–187) in Isaac Rosenfeld, *An Age of Enormity: Life and Writing in the Forties and Fifties* (New York: World, 1962). Ellen Golub, "Eat Your Heart Out: The Fiction of Anzia Yezierska," in *Jewish Women Writers and Women in Jewish Literature*, ed. Daniel Walden, Studies in American Jewish Literature 5 (Albany: State University of New York Press, 1983), 51–61, applies this same argument to Yezierska's work, where metaphysical libido is expressed through a seemingly endless stock of eating metaphors. "Vast menus of food live in her work; orality sitting in paragraphs, baked into phrases, roasted into sentences, cooked into her fiction to better articulate the sadness of a generation lost between two worlds" (60). But since "food is not food and it cannot satisfy a hunger that is not hunger" (in Rosenfeld's words), all this libidinal cathexis onto food is itself merely a sublimated yearning for a more primordial object—maternality.

15. Presciently enough, the authors offhandedly remark that Prague German (in Kafka's case) "can be compared in another context to what blacks in America today are able to do

with the English language" (17). Whether or not this does or should give a Deleuze-Guattarian twist to something as contemporarily American as the Ebonics controversy, the parallel is implicit. Rosaldo, "Politics, Patriarchs, and Laughter," sustains an admirable caution regarding such transplantation onto American space, in his topic's case, across the border separating Chicano culture from that of white America. See also José Limón's excellent discussion of the John Sayles film *Lone Star* in *American Encounters: Greater Mexico, the United States, and the Erotics of Culture* (Boston: Beacon Press, 1998).

16. See, e.g., H. G. Adler, "A '*Mischling*' Attempts to Fight for His Rights," in *Displacements: Cultural Identities in Question*, ed. Angelika Bammer (Bloomington: Indiana University Pres, 1994), 205–215, for a genuinely catastrophic reckoning with hybridity.

17. The defamiliarization of speech is imaged by the novel in another way: it is *money* that talks, capital predictably assuming a certain surplus value. "What is a man without capital?" asks one of Levinsky's grasping acquaintances. "Nothing! Nobody cares for him! He is like a beast. A Beast can't talk, and he can't. 'Money talks,' as the Americans say" (181). And later, in the same vein, with the text's own axiomatic rendering of disjunction: "Of course it's nice to be educated," he said. "A man without writing is like a deaf mute. What's the difference? The man who can't write has speech in his mouth, but he is dumb with his fingers, while the deaf mute he can't talk with his mouth, but he can do so with his fingers" (181). Levinsky himself draws a further distinction of his own later on: "Humanity seemed to have become divided into two distinct classes—those who paid their obligations in cash and those who paid them in checks" (205).

18. In St. Louis, the eminent Mr. Huntington, of the Great Bazar cloak-and-suit department, asks Levinsky, "Are you a Russian?" to which Levinsky replies, "I used to be. . . . I am an American now" (337).

19. The Italian film director Sergio Leone, for example, in his mythic cinematic fables about nineteenth-and twentieth-century America, *Once upon a Time in the West* and *Once upon a Time in America*, chooses trains and train stations as the dominant locale and emblem on which the movies' respective plots turn.

20. Emmanuel Levinas, "Reality and Its Shadow," in *Collected Philosophical Papers*, trans. Alphonso Lingis (The Hague: Martinus Nijhoff, 1987), 6, 9. For a discussion of this essay in the context of Levinas's relevance for literary studies, see Robert Eaglestone, *Ethical Criticism: Reading after Levinas* (Edinburgh: Edinburgh University Press, 1997); Jill Robbins, *Altered Reading: Levinas and Literature* (Chicago: University of Chicago Press, 1999); Adam Zachary Newton, *Narrative Ethics* (Cambridge: Harvard University Press, 1995), and *Facing Black and Jew*.

21. Indeed, in "The Kafka Effect," Réda Bensmaïa, praising Deleuze and Guattari's departure from Benjamin's approach to Kafka, which is in other ways similar, says they "make way for—perhaps for the first time—a 'joyous' reading of Kafka: a *Gaya Scienza* of Kafka's work." Réda Bensmaïa, foreword to Gilles Deleuze and Félix Guattari, *Kafka: Toward a Minor Literature*, trans. Dana Polan (Minneapolis: University of Minnesota Press, 1988), xix. It is Benjamin's Kafka, the chastened allegorist, who much more closely approximates the spirit of Cahan, Johnson, Larsen, and Yezierska.

22. Cuddihy, *The Ordeal of Civility*, 3–4.

23. Cf. also *Levinsky*: when David informs his tutor of his plan to emigrate, the ironically named Reb Sender replies, "To America! . . . Lord of the World. But one becomes a Gentile there" (61).

24. Cuddihy, *The Ordeal of Civility*, 6. In a footnote to her book on Levinas, however, Jill Robbins says that decoding a face, Goffman style, would amount to defacing it, according

to Levinas's ethical-philosophical terms, and thus, "For this reason, Goffman's analyses and decoding of 'face-work,' while immensely suggestive for a (social) idiom of face, would be derivative upon the Levinasian conception." Robbins, *Altered Reading*, 8.

25. As one definition of modernity, Cuddihy cites Talcott Parson's pattern-variable model of differentiation, which specifies a movement (passing from right to left) "from affectivity to affective neutrality, from particularism to universalism, from . . . private affect to public demeanor." Cuddihy, *The Ordeal of Civility*, 9, 13. This in turn becomes the chief burden of Jewish intellectual culture, which finds itself in the impossible vise of an apologetics for unreconstructed "Jewish" Jews on the one hand, and a jeremiad against modernity's thinly veiled secular Protestantism, on the other. See also Milton Himmelfarb, *The Jews of Modernity* (New York: Basic Books, 1973); Maurice Samuel, *Jews on Approval* (New York: Liveright, 1932) and *The Gentleman and the Jew* (New York: Alfred A. Knopf, 1950); Barry M. Rubin, *Assimilation and Its Discontents* (New York: Random House, 1995); and, more disturbing, Alan Dershowitz, *The Vanishing American Jew: In Search of Jewish Identity for the Next Century* (New York: Little, Brown, 1997).

26. Walter Benn Michaels, *Our America: Nativism, Modernism, and Pluralism* (Durham, N.C.: Duke University Press), 117, 118.

27. Sigmund Freud, "The 'Uncanny'" (1919), in the *Standard Edition of the Complete Psychological Works of Sigmund Freud*, trans. and ed. Lytton Strachey (London: Hogarth Press, 1955), 217–256; Otto Rank, *The Double: A Psychoanalytic Study*, trans. and ed. Harry Tucker Jr. (Chapel Hill: University of North Carolina Press, 1971).

28. Erving Goffman, *Stigma: Notes on the Management of Spoiled Identity* (Englewood Cliffs, N.J.: Prentice-Hall, 1963).

29. Samuel, *Jews on Approval*, 9; quoted in Cuddihy, *The Ordeal of Civility*, 14.

30. Compare Henry Louis Gates Jr., "The Trope of a New Negro and the Reconstruction of the Image of the Black," *Representations* 24 (Fall 1988): 129–155; Michael Rogin, *Blackface, White Noise: Jewish Immigrants in the Hollywood Melting Pot* (Berkeley: University of California Press, 1996); Alain Locke, "Harlem: Mecca of the New Negro," *Survey Graphic* 1 (1925); and Hasia R. Diner, *In the Almost Promised Land: American Jews and Blacks, 1915–1935* (Westport, Conn.: Greenwood Press, 1977).

31. See Emile Benveniste, *Problems in General Linguistics*, trans. Mary Elizabeth Meek (Coral Gables, Fla.: University of Miami Press, 1966); Philippe Lejeune, *On Autobiography*, ed. Paul John Eakin, trans. Katherine Leary (Minneapolis: University of Minnesota Press, 1989); Alice Yaeger Kaplan, "On Language Memoir," in *Displacements: Cultural Identities in Question*, ed. Angelika Bammer (Bloomington: Indiana University Pres, 1994), 63–90; and Paul de Man, "Autobiography as Defacement," in *The Rhetoric of Romanticism* (New York: Columbia University Press, 1984), 67–81.

32. This is particularly evident in *Levinsky*, where the narrator speaks floridly of "discovering America" and emulating Columbus. The *iterability* of immigration narratives, the sense of their being a *borrowed* construction, of course, merely compounds the generic redundancy of the *apologia* form. And when Levinsky jeopardizes his cutting job at Mannheimer brothers by literalizing a cliché—he spills a bottle of milk and decides not to cry over it, but change his luck instead—the prefabricated nature of his whole narrative enterprise becomes unmistakable. Henry Louis Gates Jr. makes a similar point about black autobiography in "Bad Influence," *New Yorker*, 7 March 1994, 94–98.

33. M. M. Bakhtin, "Author and Hero in Aesthetic Activity," in *Art and Answerability: Early Philosophical Essays*, ed. Michael Holquist and Vadim Liapunov, trans. Vadim Liapunov (Austin: University of Texas Press, 1990), 30; Levinas, "Reality and Its Shadow," 2–10.

34. Compare the father's biting remark in "Children of Loneliness": "You think you got a different skin from us because you went to college?" (145).

35. In showing how identity marks a border between private and public worlds, both shaped and deformed by a recognition granted by others, Charles Taylor explains how a politics of difference grows out of but may still be at odds with a politics of universalism; Taylor, *Multiculturalism and "The Politics of Recognition": An Essay* (Princeton: Princeton University Press, 1992). But as a broadly sociological phenomenon without specific regard to ethnicity, what Yezierska calls soap and water translates into the variety of disinfectant maneuvers called into practice by the sheer power of stigma.

36. Anzia Yezierska, *Bread Givers: A Novel: A Struggle between a Father of the Old World and a Daughter of the New* (Garden City, N.Y.: Doubleday, Page & Co., 1925); quoted in Michaels, *Our America*, 69. Michaels's brief discussion of Yezierska underscores the theme of his book: the changing fortunes of Americanness, of blood ties and the values of race and culture reflected in a literary moment he calls nativist modernism, when categories of individual and collective identity were undergoing often startling revisions and chiastic reversals. Thus, when the heroine of *Bread Givers* marries an Americanized landsman who has moved not only transversely on the plane of culture but also vertically in the hierarchy of class, a ritual of consent magically and unexpectedly resolves exigencies of descent, as Sara Smolinski becomes similarly transposed through a reconciliation with her father, Reb Smolinski, and the Old World he represents. "Through the restoration of the child to her father," writes Michaels, "Jewishness is made Jewishness again; the claim to one blood becomes the claim to difference . . . rewriting the critique of racial identity as the commitment to racial identity." *Our America*, 72.

37. "One day the White Master, *without conflict*, recognized the Negro slave. But the former slave wants to *make himself recognized*" (Frantz Fanon, *Black Skin, White Masks* [1967; reprint, New York: Grove Press, 1982], 217). As Shamoon Zamir explains in his important study of W. E. B. Du Bois's place in American philosophy, *Dark Voices: W. E. B. Du Bois and American Thought* (Chicago: University of Chicago Press, 1995), Fanon, Orlando Patterson, and many modern critics of Hegel's *Phenomenology* misconstrue recognition in the dialectic of lordship and bondage. "What the master recognizes primarily is not the slave or his humanity but rather that his own freedom is a determined one, materially contingent on the labor that the slave produces. The slave, reciprocally, recognizes the possibility of his own independent consciousness. The recognition, in other words, is a mutuality, a co-construction" (130).

38. See Mary V. Dearborn, *Love in the Promised Land: The Story of Anzia Yezierska and John Dewey* (New York: Free Press, 1988).

39. *The Philosophy of John Dewey* (1928; reprint, New York: Putnam, 1973).

40. Cornel West, *The American Evasion of Philosophy: A Genealogy of Pragmatism* (Madison: University of Wisconsin Press, 1989), 106.

41. *The Philosophy of John Dewey*.

42. What one wants, rather, is a Du Boisian sense of history making as culture-making—that is, a belief in "ethnic agency." "To what degree," West paraphrases, "have the demands of blacks fostered and expanded American democracy? In that way is democracy dependent on these demands, given their spin-off effects in demands made by larger ethnic groups?" (West, *The American Evasion of Philosophy*, 147). And again, "Creative powers reside among the wretched of the earth even in their subjugation, and the fragile structures of democracy depend, in large part, on how these powers are ultimately exercised" (148). Zamir's study of

self-consciousness in Du Bois's *Souls of Black Folk* also illuminates the comparative deficits of Dewey's Hegelian optimism and centrism when measured against Du Bois's harder-edged sense of "the negativity of historical experience," which embodied a racially specific "unhappy consciousness" in the souls of black folk. Zamir, *Dark Voices*, 115.

43. Dewey, 615. The figure of in-betweenness here cuts at least two ways, one being merely a stock immigrant trope. In Samuel Raphaelson's short story "The Day of Atonement," on which the movie *The Jazz Singer* was based, the narrator intones, "Jakie was simply translating the age-old music of cantors—that vast loneliness of a race wandering 'between two worlds, one dead, the other powerless to be born.'" But Yezierska's betweenness also recalls the cultural fissure between *Yiddishkayt* and civility discussed earlier, something to which its own racist provenance can be tracked—back, for example, to Matthew Arnold's distinction between Hebraism and Hellenism in *Culture and Anarchy*, and even beyond to Renan, Gobineau, and Herder. When Dewey uses the word "culture," it has neutral and pragmatist implications. When Yezierska's heroines pronounce on their own cultural misfit, they tap (however unwittingly) into a reservoir of long standing: the anthropological, racist underpinnings of high culture versus low, active versus moribund, Semitic versus not-Semitic. See again in this connection Michaels, *Our America*, especially the final chapter, on Melville Herskovits, Waldo Frank, and pluralism; also Nathan Glazer, *We Are All Multiculturalists Now* (Cambridge: Harvard University Press, 1996), for an illuminating analysis of the differential treatment accorded American Jews and African Americans by Dewey as "meltable" Americans.

44. Karl Mannheim coined the phrase "fresh contact" to describe both the individual and the generational shift within a given culture. See Mannheim, "The Problem of Generations," in *Essays on the Sociology of Culture*, ed. Karl Mannheim (London: Routledge, 1992).

45. Not coincidentally, the in-between generation bodied forth by Yezierska's heroines is the same one that, on a larger cultural scale, was determined to shift the modern American woman's body concept from full to lean. As this was *comme il faut* for WASP culture of the 1920s, Jews—and blacks—could claim a necessarily ambivalent relation to such a combined politics of diet and identity. For a discussion of this cultural moment, specifically in relation to Gertrude Stein and Fannie Hurst, see Ann Douglas, *Terrible Honesty: Mongrel Manhattan in the 1920s* (New York: Farrar, Straus, and Giroux, 1995).

46. Luc Sante, *Low Life: Lures and Snares of Old New York* (New York: Vintage Books, 1992), observes of the mixed architectural blessing that was the airshaft in tenements after the 1880s: "Even when two adjacent houses were so equipped and their shifts happened to be contiguously positioned, the resulting hole was laterally no more than the size of a man's coffin, and the pathway from sky to window was so constrained that sunlight could not make its way below the top story except at high noon." Sante, *Low Life*, 40. Rachel's focused revulsion at the interior of her apartment elides the fact that the airshaft itself functioned commonly as a public dumping ground, and thus obscures class self-consciousness under the sign of the hyphen.

47. Golub, "Eat Your Heart Out," 60.

48. In his autobiography Cahan writes, "I felt at home with my Russian-speaking friends. But I felt a strong attraction to the Yiddish language, more than I had ever felt in Russia. . . . In was in Yiddish, one day, that I greeted in the street the carver from the old country who, in another world, had promised to teach me a trade." Abraham Cahan, *The Education of Abraham Cahan*, trans. A. P. Conan, L. Davison, and L. Stein (Philadelphia:

Jewish Publication Society, 1969), 281. Being "in" Yiddish momentarily solves having moved out and away from that other world.

49. Henry James, *The American Scene* (New York: Harper and Brothers, 1907), 85, 86.

50. Ibid., 122.

51. Ibid., 138–139. James's belletristic shock takes on an interesting dimension when read in conjunction with the varieties of opinion expressed by Jewish-Americans in a symposium, "The Jewish Writer and the English Literary Tradition," *Commentary* (September–October 1944): 209–219, 361–370. Compare additionally the essay by Leslie Fiedler earlier the same year, "What Can We Do About Fagin?" *Commentary* (May 1944): 411–419. But ethnic literary context aside, James's sense of the "face-to-face" here invites comment. In another section of *The American Scene*, the author stops to look at some Italian ditchdiggers, who return his stare. Instead of "the play of mutual recognition" he would expect in a similar street scene in Europe, with "some impalpable exchange" for a consequence, he reads instead "sterility" and "staring silence" between himself and the mandarin faces that look up at him (118–119). Interpreting that very scene, Boelhower ascribes a prescient postmodernism to James, who, instead of merely dichotomizing monocultural and multiethnic perspectives, "weaves between both paradigms by dislocating the fixed point of view, by making the relation rather than the immobile subject central" (23). But in fact, we never hear from the ethnics in this tableau, so we really cannot know the status of any lived relationality. Moreover, the asymmetry of James at street level and diggers and ditchers below him is hard to finesse. Sante's analysis of the "face" presented by the New York tenement far more concretely and justly renders "the fixed point of view" from street level—that is, how a *material* ethnic and working-class immobility might signify to critically inquisitive eyes. Sante corrects for James's (and Boelhower's) privileged gaze by reading humanity out from behind the nonhuman face of the cityscape. James, by contrast, makes ethnically particular faces unreadable, while Boelhower liberates their semiotic possibilities within the frame of the postmodern.

52. James, 375, 376. Far more acutely than Boelhower, Michaels offers this observation of James's play of near and far in *The American Scene*: "If, from one standpoint, this fear of intimacy with the Negro suggests James's complicity with the new racism, from another standpoint, it suggests his inability to recognize the potential of that racism as an organizing principle of social life" (*Our America*, 56–57).

53. Deborah E. McDowell, introduction to Nella Larsen, *"Quicksand" and "Passing"* (New Brunswick, N.J.: Rutgers University Press, 1986), consistently refers to Irene as an "unreliable narrator." In fact, the text is focalized through her, but she is not its narrating voice; passages of free indirect style alternate with direct discourse and psychonarration. One could argue for hyphenate identity as making itself felt on a purely textual level in a modernist text like this, where the narrating consciousness and the color line–driven protagonist place themselves in varying degrees of proximity to one another, sometimes merged and sometimes quite distinct. Pamela Caughie, "'Not Entirely Strange . . . Not Entirely Friendly': *Passing* and Pedagogy," *College English* 54, no. 7 (November 1992): 775–793, reads above the text's ambiguating and blurred enigmas of race and gender for differences that "are accidental, acquired, and alterable—such as social and interlocutionary positions" (782). Even while the novel cleverly makes racial difference and sexual difference incommensurate and nonsubstitutable, it points beyond the simply textual noncoincidence of metaphor and metonymy to a politics of conversation and (mis)recognition.

54. The "secrets" the novel keeps on the level of story—did Clare fall from the window or was she pushed? did she have an affair with Brian? is Irene sexually attracted to Clare?—

contrast with the looseness and immodesty that characterize so much of the discourse, by turns defamatory and talebearing.

55. Zora Neale Hurston, *I Love Myself When I'm Laughing . . . and Then Again When I Am Looking Mean and Impressive* (Old Westbury, N.Y.: Feminist Press, 1979), 152–155. See also Hurston, "Characteristics of Negro Expression" (in *Within the Circle: An Anthology of African American Literary Criticism from the Harlem Renaissance to the Present,* ed. Angelyn Mitchell [Durham, N.C.: Duke University Press, 1994], 87), in which she remarks, "The Negro, the world over, is famous as a mimic," and her autobiography, *Dust Tracks on a Road: An Autobiography* (Urbana: University of Illinois Press, 1970), particularly the chapter titled "My People, My People" (215–237). The essay on mimicry is especially relevant for Larsen's novel in its correlation of class identity and racial identification, its differentiations along both axes dependent, in Michaels's cogent reading of it, on the distinction between being something and trying to be the thing one is. See Michaels, *Our America,* 87–90.

56. Levinas, "Reality and Its Shadow," 10.

57. McDowell argues that a lesbian subtext adds sexual identity to race as another dimension in which Larsen's novel parses the politics of passing; readers risk colluding with the characters if they collapse one into the other. But the question posed here encompasses that undecidability since it raises a problem intrinsic to the ethnic text in general: if identity *within* the text means self-difference, does a corresponding division or doubling impinge on readers as well? That is, in addition to selecting out different audiences—inside versus outside, minority versus nonminority—does a novel such as *Passing* produce a splitting in *any* attentive reader insofar as the burden of recognition in regard to character or event is assumed? Detection and misrecognition, the dual risks incurred by Clare Kendry in passing, can also be said to define the hermeneutic stakes here. For his confession of liberal guilty conscience around this text, see also Peter Rabinowitz, "Betraying the Sender: The Rhetoric and Ethics of Fragile Texts," *Narrative* 2, no. 3 (October 1994): 254–267.

58. Compare Clare's philoracist remark, "You don't know, you can't realize how I want to see Negroes, to be with them again, to talk with them, hear them laugh" (200).

59. Michaels, *Our America,* 115.

60. It is, incidentally, in this same section that reference is made to a light-skinned black man who passes even a further step beyond, who "was no longer a Negro or a Christian but had become a Jew" (169). In this vein one thinks also of the liminal moment in *The Jazz Singer* when Jolson, "hearing the song of his race," dons blackface, obscuring Jew by means of black.

61. On an anthropologic and ethnographic sidepoint, both Melville Herskovitz and Franz Boas distinguished between (American)-Jewish and African-American experiences of migration. Barbara Kirshenblatt-Gimblett, "Spaces of Dispersal," *Cultural Anthropology* 9, no. 3 (Summer 2000): 339–344, observes, "Both of them denied the existence of Jewish particularism (because of diaspora) while valorizing African American difference (in spite of diaspora)." And again, "Herskovits could write *The Myth of the Negro Past* but could not imagine a comparable Myth of the Jewish Past, or rather, the task was to demonstrate that there *was* a Negro past and to question claims made for a Jewish past" (341). Thus, Herskovits, "When Is a Jew a Jew?" *Modern Quarterly* 4 (1927): 109–117: "A Jew is a person who calls himself a Jew, or is called Jewish by others. . . . I fail to see anything particularly unique in the Jew as Jew" (116–117). See also Michaels's study of Herskovits in the final chapter of *Our America* and in "Race into Culture: A Critical Genealogy of Cultural Identity," *Critical Inquiry* 18 (Summer 1992): 669–690.

62. Bakhtin, "Author and Hero in Aesthetic Activity," 143. Bakhtin earlier speaks of "purifying the reflected face," a figure for exterior perception of self-identity ("Author and Hero in Aesthetic Activity," 30–35), and addresses the problematics of confession again in the late essay "Toward a Reworking of the Dostoevsky Book," in M. M. Bakhtin, *Problems of Dostoevsky's Poetics* (Minneapolis: University of Minnesota Press, 1984), 283–301.

63. Ibid., along with M. M. Bakhtin, "The Problem of Speech Genres," and "From Notes Made in 1970–71," in *Speech Genres and Other Late Essays*, trans. Vern W. McGee (Austin: University of Texas Press, 1986), 87–100 and 143–149, respectively.

64. Levinsky will typically employ locutions such as "But this is a common trait among our people" (5) and "the blood of my race" (4) or make coded references such as "the Hebrew Old Testament." The Ex-Colored Man will speak of "trying to catch the spirit of the Negro in his relatively primitive state" (173). Werner Sollors explains the Baedeker impulse so common to early modernist ethnic fiction in *Beyond Ethnicity*, also pointing to the oversound of authorial perspective in *Levinsky* and *Ex-Colored Man* bracketing the narrators in each text. See also Johnson's and Cahan's own autobiographies, *Along This Way* (1927) and *The Education of Abraham Cahan* (1926).

65. The recognition scene dramatizes Fanon's observation that "the Negro is a phobogenic object, a stimulus to anxiety" (Fanon, *Black Skin, White Masks*, 151) and represents another potent instance of the ethnic Uncanny: "Then I told her, in what words I do not know, the truth. I felt her hand grow cold, and when I looked up, she was gazing at me with a wild, fixed stare as though I was some object she had never seen. Under the strange light in her eyes I felt that I was growing black and thick-featured and crimp-haired. She appeared not to have comprehended what I said. Her lips trembled and she attempted to say something to me, but the words stuck in her throat" (204–205).

66. The theater locale is entirely in keeping with the theme of blacks (and tragic mulattoes especially) as simulacra. Of a minstrel, the narrator observes, "Here was a man who made people laugh at the size of his mouth, while he carried in his heart a burning ambition to be a tragedian; and so after all he did play a part in a tragedy" (106).

67. Ralph Ellison, *Invisible Man* (1952; reprint, New York: Vintage, 1990), 14. Ellison's narrator is, to be sure, no model of innocent rhetoric himself. But compare Fanon here: "Man is human only to the extent to which he tries to impose his existence on another man in order to be recognized by him. As long as he has not been effectively recognized by the other, that other will remain the theme of his actions" (217). For a discussion of Johnson's novel as precursor to Ellison's, see Houston A. Baker Jr., *Long Black Song: Essays in Black American Literature and Culture* (Charlottesville: University Press of Virginia, 1972).

68. The term belongs to Werner Sollors. See also Roger Rosenblatt's reading of Johnson's novel in Rosenblatt, *Black Fiction* (Cambridge: Harvard University Press, 1974); Stephen Ross, "Audience and Irony in Johnson's *The Autobiography of an Ex-Colored Man*," *CLA Journal* 18 (December 1974): 198–210; Simone Vathier, "The Interplay of Narrative Modes in James Weldon Johnson's *The Autobiography of an Ex-Colored Man*," *Jahrbuch für Amerikastudien* 18 (1973): 173–181.

69. Bakhtin, "Author and Hero in Aesthetic Activity," 32, 33.

70. "For racial identity to become a project, it must turn to culture; for cultural identity to become a project, it must turn to race. The Ex-Colored Man's ambition to make a Negro out of himself provides a kind of rehearsal for a broader range of identitarian ambitions. Because he can pass for white, he can choose to be black—biology is supplemented by behavior, race is supplemented by culture. But because he cannot choose to be white—he can

only pretend to be white—behavior can never replace biology, culture cannot replace race." Michaels, *Our America*, 122.

71. See Zamir, *Dark Voices*.

72. W. E. B. Du Bois, *The Souls of Black Folk*, 6, 173.

73. Hurston, "Characteristics of Negro Expression." That essay's whole discussion of race and culture, class and behavior bears profoundly on the Ex-Colored Man's artistic aspirations and the double bind that makes him adhere to what he believes he can detach himself from.

74. Philippe Lejeune writes, for example: "'Identity' is a constant relationship between the one and the many. Linguistically, this problem of identity . . . at the lexical level . . . is 'resolved' by the class of 'proper names,' to which in the final analysis the personal pronouns refer. The name is the guarantor of the unity of our multiplicity: it federates our complexity in the moment and our change in time" (*On Autobiography*, 34).

75. Of such unsatisfiable nostalgia for hunger, Isaac Rosenfeld remarks, "Precisely because the desires [for relief and betterment] are formed under its sign, they become assimilated to it, and convert it into the prime source of all value, so that the man, in his pursuit of whatever he considers pleasurable and good, seeks to return to his yearning as much as he does to escape it" (*An Age of Enormity*, 277).

76. It can also be understood as underpinning the just-as-frequent scenes of "social acting" in the text in restaurants, on trains, and in conversation, when Levinsky shuttles back and forth (or up and down) between hyphenate-identity halves. Such social acting, however, does not belong exclusively to the domain of ethnicity at this particular moment in American literary history. See the earlier note about "acting" in *Ex-Colored Man* and Philip Fisher's relevant treatment of Dreiser in *Hard Facts: Setting and Form in the American Novel* (New York: Oxford University Press 1985).

77. Compare Cahan's own continued *heymisch* attachment to Yiddish as a place all its own in *The Education of Abraham Cahan*: "I loved Yiddish and often fought for it. . . . It was in Yiddish, one day that I greeted in the street the carver from the old country, who in another world, had promised to teach me a trade" (281), the prepositional marker "in Yiddish" topographically subsuming all the other degrees of location in the sentence. See also Boyarin's more theoretically pointed *Thinking in Jewish*, 1–7.

78. This question of heteroglossia (which Deleuze and Guattari do not take up in respect to Kafka) is not insignificant for a text such as *Levinsky*. Unlike, say, Henry Roth's *Call It Sleep*, which makes language difference structurally integral, Cahan makes very little attempt to render Yiddish per se except in terms of the linguistic tensions that Levinsky experiences in the company of his Yiddish-speaking love interest, Dora, and her English-speaking daughter, Lucy. Nevertheless, it is understood that Levinsky is a gypsy and refugee in another language and is thus palpably alienated—deterritorialized by circumstance, not choice. *Mutatis mutandis*, Tevkin the Hebrew poet, through a curious back-projection, is himself deterritorialized within the Yiddish-speaking subculture of the Lower East Side in which poets such as Moishe-Leib Halpern or Yankev Glatstein would have far more currency. The text, however, does make positive reference to the revival of Hebrew as "the living tongue of the Zionist colonists in Palestine" (463), and a dedicated coterie of American Hebraists had found its voice through several small journals published at this very juncture.

79. See Philip Barrish, "'The Genuine Article': Ethnicity, Capital, and *The Rise of David Levinsky*," *New Literary History* 5, no. 4 (1994): 643–662, for a comprehensive discussion of

the novel's several economies. Barrish convincingly analyzes Levinsky's self-division, contrary to readings of the text as cautionary tale, as that mechanism ultimately underwriting rather than undercutting his rise "in both its cultural and economic aspects" (645). I would complicate the view of Levinsky's "ethnic real" as the sum of broken, "iterable" fragments (Barrish's overarching argument requires the accumulation of capital on every level of the text). "Genuine articles" of a manipulable Jewish past need not be seen in the capacity of so many quotidian shards and sparks, but rather as something almost fugal, contrapuntal—that is, ongoing—in their motivic recirculation, a central feature a generation later of Henry Roth's *Call It Sleep*.

80. See the preface to Newton, *Facing Black and Jew*, for an explication of this term and method.

81. Compare Cahan, *The Education of Abraham Cahan*, 281.

82. The two are even conflated: "I found myself in the vicinity of City College. As I passed that corner I studiously looked away. I felt like a convert Jew passing a synagogue" (207). And again, shortly thereafter: "The Talmud tells us how the destruction of Jerusalem and the great Temple was caused by a hen and a rooster. The destruction of my American temple was caused by a bottle of milk. . . . To me it is a sacred spot . . . the sepulcher of my dearest ambitions, a monument to my noblest enthusiasm in America" (215–216).

83. D. H. Lawrence, *Studies in Classic American Literature* (New York: Penguin, 1977), 6.

84. Ellison, *Invisible Man*, 14.

85. Paul Gilroy, *The Black Atlantic: Modernity and Double Consciousness* (Cambridge: Harvard University Press, 1993), 211. Henry Louis Gates Jr., "'Authenticity,' or the Lesson of Little Tree," *New York Times Book Review*, 24 November 1991, 29. See also R. Radhhakrishnan, "Ethnic Identity and Post-Structuralist Difference," in *Cultural Critique* (Fall 1987): 199–221; Homi K. Bhabha, "Frontlines/Borderposts," in *Displacements: Cultural Identities in Question*, ed. Angelika Bammer (Bloomington: Indiana University Press, 1994), 269–272, and, more extensively, *The Location of Culture*.

86. Emmanuel Levinas, "Means of Identification," in *Difficult Freedom: Essays on Judaism*, trans. Seán Hand (Baltimore: Johns Hopkins University Press, 1990), 50. I discuss this essay in "Is Jew/Greek Greek/Jew; or does 'Hebrew' Mean Cross-Over? The Tightrope, the Window, and the Text: An Excursus on Identity," *Social Identities* 2, no. 1 (February 1996): 93–107, and *The Fence and the Neighbor: Emmanuel Levinas, Yeshayahu Leibowitz, and Israel among the Nations* (Albany: State University of New York Press, 2001).

87. Levinas, "Means of Identification," 50.

88. Michaels, *Our America*, 141.

89. Some version of this paradox (if not fully in support of Michaels's claim, then at least an exploration of it) can be seen in Philip Roth, *The Human Stain* (New York: Houghton Mifflin, 2000), a fin-de-siècle composite of *Ex-Colored Man, David Levinsky*, and *The Scarlet Letter*, and a late exercise in the allegorical possibilities of "black-Jewish relations." Roth's protagonist, Coleman Brutus Silk, is sufficiently light-skinned to refashion his African Americanness as Jewishness—ex-ing the blackness of Silk under the guise of the "Ellis Island attenuation of Silberzweig" (130). His provisional solution to the opposing claims of race and culture is "the raw I" and its power to keep secrets: "Not the tyranny of the we that is dying to suck you in, the coercive, inclusive, historical, inescapable moral *we* with its insidious *E pluribus unum*. . . . Instead the raw I with its agility . . . Singularity. The sliding relationship with everything . . . Self-knowledge but *concealed*. What is as powerful as that?" (108). The question is posed more dubiously a few pages later in Silk's own manifesto of eth-

nic semiosis: "To be two men instead of one? To be two colors instead of one? To walk the streets incognito or in disguise, to be neither this nor that but something in between? To be possessed of a double or triple or quadruple personality" (130)? Of course, this seemingly Larsenlike rhetoric has been distilled through a machinery of authorial hide-and-seek unavailable to Cahan, Johnson, Yezierska, or Larsen, against the backdrop of an America corresponding to a very different "our" than Roth's "we" or "they."

A Jewish New World in
Jacob Glatshteyn's "Sheeny Mike"

■

The greenhorn in the Automat fed nickel after nickel into the apple-pie
slot. His friend exclaimed, "Are you crazy, you *chozzer*? You have already
fifteen pies!" Said the greenhorn, "Why should it bother you if I keep
winning?"

—QUOTED IN LEO ROSTEN, *The Joys of Yiddish*

The gangster is a familiar, albeit shady, inhabitant of American literature and popular culture. Indeed, the cultural critic Robert Warshow maintained in 1948 that
"the experience of the gangster *as an experience of art* is universal to Americans.
There is almost nothing we understand better or react to more readily or with
quicker intelligence."[1]

By the turn of the twentieth century, "quick intelligence" had dictated that
gangsters are inherently ethnic, inherently urban, inherently male, and inherently
modern—in contrast with legendary "outlaws" such as the James brothers, Ma
Barker, Pretty Boy Floyd, or Bonnie Parker and Clyde Barrow, whose setting was
rural or small-town America. In a variety of popular media, gangsters came to serve
as markers, even admonitions, of the dangerous potential in each of these qualities.
Explicitly patriotic propaganda is highlighted in such important gangster films as
The Public Enemy (1931) or *Little Caesar* (1930),[2] for instance: through intrusive
prologues, afterwords, and set pieces, the audience is warned about immigrants
who disgrace their communities, about mass media that only seeks to sensational-
ize, and about men who prove their toughness by lack of respect for even "their
own" women. But as moviegoers watched somber words scroll across the screen,
declaring that *Little Caesar* should stand as a warning to good Americans, many, of
course, still found themselves rooting for, and choosing to identify with, the characters carefully marked as villains: the newcomers and outsiders in what was clearly
a social war.

This apparent contradiction is extremely consequential, for such moments
of contest can be uniquely revelatory concerning cultural identity formation.
Jacob Glatshteyn's long poem "Sheeny Mike," which was written in Yiddish in
1929 and tells of a dead Jewish gangster in New York, both describes and enacts
just such a moment of cultural collision: the gangster Mike has been living large in
two worlds—that of traditional Jewishness, and that of modern Americanness—

while maintaining a need to reject, and be rejected by, both. The purpose of this essay is to examine the ways in which the figure of the Jewish gangster, precisely because he is cast in ambivalence and ambiguity, becomes a tool for metaliterary investigation by Glatshteyn of the place of the Jew—and Jewish literature—in modern America.

Glatshteyn was eighteen years old when he immigrated to the United States from Russian Poland; it was in Europe that he first encountered the world of literature and made his first literary ventures. Once in the United States, he (along with his contemporaries in the modernist American Yiddish literary movement known as In Zikh) absorbed both high and popular American culture in addition to ideas about art that were developed in a host of avant-garde movements, including Russian and Italian futurism, German expressionism, and Anglo-American imagism.[3]

Glatshteyn's migrant status is emblematic rather than unique; cross-fertilization, carried by polyglot immigrants, was commonplace, and Glatshteyn's bicontinental set of influences can be said to concretize a fertile East Side connection between American and Russian literature and culture.[4] The extensively intertextual nature of Glatshteyn's poem, which invokes and revises a contemporary body of gangster literature both Eastern European and American, positions the character of Sheeny Mike (and the text of the poem) at a complicated crossroads. The variety of subtexts engendered by Glatshteyn's transnational gaze demonstrates the internal contest of loyalties facing the Jew in America. At the same time, the echoes and revisions of earlier texts emphasize the creation of national identity as an ongoing process in which Jewish writers play a part. Ultimately the Jewish gangster becomes both sign and signified, as his historical, literary, and stereotypical functions serve as a catalyst for Glatshteyn's discussion of ethnicity and literary power in America.

Glatshteyn's poem is framed by its title (and its hero by his name) in ambivalence. The name "Sheeny Mike" has obviously been given to this Jewish man by his Gentile associates.[5] It serves at once to denote Mike's Jewish otherness—"sheeny" is an offensive epithet—and his assimilation—"Mike" is an Americanized version of a nickname that probably was originally "Mechele."

It is significant that Mike's Jewishness is first indicated from the external perspective of non-Jews. Mike's gang name, "sheeny," was also a slang term for a pawnbroker or a frugal man and therefore is indicative of the old stereotype of Jews as mercantile.[6] Mike's noisily grieving parents are likewise reduced by synecdoche to those overtly Jewish qualities—the mother's ritual wig (*der mammas shaytl*) and the father's long beard (*dem tatns olter bord*)—that would serve as anti-Semitic stereotypes. By using popular (if derogatory) "American" definitions of Jewishness to mark Mike's ethnicity, Glatshteyn deconstructs essentialist nationalist categories that he and his In Zikh colleagues found artistically damaging:

> But if they say to me: "Jewish Art," with the emphasis on the first word,
> I don't know what it is at all. Even more, I feel some kind of instinctive
> peril from such an emphasis. . . .

I do not pretend to be naive. I know what Mr. Nigger [pseudonym
of the foremost Yiddish literary critic in the United States; usually
transliterated S. Niger] wants. He speaks of the inner content of this literature and he wants Yiddish literature to have an explicit, inherently
Jewish content.

But what does this mean? An idea? A mission? Does Mr. Nigger want
Yiddish literature to have a missionary function? . . . This is a mistake. A
bad, dangerous mistake.[7]

The notion of Jewishness as an externally imposed category of otherness that
is internalized by Jews themselves is consonant with Glatshteyn's conception of the
American Jew as forever alien—a conception that came to dominate Glatshteyn's
later work, notably his bitter *Gute Nacht, Velt* (Good Night, World). Indeed, the
figure of the gangster stands by definition at a problematic crossroads. Sheeny
Mike is born of American conditions and is quite willing to exist in—and profit
from—the American system, to which he has no ideological objections. Yet at the
same time he remains marginalized by society because he is a criminal, representing, as Warshow notes, rejection of "the qualities and demands of modern life . . .
'Americanism' itself."[8]

It is precisely this duality—the simultaneous dependence upon mainstream
society and rejection of and by it—that Isaac Babel explores in his stories about
Benya Krik, the Jewish gangster from Odessa, which he wrote between 1921 and
1924. Benya Krik's position becomes emblematic of that of the most estranged
minority in imperial Russia: the Jews. Bakhtin's notion of "chuzhaya rech'," or the
alien voice, best conveys the extraordinary nature of Benya Krik's speech acts, for
although Babel wrote in Russian rather than his native Yiddish, Benya's linguistic
difference is striking. His use in spoken Russian of a combination of thieves' jargon
and Yiddishisms sets him off from the Russians:

—*Kto ty, otkuda ty idesh' i chem ty dyshish'?*
—*Poprobui menya, Froim,—otvetil Benya,—i perestanem razmazyvat'
beluyu kashu po chistomu stolu.*[9]

[Rook asked him: "Who are you, where do you come from, and what
do you use for breath?"
"Give me a try, Ephraim," replied Benya, "and let us stop smearing
kasha over a clean table."]

One character even remarks that Benya does not say much, but what he does
say is "savory" (*smachno*). Indeed, his trade name, Krik, which translates literally as
"yell," refers to an aggressive vocalization. Consistently, Benya Krik distinguishes
himself not only through his active control of language, but also through his vernacular assault on "standard" Russian.

In addition to scrupulously depicting the particularities of Jewish Russian, Babel also demonstrates Jewish exclusion from the "mainstream" cultural world by playing with conventions of Russian fairy tales. A stock ending of the Russian fairy tale is, approximately, "How do I know this? Why, I was there, and ate and danced until dawn." Recognition and understanding of such phrases (which are akin to the "Once upon a time" of English fairy tales) implies membership in a common community. But Babel's Jewish narrator twists the convention: "Ya ne byl pri etoi ssore. No te, kto byl, te pomnyat" (*DDR*, 252: I wasn't present at this quarrel, but those who were remember it). In other words, he invokes a shared cultural fund in order to say he wasn't fully part of it. Like Babel, Glatshteyn also uses the stock phrases and characters of fairy tales in order to undercut the assumption of commonality on which the stories depend; Sheeny Mike is "der eydlman, / Der raytndiker riter, / Der temper yung, / der shiker" (the nobleman, / the knight on horseback, / the dumb guy, / the drunkard).[10]

Although Glatshteyn's poem is preoccupied with its own "Americanness," the Benya Krik stories operate as a crucial subtext. Like Glatshteyn, Babel makes the gangster-hero's professional nickname the title of the story, underscoring its ironic implications. Benya Krik is called "The King"—a term repeatedly associated with Sheeny Mike:

Dem tatns bord un der mames shaytl
Hobn zey den gevust az unter eyn dakh
Voynt a kinig . . . ("SM," 244)

Papa's beard and mama's *shaytl*—
Did they know that under the same roof
Lived a king . . . ("SM," 245)

It is at a gangster funeral that Benya Krik is first called "The King." Sheeny Mike is even more ironically first called a king at his own funeral.[11]

This allusion to Babel serves several purposes. In the first place, it functions as a kind of literary shorthand invoking the historically alien state of Jews worldwide. But Glatshteyn does not merely invoke as precedent Babel's famous treatment of the Jewish gangster-hero. He also expands the portrait to accommodate the particular situation of an American Jew. Babel's most well-known Benya Krik story is called "Kak eto sdelalos' v odesse" (How It Was Done in Odessa). By echoing this formulation of "how it was done," Glatshteyn revises the question to ask how it is done in *America*:

Vi ozoy hot er oysgekholomt zeyn malukhe
Vi ozoy hot er geveltekt
Vi ozoy gehersht
Vi ozoy hot er porunterteynikt

Vi ozoy faryokht
Zeyn pitsl velt . . . ("SM," 244)

How did he dream up his kingdom
How did he govern
How did he rule
How did he subdue,
How did he harness
His little world . . . ("SM," 243)

Glatshteyn's theme of the gangster funeral has recognizable historical as well as literary roots. In 1908 the Jewish community of New York had been deeply shaken by an article written by the police commissioner, Theodore Bingham, alleging that Jews comprised at least half the city's criminals. Though Bingham ultimately retracted much of his article, the notion of a Jewish underworld remained an issue inside and outside the Jewish community. This became even more prominent in 1912 after the shooting of Herman "Beansey" Rosenthal, a gambler who was a friendly witness for the New York district attorney's office in an investigation of police corruption. While most of the "mainstream" press focused their coverage of the murder on issues of police and municipal corruption, the Jewish press was far more concerned with the fact that implicated in the crime were twelve Jews, including the victim and nearly all the gunmen who committed the murder. Newspapers from the ultrareligious *Judisches Tageblatt* to the socialist *Jewish Daily Forward* were determined to unearth causes for what everyone wanted to think was a departure from the Jewish historical experience.[12] The New York Jewish community, as Jenna Joselit puts it, became obsessed with "What, then, had gone awry? How was one to reconcile the promise of America with the reality of a Lefty Louie?"[13]

Ironically, for Sheeny Mike it is both the promise of the American dream and the historical exclusion from the dream of Jewish immigrants such as his old father that lead him into the world of crime. The dream of Mike's kingdom is his hope to escape his father's immigrant fate:

Der mames porshaverte bentshlaykhter
Der oremer shabbes in hoyz
Di faykhte vegt
Dem tatns bord un der mames shaytl . . . ("SM," 244)

Mama's rusty candle holders
The poor sabbath at home,
The damp walls . . . ("SM," 245)

Here, in belletristic fashion, Glatshteyn, who supported himself as a journalist for the Yiddish daily *Morgen-zhurnal* (which Arthur Goren characterizes as

"Orthodox but Anti-Zionist and conservative on social issues"),[14] enters an ongoing and broad investigation of "the environmental roots of Jewish criminality."[15]

The year before "Sheeny Mike" was written, New York was preoccupied by the murder at the age of forty-six of the powerful Jewish gangster Arnold Rothstein, purportedly by Jewish gunmen (although the case remains unsolved). The resulting uproar revived the question of whether Jewish crime was a Jewish or an American problem—although, unlike Rosenthal or "Little Augie" Orgen, Rothstein was eulogized in both the Jewish and the "mainstream" press as an urbane "American" criminal who was one of the founders of the new "business"-type gangsterism.[16]

Rothstein's sensational death was not the first event that thrust his name into the national press. The most famous (or infamous) incident connected to Rothstein was his alleged responsibility for the "fixing" of the 1919 World Series. Although it now appears that Rothstein was not actually involved in the plot, the press accused him of masterminding the entire "Black Sox" scandal. Henry Ford seized upon these stories and used them in his *Dearborn Independent* in a series of articles with titles such as "The Jewish Degradation of American Baseball" and "Jewish Gamblers Corrupt American Baseball" to represent a larger cultural construct: the foreign Jew corrupting America.[17]

This notion of Rothstein as alien Jew corrupting American values and institutions significantly informs F. Scott Fitzgerald's characterization of Meyer Wolfsheim in *The Great Gatsby*. Wolfsheim, a gambler, is identified by Jay Gatsby as "the man who fixed the World Series back in 1919."[18] Though Fitzgerald obviously bases his character upon Rothstein, he makes Wolfsheim appear far more "foreign" than Rothstein, who grew up on New York's Upper West Side rather than the Lower East Side. Although Rothstein was known for his "good looks, polished manners and 'abundant personal charm,'"[19] Wolfsheim speaks in a caricature of Yiddish-influenced English: "It was six of us at the table, and Rosy had eat and drunk a lot all evening"; "I understand you're looking for a business gonnegtion"; "He went to Oggsford College in England. You know Oggsford College?" (*GG*, 70, 71, 72). Moreover, Wolfsheim's first name, Meyer, is far more stereotypically Jewish than is "Arnold." While Rothstein was a handsome and dapper playboy who moved comfortably in high society, Wolfsheim is unappealingly described as "a small, flat-nosed Jew" with "a large head" (*GG*, 69). Fitzgerald also dwells upon Wolfsheim's profusion of nose hair (*GG*, 69–70).[20] Thus, for Fitzgerald, Wolfsheim—as well as, by extension, Rothstein—is not merely a particular man who fixed the World Series, but rather *the* generic Jew, both alien and repulsive, who attacked an important icon of American life: "The idea staggered me. I remembered, of course, that the World's Series had been fixed in 1919, but if I had thought of it all I would have thought of it as a thing that merely happened, the end of some inevitable chain. It never occurred to me that one man could start to play with the faith of fifty million people—with the single-mindedness of a burglar blowing a safe" (*GG*, 74). Nick Carraway is stunned when Wolfsheim talks business practically in the same breath in which he relates the grim fate of those involved in the Rosenthal affair: five men went to the electric chair.

Five years later, Mike Gold would add his infamously bellicose voice to the debate: "Gyp the Blood, who burned in the chair for the killing of the gambler Rosenthal, was in my class at public school. He was just the ordinary rugged East Side boy."[21] Gold also addresses the notion Fitzgerald rehearses of the Jewish gangster's polluted speech (the historical consequences of which are the subject of Sander Gilman's *Jewish Self-Hatred*) polemically elevating Yiddish as "Elizabethan" (*JWM*, 112).[22] This linguistic movement is of great import: though language, the behavioral choice of the Jewish gangster as outcast and rebel becomes a literary choice. Indeed, the idea that gangsterism is a literary choice informs Gold's novel throughout: in the third chapter, for instance, Mikey's "gang of little Yids" (*JWM*, 16) chases a sightseeing bus and pelts it with dead cats, rocks, and garbage, because "What right had that man with the megaphone to tell them lies about us?" (*JWM*, 55). Thus an unruly gang, led by a future criminal with the only-in-America nickname "Nigger," manages to challenge and overcome a mainstream narrative of lies. At the same time, Gold takes a blow at any curatorial, sentimental attraction the ghetto might have held for outsiders (an attraction that could produce works such as Hutchins Hapgood's 1902 philo-Semitic *The Spirit of the Ghetto: Studies of the Jewish Quarter of New York*)—and also perhaps at any titillation his own readers might seek: "What right had these stuckup foreigners to come and look at us?" (*JWM*, 55).[23]

By virtue of existing outside decorum—and thereby claiming access to an agency denied other East Side Jews—criminals can act as public servants. The notion of transgression as self-assertion is crucial to Jewish gangster literature; in the works of Samuel Ornitz, Mike Gold, and others, brutal gangs frequently (if briefly) become local heroes for defending Jews—usually pious, older, and frightened ones—from attacks by anti-Semitic tormenters.

Daniel Fuchs, in his three novels of the 1930s—*Summer in Williamsburg* (1934), *Homage to Blenholt* (1936), and *Low Company* (1937)—also envisions criminals as perfect American blenders and typifiers—although with a measure of contempt and despair so deep that it approaches the dystopian.[24] In *Summer in Williamsburg*, a vicious and wholly unsympathetic gangster called Papravel has intelligently if coldly mapped out a strategy for advancing in the New World. Fuchs, like Samuel Ornitz, creates criminals who are utterly at home in the teeming metropolis. Correspondingly, gangster activity has a "deracinating" effect. Fuchs emphasizes the multinationality of an organization that seems to be based partially upon the notorious Murder, Inc. Over and over, almost musically, his narrator recites the makeup of Papravel's group of "boys": "Gilhooley, two Jews, one Negro and three Italians." Thus, by "doing business" their way, Jewish gangsters become neat representatives of their multinational society—and less Jewish. (Years later, the gangster Meyer Lanksy remarked in his memoirs that he became a criminal and committed acts of violence in order to move into the American mainstream.)[25] *Homage to Blenholt* is organized around exhibitionist funeral, recalling once again Arnold Rothstein's—and his casting as an American business innovator.

Rothstein's funeral struck a deep chord in the public imagination because it was Orthodox as well as its lavish. Irving Howe and Jenna Joselit both note the tendency of Jewish gangsters to be buried according to Orthodox rules. Rites of death, furthermore, are the ones that Jews of various denominations are most likely to be conservative in following.

But despite the exaggerated traditionalism of Sheeny Mike's parents, his funeral, unlike that of Arnold Rothstein or those of the two gang members who die in the Benya Krik stories, departs in several striking ways from Jewish tradition. In the first place, Mike is buried in a coffin of bronze ("in a bronzenem orn"; "SM," 240). Although the Yiddish term *orn* explicitly signifies a casket for a Jew, this casket is bronze, not the plain wooden box generally used in traditional Jewish burials. This contradiction amplifies the poem's essential conflict: Mike's Jewishness and his deviation from it.

The use of a bronze casket also functions as a literary allusion to the caskets made of precious metals in Shakespeare's *Merchant of Venice*, a play with the repudiation of Judaism at its dramatic climax. During the early 1920s the Yiddish theater in New York put on a popular Jewish version of Shakespeare's play in which "Shylock, the poor little Jew alone in a land of lynchers, the butt of the wit and spittle of every ignorant yokel or young aristocratic punk," is betrayed by his daughter, Jessica, to "the cruel and murderous enemy."[26] Glatshteyn further revises the tale so that it is the child who is somehow betrayed and lies dead of it. His casket is not made of gold or silver—the two wrong choices in Shakespeare's play—but neither is it made of "proper" base materials—the humble lead box in *Merchant of Venice* or the simple wood of Jewish tradition. Sheeny Mike's bronze casket signifies a third choice of neither traditionalism nor complete assimilationism and establishes his membership in a new age (gold, silver, and bronze together recall their common usage to classify and evaluate periods of time). The notion of a metallic series of ages, borrowed from classical Greek poets, is suggestive in terms of "Sheeny Mike" because it depicts the progressive degeneration of races.[27] The Bronze Age, according to the ancient Greeks, was a time of fairly advanced moral deficiency. Hesiod accuses the "bronze race" of being the first to forge the sword; its members supposedly admired the works of Ares, god of war. But their biggest crime was cannibalism, and eventually they were destroyed by their own hands. Glatshteyn, through his journalistic work, knew that the murders of New York Jewish gangsters shocked the Jewish community for the picture of Jews killing—consuming, as it were—each other as well for as the general violence of the situation. Interestingly, the warmaking Ares, hero of the Bronze Age race, is imprisoned at one point for his violent transgressions in a vessel of bronze.[28]

The idea of a clash between historical periods commands the central position in one of Glatshteyn's Russian-Jewish subtexts, Ilf and Petrov's humorous novel of Soviet gangsterism *12 Stul'ev* (The Twelve Chairs). The title of Ilf and Petrov's novel is encoded within the second stanza of "Shini mayk," in which the words "twelve" and "chair" are repeated. In any case, the novel's Jewish rogue-hero, Ostap Bender, can effectively be argued to be Sheeny Mike's Soviet counterpart. He is young (in his early twenties); the nobleman Vorobyaninov and the priest Vostrikov act as his foils in the old regime/new regime dichotomy in the same way that Sheeny Mike stands out as a new modern man in contrast with his elderly parents. Bender thinks he can fit into the new Soviet society and beat it at its own game. He manipulates the particular vulnerabilities of the Soviet bureaucracy, convening, for instance, meetings of a "trade union" for pickpockets and other criminals. Sheeny Mike, for his part, is very much a product of American capitalism. Mike and Ostap Bender both end up dead, just after seeming to ascend from the level of petty thief to great heights of criminal power. Glatshteyn lends the gangster's ascent mythical proportions which he immediately undercuts: Sheeny Mike is king and ruler "iber di gantse arum un arun tsvelf blok" ("SM," 242; of twelve whole blocks).

The distancing effect of Glatshteyn's brassy inflation, and subsequent deflation, of Sheeny Mike's "success" is Brechtian in tone as well as theme. Brecht and Weill's production of *Die Dreigroschenoper* (The Threepenny Opera), which opened at the Berlin Schiffbauerdamm Theater in 1928, was an immediate hit. One of the most accessible models for Sheeny Mike is Mack the Knife, the rogue-hero of an organized kingdom of beggars and criminals. In farcical fashion, Brecht trumpets the environmental causes of crime that Glatshteyn laments:

> *Ein guter Mensch sein! Ja, wer wär's nicht gern?*
> *Sein Gut den Armen geben, warum nicht?*
> *Wenn alle gut sind, ist Sein Reich nicht fern*
> *Wer säße nicht sehr gern in Seinem Licht?*
> *Ein guter Mensch sein? Ja, wer wär's nicht gern?*
> *Doch leider sind aut diesem Sterne eben*
> *Die Mittel kärlglich und die Menschen roh.*
> *Wer möchte nicht in Fried und Eintract leben?*
> *Doch die Verhältnisse, sie sind nicht so!*[29]

> To be a good man! Sure, who wouldn't like to be one?
> To share one's belongings with the poor, why not?
> When all is good, *His* kingdom is not far
> Who would not like to bask beneath His light
> To be a good man? Sure who wouldn't like to be one?
> But sad to say, you see, upon this planet
> Our means are sparse and Man is coarse.
> Who wouldn't want to live in peace and concord?
> But circumstances just aren't so.

The tension between religious morality and economic reality is echoed in "Sheeny Mike":

> *Di avos, di frume vaserteger un fargrebte gotfortike katsovim*
> *Zeynen poblibin ach di beysoylemis fun yener zeyt.*

Pobn zey zikh nit gemit
Ven der tata mit di royte oygen hot bahahovidik
Bozetst dem dullus in hoyz mit zeyn gazang ("SM," 242)

The forefathers, the pious waterbearers and coarsened God-fearing
　　butchers,
Stayed behind in the cemeteries over there.
They did not intercede
When Papa with his red eyes generously
Furnished the house with chanting ("SM," 243)

The difference is that while Brecht implies that things have always been so—

Doch leider hat man bisher nie vernommen
Daß etwas recht war—und dann war's auch so! (*DGO*, 11)

But sad to say one never yet has heard of
That what is right really come about!

—Glatshteyn sets up an Old World–New World dichotomy, in which Jewish morality, along with Jewish traditions, has become atavistic.

　　Glatshteyn's simultaneous legend-making and legend-smashing in "Sheeny Mike" make use of *Verfremdung*, a technique mostly associated with Brecht. For instance, each time the stature of Glatshteyn's "king" rises, the ludicrousness of his kingdom of twelve blocks is stressed. This process is particularly striking in the poem's final stanza, which describes Mike's sweetheart weeping over his coffin. His appeal to her as dashing and noble is coupled with attributes that contradict this appeal:

Iz er geven der eydlman
Der raytndiker riter,
Der temper yung, der shiker ("SM," 244)

He was the nobleman,
The knight on horseback,
The dumb guy, the drunkard ("SM," 245)

　　In this stanza Mike as a character, along with the little we know about him, has disappeared. Instead of a picture of Mike smiling in a casket of bronze, there is just the casket of bronze.

　　Mike's approaching girlfriend also inverts a story from the Torah about the Rabbi Akiba, a poor shepherd who becomes a great teacher of Jewish law. The young Akiba is cast out after secretly becoming betrothed to his boss's daughter; he devotes twelve years (echoed in the twelve blocks) to studying and teaching before returning as a famous sage. After he has finally revealed himself to his beloved's father as a great scholar of the Law, he approaches his betrothed, who attempts to draw near him through a crowd and is held back. Akiba calls out to let her pass, just as the narrative voice of "Sheeny Mike" repeats in this final stanza, "Lozt zi tsu tsum brondzenes arum" ("SM," 244; let her through to the coffin of bronze). That this modern Akiba, Sheeny Mike, is on the other side of the law adds a bitter note to the legend.

The inclusion and subsequent pushing away of the reader is reinforced by the poem's rhythmical structure. In the first poem Mike is described as "Der shrek un der hiter, der meylehk un gebiter" ("SM," 240; the terror and guardian, the ruler and king). The regular rhythm and internal rhyme of this line give it a sing-song sound that is comforting in its simplicity. The lulling effect is immediately interrupted with the jarring strophes "arum tsvelf blok" ("SM," 242; of twelve whole blocks).

Sheeny Mike's mythologized and degraded ascent toward realization of "the dream of his kingdom" is couched in the poem's second stanza in specifically biblical terms. Mike's youthful dreaming on the rooftops is reminiscent of Jesus' temptation by Satan:

> Once more the devil led him to a very high mountain and showed him
> all the kingdoms of the world and their glory, and said to him: All this I
> will give you if you will throw yourself down and worship me.[30]

> *Do, Af dem dakh hot er dokh dem kholem fun zayn kinigraykh derzen.*
> *Di tsiteldiker vesh afn di shtreyk*
> *Zeynen geven zeyne langen* ("SM," 242)

> Here, on the roof, he saw the dream of his kingdom.
> The flapping sheets on the lines
> Were his plains ("SM," 242)

This equation of American commercial success with worldly temptation establishes Mike as the corrupted, not the corrupter. Furthermore, the ironic association Glatshteyn is making of a small-time gangster with the Christian messiah places him in the company of modernist writers, such as Antonin Artaud, and painters, such as Joan Miró, who experimented in their work with the forms and rituals of hagiography in their own renderings of "modern" life.

The metaphor of Christ also allows the figure of Mike to stand in once again for the position of American Jews as a people. Christ was, after all, a Jewish boy whose birth and death served for centuries as an excuse for the Christian persecution of Jews. As has already been noted, the "mainstream" press in New York presented examples of Jewish gangsters like Sheeny Mike as empirical evidence of Jewish moral inferiority. The question that remains is, of course, "Who crucified Sheeny Mike?"

Glatshteyn is not alone in his invocation of the sacrificial to characterize the social position of the Jewish gangster. A particularly resonant image in Gold's *Jews without Money* encompasses the fluctuating identity of victim versus victimizer in its entirety: that of the saloon goat who lies on the sidewalk outside the bar, lazily munching whatever comes to hand, including scraps of newspaper. As James Bloom points out, the goat "obviously and comically . . . exhibits the critical outsider's hunger for culture that characterizes proletarian writing of the thirties, from Gold's *Jews Without Money* to Richard Wright's *Black Boy*."[31] But the goat is just as obviously (and comically) performing a slapstick act of cultural resistance, made even more suggestive for our purposes by the fact that at one point the goat chews up a copy of the *Police Gazette*. Gold's narrator has already stated that a certain cop—whom he goes so far as to mention by name—"tipped the balances that swung Nigger into his career of gangster" (*JWM*, 29). The goat, both consuming and pulverizing, represents the sacrificial as well as the resistant aspect of the gangster: in Jewish folklore, a pure white kid is akin to the Christians' snowy Lamb of God. Furthermore, at that time (indeed, to this day) the single most popular Yiddish song was Goldfaden's "Rozhinkes mit mandlen" (Raisins and Almonds)—a song Gold names as having been his father's favorite.[32] In it a mother sings to her child that while he sleeps, a kid will go to market to bring him raisins and almonds. While it is pretty to think of the white goat returning with a basket of goodies over its arm, that is not how goats fetch food: it has been slaughtered and sold. Thus, the masticating saloon goat is both innocent sacrifice (to the marketplace) and survivor—it is able to live on cast-off garbage and breaks the skull of a drunken sailor who confronts it. As well, the goat image strongly evokes Ornitz's *Haunch Paunch and Jowl*, in which the Jewish gangster-protagonist carries the childhood nickname of Ziegelle, or little goat. (Mikey also describes Nigger "leap[ing] gaps between the tenements like a mountain goat" [*JWM*, 28].)

That this whole tension operates among these writers on such a self-consciously literary—and metaliterary—level further indicates the importance of the gangsters to a literary enterprise: addressing the contest of loyalties facing the Jewish writer in America, in modernist literature, and in the sphere of the modern generally. Glatshteyn's language in "Sheeny Mike" reproduces the contest of loyalty that it portrays. Glatshteyn and his circle chose to write in Yiddish as a muscular cultural assertion. This structural choice, they felt, identified their work as *Jewish* poetry: "We are 'Jewish poets' simply because we are Jews and write in Yiddish. No matter what a Yiddish poet writes in Yiddish, it is ipso facto Jewish. One does not need any particular Jewish themes."[33] At the same time, these poets lamented the fact that their choice of language alienated them from the American community that they felt a part of and (at least initially) embraced. Because they write in Yiddish, they remain in internal exile: "So many years in America, such a fine literature created here, and we remain strangers to our neighbors as if we had lived in Siam, or had written in some Eskimo dialect."[34]

Glatshteyn's Yiddish plays out semantically the choices that face American Jews. "Sheeny Mike" contains within it an unusual number of Hebrew words (even when there is a Yiddish alternative)—and a large number of English words. Similarly, Sheeny Mike's Yiddish-speaking father struggles to translate from Hebrew into English: "Oy, sculchon—a taybel, un Keesay—a chair" ("SM," 242).

As Harshav points out, the profusion of foreign and Hebrew words underlies the linguistic and cultural richness of the Yiddish language, the Yiddish poet and the Yiddish readership, a richness Glatshteyn and his contemporaries were anxious to demonstrate.[35] But such considered emphasis on the contradistinct presence within American Yiddish of different language forms throws into sharp relief the clash between worlds. As well, the linguistic Otherness of Jews, and particularly of the Jewish poet, is underscored by the resultant strangeness of all three languages. Furthermore, the linguistic triplet that emerges in the poem—Ancient Hebrew, Yiddish, and American English—recalls the three ages inferred (gold, silver, and now bronze).

A complicated language system is a necessary component of Glatshteyn's poetics. Over the course of his poetic career, Glatshteyn returned repeatedly to the phrase *velt-plonter*, or tangle of the world. The In Zikh poets, in their poetry as well as in their theoretical articles, asserted that a straightforward approach was impossible. Not only would it be boring (Glatshteyn warned against "monotony" in poetry on more than one occasion)[36]—but it could not adequately represent the complicated internal life of Jews ("A Yiddish poet's song must be confused," Glatshteyn's friend and In Zikh colleague Aaron Glanz-Leyeles (who used the pseudonym A. Leyeles) had written three years earlier).[37]

The irregular, multidimensional "kaleidoscope technique" that the Inzikhim found particularly adaptable to the Jewish experience was a central part of the cultural aura of the 1920s. The expressionists had already noted that being true to the world demanded no less than chaos. In the Yiddish journal *Albatross* (Warshow, 1922), Uri Zvi Grinburg, who had been a soldier and deserter in World War I, wrote:

> This is how things are. Whether we want it or not. We stand as we are: with slash-lipped wounds, rolled up veins, unscrewed bones, after artillery bombardments and cries of "Hurrah," after gas-attacks; after bowls filled with gall and opium and daily water: disgust. And the foam of decay covers our lips.
>
> Hence the atrocious in the poem.
> Hence the chaotic in the image.
> Hence the scream in the blood.
>
> . . . It is imperative to write such poems. Atrocious. Chaotic. Bleeding.[38]

Similarly, the Italian and Russian futurists called for the breaking down of artificially imposed temporal and spatial boundaries. And Henri Bergson's theory of simultaneity informed the theory of all avant-garde art. Glatshtyen found the intersecting planes of influence, the chaos, within the fluid identity of Sheeny Mike.

If the New World experience molded the criminal character of Sheeny Mike, then why invoke the presence of gangsters back in Eastern Europe? It is unlikely that Glatshteyn ever fully resolved this tension. In 1934 he returned briefly to Europe and felt distanced from the Old World; in 1938 he wrote "Good Night, World," bitterly rejecting Western cultures in general and American culture in particular. In "Sheeny Mike" Glatshteyn seems to indicate that plainly, Jews have come to America—for better or worse they have "cut through the dirty water" on the journey to the New World. But although this ambiguous journey will shape their individual and collective identity, they do come dragging cultural baggage. Their vessels are "schvere schlepshifen" ("SM," 242; heavy tugboats), and the cargo cannot be omitted from considerations of Jewish ethnicity.

At the same time Glatshteyn is anxious to dispense with cultural positions that posit Jewish ethnicity in a rigid or reductive fashion. In the figure of the gangster Glatshteyn finds a model that is sufficiently fluid for his purposes. This heroic and marginalized figure allows him to connect his poetry to both Jewish and non-Jewish literary works, as well as both American and European ones, in which the figure of the gangster is important—while taking into account the peculiar conditions of New York's Lower East Side.

At the end of the twentieth century, the aesthetic experience of the Jewish gangster is still capturing the public imagination—particularly, it seems, on the screen. Americans have witnessed a host of recent offering—such as *Bugsy* (1991), *Billy Bathgate* (1991), *Miller's Crossing* (1990), *The Plot against Harry* (1989), and *Once upon a Time in America* (1984). Similarly, glasnost and the subsequent social and economic developments in the (former) Soviet Union brought a spate of new movies about black-marketeers and other organized criminals. But the focus is different. Gone is the intense inner debate about what it means to be a Jew while crafting a New World identity. The metaphor of transgression (social and literary) provided by the gangster no longer has the same direct poignancy. For instance, in E. L. Doctorow's 1989 novel *Billy Bathgate*, the gangster Dutch Schultz speaks in the same Yiddish-inflected English that Fuchs's Shubunka or, for that matter, Fitzgerald's Wolfsheim uses: "Show her how you can't do certain things anymore in your life, Bo. Show her how the simplest thing, crossing your legs, scratching your nose, it can't be done anymore by you."[39] But Schultz (whose real name was Arthur Fleigenheimer) was a German Jew whose first language would not have been Yiddish. The point is not that Doctorow has made a mistake, but rather that his concerns are elsewhere: the relationships among Jewishness, criminality, and linguistic power have lost their immediacy, and Schultz's characterization as a Jewish criminal has become somewhat of a stylistic question of association for modern readers. To put it simply, Doctorow is marking the thief as a Jew, rather than the Jew as a thief. The impact of World War II certainly had much to do with inserting a whole new set of reference points for meditations on the position of the Jew and the Jewish writer in society.

Critical work under the rubric of "ethnic studies" has usefully located the creation of criminal or near-criminal types by "ethnic" American writers (for example, the African American "badman" or the Chicano *pachuco* or *vato loco*) at the center of literary traditions striving to negotiate a position that can encompass the feeling of "double consciousness" articulated by W. E. B. Du Bois. Regarded in this way, Glatshteyn's use of a criminal Jew, represented as caught between words and worlds, becomes a complicated reflection on monolingualism in the United States. If crime movies taught the American public "to look over our shoulders at night,"[40] perhaps Glatshteyn and Sheeny Mike can teach us to do the same thing as readers and scholars. American literary studies may as a result indeed be better off.

■ NOTES

Portions of this essay appear in my book, *Jewish Gangsters of Modern Literature* (Urbana: University of Illinois Press, 2000).

1. Robert Warshow, *The Immediate Experience* (New York: Atheneum, 1970), 130.

2. *Little Caesar*, dir. Mervyn LeRoy (Warner Brothers/First National, 1930). *The Public Enemy*, dir. William Wellman (Warner Brothers, 1931).

3. The name "In Zikh" (literally, "in the self") is translated as "Introspectionism." For more on the introspectionists, see Benjamin Harshav, "Introspectivism: A Modernist Poetics," in *American Yiddish Poetry: A Bilingual Anthology*, ed. and trans. Benjamin Harshav and Barbara Harshav, with Kathryn Hellerstein, Brian McHale, and Anita Norich (Berkeley: University of California Press, 1986), 36–44.

4. Werner Sollors argues suggestively in *Beyond Ethnicity: Consent and Descent in American Culture* (New York: Oxford University Press, 1986), 247–248, that connections with experimental artistic movements in Europe frequently made ethnic writers in the United States "modern" faster or earlier than their more "mainstream" contemporaries who lacked this access.

5. There was a "real life" Sheeny Mike in New York: Michael Kurtz, who was known by that name during the 1880s, was allegedly the "champion burglar of America" (Moses Rischin, *The Promised City: New York's Jews, 1870–1914* [Cambridge: Harvard University Press, 1962], 89).

6. Leo Rosten, *The Joys of Yiddish* (New York: McGraw Hill, 1968), 334.

7. A. Leyeles, "Jewish Art," in Harshav and Harshav, *American Yiddish Poetry*, 789.

8. Warshow, *The Immediate Experience*, 130.

9. Isaak Babel, *Detstvo i drugie rasskazy* [Childhood and Other Stories] (Jerusalem: Aliya, 1979), 247; hereafter cited parenthetically in text as *DDR*. Translations of Babel are by Walter Morison in *The Collected Stories of Isaac Babel*, trans. and ed. Walter Morison (New York: New American Library, 1955); hereafter cited parenthetically in text as *CSIB*. Babel was later attacked by members of Stalin's administration for having done harm to the Russian language through his inclusion of *chuzhaya rech*.' In his *Style and Structure in the Prose of Isaac Babel*, Efraim Sicher explicates in some detail the linguistic interference in Babel's short fiction of various vernacular forms: Yiddish dialects, criminal slang, Odessan slang, and so forth (see Efraim Sicher, *Style and Structure in the Work of Isaac Babel* [Columbus, Oh.: Slavica, 1985]).

10. Jacob Glatshetyn, "Sheeny Mike," in Harshav and Harshav, *American Yiddish Poetry* (241–247); hereafter cited as "SM."

11. Of course, there is a long-standing literary tradition that makes use of such "inverted kingdoms," stretching back at least as far as Shakespeare (especially Falstaff's role-playing in the Henriad)—for instance, Fagan's "little kingdom" in Charles Dickens's *Oliver Twist*. This inversion implicitly and explicitly calls into question, indeed criticizes, social hierarchy.

12. Jenna Weissman Joselit, *Our Gang: Jewish Crime and the New York Jewish Community, 1900–1940* (Bloomington: Indiana University Press, 1983), 84.

13. Joselit, *Our Gang*, 77.

14. Arthur Goren, *New York Jews and the Quest for Community: The Kehillah Experiment, 1908–1922* (New York: Columbia University Press, 1970), 26.

15. Joselit, *Our Gang*, 20.

16. Ibid., 140–141. The first movie about Arnold Rothstein, *King of the Roaring Twenties: The Story of Arnold Rothstein*, dir. Joseph M. Newman (Allied Artists, 1961), manages to convey Rothstein's stylish good looks. More recently, *Eight Men Out*, dir. John Sayles (Orion, 1988), which blames the White Sox scandal on Rothstein, replicates the Fitzgerald model of the criminal Jew: Rothstein is presented as fat and sloppy and appears onscreen almost exclusively while eating rapaciously.

17. Joselit, *Our Gang*, 145. This vision of immigrant pollution of "real" American culture had its academic proponents as well. A notable example was Van Wyck Brooks, who expressed open dismay over the fact that, as he saw it, the influx of non-English-speaking immigrants as well as the younger generation of critics from immigrant stock (including H. L. Mencken) had taken over, destroying the New England cultural community with their detachment from American past. Brooks expresses a futile and xenophobic desire to elevate what he calls the "hereditary American" ("America's Coming-of-Age," 134). The activities of the Immigrant Restriction League, capped by the 1924 National Origins Act limiting immigration, depended upon similar reasoning.

18. F. Scott Fitzgerald, *The Great Gatsby* (1925; reprint, New York: Charles Scribner's Sons, 1953), 74; hereafter cited parenthetically in text as *GG*.

19. Joselit, *Our Gang*, 142.

20. For a detailed treatment of the Jewish nose as a marker for perversion, see Sander Gilman, *The Jew's Body* (New York: Routledge, 1991).

21. Mike Gold, *Jews without Money* (1930; reprint, New York: International, 1942), 125; hereafter cited parenthetically in text as *JWM*.

22. Likewise, he characterizes the dance of a ghetto child to a street organ-grinder as a Morris dance (32). In *Call It Sleep*, Henry Roth accomplishes the same elevation of Yiddish by rendering it into a lyrical, lovely English, while representing the Jewish characters' actual spoken English as halting and rough (1934; New York: Farrar, Straus, and Giroux, 1991).

23. A 1965 reissue of *Jews without Money*, perhaps heedless of this warning, screams in headline type across the back cover "NEW YORK'S TENEMENT POOR" and goes on to promise the "anguished sound of . . . thieves, whores, pimps, gangsters, and the honest oppressed."

24. Daniel Fuchs, *Three Novels by Daniel Fuchs: "Summer in Williamsburg," "Homage to Blenholt," "Low Company"* (New York: Basic Books, 1961).

25. See Joselit, *Our Gang*, 169–170.

26. Michael Folsom, ed., *Mike Gold: A Literary Anthology* (New York: International, 1972), 312.

27. Hesiod discusses the various "Ages of Man" in the "Works and Days" (*Poems of Hesiod*, trans. R. M. Frazer [Norman: University of Oklahoma Press, 1983], 92–142). Subsequent

loci classici for this conception, which was a common one in Greek and Roman poetry, include Aratus, Lucretius, Catullus, and Vergil.

28. H. J. Rose, *A Handbook of Greek Mythology* (New York: E. P. Dutton, 1959), 157–158.

29. Berthold Brecht and Kurt Weill, *Die Dreigroschenoper* (1928; New York: CBS Masterworks, 1982), 11. The translation is by Guy Stern.

30. Matthew 4:8–9, *The Four Gospels and the Revelation*, trans. Richmond Lattimore (New York: Pocket Books, 1979), 49.

31. James Bloom, *Left Letters* (New York: Columbia University Press, 1992), 37.

32. Folsom, *Mike Gold*, 304.

33. Glatshteyn, Leyeles, and Minkov, "Introspectivism" (Manifesto of 1919), in Harshav and Harshav, *American Yiddish Poetry*, 774.

34. A. Leyeles, "Yiddish Literature and the World," in Harshav and Harshav, *American Yiddish Poetry*, 801.

35. Harshav, *The Meaning of Yiddish* (Berkeley: University of California Press, 1990), 72.

36. Glatshteyn, "Chronicle of a Movement: Excerpts from Introspectionist Criticism," in Harshav and Harshav, *American Yiddish Poetry*.

37. A. Leyeles, "Autumn," in Harshav and Harshav, *American Yiddish Poetry*, 123.

38. Quoted in Harshav and Harshav, *American Yiddish Poetry*, 40.

39. E. L. Doctorow, *Billy Bathgate* (New York: Harper and Row, 1989), 27.

40. Carlos Clarens, *Crime Movies: An Illustrated History* (New York: W. W. Norton, 1980), 14.

Beware of Signs; or, How to Tell the Living from the Dead

Orality and Writing in the Work of Pedro Pietri

■

I first met Pedro Pietri's voice on a recording of a performance at the Casa Puerto Rico in New York. Over a background of talking and laughing voices, applause, cheering, and an occasional crying child, Pietri chanted, shouted, laughed, sang, whispered, and groaned his "Puerto Rican Obituary" and other poems, going back and forth across the blurred order of English and Spanish as shaped by the Nuorican experience.[1] Ten years later I met him again, in person, after a performance of his play *No More Bingo at the Wake*, which also explores the forms and genres of the oral collective voice of his community.

On the record, Pietri begins by introducing the shopping bag in which he carries his manuscripts and then launches into his first poem: "Beware of signs that say / 'Aqui se habla Espanol.'" The Spanish words are delivered with a thick Anglo accent: the stress on the wrong syllable ("Espànol"), the retracted English /l/, the inability to pronounce the Spanish /ñ/. This was Pietri's way of making us aware that we were not merely hearing the oral rendition of a written text (a "poetry reading"), but listening to a performance in which orality is inherent to meaning: a poem inspired by the sounds of speech and conceived to be communicated by the living voice.

The Anglo accent, of course, stands for the distorted communication generated by an unequal social relationship. But meaning goes deeper than that. In fact, the question it raises is: How can a *sign* have an *accent*? In fact, how can a written sign *say* anything?

Chirographic and typographic cultures have generated the metaphor that written texts "speak," that they have something to "say": a useful one, but still only a metaphor, one that enjoyed its greatest vogue and relevance in late-eighteenth- and early-nineteenth-century literature in such different genres as the satires of Jonathan Swift and Washington Irving, on one hand, and the autobiographies of such Africans and African Americans as James Albert Ukawsaw Gronniosaw and John Marrant.[2] The meanings are not necessarily the same, and in Third World and ethnic writing the "trope of the talking book" usually implies a confrontation with the dominant culture. In the archetypical episode, when Spanish missionaries handed him a Bible, the Inca Atahualpa threw it to the ground, declaring that the book "didn't say anything to him, didn't say a word."[3]

The metaphor acquired literal credibility as writing gradually expropriated the spoken word of its cultural power and became the only legitimized way of "saying" anything that is worth being "heard." Pedro Pietri's wordplay, then, reminds us of our distorted perception of *all* "signs," not just those in store windows, and of the active presence of orality in our time and culture.

While most critics describe only two types of orality—the "primary" one of traditional cultures, and the "secondary" one of electronics and mass media—the most fascinating, complex, and advanced functions of orality are expressed in the intermediate stages, where the spoken, the written, and the electronic word coexist and influence each other. The poetry of Pedro Pietri is an expression of this stage. It is an example of the "powerful and beautiful verbal performances of high artistic and human worth" that Walter J. Ong concedes can be produced by oral cultures but avails itself of writing (the manuscripts in the shopping bag) and of electronics (the record).[4] Thus, Pietri cannot be labeled either a "writer" or an "oral poet." His works are not composed purely in memory or in performance, as those of strictly oral cultures are, and yet they are shaped by the experience and perspective of orality; they are printed on books, told at performances, and recorded on LPs, their ultimate form. The "technologies" of the word do not replace one another in linear chronological progress but coalesce in the process of composition in the finished "text" and in the forms in which it is communicated.

Says Pietri:

> I was writing poetry since 1957. . . . There was this group called Frankie Lymon and the Teenagers. Frankie Lymon and the Teenagers was a rock group; they did "Why Do Fools Fall in Love." We used to live near those people, we used to play baseball with them. And the fact that he wrote that song gave us a motive to survive—it doesn't have to be that bad if we get a rock and roll group, we sing good, we can survive in society. So that's where I got my first inspiration for writing.[5]

As Pietri's poetry would be, "Why Do Fools Fall in Love" is a convergence of technologies of the word: composed orally, tried out at street corners, recorded, and broadcast, it finally inspired one of the neighborhood kids to write.

Pietri recalls Amsterdam Avenue in East Harlem, where he used to live, as a multicultural society, where cultures and languages interacted. He was exposed to them all, and yet was taught that he had no language and culture of his own: most of his Spanish was soon lost; his English was not good enough to enable him to pass the civil service tests, and it did not sound right to his teachers.

> Like I said, it was in 1957 when I started in oral tradition by memorizing all the poems I wrote. A few rock and roll songs. And then from the experience of the factory. I started writing about this, you know. . . .

Yeah, I used to memorize all my poems. And I'd sit in parties, and bars—they were just poems to make people feel good. There were my aunts and uncles, the men in the family used to know these songs that went on for hours and they were singin' it and singin' it, you know.

Even after he came in contact with the world of books, working at the library of Columbia University and meeting poets such as Allen Ginsberg, Amiri Baraka, Ted Jones, and Gregory Corso, Pietri retained the sound of speech as a criterion for poetry: "I was introduced to Langston Hughes, who became one of my favorite poets. . . . I mean, he was a poet; he wasn't about words, he was a poet, he had rhythm." So does Pedro Pietri. By means of rhythm, tone, volume, and accent, he incorporates in his performance all the personae of the oral bards and verbal artists of his culture. His chanted delivery ranges from mimicry of the monotone of the written word to the impersonality of the ballad singer; from the straight face of the standup comedian ("September Hangover") to the incantatory patterns of preaching, praying, and nursery rhyming (and the respective parodies: "Himno de Papa Dios," the fortune teller in "Puerto Rican Obituary"); from the dirty "dozens" ("Sex and the Virgin Mary") to soap-box oratory (and its parody again: "Himno"). The choral, antiphonal patterns of formalized collective speech, stylized and thematized in his play *No More Bingo at the Wake* (1985), amplify the voice of the community shouting in slogans, mumbling litanies, and calling the numbers of the Bingo game.

Sound is at the center of this poetry. The voice changes pace suddenly after a long monotone; it soars to a scream and drops to a whisper and a groan. Rhythms break and change, pauses arrive—or fail to arrive—unexpectedly. Rhyme and assonance pile up words into hammered riffs that establish a rhythmic urgency only to break it into ironic relief as the patter broadens, changes, or just dissolves:

I hate the world
I am dejected
I am neglected and disrespected
ever since these damn liberals got elected
and corrected nothing really important
("Suicide Note of a Cockroach in a Low Income Housing Project")

The humor is based on the sound shape of language and on its relationship to time. The interplay of English and Spanish sounds underlines the ironic contrast between the formulaic speech of television, advertising, politics, organized religion, and the flow of everyday street sounds. The wordplay of punning and the associations of incompatible words and ideas ("the make-believe steaks / and the bullet-proof rice and beans" in "Puerto Rican Obituary") rely for effect on time: they must be quick, sudden, self contained; they must follow each other in quick succession, like the one-liners of the stand-up comedian. Clearly, this device is much more at home in a time-related medium such as orality than in spatial, simultaneous writing.

This type of orality is, however, far from a carryover from archaic cultures or a nostalgia for a mythical past. Though Pietri is also related to the folk tradition, his voice and poetry are shaped by the contemporary urban experience. "Suicide Note of a Cockroach in a Low-Income Housing Project" has roots in the classics of oral tradition, such as "The Ballad of the Boll Weevil": the project dweller identifies with the insect that infests his apartment, much as the black sharecropper identified with the insect that destroyed his crop. But the poem is also reminiscent of Amiri Baraka's (a friend of Pietri's) *Preface to a Twenty-Volume Suicide Note*—a relationship ironically stressed by the bulk of the suicide note that, in his spoken introduction on the record, Pietri says was found lying at the side of the insect's dead body.

As is always the case in oral tradition, old forms in new contexts express new functions and meanings. Though Pietri's later poetry (as collected in *Traffic Violations*)[6] is much more personal and literary, we can still detect there all the verbal devices of oral poetry: parallelism and paratacticism; strophic structures connected by anaphoric links (refrains); alliteration, repetition, and word lists. In the title poem, Pietri uses incremental repetition to create a surrealistic atmosphere; in "Intermission from Monday," repetition in the form of tautology represents a radical dislocation of reality, where things are no longer themselves. Both the nightmarish atmosphere and the paratactic accumulation of glimpses of vision in "Fifth Untitled Poem" and many others remind us of another oral poet of the electronic age, Bob Dylan. Indeed, many of Pietri's titles—"April 15th until Further Notice" or "Manual Typewriter Revisited"—have a Bob Dylan flavor.

The relationship between Pietri's perception of contemporary reality and his preoccupation with words, sounds, and signs is best revealed by a key poem such as "Do Not Observe the No Smoking Sign":

I once met a Bus Driver
With fifty fifty vision
Who had a sign on his neon mind
Informing the passengers
The exact fare to go somewhere

On this bus will be announced
A few weeks after the trip ends
DO NOT OBSERVE THE NO SMOKING SIGN
Anyone caught using seatbelts on the bus
Will not be allowed to ride with us.

Conflicting messages, signs telling us not to obey signs, generate chaos and rebellion; only at the end of the ride will we know what its cost was. To understand this poem, we must go back to the source of Pietri's surrealistic vision: the presence of death in the midst of life, the blurring of life and death in contemporary urban society, and the roots of life and death in the immigration experience. "It goes back to a long time ago," Pietri remembers. "It goes back to 1945; when my parents, right, they left paradise looking for paradise. . . . During the adventure of Operation Bootstrap, a lot of people were brainwashed to believe that if they leave there you can have a better life over here." Only at the end of the plane ride is the "fare" announced; only after they land into their "broken English dream" (another Pietri title) do the immigrants begin to glimpse what the trip cost.

"Here you have all these changes of season, and they didn't know the language, the education that they received there was what you would call an education to survive there, not to survive here." They could not read the endless, threatening signs that greeted them at the airport:

> We follow the sign
> that says welcome to america
> but keep your hands off the property
> violators will be electrocuted
> follow the garbage truck
> to the welfare department
> if you cannot speak english
> ("The Broken English Dream")

In America streets are lined with "funeral parlors with neon signs that said / Customers wanted No experience necessary."

> My grandfather committed suicide in '48, he came here in '47. My father died of double pneumonia in '49, because of the change in atmosphere, they didn't know how to dress properly for the weather, so, let's say a few years after the migration we started going to all these funerals, because people couldn't adapt, either they committed suicide or they died because they did not understand the climate. . . . So at a very early age, we were constantly in mourning, for my father in '48, for my grandfather in '49, for some relatives in '50. And I was very young, and I said, is this what life is all about.

Later, he would write about "the metaphor of being alive" ("I Hate Trees"). His poetry describes the presence of death all around us as a metaphor for mental death into assimilation, subordination, frustration, despair—in "the nervous breakdownstreets / where the mice live like millionaires / and the people do not live at all" ("Puerto Rican Obituary"). This is "the world of walking canes and pace makers" ("April 15th until Further Notice"): the pun hints that in this world things walk around as if they were alive (*walking* canes!), while humans are turned into part-machines, and their movements (their "pace") are "made" by the machine inside them. In this pre-cyberpunk vision, human beings become walking corpses, while inanimate things develop a soul and a will of their own; things are in the saddle, and the people turned into things come back as zombies to haunt us—like

"Your dead english teacher who keeps coming / back to life to make sure you don't get a raise or promotion" ("Intermission for Friday"). This is Pietri's metaphor for the fetishism of commodities and the acquisitive society.

In this process, signs play a key role. The bus driver's mind becomes a neon sign—another human is turned machine.[7] He finally disappears, but after the ride, signs come back to haunt us: "The following morning / All the passengers read in the newspaper / THIS HAS BEEN A RECORDING." The telephone operator's message has an "aural" aspect, but it also possesses the repetitive, detached, impersonal fixity of writing. This is why it is so easily picked up by the newspapers: it is a mechanical, disembodied voice—a *sign* that *speaks*, like the ones Pietri has been telling us to beware of, and like the ghostly, disembodied voices of computers, constructs, and artificial intelligence in the postmodern science fiction of William Gibson.[8] Like the trip the fare for which will be announced only after its completion, so the recorded message reveals its true nature only after it has deceived us into thinking it was "live." Most important, you cannot talk back to it, just as you cannot talk back to a book: "There is no way directly to refute a text," writes Walter J. Ong: "After absolutely total and devastating refutation, it says exactly the same thing as before."[9] Finally, by telling us not to obey it, the message puts us in a double bind: there is no way of escaping the power of signs. Whether we smoke or not, we will still be following a sign's direction. The message all signs share is our subordination to them—and to those who own them.

Signs, then, become the battleground of the class struggle between life and death. In the poems of *Puerto Rican Obituary* Pietri explores the life-giving possibilities of private and communal orality; in the much more personal and "written" *Traffic Violations*, though he still seems to assume oral performance as a setting (in "Eleventh Untitled Poem" he speaks of hearing the poem in "an auditorium"; in "Poem for My Daughter" he writes "recite" a poem), Pietri scrutinizes the act and experience of writing: the solitude of the writer-poet is described in the confrontation with the "flawless blank page," "the "magnificent blank page" ("1st Untitled Poem"). A lifeless object that resists our need to speak, the blank page becomes at times a representative of hostile institutions ("the official blank page," in "13th Untitled Poem"). But it is also the innocent target of the writer's aggression: he will cause it to lose the "privilege to be blank" ("8th Untitled Poem"). The sexual overtones in the struggle between the flawless blank page and the thin pencil (again and again dropped to the floor) heighten the conflict within the writer: one cannot possess innocence without violating it and losing one's own, and the poet knows that he will be turned into a speaking sign if he writes but will be silenced if he does not.

> I know it will be very unwise of me
> To lose sleep over writing this poem
> When the correct thing for me to do
> Is to lose sleep over keeping the page blank
> ("1st Untitled Poem")

The contradiction is inherent in the terms he uses: keeping the page blank is "correct" because it will keep it from becoming a sign; but the very idea of doing the "correct" thing sends us ironically back to the world of rules and grammar. Thus, the only way of resisting a system that negates us by means of signs is to upset their "correct" order.

"To the United States we came" / To learn how to misspell our names" ("The Broken English Dream"); the factory gave us "punched cards with out names misspelled" ("I Hate Trees"). "Newspapers / that misspelled mispronounced / and misunderstood our names" taught the immigrants that they have no identity nor real citizenship. The poet reacts by turning the disruption into an offensive weapon: he proclaims that "the end has come to the correct spelling of words" ("Missing in Action") and teaches his daughter the importance of "misspelling words correctly" ("Poem for My Daughter"). "There is no alphabetical order / To restrain the element of surprise," he declares, in a poem called "Last Days of Up and Down," printed upside down, like a literally sub-verted sign, playing with type as he has played with sounds.[10]

Yet, the battle is far from won: in fact, the signs, so to speak, are not encouraging. In "Purple Pedestrian," while an old woman offers a child a piece of paper "With all the names / Of his friends & enemies/ Misspelled perfectly," the losers go on "slurring and staggering / All the way to the last / Letter of the alphabet" and back to their rooms, where they lie in the dark with their eyes open and a "blank expression." They have become blank pages, and one can imagine how their faces in the dark reflect the changing lights of the neon sides outside the window.

The tension between the sound of names and their spelling, the battle between orality and writing over identity, turns out to be another form of the blurring of life and death, the blurring of the line between lifeless objects and animated beings. Pietri seems to feel that writing has vampirized us: things learned to speak and made us speechless. They now speak to us, write upon us, and we can neither talk back nor talk to one another.

Communication with the dead (the fortune teller in "Puerto Rican Obituary"; "I Hate Trees") becomes a metaphor of the yearning to communicate with the living, who have become indistinguishable from the dead. But we cannot communicate with others unless they are alive, and they can prove they are alive only by communicating with us. If our message meets with no response, if no one talks back to us, then we are no better than recorded messages—we are dead, too.

Signs, then, are dangerous when they only communicate in one direction. To the frozen, unilateral messages of the dominant culture, Pietri opposes the flexible, multilateral communication of orality. The live performance of poetry, the call and response of antiphonal speech forms, the exchange of conversation, become metaphors of survival. "Adults . . . are buried," he writes, "when the conversation is dropt" ("Poem for My Daughter").

Let us "beware of signs," then: on the lower frequencies, Pedro Pietri speaks for us. Like the immigrants in the last lines of "Puerto Rican Obituary," we are dead, he warns us, we are dead, and we shall not return from the dead until we stop "neglecting the art of our dialogue for broken-English lessons."

■ NOTES

1. *Aquí se habla Español,* discos Coqui Stereo CP 1203. Among Pedro Pietri's other records on the Folkways label are *Loose Joints* and *One Is a Crowd.*

2. Henry Louis Gates Jr., "The Trope of the Talking Book," in *The Signifying Monkey: A Theory of Afro-American Literary Criticism* (New York: Oxford University Press, 1988), 127–169.

3. Anita Seppilli, *La memoria e l'assenza: Tradizione orale e civiltà della scrittura nell'America dei conquistadores* (Bologna: Cappelli, 1979), 30.

4. Walter J. Ong, *Orality and Literacy: The Technologizing of the Word* (London and New York: Methuen, 1982), 15–16.

5. Interview with Pedro Pietri, New York, 22 November 1983. All subsequent quotes are from this interview, which is published in full as part of A. Portelli, "Come distinguere i vivi dai morti: La poesia nelle strade del barrio," *I giorni cantati* 5 (Spring 1984): 7–12.

6. Pedro Pietri, *Traffic Violations* (Maplewood, N.J.: Waterfront Press, 1983).

7. The same image appears in "April 15th until Further Notice": "Your vacancy neon sign mind."

8. William Gibson, *Neuromancer* (New York: Ace Books, 1984), 12, 138. "Real" phone operators in the United States are trained, in fact, to sound as much as possible as if they were recorded messages. They transmit formulaic messages in an impersonal style to convey the impression that the user is not speaking to individual persons but to the company, which speaks through its representatives.

9. Ong, *Orality and Literacy,* 70.

10. "Up" and "down," of course, are themselves directive signs. As such, they are included in "Do Not Observe the No Smoking Sign."

FRITZ GYSIN

Centralizing the Marginal

Prolegomena to a Study of Boundaries in Contemporary African American Fiction

> *Q.* An obscure legal document states that Lake Webster in the south-central Massachusetts town of Webster is "also known as Lake Chargog-gagoggmanchaugagoggchaubunagungamaug." Is this true and, if so, what does it mean?—J. K., West Newton
>
> *A.* 'Tis true. According to the *Encyclopedia of New England*, the word— of Algonquin Indian origin—roughly translates to "you fish on your side, I fish on my side, and nobody fish in the middle."
> —BOSTON GLOBE, 6 July 1990

This essay addresses the need for an analytical conception of *boundary*, a need that becomes imperative if one wants to pay tribute to the dynamic function of boundaries as a phenomenon in recent African American fiction. In the introduction to *The Location of Culture*, Homi Bhabha starts out with a quotation from Martin Heidegger: "A boundary is not that at which something stops but, as the Greeks recognized, the boundary is that from which *something begins its presencing*."[1] And Bhabha supports his proposal "to move away from the singularities of 'class' or 'gender'" with a statement that, like Heidegger's, is just as fascinating as it seems problematic:

> What is theoretically innovative, and politically crucial, is the need to think beyond narratives of originary and initial subjectivities and to focus on those moments or processes that are produced in the articulation of cultural differences. These "in-between spaces" provide the terrain for elaborating strategies of selfhood—singular or communal—that initiate new signs of identity, and innovative sites of collaboration, and contestation, in the act of defining the idea of society itself.[2]

The statement is fascinating because it shows one of the foremost thinkers of postcolonial theory addressing an issue that has been prevalent in African American writing for quite some time as well as promising to take it a considerable step further by discussing it in an international context; it is problematic inasmuch as it appears, at a first glance, to be informed by a too vague and therefore rather confusing conception of boundary. To appreciate the challenge Bhabha's "inversive" and subversive privileging of boundaries provides to cultural performance in an African American context, I think it is necessary to take a more analytical look at the concept. As I am no cultural theorist, I shall try to stick as much as possible to my own field of critical interest, which is recent fiction, but I will pay attention to certain developments in the discussion of culture and ethnicity during the last two decades.

In one of his later novels, *Painted Turtle: Woman with Guitar*,[3] the African American writer Clarence Major—to my knowledge for the first time in African American fiction[4]—crosses an important cultural boundary and places his story exclusively among Native American protagonists in the Southwest of the United States. Painted Turtle is a Zuni woman on the way to folk-singing stardom;[5] in a series of flashbacks covering the story of her life, the novel traces her complex journey from one seedy night spot and motel room to the next, recording her attempts to negotiate a viable relationship with the ancient traditions of her tribe. Her experiences are recounted by Baldwin Saiyataca, who finally becomes her lover and companion. This narrator is a "half breed," the son of a Hopi mother and a Navajo father, who grew up on the Hopi reservation but was educated by his father to be a Navajo, which "wasn't exactly a picnic."[6] What is especially astounding is the central geographical location in which this narrator is said to have experienced his social marginality: alone in the middle of the Hopi reservation, which is located in the middle of the Navajo nation, surrounded, in turn, by white America.[7] Needless to say, the complexity of the woman's life story warrants an equally complex narrator. Yet such an explicit positioning of Baldwin Saiyataca's descent is rather extraordinary; it suggests an elaboration on Native American fictional thematics that more exactly reflects the concerns of the African American writer: the continued preoccupation with boundaries and the centralizing of marginality.

To what lengths the contemporary African American writer will go in his preoccupation with boundaries shall be illustrated by a quotation from William Melvin Kelley's novel *Dunfords Travels Everywheres*,[8] which begins with the description of a group of American students, one of whom is ostensibly black, in a fictitious Southern European town vaguely reminiscent of Madrid as depicted in Ernest Hemingway's *The Sun Also Rises*. There are several noteworthy differences, however. One of them has to do with a native custom of dressing:

> Many cafés fronted the beulward under the oak trees. In each café, by use of a bell-bedecked white wire supported at one end by a ring in the outside wall of the café, and at the other by a white standard, the management had divided the sidewalk tables into two sections.
> On the right side of the ringing wire, the native men and women of that country wore suits, jackets, pants, dresses, skirts and shirts in hues and mixtures of blue and red. On the left side, the natives wore combina-

tions of yellow and red. Neither side's colors appeared all bright, or drab, all new or all old; but when Chig squinted, the colors blended that way.

One of that country's oldest traditions, many foreigners found it difficult to understand. None of the natives on either side of the wire owned wardrobes composed entirely of one side's colors. In the morning, each native in the country would pick an outfit for that day. He might choose blue-red or yellow-red, making himself, for the day, an Atzuoreurso or a Jualoreurso.

In the street, each native lived the day his morning choice had dictated. The government reserved parts of the subway and autobus for Atzuoreursos, parts for Jualoreursos. Employers divided their offices and factories in this way. No citizen worked at a permanent desk or machine. Each used that section of the room where The Morning Choice, Lua Madjona Cheursa, had led him. Most married couples wore the same colors, to ride public transportation or take coffee together. Some couples did not, leading separate lives until they had returned home, locked their doors, and disrobed.

Four or five of Chig's twenty or thirty friends had tried to live by that tradition, dividing their closets and making their choice. But soon, each and all found it impossible to continue; some situation always developed which forced them to cross the white wire. Still, they tried their best not to disturb the natives. If, as a body, they attended a movie or a play, they would decide beforehand to dress either Atzuoreurso or Jualoreurso.[9]

An early instance of the projection of an indigenous thematics onto foreign territory,[10] this passage offers itself as a paradigm of the paradoxical treatment of boundaries in contemporary African American fiction. The voluntary but daily changing observance of apartheid among the natives may be said to reflect a stage in a long process of transformation from racial barriers to ethnic boundaries. The combination of determinism and free choice suggests a black variant of the dichotomy between descent and consent,[11] whereas the linking of ritual seriousness and absurdity, epitomized in the "bell-bedecked white wire" that enacts the spatial fixation of a temporary choice, may be found to reveal some of the dilemmas African Americans encounter in their need to choose between the melting pot and cultural pluralism. Furthermore, by displacing segregation to an exotic terrain, the text offers its American characters a negative exemplum of their own country's racial mores, but at the same time the cultural boundary prevents them from perceiving the analogy. The tension between their anxious readiness to observe the foreign custom and their practical incapability of total adjustment—and the ensuing frustration—enhances the absurdity of their own situation.

The passage gains in significance when it is seen in the context of the novel. *Dunfords Travels Everywheres* has two plots, one covering the adventures of Charles (Chig) Dunford, a Harvard-educated middle-class African American on his return home from a stay in Europe, the other relating the experience of Carlyle Bedlow, a

Harlem-educated hustler, thief, and dope peddler. Chig Dunford accidentally stumbles on a sinister shipment of slaves in the hold of the ocean liner; the seemingly white American girl he pursues with his attentions is killed by the modern slave traders as their chief opponent, and he feels guilty at not having realized that she was colored. Carlyle Bedlow victimizes a black bourgeois dentist, who engages his help in divorcing his wife, but pulls out all stops to rescue his photographer friend, who is threatened by a loan shark posing as the devil. The two protagonists have only one chance encounter toward the end of the novel, when they visit the same bar.

Their deeper relationship, however—one that has encouraged critics to treat them as two sides of the same coin—is provided by an ingenious device, which Kelley borrowed from James Joyce:[12] both characters go through similar experiences of waking dreams, in which they slowly move toward each other; each gradually realizes that he possesses an inner self that rejects his surface life, which in Chig's case is dominated by his attraction to white women, in Carlyle's by his egotism and his delight in tricking and deceiving others. These dream sections are written in an artificial language, fraught with allusions to *Finnegans Wake* and to Scandinavian mythology and making distorted use of a conglomerate of Bantu, pidgin English, and Harlem jive talk. In chapter 8 we thus read a kind of lecture meant to wake up Chig's and Carlyle's, thus "Chigyle's," and by extension the black man's, consciousness to his situation:

> Witches one Way tspike Mr. Chigyle's Languish, n curryng him back
> tRealty, recoremince wi hUnmisereaducation. Maya we now go on wi
> yReconstruction, Mr. Chuggle? Awick now? Goodd, a'god Moanng
> agen everybubbahs n babys among you, d'yonLadys in front who always
> come vear too, days ago, dhisMorning we wddeal, in dhis Sagmint of
> Lecturian Angleash 161, w'all the daisiastrous effects, the foxnoxious
> bland of stimili, the infortunelessnesses of circusdances which weak to
> worsen the phistorystematical intrafricanical firmly structure of our dis-
> tinct coresins: the Blafringo-Arumericans.[13]

As Grace Eckley explains, "The *heard* or spoken level of this language conveys the linguistic adjustments of the black American; the *seen* or reading level of this language reinterprets the mythologies of the west, particularly the Eddic, to establish contrast between the dominant 'chill' of the North and the 'sun-energy' of Africa." In the context of the waking dream, the "Languish" is that "of the transported Africans, the 'Blafringro-Arumericans,' who now live in 'New Afriquerque,' the black American nation."[14] "New Afriquerque" is thus not to be taken as an actual location within the fictional context but as an ideal or utopian country to fill the space between the oral and the written traditions, to be built by the people the two characters represent, and to make possible a new mode of existence. In order to build this new land, a land of freedom and creativity, the "annihilation of the disastrous effects of acculturation (the Blafringo Arumerican) and [the] reconstruction (africurekey) of the original African self (the phistorystematical intrafricanical structure)" is necessary.[15] Kelley uses Joyce to give words to his vision of a new black America, but it is only by going back to their African roots that his characters are able to reach the collective unconscious common to all mankind. Again, the combination of assimilationism (in this case represented by the use of white literary models) and pluralism (represented by an insistence on the African dimension of black American language and thinking) reflects the complex manner in which the deep rift between the two African American ways of life might, if ever, be patched up.

Thus, in the light of the novel's cultural strategy, it becomes increasingly clear that through his slightly sardonic depiction of the activities relating to the "bell-bedecked white wire" in the passage quoted above, Kelley is not only troping on various aspects of segregation between black and white in America but also on the visible and invisible boundaries between the assimilationist and separatist segments in the African American population. The novel ends in circular fashion, with a promise of the reconstruction of Chick Dunford. In an extension of the structural balance between the two attitudes, the hermetic boundary created by the artificial language[16] may be said to hide (and reveal?) the fact that there is another "assimilationist" agenda that has to be included in our discussion of boundaries, that of Afrocentrism.

■ Two Hypotheses

The issues of boundary and marginality have been essential in African American writing from its beginnings. If one considers the lack of attention that black writing was given in the United States until the recent past,[17] if one looks at the multiple echoes W. E. B. Du Bois's famous dictum about the color line as the problem of the twentieth century has found in African American literature and its criticism,[18] or if one pays attention to the many cases of marginal existence and outsiderdom that populate the lists of titles and the dramatis personae of African American writing,[19] one may feel justified in assuming that marginality is one of the major differentiae in the definition of this literature. Especially after the 1920s, when, under the influence of expressionism and modernism in European and American literature the outsider ceased to be a role for the alienated romantic artist and became a universal symbol of man, the topic of the social marginality of the black individual in the United States gained in importance in black as well as in white writing. The advent of existentialism added a philosophical dimension to the phenomenon of marginality; titles such as *Beetlecreek, Strangers and Alone, Invisible Man, The Outsider, The Primitive, A Different Drummer,* and *Another Country* reflected, among other things, the impact of Jean-Paul Sartre's *Nausea* and Albert Camus's *The Stranger,* and life "on the boundary," to paraphrase a famous title by Paul Tillich,[20] assumed transcendental significance.

The 1960s and 1970s brought black power and black nationalism, with their concomitant cultural programs, the black arts movement and black aestheticism. These, in their most outspoken manifestations, rejected the concepts of black marginality as well as Du Bois's "double consciousness" and emphasized instead the black community, black solidarity, the healing function of blackness, and pride in one's African roots. The outsider ceased to be a victim and rather became a hero in his fight against the American mainstream; in other words, the shift of focus turned the marginal person into a central one, celebrating his or her feats against the majority where before he or she had been treated as a tragic or absurd victim of racial and social exclusion.[21]

In the fiction of the last twenty-five years, however—and this may be considered my first hypothesis—the centralizing of the black community, the black family, black history, the cultural interest in Africa, in roots, and so on is accompanied by a new—or a renewed—concern with inner and outer boundaries, which sometimes even appear in places where, and at moments when, one least suspects them, or where there seems to be no direct motivation for them in the plot or in characterization. This seems to be happening in contrast to some of the continuing trends in the development of African American literary ethnicity, that is, the emphasis on unity of purpose, on genealogy and roots, on the folk and its healing lore, on brother and sister bonding, and so on, as well as in defiance of all those forces that—for better or for worse, for altruistic or egoistic reasons—advertise the breaking down of walls and the fusion of cultures into one big ethnic stew. To do justice to this new writing, it would be necessary to investigate the ways in which the centralizing of marginal existence and the marginal point of view affects the representation or creation, the elaboration or negotiation of psychological, social, political, ethnic, cultural, or spiritual boundaries in some of the major African American fictional texts of the 1970s, 1980s, and 1990s, as well as to establish how far these boundaries can still be seen as manifestations of Du Bois's double consciousness or—as the more recent terminology has it—of a "double-voiced discourse," and how far they suggest a different attitude in the making.

As these texts are not only—and not merely—cultural documents but also—and primarily—works of art, such an investigation would also have to consider the aesthetic aspects of the phenomenon; it would, for example, have to deal with matters of structure, imagery, and rhetoric. But here as well it would have to pay close attention to the idiosyncrasies of African American culture and writing. My second hypothesis is thus that the materials appropriated and utilized in the literary formation of boundaries derive (on the African American side) from an indigenous culture, which, apart from possessing its own century-old tradition, from early on has consisted of a fusion of black *and* white elements, a fusion that did not take place in Africa or in Europe but in America. A stylistic trait borrowed from African American music may illuminate this proposition. One of the defining rhythmical elements of jazz is "swing." It should not be confused with the style known as Swing; it is an aesthetic phenomenon, a peculiar rhythmical quality, which has been variously explained as the result of a "conflict between a fixed pulse and the wide variety of actual durations and accents that a jazz performer plays against that pulse";[22] as the superimposition of an African onto a European time scheme; as the mixture between African and South American polyrhythm on the one hand and the linearity of so-called classical music on the other; and as an element that helps produce an extraordinary combination of rhythmical power and freedom. Swing is definitely a hybrid element; in the sense employed here, neither European music nor African music swings. The term is not only used in a technical sense but very often in an evaluative one, in order to discriminate between good and bad playing. Its significance in our context is due to the fact that this "cultural blend" has also been—and sometimes still is—used by African American jazz musicians as well as by critics to define black jazz and to criticize white performance and white innovation in jazz; in this way it is quite consciously deployed for the purpose of boundary formation.[23] This musical example thus suggests a more complex model of boundary formation, one in which the cultural blends within an ethnic group are exploited to formulate the dividing issues within the same group as well as between this group and the mainstream or the majority at large.

■ Culture and Ethnicity

To designate the phenomenon I am focusing on, I have chosen the term "boundary," rather than "border line" or "line of demarcation," because "boundary" is not limited to two-dimensional models and because it combines the denotations of "division" and "periphery," a combination that is so important to the "minority" experience of marginality. In fact, the term has been used for years in discussions of ethnicity and can thus provide a link between the literary phenomena and the sociopsychological and sociocultural contexts it represents, reflects, responds to, constructs, or reconstructs. However, this terminological choice also entails some conceptual difficulties due partly to the term's increase in "metaphorical visibility" over the last years, resulting in a great variety of (often different and differing) applications; and partly to the paradox at the bottom of American conceptions of ethnicity, in which it plays a significant role. It is the latter paradox I should like to address first. Although this is not the place to reiterate all the recent definitions and discussions of ethnicity, some of its complexities must nevertheless be mentioned in order to situate the phenomenon of boundaries in its immediate social and cultural context before we can proceed to a discussion of its forms of manifestation.[24]

In *Ethnic Identity: Strategies of Diversity*, Anya Peterson Royce supplies a number of definitions that are simple and clear enough to be used as a starting point in a brief enumeration of arguments in the discussion of ethnicity pertinent to our concern with boundaries:

> An "ethnic group" is a reference group invoked by people who share a common historical style (which may be only assumed), based on overt features and values, and who, through the process of interaction with others, identify themselves as sharing that style. "Ethnic identity" is the sum total of feelings on the part of group members about those values, symbols, and common histories that identify them as a distinct group. "Ethnicity" is simply ethnic-based action.[25]

Elaborating on her definition of "ethnicity," Royce then refers to a Social Science Research Council Symposium that took place in 1973:

> For the scholars in the symposium, ethnicity seemed to involve:
> 1. a past-oriented group identification emphasizing origins
> 2. some conception of cultural and social distinctiveness
> 3. relationship of the ethnic group to a component unit in a broader system of social relations
> 4. the fact that ethnic groups are larger than kin or locality groups and transcend face-to-face interaction
> 5. different meanings for ethnic categories both in different social settings and for different individuals
> 6. the assumption that ethnic categories are emblematic, having names with meaning both for members and for analysts.[26]

These differentiae, useful as they are to the general anthropologist, conceal or ignore some controversial and complex issues that for quite some time have been the concern notably of scholars of *American* ethnicity. As a matter of fact, it seems to have become common practice today to include in the definitions of American ethnicity concepts of attitude and behavior that are downright contradictory. Discussions of the term usually resort to opposing expressions such as center and edge, fusion and fragmentation, union and secession, descent and consent, norm and deviation, and organicity and artificiality. In an article in the *American Quarterly*, Werner Sollors suggests that the term may stand for "peoplehood" as well as for "otherness," that "in America, ethnicity can be conceived as deviation *and* as norm, as characteristic of minorities *and* as typical of the country."[27] This view is corroborated by several opposing theoretical entries in the *Harvard Encyclopedia of American Ethnic Groups*, notably those by Harold J. Abramson, Philip Gleason, Michael Novak, and Michael Walzer, and Sollors himself. In *Beyond Ethnicity*, Sollors approaches American ethnicity and culture by means of the terminology of consent and descent, implying "the conflict between contractual and hereditary, self-made and ancestral."[28] His thesis plainly emphasizes the significance of consent, reflecting his "theoretical interest in American-made ethnicity."[29] Moreover, he holds that Americans have more in common than they would generally admit; therefore they are able to "dramatize their differences comfortably. Ethnicity is thus constantly being invented anew in contemporary America."[30] And his well-documented observations on parallels and fusions of typology and regeneration with ethnogenesis, as along with his assessment of the amount of myth-making involved in these processes, let him conclude that "even supposedly pure descent definitions are far from natural, being largely based on consent construction."[31]

Significantly, however, Sollors returns to the paradoxical kernel of ethnicity at the end of his book, allowing that "the same ligament constructions that spelled consensus among Americans could also be adapted to formulate secessionist and separatist peoplehoods. At times, the very glue could become dynamite."[32] This is exactly what happened in the 1960s, when to the surprise of scholarly observers,[33] the proportion of ethnicity to Americanism was inverted.[34] As Sollors phrased it in 1980, "Ethnicity has been transformed from a heathenish liability into a sacred asset, from a trait to be overcome in a conversion and rebirth experience to an identity to be achieved through yet another regeneration."[35] Thus, what is at stake here is no longer the preponderance of consent over descent, but the difference between two fundamental choices a "consenting" group makes with regard to its relationship to other groups; in other words, it is a question of the choice between separatism and assimilationism, between pluralism and the melting pot.

Again, the conflict is as old as, if not older than, the United States; however—as recent studies have shown—the matter is more complex than it seems at first sight. In his "Critique of Pure Pluralism," which he offered in the same year he proposed to go *Beyond Ethnicity*, Sollors demonstrates how in discussions of these issues since the 1920s the cultural and political agendas of the major spokesmen have often been at cross-purposes in ascribing meanings to the two terms. The political atmosphere, for example, in which Horace Meyer Kallen coined the phrase "cultural pluralism,"[36] was informed by a "literary polemic which equated all forms of assimilation and acculturation with hard-core racism" and "Anglo-conformity,"[37] whereas Kallen's later self-styled Zionism "absorbed concepts from the surrounding culture (the American idea), but gave it an ethnic name (the Jewish idea)."[38] Furthermore, as developments since the late 1960s have shown, pluralism has been divested of its redemptive cloak; far from being a panacea for prejudice, it has, in fact, come to imply purism.[39] On the other hand, if Albert Murray, at the height of the black separatist controversy in the United States, insists that "even [the] most extreme and violent polarities represent nothing so much as the natural history of pluralism in an open society," he comes down strongly on the side of assimilationism, insisting, however, that "American culture, even in its most rigidly segregated precincts, . . . is . . . incontestably mulatto"[40] and even that "there is no standard Melting Pot for the American Image."[41]

One of the conclusions to be drawn from the hopelessly intertwined crosscurrents between the two behavioral patterns is that they are, in strange and often contradictory ways, interdependent. William Boelhower, referring to Gregory Bateson, proposes an "inclusive 'transcontextuality' or contextural structure whereby to act as one of two terms (assimilation and Americanization versus pluralism and ethnification) of a structure of interaction means immediately to summon the other term."[42] Another model that might help to elucidate the interdependence of the two patterns is the one that informs W. E. B. Du Bois's treatment of "double consciousness," when, after his famous definition of the term, he speaks of the American Negro's "longing to attain self-conscious manhood, to merge his double self into a better and truer self. In this merging he wishes neither of the older selves to be lost."[43] Significantly, Du Bois makes use of the Emersonian concept of "bi-polar unity,"[44] which Harold Waskow, for example, has found to be a structural principle of Walt Whitman's poetry;[45] by locating his different and differing black paradigm in the American mainstream, Du Bois allows us to read his definition of "double consciousness" as an enactment of the model it promotes. Such models offer a less "pure" view of pluralism as well as a concept of ethnicity that is basically American; they also point to the dynamic and kinetic character of ethnic relationships and thus appear to be more fitting in a country that prides itself on the transitional character of its social and cultural life.[46]

There is one aspect of assimilationism, however, that oddly enough seemed to be ignored or neglected for a long time in the debate among cultural critics and theoreticians, namely the possible existence or invention of other melting pots. In the light of demographic developments in the 1980s and 1990s, such as the swift increase in Hispanic immigration, this neglect seems rather surprising; it can only be explained by the strong appeal that the American identity, as a conglomerate of numerous predominantly white ethnicities, exerts on potential converts and scholars alike. Anthropologists, to be sure, are aware of this gap. In the words of Anya Peterson Royce: "We saw uniform assimilation, or tried to impose it, where the reality was much more complicated. We posited one melting pot where in fact there were many."[47] As we are here primarily concerned with the cultural expression of African Americans, it is necessary to include in our discussion the often hypothetical or mythical possibility of another melting pot, one that is regularly evoked to compete with the mainstream for attraction among the black citizens of the United States: that of Afrocentrism.

In the first chapter of *The Afrocentric Idea*, Molefi Kete Asante makes the following programmatic statement:

> In establishing this perspective, you can see that I am proposing not only a new perspective but a different framework for understanding human behavior. A people who have been relegated to the fringes of the society must now be looked upon as players in the field, albeit players who have operated from a position of less power for the past four hundred years. Only an ample metatheory can adequately consider the multidimensions of the black communicative experience; and this metatheory is founded on Afrocentric bases.[48]

Drawing on earlier scholars[49] and writers[50] who either endorsed and justified the concepts of pan-Africanism and négritude or encouraged the need to examine the African sources and the African elements in black American culture, Asante proclaims a sort of African syncretism that no longer sees any need for European values nor for the American syncretism of the melting-pot kind. His metatheory is chiefly concerned with essences or nuclei, which he finds reflected in rhythm, styling, and sound in language; in word magic, call-and-response patterns, and improvisation; in the priority of rhetoric, in personalism and collective power; and in organicity, harmony, and spirituality. Consequently, his definition of Afrocentricity is quite radical:

> *Afrocentricity* is the most complete philosophical totalization of the African being-at-the-center of his or her existence. It is not merely an

artistic or literary movement. Not only is it an individual or collective quest for authenticity, but it is above all the total use of method to effect psychological, political, social, cultural, and economic change. The Afrocentric idea is beyond decolonizing the mind.[51]

In accordance with the philosophy of emancipation intrinsic in much of modern African ideology, be it the ecumenical movement, the African personality, négritude, or pan-Africanism,[52] Asante puts quite a bit of emphasis on the liberating and healing functions of Afrocentric thought and behavior, which he offers as a cure for all the harms caused by what he calls "Eurocentric" cultural domination. In fact, the Afrocentric argument tries to replace the Western historical assumption of American cultural derivation from Europe with the hypothesis of Europe's cultural derivation from Africa.[53] Needless to say, this approach demands a strong effort to suppress differences of values and customs causing many of the problems in historical and contemporary Africa, as well as a strong emphasis on unity, harmony, and solidarity.[54]

But Asante's agenda has much more to do with American Africanism than with the universal variety. Thus, whereas one of the final theoretical goals of his vision is the union—and thus the relative assimilation or melting—of all African people and peoples (and their cultures), his preoccupation with the praxis of black American culture forces him to cope with certain traits that can only be called "ethnic" even from an Afrocentric point of view. I am thinking of the comparative absence of creation myths[55] and of the importance of messianism[56] and apocalyptic rhetoric[57] in African American culture. At one point he even suggests that the Afro-American is "a new African ethnic group."[58] As a matter of fact, if we ignore for a moment the concept of the imaginative return to the source that informs much of Afrocentric thinking,[59] there actually seems to be little difference between the African antithesis of unification and separatism or ethnicity, on the one hand, and the American antithesis of melting pot and cultural pluralism, on the other. Even the crisscrossing of values and meanings can be observed. Consider the following quotation from Asante: "Blackness is more than a biological fact; indeed, it is more than color; it functions as a commitment to a historical project that places the African person back on center and, as such, it becomes an escape to sanity. Therefore, when the Kenyan writer Ngugi Wa Thiong'o gives up writing in English to write in Gikuyu, he is on the path to Afrocentricity."[60] Whereas the first sentence locates the concept of blackness surprisingly close to the realm of consent ("blackness" assuming the all-embracing character that "America" has for the assimilationist), the second one directs the choice toward descent and a separate language (but it is nevertheless a choice). The non sequitur that can be read into the sequence parallels a dilemma that should by now be familiar to the student of American ethnicity.[61]

Therefore, if we grant the Afrocentric idea as a potentiality the attention in scholarship that it is already enjoying in public life, we must make allowance for the additional complexity arising from the opposition of *two* antitheses, one between the American idea of the melting pot and cultural pluralism and the other between the Afrocentric idea and African ethnicity, as can be seen in the following model:

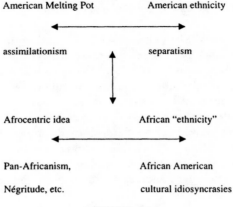

FIGURE 1

In the case of African American culture, it may be said that the two groups of terms on the right side coincide—that is, African Americans have the choice to experience their ethnicity as American ethnicity or as African ethnicity or as both. On the other hand, they may be attracted by the American or by the African melting pot, and they may opt for a consent-oriented composite peoplehood or for a descent-oriented one. Barbara Johnson's misgivings about "the fallacy of spatialization"[62] notwithstanding, the two melting-pot cultures can also be represented as two overlapping squares, with African American culture forming the segment claimed by either idea:[63]

```
aaaaaaaaaaaaaaaaaaaaaaaaaaaaaaaaaaaaaaaaaaaaa
a                                        a
a   American Melting Pot                 a
a   Culture,                             a
a   Assimilationism                      a
a                                        a
a                                        a
a       bbbbbbbbbbbbbbbbbbbbbbbbbbbbbbbbbbbbbbbbbb
a       b                                a       b
a       b                                a       b
a       b   African American             a       b
a       b   Culture                      a       b
a       b                                a       b
aaaaaaaaaaaaaaaaaaaaaaaaaaaaaaaaaaaaaaaaaaaaa       b
        b                                        b
        b                        African Melting Pot   b
        b                        Culture, Afrocentrism  b
        b                                        b
        bbbbbbbbbbbbbbbbbbbbbbbbbbbbbbbbbbbbbbbbbbbbbbbbbbb
```

FIGURE 2

This is where the concept of boundary comes in. Whereas it is a general premise of melting-pot theory that boundaries should be ignored, dissolved, or crossed, it is part of the strategy of the *particular* melting pot to get rid only of the boundary (or boundaries) within its circumference; opening up the circumference is a much more difficult undertaking.[64] Thus—to remain for a moment within the simplified and hypothetical scenario of the spatial model—adherents of the American melting pot would ideally ignore the boundary created by the Afrocentric approach (in our model marked "b"), whereas proponents of the Afrocentric approach would ignore the particularly American boundary (in our model marked as "a"). In the absence of an agreement about the common boundary, we would have to postulate the existence of a hidden boundary somewhere between the two realms. On the other hand, "inhabitants" of the overlapping segment—that is, agents of African American culture—would find themselves under the obligation of maintaining boundaries on either side ("a" as well as "b") unless they let themselves be coopted by one of the assimilationist modes. Paradoxically, if they ignored both boundaries, they would turn into embodiments of the hidden boundary between the two realms, which would be another and maybe a more radical version of double consciousness. This goes to show that the suggestion of two overlapping melting pots helps to put our topic into a better focus: when the concept of Afrocentricity is introduced to counterbalance the concept of the American melting pot, African American culture moves from a marginal to a central position; at the same time, the boundary experience takes on a new significance. Our next task will therefore consist in assessing some of the criteria that have been established in scholarly discussions of ethnic boundaries, criteria that bear on the treatment of such boundaries in African American fiction.

Boundary and Ethnicity

It has become common practice among anthropologists and cultural theoreticians to trace the emphasis on boundaries in the discussion of ethnicity back to Fredrik Barth's introduction to *Ethnic Groups and Boundaries: The Social Organization of Culture Difference.*[65] Emphasizing context and interaction, Barth challenges social and cultural models of "ethnic groups" that solely insist on content and essence,[66] proposing instead to focus his analysis on the boundaries between such groups. Much of his preoccupation with the maintenance of boundaries, however, depends on his distinction between the social and the cultural domains involved in this process, which is not always quite consistent. His major assertions are that "boundaries persist despite a flow of personnel across them";[67] that "ethnic distinctions do not depend on an absence of social interaction and acceptance, but are quite to the contrary often the very foundations on which embracing social systems are built"; and that "cultural differences can persist despite inter-ethnic contact and interdependence."[68] On the other hand, he insists that "a drastic reduction of cultural differences between ethnic groups does not correlate in any simple way with a reduction in the organizational relevance of ethnic identities, or a breakdown in boundary-maintaining processes"[69] and that "most of the cultural matter that at any time is associated with a human population is *not* constrained by this boundary; it can vary, be learnt, and change without any critical relation to the boundary maintenance of the ethnic group."[70] What this amounts to is a model in which "ethnic boundaries are maintained in each case by a limited set of cultural features. The persistence of the unit then depends on the persistence of these cultural differentiae, while continuity can also be specified through the changes of the unit brought about by changes in the boundary-defining cultural differentiae."[71]

Barth's emphasis on the significance of boundaries in the scholarly discussion of ethnicity has not gone unchallenged.[72] But at the same time he has rightly been praised for focusing not only on the survival of ethnic consciousness but also on its emergence.[73] What is even more crucial for an analysis of boundaries in fiction, however, is his interest in the emergence of the boundaries themselves and in the circumstances of their creation or invention.[74] Furthermore, his distinction between "ascription" and "performance"[75] may have been instrumental in the development of Royce's concept of the "double boundary":

> Barth called for closer attention to the boundaries that signal ethnic dichotomies, but we can go further and speak of double boundaries; that is, the boundary maintained from within, and the boundary imposed from outside, which results from the process of interaction with others. Individuals enclosed by the inner boundary share a common cultural knowledge; hence, their interaction may be varied and complex and tolerate a great deal of ambiguity. Interaction across the outer boundary is much more limited because of the lack of shared knowledge.[76]

Needless to say, this distinction between boundaries from within and boundaries from without not only facilitates Royce's own (anthropological) discussion of ethnic symbols and stereotypes;[77] it is also particularly helpful for the interpretation of fiction.[78] Psychologically speaking, the difference between "walling in" and "walling out"[79] may also be a matter of perception—hence its significance in the fictional discourse, where the shift between focalizers can determine the nature of the boundary.

A related criterion of ethnic identity is the interaction between groups and individuals. Royce, who has structured her entire book to reflect what she calls a "dichotomy," stipulates that "persons make choices as individuals but if they are to have any saliency in an ethnic identity they must have an ethnic group as a referent."[80] Putting this insight into a psychological context, Roberta Rubenstein comments on the relationship between personal and social boundaries: "Beginning with what D. W. Winnicott terms the psychic 'membrane' in each individual across which the dialectic between inner and outer occurs, social organization and culture are the result of innumerable individual and collective mediations of boundary."[81] Rubenstein's analysis of the work of several women writers demonstrates how helpful this criterion is for an understanding of boundaries in fiction; on the other hand, it also illustrates the dilemma caused by a loose definition of the term. If group boundaries are primarily related to ego boundaries, the defining and protective functions of the concept may be given undue priority. This may work with some authors, but with others it may impede the perception of complex images and structures.[82] Besides, the establishment of ethnic or social boundaries may be experienced by the individual as a violation of the boundaries of the self, whereas an assertion of one's personal boundaries can result in a transgression of social or ethnic boundaries. It is therefore necessary to postulate a model in which the relationship between personal and ethnic boundaries allows for affinity as well as for tension and contradiction.

Contrary to earlier cultural theories, some of the more recent studies insist on—or at least take for granted—the dynamic quality of social and ethnic boundaries.[83] In other words, boundaries can be limited or extended; they can shift back and forth, depending on the social, economic, or psychological constellations of the bordering groups. During the struggle for civil rights in the 1960s, for instance, the lines of segregation were not immediately abandoned; they were often moved to other, less conspicuous areas of social or economic contact. Moreover, boundaries can always be weakened or strengthened; they can be made more or less permeable, even fluid.[84] In addition, they can also be extended or limited with respect to the different levels of contact or they can shift between these levels. Barth's assertion of the persistence of boundaries "despite a flow of personnel across them"[85] is a case in point. Acceptance of this criterion in a model of boundaries allows for the transfer of boundaries to other areas of experience and would thus be crucial to an analysis of this phenomenon in African American fiction.

A very important aspect, which is related to their pliability, is the frequent use of boundaries for strategic purposes. Paradoxically, this includes the activities of crossing and recrossing as well as of straddling them. In her discussion of what she calls "situational ethnicity,"[86] Royce calls attention to specific behavioral tactics that implicitly have to do with the crossing of boundaries: "Impression management is the manipulation of identity to an individual's advantage, while alter casting is the manipulation of an interaction. If, for example, you hold the dominant status in terms of social class but not ethnic group, it is to your advantage to recognize the other person in terms of his or her class rather than ethnic group."[87] The complex social and psychological processes involved here are carried out on the basis of "ethnic cues and clues," that is, given ethnic features and adopted ones.[88] An illustration of the intricacy of such shifts can be found in Murray's description in 1970 of processed or "conked" hair being a feature of "unmistakably Negro-idiom oriented" blacks, whereas "natural" hair is worn by blacks who "are clearly most interested in integration and assimilation."[89] In literature, emphasis on the crossing or recrossing of boundaries as well as on "switching identities"[90] may have an opposite effect: rather than eliminating boundaries or causing them to be ignored, it may also highlight them.

Finally, as Hartwig Isernhagen suggests in an article about Native American writing, boundaries "are fostered and supported by power relations and differentials," and especially in boundaries between "white" and "non-white" groups, these power relations are frequently asymmetrical.[91] This observation helps to explain some of the activities across boundaries, as suggested above: frequently the transgression or trespassing does not necessarily aim to eliminate the boundary itself but is intended to redress the balance of the adjoining power units or to invert their ratio. This means that crossing and straddling of boundaries may in some cases contribute to their maintenance.[92] Practical approaches, such as those described by Thomas Kochman in *Black and White Styles in Conflict*,[93] suggest ways in which it would be possible to establish such a balance of power at the boundary, to make ethnic coexistence possible and fruitful by creating a cultural equilibrium.

◼ Some Forms of Boundary

After taking account of a number of significant ethnological and sociological criteria related to the concept under investigation, it is now necessary to look at some of the more basic forms underlying its complex manifestations. It goes without saying that pure forms such as those presented below rarely occur, neither in "reality" nor in literature. But paying attention to the basic patterns may help us understand the often confusing applications of the term. As these forms are not limited to a particular ethnic experience, some of them can be illustrated by examples from mainstream poetry. Depending on the principles of distinction, we can distinguish four or five different basic forms of boundary.

1. Boundary as Dividing Line

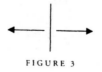

FIGURE 3

The form related to the most common use of the term is the *dividing line*, a kind of wall put up between two contiguous realms, cultures, forms of behavior, and so son, which it separates or is supposed to separate or keep apart. Depending on the focus, it includes or excludes, protects or restrains. It can be crossed, but this is not its main purpose: it should safeguard the purity of cultural identity by allowing representatives of one side to ignore those on the other side. Essentially it functions like a watershed. In the social reality this form of boundary is very difficult to achieve or maintain, but it does exist as a questionable ideal in specific cultural or literary situations. Robert Frost's ironic use of the proverb "Good fences make good neighbors" in his poem "Mending Wall" is a case in point. Some positions in the black aesthetic favor this model. After all, it reflects the goals of separatism.[94]

2. Boundary as Area of Contact

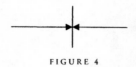

FIGURE 4

The second form is closer to the actual cultural situation; it represents a zone of ethnic interaction and is characterized by cultural clash, superimposition, cross-fertilization, fusion, and so on. The most concrete example is the territorial border, that is, a line or band on a horizontal plane, where citizens of adjoining nations exchange or oppose customs or ideas. "Minority" existence often entails the experience of this kind of boundary. To the extent that an assimilationist approach can accept the concept of boundary at all, it is this form that it has to deal with. A highly complex image of this form of boundary occurs in Walt Whitman's poem "As I Ebb'd with the Ocean of Life," in which the speaker experiences himself as a piece of "sea-drift" that is claimed by the sea and the land, the mother and the father, as part of the line of demarcation between death and life.[95]

3. Unilateral Boundary

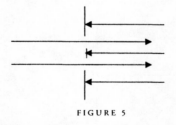

FIGURE 5

An asymmetrical variant including elements of the first two forms, the unilateral boundary is pervious (a) from one side only, (b) in one direction only, and (c) for agents of one side only. It can be illustrated by a situation in which people of one group have access to or control of the living space of the other group, but not vice versa. Interactions do not take place on the boundary but behind it, if at all. In social reality, this situation is often complemented by its inversion on another level. For example, for quite some time white Americans claimed they had considerable insight into the economic situation of black Americans, without allowing the blacks insight into white economic dealings; on the other hand, black Americans claimed that their need to survive as underdogs forced them to learn and understand the behavioral patterns of white Americans, whereas most white Americans remained comparatively ignorant of behavioral patterns of black Americans.[96] In each case the boundary was considered pervious in one direction only.

4. Boundary as Brink or Edge

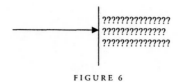

FIGURE 6

The form of boundary that functions as a brink or edge represents the outskirts of a familiar, known, accepted area, beyond which it is difficult or dangerous to go. The other side may be unknown, forbidden, or nonexistent. Depending on the nature of that other side, the boundary may be seen as locking in or locking out. A "no trespassing" sign, it nevertheless invites adventure and exploration, usually at a high risk. This is the form of boundary that in the Puritans' imagination divided their settlements from the "howling wilderness" of uncivilized nature. But the most typical boundaries of this sort are of the metaphysical kind; they separate this world from the next. Stories of closure and (less frequently) of quest operate with this form of boundary.

5. Boundary as Threshold

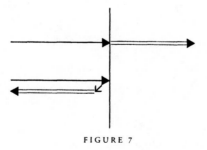

FIGURE 7

Closely related to the fourth form is the boundary that functions as a threshold, the difference being that the boundary zone acts as a locus of transformation. Again, depending on the nature of the "other" side, the boundary can be crossed (in which case the crossing entails the change), or it is experienced as an outermost region, from which one returns changed. Commonly related to the process of initiation, it manifests itself in psychological, social, cultural, and ethnic contexts, but it also frequently implies metaphysical dimensions. In literature it often appears in quest stories, usually in several varieties at the same time. It is related to, but not the same as, Victor Turner's concept of liminality.[97]

An analysis of the matter of boundaries in fiction will have to take into account the ways in which these five models are employed, mixed, superimposed upon one another, exchanged, transformed, and so forth. However, there is at least one further principle according to which fictional boundaries can be classified. It is what I propose to call a division into "horizontal" and "vertical" boundaries. The first category would include boundaries on a horizontal plane; topographical, historical, social, and political ones. Simple examples would be the Ohio River, the Mason-Dixon line, Frederick Jackson Turner's frontier, the railroad tracks in a small southern town, the city boundary separating urban and rural areas, boundaries between the rich and the poor or between old inhabitants and newcomers, and the like. The second category would include boundaries in the philosophical, psychological, and religious realms, involving fields such as myth, ritual, possession, conjuring, demonology, and insanity—boundaries between life and death, the secular and the spiritual, the rational and the irrational, and such. As they are not to be contained within a two-dimensional model, they often consist of areas, such as sacred places, inner sanctums, no-man's lands, mountains, chasms, or cellars, that are sometimes inhabited by characters or creatures that are personifications of the boundary. It goes without saying that their usage in fiction often transplants and transforms elements from one category into the other, and it would be particularly exciting to see how this is done.

But let us return for a moment to Homi Bhabha and his proposal to consider "border lives" as "the art of the present" (his subtitle).[98] By staking a claim for what some have begun to call "emergent literatures," Bhabha zeroes in on the second type of boundary I have discussed above and then combines this with a vertical dimension, that is, he foregrounds hybridity as *the* location of culture and treats its subversive quality as a creative asset. Such claims have been staked before by proponents of a literature of exile, which usually foregrounded the solitary individual in a new and confusing political context, but now the mandate is extended to larger (new) cultural groups, such as migrants, refugees, or even denizens of geographical border regions. Bhabha's problem is not only that despite his references to the "beyond,"[99] that is, to the boundary as edge (type 4), he focuses almost exclusively on the boundary as an area of contact and tends to downplay the other types; but his new cultural groups have an as yet rather precarious historical claim to their own new boundaries, which allows the strategic transformation of the boundary into a Heideggerian bridge[100] (something different from a threshold). Whereas such postcolonial plotting permits the inversion of inside and outside, the treatment of the "ex-centric" as the "in-between" (and thus as the "beyond") or what I have called the centralizing of the marginal, in an African American context it only makes sense if and when we pay attention to the fact that what is centralized is exactly the condition of the boundary in all its diverse manifestations.[101]

■ Spaces of Contradiction

In 1989 the question of boundaries seemed to hover in the background of a conference held at the University of Pennsylvania concerned with programs, predictions, and prophecies regarding the future of African American literature, as can be seen in the publication of its proceedings under the title *Afro-American Literary Study in the 1990s.*[102] Even from the point of view of the present, some of these prescriptions and predictions remain remarkably accurate and to the point. The specter of African American critical and theoretical separatism is raised at the beginning of the book, where Henry Louis Gates claims to be witnessing "a moment of literary liminality in the African-American Tradition"[103] and proposes—once again—a literary theory based on the "black vernacular" and the "oral tradition," which he considers to be basically African paradigms.[104] Rejecting what Anthony Appiah calls "the Naipaul fallacy," he recommends isolating "the signifying black difference through which to theorize about the so-called discourse of the Other."[105] Subsequent contributions openly or covertly take issue with Gates about cultural separatism in literature, rejecting his "fallacy of spatialization"[106] or insisting on the difference between African and African American ways of seeing things,[107] proposing to "move the discourse to other territories,"[108] or persisting in the African American critic's commitment to "exploring the blackness of black texts."[109]

The boundary between the two views, that of the black separatist and that of the assimilationist critics, is successfully problematized by Kimberly Benston in a comparison of the attitudes toward ethnicity expressed in Ralph Ellison's *Invisible Man* and Amiri Baraka's *Dutchman:*

> In this sense, the Ellison-Baraka contrast offers us a mechanism—an enabling allegory, if you will—for resituating the critical opposition of "blackness" and "universality" on a ground internal to Afro-American discourse itself. Ellison and Baraka offer models of the black text which imply that such an opposition is, indeed, constituent of Afro-American poetics. If this is so, then criticism might make the opposition its own subject.[110]

Borrowing a comment by Hortense Spillers out of context—"We are called upon, then, to articulate the *spaces* of contradiction"[111]—one may say that what is especially noteworthy in Benston's argument for his "enabling allegory" is that it locates the contradicting elements *within* the African-American critical discourse, thus providing a parallel—on the level of theory—to the urge, formulated in my second hypothesis, to look for the components of fictional boundaries *within* the indigenous culture.

Drawing on such indigenous cultural features, it is possible to analyze the boundaries in recent African American fiction along at least three "dimensions": somatic, aesthetic, and historical. In the somatic dimension it is the treatment of skin color that warrants special attention; in the aesthetic dimension it is the deployment of elements of jazz; and in the historical dimension it is the treatment of slavery. As far as skin color is concerned, we witness a new interest in the mulatto and the process of passing,[112] together with a shift toward the albino as a kind of meta-outsider, as an inversion of the black man who is white inside, and as an archetype of black suffering; Raymond Andrews, Charles Johnson, and John Edgar Wideman have offered texts that may become paradigmatic in this respect.[113] Elements of jazz that are either directly utilized in fiction or used as analogies or models include the blues as a "philosophical" attitude, poetic genre, and musical form; the rhythmical phenomenon of swing as described earlier; and bebop as a style obsessed with boundaries. The fiction of Albert Murray, Gayl Jones, John Edgar Wideman, and Nathaniel Mackey,[114] to name only a few, adopts central issues from this music and applies them to structure, characterization, and imagery. The topic of slavery finally has not only caught the renewed interest of American historians, but has preoccupied the authors of some of the most significant fictional texts in the last two decades. Ishmael Reed, David Bradley, Charles Johnson, Sherley Anne Williams, and Toni Morrison, among others, explore slavery in new and unusual ways,[115] drawing on the wealth of well-known and recently discovered slave narratives. The reason for this is obvious. To quote Werner Sollors once more: "In the terms of Fredrik Barth, slavery is not just a boundary but one of the most extreme forms of social boundaries constructed between people who considered themselves full human beings and cast others into the category that Orlando Patterson has forcefully described as 'social death.'"[116]

Conclusion

While analyzing and interpreting the representation and creation of boundaries in literature, we must always remain aware of their paradoxical quality. As Roberta Rubenstein reminds us,

> The irreducible paradox of boundary is that it indicates the figurative
> line of both separation and connection between contiguous entities.
> That which demarcates, whether construed in an interpersonal, cultural, or geographical sense, may exclude or include, depending on the
> position and perception of the observer. As Robert Lifton has written in
> a somewhat different context, "Boundaries can be viewed as neither permanent nor by definition false, but rather as essential and yet subject to
> the fundamental forces for change characterizing our age. We require
> images of limit and restraint, if only to help us grasp what we are transcending."[117]

The significance of this statement cannot be overestimated. In the light of the pressures exerted by various movements of accommodation, assimilation, and even unification on behavioral, social, economic, and political levels, there is a tendency, on the part of proponents of an American melting pot as well as on that of adherents of the Afrocentric Idea, to accentuate only the sinister side of cultural boundaries, to attack their "reification" and treat them as manifestations of bad faith while either tacitly assuming the superiority of one form of assimilation only or embracing a too-gratuitous and rather formless kind of cultural syncretism reminiscent of the hotchpotch that often graces American folklore festivals, with their combinations of "ethnic food," "ethnic rock music," and "ethnic dancing." If we accept John Clifford's norms of culture as being "beauty, truth, and reality,"[118] if we concentrate on literature as a value-charged category,[119] and especially if we deal with a literature as vital as that of the African Americans, we must accept the existence of, as well as the serious concern with, boundaries as a result of the centralizing of marginality. The universal significance of this view, its topical importance even, is articulated in an article by John Edgar Wideman, in which he appeals to his American readers to "attend to the *chaos which lives within the pattern* of our certainties," and which I offer by way of conclusion:

> When a culture hardens into heliocentricity, fancies itself the star of creation, when otherness is imagined as a great darkness except for what the star illuminates, it's only a matter of time until the center collapses in upon itself, imploding with sigh and whimper.
>
> Minority writers hold certain, peculiar advantages in circumstances of cultural breakdown, reorientation, transition. We've accumulated centuries of experience dealing with problems of marginality, problems that are suddenly on center stage for the whole of society: inadequacy of language, failure of institutions, a disintegrating metropolitan vision that denies us or swallows us, that attracts and repels, that promises salvation and extinction. We've always been outsiders, orphans, bastard children, hard pressed to make our claims heard. In order to endure slavery and oppression it has been necessary to cultivate the double-consciousness of seer, artist, mother. Beaten down by countless proofs of the inadequacy, the repugnance of our own skin, we've been forced to enter the skins of others, see the world and ourselves through the eyes of others. The reality carried around inside our skulls is a sanctuary. Imagination has evolved as discipline, defense, coping mechanism, counterweight to the galling facts of life. We've learned to confer upon ourselves the power of making up our lives, changing them as we go along.[120]

███ NOTES

1. Homi K. Bhabha, *The Location of Culture* (London: Routledge, 1994), 1. The quotation is from Martin Heidegger, "Building, Dwelling, Thinking," in *Poetry, Language, Thought* (New York: Harper and Row, 1971), 152–153.

2. Bhabha, *The Location of Culture*, 1–2.

3. Clarence Major, *Painted Turtle: Woman with Guitar* (Los Angeles: Sun and Moon Press, 1988).

4. An earlier African American novel that introduces an American Indian character is Ishmael Reed, *Flight to Canada* (New York: Random House, 1976): Princess Quaw Quaw Tralaralara is introduced in chapter 15.

5. A more upbeat character with the same name appears in the first half of an earlier novel, *My Amputations* (New York: Fiction Collective, 1986). She is the protagonist's lover in New York but disappears and is later briefly spotted by him on a speaking engagement at the University of Colorado at Boulder, in the company of a fellow who always sniggers at his talk (74). In *Painted Turtle* she is the central character.

6. Major, *Painted Turtle. Woman with Guitar*, 147, 144.

7. "Still, I didn't want to get angry that night—and I would have had I started talking about how it had been growing up half Navajo among Hopis, who, after all, live on a postage stamp-size piece of land smack in the middle of the Navajo reservation—which is the largest one, as far as I know, anywhere" (147).

8. William Melvin Kelley, *Dunfords Travels Everywheres* (Garden City: Doubleday, 1970).

9. Kelley, *Dunfords Travels Everywheres*, 2–3.

10. Kelley's preference for fictitious landscapes already shows in his first novel: *A Different Drummer* (Garden City: Doubleday, 1962) takes place in a fictitious state in the Deep South, bordering Tennessee to the north, Alabama to the east, and Mississippi to the west; its southern border is the Gulf of Mexico. In other words, Kelley, as it were, explodes the borderline between Mississippi and Alabama into a new state, which he then makes resemble the state of Louisiana.

11. Cf. Werner Sollors, *Beyond Ethnicity: Consent and Descent in American Culture* (New York: Oxford University Press, 1986).

12. Grace Eckley, "The Awakening of Mr. Afrinnegan: Kelley's *Dunfords Travels Everywheres* and Joyce's *Finnegan's Wake*," *Obsidian* 12 (Summer 1975): 27–41; Marieme Sy, "Dream and Language in *Dunfords Travels Everywheres*," *CLA Journal* 25, no. 4 (June 1982): 458–467; Valerie M. Babb, "William Melvin Kelley," in *Afro-American Fiction Writers after 1955*, ed. Thadious M. Davis and Trudier Harris (Detroit: Gale, 1984), 135–143; Bernard W. Bell, *The Afro-American Novel and Its Tradition* (Amherst: University of Massachusetts Press, 1987), 296–299.

13. Kelley, *Dunfords Travels Everywheres*, 49.

14. Eckley, "The Awakening of Mr. Afrinnegan," 28. Cf. also Babb, "William Melvin Kelley," 142.

15. Sy, "The Awakening of Mr. Afrinnegan," 461.

16. Cf. Bernard Bell's comment: "Unfortunately, many readers will probably find that it takes too much time and effort to understand Kelley's word games and multilevel puns, and will not adequately appreciate the richness of his comic imagination and ironic reconstruction of myth" (*The Afro-American Novel and Its Tradition*, 299).

17. See Fritz Gysin, *The Grotesque in American Negro Fiction: Jean Toomer, Richard Wright, and Ralph Ellison* (Bern: Francke, 1975), 11–21; cf. Werner Sollors, "A Critique of Pure Pluralism," in *Reconstructing American Literary History*, ed. Sacvan Bercovitch (Cambridge: Harvard University Press, 1986), 250–258, 278–279; cf. Robert Stepto, "Afro-American Literature," in *The Columbia History of American Literature*, ed. Emory Elliott (New York: Columbia University Press, 1988), 785–799.

18. W. E. B. Du Bois, "The Forethought," in *The Souls of Black Folk: Essays and Sketches* (1903; reprint, New York: Fawcett, 1961), v.

19. E.g., *Nobody Knows My Name* (Baldwin), *Preface to a Twenty-Volume Suicide Note* (Baraka), *Soul on Ice* (Cleaver), *Beetlecreek* and *The Catacombs* (Demby), *Invisible Man* (Ellison), *The Primitive* (Himes), *The Autobiography of an Ex-Coloured Man* (Johnson), *A Different Drummer* (Kelley), *The Outsider* (Wright), etc.

20. Paul Tillich, *On the Boundary: An Autobiographical Sketch*, introduction by J. Heywood Thomas (London: Collins, 1967); cf. also Santiago Rodriguez de la Fuente, "Grenzbewusstsein und Transzendenzerfahrung: Eine Studie ueber die philosophische Theologie von Karl Jaspers" (Ph.D. dissertation, Munich, 1983).

21. A belated example of this attitude in criticism is Joyce Ann Joyce's redefinition of tragedy in her interpretation of *Native Son*. Cf. Joyce, *Richard Wright's Art of Tragedy* (Iowa City: University of Iowa Press, 1986).

22. *The New Grove Dictionary of Jazz*, ed. Barry Kernfeld (London: Macmillan, 1988), 2:508. Cf. also Albert Murray, *Stomping the Blues* (New York: McGraw Hill, 1976); John Gennari, "Jazz Criticism: Its Development and Ideologies," *Black American Literature Forum* 25 (Fall 1991): 449–523; Reginald T.Buckner and Steven Weiland, eds., *Jazz in Mind: Essays on the History and Meanings of Jazz* (Detroit: Wayne State University Press, 1991); Paul F. Berliner, *Thinking in Jazz: The Infinite Art of Improvisation* (Chicago: Chicago University Press, 1994); Jim Merod, ed., *Jazz as a Cultural Archive, boundary 2* 22, no. 2 [special issue] (Summer 1995).

23. Cf., e.g., the use of the term in Feather's criticism of André Hodeir in Leonard Feather, *The Book of Jazz* (New York: Horizon Press, 1957), 54. Cf. also Bhabha, *The Location of Culture*: "The social articulation of difference, from the minority perspective, is a complex, on-going negotiation that seeks to authorize cultural hybridities that emerge in moments of historical transformation" (2).

24. Pertinent information about research till 1980 can be found in Steven Thernstrom, Ann Orlov, and Oscar Handlin, eds., *The Harvard Encyclopedia of American Ethnic Groups* (Cambridge: Harvard University Press, 1980). Cf. esp. Harald J. Abramson, "Assimilation and Pluralism," 150–160; Philip Gleason, "American Identity and Americanization," 31–58; Michael Novak, "Pluralism: A Humanistic Perspective," 772–781; William Petersen, "Concepts of Ethnicity," 234–242; Werner Sollors, "Literature and Ethnicity," 647–665; Michael Walzer, "Pluralism: A Political Perspective," 781–787. For more recent discussions of "ethnicity" cf. Werner Sollors, "Theory of American Ethnicity, or: '? S ETHNIC?/TI AND AMERICAN/TI, DE OR UNITED (W) STATES S S1 AND THEOR?,'" *American Quarterly* 33, no. 3 (1981): 257–283; Anya Peterson Royce, *Ethnic Identity: Strategies of Diversity* (Bloomington: Indiana University Press, 1982); William Boelhower, *"Through A Glass Darkly": Ethnic Semiosis in American Literature* (Venice: Edizioni Helvetia, 1984); Sollors, *Beyond Ethnicity*; Werner Sollors, "A Critique of Pure Pluralism," in *Reconstructing American Literary History*, ed. Sacvan Bercovitch (Cambridge: Harvard University Press, 1986), 250–279; Winfried Siemerling and Katrin Schwenk, *Cultural Difference and the Literary Text: Pluralism and the Limits of Authenticity in North American Literatures* (Iowa City: University of Iowa Press, 1996); Samira Kawash, *Dislocating the Color Line: Identity, Hybridity, and Singularity in African-American Literature* (Stanford, Calif.: Stanford University Press, 1997).

25. Royce, *Ethnic Identity*, 18. Royce defines "style" as follows: "I use it to refer to a complex of symbols, forms, and value orientations that, when applied to ethnic groups, signals both the overt cultural contents and the underlying subjective values and standards by

which performance is judged. . . . [It] also implies that individuals have a choice in selecting appropriate styles" (28).

26. Royce, *Ethnic Identity*, 24.

27. Sollors, "Theory of American Ethnicity," 261.

28. Sollors, *Beyond Ethnicity*, 5–6.

29. Ibid., 11.

30. Ibid., 13–14.

31. Ibid., 234.

32. Ibid., 259.

33. Petersen, "Concepts of Ethnicity," 238.

34. Sollors, "Literature and Ethnicity," 649.

35. Ibid., 649.

36. Horace M. Kallen, *Culture and Democracy in the United States: Studies in the Group Psychology of the American Peoples* (New York: Boni and Liveright, 1924).

37. Sollors, "A Critique of Pure Pluralism," 258–259.

38. Ibid., 265.

39. Ibid., 273.

40. Albert Murray, *The Omni-Americans. Some Alternatives to the Folklore of White Supremacy* (New York: Outerbridge and Dienstfrey, 1970; reprint, New York: Da Capo Press, 1989), 22.

41. Ibid., 52.

42. Boelhower, *"Through a Glass Darkly"*, 33.

43. Du Bois, *The Souls of Black Folk*, 17.

44. Ralph Waldo Emerson, *Journals*, ed. W. E. Forbes and E. W. Emerson, 10 vols. (Boston: Houghton Mifflin, 1910–1914), 5:206.

45. Harold Waskow, *Whitman: Explorations in Form* (Chicago: Chicago University Press, 1966), 16, 22–48.

46. Cf. also "Double Consciousness: The Marginal Perspective in Language, Oral Culture, Folklore, Religion," in Berndt Ostendorf, *Black Literature in White America* (Sussex: Harvester Press; New Jersey: Barnes and Noble, 1982), 14–64. Cf. also James Clifford, *The Predicament of Culture: Twentieth-Century Ethnography, Literature, Art* (Cambridge: Harvard University Press, 1988): "The increased pace of historical change, the common recurrence of stress in the systems under study, forces a new self-consciousness about the way cultural wholes and boundaries are constructed and translated" (231).

47. Royce, *Ethnic Identity*, 133.

48. Molefi Kete Asante [Arthur L. Smith Jr.], *The Afrocentric Idea* (Philadelphia: Temple University Press, 1987), 32.

49. Cf., e.g., Cheikh Anta Diop, *The Cultural Unity of Black Africa: The Domains of Patriarchy/Matriarchy in Classical Antiquity* (London: Karnak House, 1989); Melville Herskovits, *The Myth of the Negro Past* (1941; reprint, Boston: Beacon Press, 1958).

50. Cf., e.g., Janheinz Jahn, *Muntu: The New African Culture* (New York: Grove Press, 1961); Imamu Amiri Baraka [LeRoi Jones], *Blues People* (New York: Morrow 1963); Haki Madhubuti, *Earthquakes and Sunrise Missions* (Chicago: Third World Press, 1984). The idea is as old as the history of black people in America. Martin R. Delany, Marcus Garvey, and Malcolm X are only three of its most conspicuous proponents.

51. Asante, *The Afrocentric Idea*, 125.

52. Cf. John S. Mbiti, *African Religions and Philosophy* (Garden City, N.Y.: Doubleday, 1969), esp. 348–353.

53. Cf. Cheik Anta Diop, *Precolonial Black Africa*, tr. Harold J. Salemson (Trenton, N.J.: Africa World Press Edition, and Westport, Conn.: Lawrence Hill, 1987); Martin Bernal, *Black Athena: The Afroasiatic Roots of Classical Civilization* (London: Free Association Books, 1987); St. Clair Drake, *Black Folk Here and There: An Essay in History and Anthropology* (Los Angeles: Center for Afro-American Studies, University of California, 1987); Molefi K. Asante, *Kemet, Afrocentricity, and Knowledge* (Trenton, N.J.: Africa World Press, 1990); K. K. Dompere, *Africentricity and African Nationalism: Philosophy and Ideology for Africa's Complete Emancipation* (Langley Park, Md.: I.A.A.S., 1992); Herbert Edwe-Ekwe and Femi Nzegwu, *Operationalising Afrocentrism* (Reading, Pa. : International Institute for Black Research, 1994); Errol Anthony Henderson, *Afrocentrism and World Politics: Towards a New Paradigm* (Westport, Conn.: Praeger, 1995). Mary R. Lefkowitz, *Not Out of Africa: How Afrocentrism Became an Excuse to Teach Myth as History* (New York: Basic Books, 1996); Dhyana Ziegler, ed., *Molefi Kete Asante and Afrocentricity: In Praise and in Criticism* (Nashville, Tenn.: James C. Winston, 1995).

54. "In fact, it is when the undiscriminated past is dwelt upon that ethnicity becomes crippling" (Royce, *Ethnic Identity*, 220). "And besides, look at what actually happened to the Africans who remained at home with their culture intact. Some 'African bag' polemicists cop out at this point" (Murray, *The Omni-Americans*, 185). For a caustic early rejection of a pan-African appropriation of African American writing, see James Baldwin, "Princes and Powers," in *Nobody Knows My Name: More Notes of a Native Son* (New York: Dial, 1961), 24–54. One of the best studies of the problem from the African point of view is Abiola Irele, *The African Experience in Literature and Ideology* (London and Exeter, N.H.: Heinemann, 1981; reprint with new introduction, Bloomington: Indiana University Press, 1990). For a positive vision of an Afrocentric literature, see also Melvin Dixon, "Toward a World Black Literature and Community," in *Chant of Saints: A Gathering of Afro-American Literature, Art, and Scholarship* ed. Michael S. Harper and Robert B. Stepto (Urbana: University of Illinois Press, 1979), 175–194.

55. "Creation myths of the type found in traditional African and European cultures are not present in the African American cultural experience, if we take the formal arrival of Africans in the Virginia colony in 1619 as a point of departure"; Asante, *The Afrocentric Idea*, 98.

56. "Yet messianism has no tradition in Africa; it became for the African in America, enslaved and abused, the one tenet of an apocalyptic-Judaic-Platonic heritage that immediately made sense"; Asante, *The Afrocentric Idea*, 127.

57. Cf. the section on Nat Turner's messianism in Asante, *The Afrocentric Idea*, 128–139.

58. Asante, *The Afrocentric Idea*, 183.

59. Gleason emphasizes the "future orientation" of American nationality and the "assimilationist idea" ("American Identity and Americanization," 33), thus distinguishing it from ethnicity and its regressive quality. Afrocentrism, it seems to me, despite its concern with roots, also contains a programmatic, future-oriented element, so that the comparison is not as far-fetched as it may appear at first sight. Cf. Clifford, *The Predicament of Culture*: "It is becoming common to distinguish two negritudes. Senghor's looks back to tradition and eloquently gathers up a collective 'African' essence. Césaire's is more syncretic, modernist, and parodic—Caribbean in its acceptance of fragments and in its appreciation of the mechanism of collage in cultural life" (173). For more recent contributions to the theme of Afrocentricity, consult Molefi K. Asante, *Kemet, Afrocentricity, and Knowledge* (Trenton, N.J.: Africa World Press, 1990); Dompere, *Africentricity and African Nationalism*; Herbert Edwe-Ekwe and Femi Nzegwu, *Operationalising Afrocentrism* (Reading: International Institute for

Black Research, 1994); Errol Anthony Henderson, *Afrocentrism and World Politics: Towards a New Paradigm* (Westport, Conn.: Praeger, 1995); Lefkowitz, *Not Out of Africa*; Ziegler, *Molefi Kete Asante and Afrocentricity*; Linda James Myers, *Understanding an Afrocentric World View: Introduction to an Optimal Psychology* (Dubuque, Iowa: Kendall/Hunt, 1988, 1993); Edward Scobie, *Global African Presence* (Brooklyn: A and B Books, 1994); Clovis E. Semmes, *Cultural Hegemony and African American Development* (Westport, Conn.: Praeger, 1992).

60. Asante, *The Afrocentric Idea*, 125.

61. Another paradox may be found in the current usage of the term "African diaspora" for American blacks. It is meant to mark the move from the margin to the center of cultural attention, but what is more marginal than a diaspora?

62. Barbara Johnson, response to Henry Louis Gates Jr., "Canon-Formation, Literary History, and The Afro-American Tradition: From the Seen to the Told," in *Afro-American Literary Study in the 1990s*, ed. Houston A. Baker Jr. and Patricia Redmond (Chicago: University of Chicago Press, 1989), 42.

63. Craig Werner uses two overlapping circles when he appropriates Elaine Showalter's "wild zone" to his analysis of African American culture, but Showalter's overlapping section seems to me too large to apply it to African Americans. Furthermore, the "crescent" he tries to interpret as the "wild zone" loses its quality of muteness when the concept of Afrocentricity is introduced into the model. See Craig Werner, "New Democratic Vistas: Toward a Pluralistic Genealogy," in *Belief versus Theory in Black American Literary Criticism*, ed. Joe Weixlmann and Chester J. Fontenot (Greenwood, Fla.: Penkevill, 1986), 50–55.

64. In the case of the American melting pot, this process would, e.g., demand the acceptance of "un-American" activities or bilingualism.

65. Fredrik Barth, ed., *Ethnic Groups and Boundaries: The Social Organization of Culture Difference* (Boston: Little, Brown, 1969).

66. Ibid., 15.

67. Ibid., 9.

68. Ibid., 10.

69. Ibid., 32–33.

70. Ibid., 38.

71. Ibid., 38.

72. "Barth takes the reasonable position that one cannot know an ethnic group by its content alone; therefore we should pay attention to its behavior, particularly its boundary-maintaining behavior. This idea was taken by many to mean that content was out and boundaries were in. It is time to return to a middle ground for the simple reason that one cannot understand let alone explain ethnic behavior without reference to both content and boundary, symbols and behavior"; Royce, *Ethnic Identity*, 7. "Moreover, I disagree with Barth's contention that the 'cultural stuff' enclosed by the boundary is not a critical focus of investigation. The 'cultural stuff' contains the very dynamics of boundary construction, whether it be an internally generated boundary, as in the case of Clachan, or one used to defend an ethnic enclave from the wider world"; Peter G. Mewett, "Boundaries and Discourse in a Lewis Crofting Community," in *Symbolising Boundaries: Identity and Diversity in British Cultures*, ed. Anthony P. Cohen (Manchester: Manchester University Press, 1986), 73. Cf. also Hans Vermeulen and Cora Govers, *The Anthropology of Ethnicity: Beyond "Ethnic Groups and Boundaries"* (The Hague: M. Nijhoff International, 1994).

73. Cf. Sollors, *The Invention of Ethnicity*, 241 n12.

74. Cf. Barth, *Ethnic Groups and Boundaries*, 18, 30.

75. "The preceding discussion has brought out a somewhat anomalous general feature of ethnic identity as a status: ascription is not conditional on the control of any specific assets, but rests on criteria of origin and commitment; whereas *performance* in the status, the adequate acting out of the roles required to realize the identity, in many systems does require such assets"; Barth, *Ethnic Groups and Boundaries*, 28.

76. Royce, *Ethnic Identity*, 29.

77. Cf. Royce, *Ethnic Identity*, 4, 6, 28, 30, 31, 145, 146, 150, 156, 230, 232.

78. Cf. Roberta Rubenstein, *Boundaries of the Self: Gender, Culture, Fiction* (Urbana: University of Illinois Press, 1987), 7.

79. Robert Frost, "Mending Wall," *Selected Poems of Robert Frost* (New York: Holt, Rinehart and Winston, 1963), 24.

80. Royce, *Ethnic Identity*, 6.

81. Rubenstein, *Boundaries of the Self*, 7.

82. Cf. Rubenstein, *Boundaries of the Self*, 4, 6, 8, 149. For a related, though in its results quite different, treatment of boundaries, see Nachman Ben-Yehuda, *Deviance and Moral Boundaries: Witchcraft, the Occult, Science Fiction, Deviant Sciences, and Scientists* (Chicago: University of Chicago Press, 1985).

83. Rubenstein, *Boundaries of the Self*, 238. Cf. also Royce, *Ethnic Identity*, 168.

84. "Paradoxically, then, the very concept of boundary itself is fluid. In the most general sense, it indicates the figurative line that divides, defines, distinguishes between two or more contiguous areas: When these areas are conceived as metaphorical rather than literal, the possibilities of meaning extend into diverse aspects of experience"; Rubenstein, *Boundaries of the Self*, 8. On the imaginary quality of the boundary, or, as he calls it, the "border," see also Jacques Derrida, "Some Statements and Truisms about Neologisms, Newisms, Postisms, Parasitism, and other small Seisms," trans. Anne Tomiche, in *The States of "Theory": History, Art, and Critical Discourse*, ed. David Carroll (Stanford, Calif.: Stanford University Press, 1987), 63–94.

85. Barth, *Ethnic Groups and Boundaries*, 9.

86. Situational ethnicity "implies the strategic use of an ethnic identity to fit particular situations"; Royce, *Ethnic Identity*, 202.

87. Ibid., 212.

88. "Ethnic cues and clues form the basis from which identities are negotiated. Cues are the features over which the individual has little or no control—skin color, hair type, body shape, and any other physical characteristic that can be used to categorize a person. Clues, in contrast, are identifying marks that people reveal during the course of an interaction in order to establish a specific identity. They may include language, dialect, origin, patterns of nonverbal communication, and in-group knowledge. Cues establish the fabric of the interaction, and clues embroider upon it"; ibid., 211–212.

89. Murray, *The Omni-Americans*, 50.

90. Royce, *Ethnic Identity*, 189, 212.

91. Hartwig Isernhagen, "Re-Orientation and Superimposition: Reinterpretations of Majority Topographies in Native American Literature," *Revue française d'études américaines* 36 (April 1988): 250, 251. Cf. also Isernhagen, "Literature—Language—Country: The Preservation of Difference and the Possibility of Relation," *Zeitschrift der Gesellschaft für Kanadastudien* 10, no. 1 (1986), and "Ethnicity, Minority, and Power: Challenges to

(American) Literary Historiography," in *The Future of American Modernism: Ethnic Writing between the Wars*, ed. William Boelhower (Amsterdam: VU University Press, 1990).

92. Royce proposes to "view any inter-ethnic situation in terms of . . . three factors": "power, perception, and purpose"; Royce, *Ethnic Identity*, 3.

93. Thomas Kochman, *Black and White Styles in Conflict* (Chicago: University of Chicago Press, 1981).

94. Cf. Amiri Baraka [LeRoi Jones], *Blues People* (New York: Morrow, 1963).

95. Walt Whitman, "As I Ebb'd with the Ocean of Life," in *Leaves of Grass: Comprehensive Reader's Edition*, ed. Harold W. Blodgett and Sculley Bradley (New York: New York University Press, 1965), 253–256.

96. "Ask any Negro what he knows about the white people with whom he works. And then ask the white people with whom he works what they know about *him*"; James Baldwin, *The Fire Next Time* (New York: Dial, 1963), 138.

97. Victor Turner, *Dramas, Fields, and Metaphors: Symbolic Action in Human Society* (Ithaca, N.Y.: Cornell University Press, 1974): "Thus, for me, *liminality* represents the midpoint of transition in a status-sequence between two positions" (237). "What I call liminality, the state of being in between successive participations in social milieux dominated by social structural considerations, whether formal or unformalized, is not precisely the same as communitas, for it is a sphere or domain of action or thought rather than a social modality"(52).

98. Bhabha, *The Location of Culture*, 1.

99. Ibid., 4.

100. Ibid., 5, 9.

101. For other recent theorizing of boundaries, see Stanton W. Green and Stephen M. Perlman, eds., *The Archeology of Frontiers and Boundaries* (Orlando, Fla.: Academic Press, 1985); Matthew Melko and Leighton R. Scott, eds., *The Boundaries of Civilizations in Space and Time* (Lanham, Md.: University Press of America, 1987); bell hooks, "Choosing the Margin as a Space of Radical Openness," *Yearning: Race, Gender, and Cultural Politics* (Boston: South End Press, 1990); D. Emily Hicks, *Border Writing: The Multidimensional Text* (Minneapolis: University of Minnesota Press, 1991); cf. also Winfried Siemerling and Katrin Schwenk, *Cultural Difference and the Literary Text: Pluralism and the Limits of Authenticity in North American Literatures* (Iowa City: University of Iowa Press, 1996). Cf. also Kawash, *Dislocating the Color Line*.

102. *Afro-American Literary Studies*. For an earlier—and actually much more contentious—demonstration of boundaries in academic discourse, see Henry Louis Gates Jr., ed., *"Race," Writing, and Difference* (Chicago: University of Chicago Press, 1986). Cf. also Gates, *Loose Canons : Notes on the Culture Wars* (New York: Oxford University Press, 1992).

103. Baker and Redmond, *Afro-American Literary Study in the 1990s*, 14.

104. Cf. also Henry Louis Gates Jr., *The Signifying Monkey: A Theory of Afro-American Literary Criticism* (New York: Oxford University Press, 1988); *Figures in Black: Words, Signs, and the "Racial" Self* (New York: Oxford University Press, 1987); *Thirteen Ways of Looking at a Black Man* (New York: Random House, 1997).

105. "We *must* not, Appiah concludes, ask 'the reader to understand Africa by embedding it in European culture'"; Baker and Redmond, *Afro-American Literary Study in the 1990s*, 27.

106. Barbara Johnson in Baker and Redmond, *Afro-American Literary Study in the 1990s*, 42.

107. Donald Gibson in Baker and Redmond, *Afro-American Literary Study in the 1990s*, 46.

108. Deborah McDowell, "Boundaries: Or Distant Relations and Close Kin," in Baker and Redmond, *Afro-American Literary Study in the 1990s*, 59.

109. Michael Awkward's response to McDowell's essay in Baker and Redmond, *Afro-American Literary Study in the 1990s*, 76.

110. Kimberly Benston, "Performing Blackness: Re/Placing Afro-American Poetry," in Baker and Redmond, *Afro-American Literary Study in the 1990s*, 174.

111. Hortense J. Spillers's response to Deborah McDowells's article in Baker and Redmond, *Afro-American Literary Study in the 1990s*, 72.

112. Cf. Werner Sollors, *Neither Black nor White yet Both: Thematic Explorations of Interracial Literature* (New York: Oxford University Press, 1997); Fritz Gysin, "Scandalous Roots: Black and White Ancestry in Recent African American Fiction," in *Families*, SPELL: Swiss Papers in English Language and Literature 9, ed. Werner Senn (Tübingen: Gunter Narr Verlag, 1996), 169–177.

113. Raymond Andrews, *Appalachee Red* (New York: Dial, 1978); Charles Johnson, *Oxherding Tale* (Bloomington: Indiana University Press, 1982), *Middle Passage* (New York: Atheneum, 1990); John Edgar Wideman, *Sent for You Yesterday* (New York: Avon, 1983); cf. Fritz Gysin, "Predicaments of Skin: Boundaries in Recent African American Fiction," in *The Black Columbiad: Defining Moments in African American Literature and Culture*, ed. Maria Diedrich and Werner Sollors (Cambridge: Harvard University Press: 1994), 286–297.

114. Albert Murray, *Train Whistle Guitar* (New York: McGraw-Hill, 1974), *The Spyglass Tree* (New York: Pantheon Books, 1991), *The Seven League Boots* (New York: Pantheon Books, 1995), *The Blue Devils of Nada: A Contemporary American Approach to Aesthetic Statement* (New York: Pantheon Books, 1996); Gayl Jones, *Corregidora* (New York: Random House, 1975); Wideman, *Sent for You Yesterday*; Nathaniel Mackey, *Bedouin Hornbook*, Callaloo Fiction Series (Lexington: University Press of Kentucky, 1986), *Djibot Baghostus's Run* (Los Angeles: Sun and Moon Press, 1993), "*ATET A.D.*: An Excerpt," *Callaloo* 19, no. 3 (Summer 1996): 690–703. Cf. Fritz Gysin, "African American Modernism and the Construction of the Blues," in *Aspects of Modernism: Studies in Honour of Max Naenny*, Andreas Fischer, Martin Heusser, and Thomas Hermann (Tübingen: Gunter Narr, 1997), 279–294; "From 'Liberating Voices' to 'Metathetic Ventriloquism': Boundaries in Recent African American Jazz Fiction," *Callaloo* (forthcoming).

115. Ishmael Reed, *Flight to Canada* (New York: Random House, 1976); David Bradley, *The Chaneysville Incident* (New York: Harper and Row, 1981); Johnson, *Oxherding Tale*, *Middle Passage*; Sherley Anne Williams, *Dessa Rose* (New York: William Morrow, 1986); Toni Morrison, *Beloved* (New York: Knopf, 1987); John Edgar Wideman, *Fever* (New York: Henry Holt, 1989), *The Cattle Killing* (Boston: Houghton Mifflin, 1996). Cf. Fritz Gysin, "John Edgar Wideman: 'Fever' (1989)," in *The African American Short Story, 1970 to 1990*, ed. Wolfgang Karrer and Barbara Puschmann-Nalenz (Trier: Wissenschaftlicher Verlag Trier, 1993), 193–204; "From Reconstruction to Deconstruction: Dessa Rose and the Flim-Flamming of the Civil War," in *Red Badges of Courage: Wars and Conflicts in American Culture*, ed. Biancamaria Pisapia, Ugo Rubeo, and Anna Scacchi, Rivista di Studi Anglo-Americani (Roma: Bulzoni Editore, 1998), 526–531; "The Enigma of the Return," in *Black Imagination and the Middle Passage*, ed. Maria Diedrich, Henry Louis Gates Jr., and Carl Pedersen (New York: Oxford University Press, 1999), 183–190.

116. Sollors, *Beyond Ethnicity*, 37.

117. Rubenstein, *Boundaries of the Self*, 238.

118. Clifford, *The Predicament of Culture*, 119.

119. Ibid., 131.

120. John Edgar Wideman, "The Architectonics of Fiction," *Callaloo* 13, no. 1 (Winter 1990), 43.

When All Met Together in One Room

Josef Jařab Interviews Allen Ginsberg

Part I

JOSEF JAŘAB: How do you feel about people saying that the whole beat movement started with you meeting [Jack] Kerouac and [William S.] Burroughs somewhere in the 1940s and ended with [Neal] Cassady's and Kerouac's deaths in the 1960s? Can we really limit it this way?

ALLEN GINSBERG: Well, you know, the notion of the "beat generation" as a literary movement has a real basis, but it's also a journalistic stereotype. It's originally just a group of friends who *later* were called the beat generation, but we did have some views in common. It was an extended circle, or an extended family. I would say that Kerouac and Burroughs were at the heart of it; myself learning a great deal from them, and other integral members were Gregory Corso, from the 1950s on, and Peter Orlovsky. That would be an inner circle of friends. But from 1948 on there were a number of other poets with whom we associated who were traditionally part of the beat generation—the anthologies, and a friendship circle. You'd have to include Gary Snyder, Philip Whalen, and Lew Welch. Gary Snyder and Philip Whalen have gone on to become accomplished Zen practitioners—Zen *sensei*, which means "teachers," and they have been given transmission so that if they continue teaching, they would be Zen masters, the first American poet Zen masters, who were, incidentally, integral to the beat generation. So there's been a great deal of development out of what was in 1960 considered sloppy home-made Buddhism but which actually was most accomplished and sophisticated. *The Dharma Bums*, Kerouac's novel about Snyder in 1957, begins a progression from Snyder going to Japan to study, and now he winds up with transmission to teach. As for myself, you know, I participated in founding the Jack Kerouac School of Disembodied Poetics at Naropa Institute, which is the first Buddhist college in the Western world accredited along with other schools and universities. That's quite an accomplishment and a development, a ripening of early interests, or as Robert Graves wrote in *To Juan at the Winter Solstice*. "Nothing promised that was not performed."

Then if you survey the galaxy of writers associated with the beat generation you find that only Kerouac died, Neal Cassady died, Lew Welch died early. Living and growing and more and more powerful artistically, and more influential finally, are Burroughs, myself, Gregory Corso, Gary Snyder, Philip Whalen, Michael McClure, Robert Creeley (who's always been a friendly associate), Peter Orlovsky (who published a book very late in 1978, his first book), also LeRoi Jones/Amiri Baraka, and Lawrence Ferlinghetti in San Francisco. And I'm going to try to name the geniuses in a second generation: Among the best poets who were students and friends of Kerouac and shared influence from the beat generation and the New York school: Anne Waldman, Ted Berrigan, Ron Padgett, Ed Sanders, Bob Dylan, among others. And in a third generation beyond that: David Cope, Antler, Andy Clausen, Patti Smith, Jim Carroll, John Giorno.

JJ: Somehow then, there's quite an extension into the present.

AG: Yeah, and you'll find we have a better survival rate than most insurance men or professors. Certainly a lot better than the academic poets of our era who have wrecked themselves drinking, like John Berryman, Delmore Schwartz, Robert Lowell, and Randall Jarrell, who committed suicide.

JJ: Sylvia Plath.

AG: Yeah. So that as distinct from the academic poets perhaps we were saved by our interest in marijuana rather than alcohol. Those of us who died early were those who had problems with alcohol. The old American . . .

JJ: Monster.

AG: Yes, the old American monster. So that I would say that the major people of the beat generation have gone on to the last forty years, the 1940s to 1980s, growing in authenticity and power. Burroughs's most recent work is his most powerful, a trilogy: *Cities of the Red Night* (1981), *The Place of Dead Roads* (1984), and *The Western Lands* (1987). My later work will take time for people to catch up, but the late 1970s work includes *Father Death Blues*, *Plutonian Ode*, and *White Shroud*. Gregory Corso's 1981 poem "Herald of the Autochthonic Spirit" is almost an international classic and will be when it's translated. It has been translated already into Russian, Chinese, and Hungarian.

JJ: Well, we'll hurry up and have our own Czech translation soon.

AG: Now for the ideas involved—recollect that Gary Snyder and Michael McClure back in the 1950s poetry readings introduced early notions of ecology. It's taken the mainstream of American society thirty-five years to catch up to those insights introduced in original beat poetry—in the tradition of Thoreau, Whitman, but formulating it as regard for nature, regard for the industrial wasting of the planet or up to the point where now we might even say that the planet itself has AIDS. The immune system of the planet is no longer able to restore the damage done by the human virus.

JJ: That's a powerful image.

AG: Yes, I mean, the immune system of the planet may not be able to cope with environmental degradation through hypertechnology and human overpopulation.

JJ: Terrifying.

AG: Well, on the other hand, there's a new theory among gay AIDS people of not "people *dying* of AIDS" but of "people *living* with AIDS"—as an attitude: not taking a negative attitude.

There's also—introduced somewhat by Kerouac—a main theme, the appreciation of Negro black culture and jazz. Another continuing theme or motif in ongoing beat literature is the reconsideration of the nature of consciousness: the introduction in literary terms and in practical, social terms of "East meets West," that is, the meeting of the Eastern and Western minds; the introduction of meditation practice, now familiar to many poets, more and more influential in the 1970s and 1980s in the American culture; even the founding of an institution to train young poets in that area of contemporary poetics, at Naropa.

So that what we've done is try to find permanent forms for these "open mind" insights. And it so happens that the particular "bohemian" insights that Kerouac had into spontaneous mind are also classical notions in Japanese, Chinese, and Tibetan poetry. It was for lack of sophistication and a sad provincialism among American and English literary scholars—even European scholars, but more the American and English scholars of the 1950s and 1960s—that they didn't recognize Kerouac's aesthetic of "first thought, best thought," as relating to calligraphy, haiku, Tao, Tibetan mind forms, the whole teaching practice of Zen and Tibetan Buddhism, in which seeing the mind is the guideline for wisdom. The discipline is in the *mind* first, not on the page revised over and over.

JJ: Yes, the apparent simplicity here is, in fact, complex.

AG: Yes, like improvised jazz. The mistaken notion of an "undisciplined" Kerouac, an "ignorant" Kerouac, by the academy misled people who did not realize that Kerouac was extremely sophisticated, intelligent, and extremely learned, and that he had a good grasp of ideas on wisdom practices. And technically, writing insights. So you could say on several levels in the psychedelic, ecological, the contemplative aesthetics, and the advanced, postmodern aesthetics, the beat generation's early practices have developed and rightfully become much more understandable now. Even Burroughs's cut-ups are understandable in terms of music television—MTV. And, of course, regarding Burroughs, Kerouac, to some extent, myself, the influence of these poets, not only in Eastern Europe as well as in China or Russia is very strong, but also in the younger generations in America. Every decade has a revival of beat generation 1940s, 1950s, 1960s texts—a reappreciation. It seems to be the main literature that survives of us in Europe, as the academic literature begins to fade for lack of energy, vividness, and adventure—and appreciation of the planetary new consciousness.

JJ: The vividness seems to be the key word with us, for instance. And it has functioned this way for decades.

AG: Another element is that a lot of the literature of the beat generation comes directly out of a classical lineage in American writing; it didn't get itself born, it didn't hatch out of an egg from nowhere. It was the line of . . .

JJ: Whitman?

AG: Whitman, of course, and Thoreau the ecologist, and Emerson the individualist. But also, Robert Creeley was engaged in correspondence about how to run a magazine, *Black Mountain Review*, with Ezra Pound. And William Carlos Williams wrote prefaces to two of my books and received me and Jack and Peter and Gregory in his living room and warned us, as he pointed out the window, "There's a lot of bastards out there." I knew Caresse Crosby and met Marianne Moore and spent time with Pound. Burroughs and I visited Louis-Ferdinand Céline in the last year of his life. And there was in America—in Chicago and New Haven and in San Francisco—Jean Genet; and of course there were Genet and others, and we met in Paris, not only Céline, but also Tristan Tzara, Benjamin Peret, Marcel Duchamp, and Man Ray, many in the cafés in the late 1950s. Actually we come from a very sophisticated lineage, both European and American.

JJ: [Guillaume] Apollinaire meant a lot for you, didn't he?

AG: Yes, when I lived in Paris I wrote an homage at his tomb. And it was supposed to be a signal to the American academics where I was coming from, but I don't think they picked up on it. So we were continuing that open form "filiation" or "lineage," Whitman through Pound and Williams, through Olson, Creeley and Kerouac, which I think is a mainstream in American letters historically; we joined that with a musical interest in black culture. The synthesis of all these themes, after us, was the very remarkable Bob Dylan, who incidentally says that it was *Mexico City Blues* that blew his mind and turned him on to poetry. Someone handed him a copy in 1958 or 1959 in St. Paul. Over Kerouac's grave, Bob Dylan told me that "it blew my mind." And I said, "Why?" and he said, "It's the first poetry that talked American language to me." So you get a line in Dylan like "the motorcycle black Madonna two-wheeled gypsy queen and her silver studded phantom lover" which comes straight out of either "Howl" or Kerouac's *Mexico City Blues* in terms of the "chain of flashing images." Kerouac's spontaneous pile-up of words. And that's the way Dylan writes his lyrics. So poetry's extended itself in its own lineage afterward into John Lennon, the Beatles (named after beats), and Dylan, so that it's gone around the world. And I think after the wave of Whitman and then maybe another wave of Pound, it's probably the strongest wave of American influence on world literature—the combination.

JJ: Definitely in our part of the world from the 1960s onward.

AG: Well, it's the same in China. And India and Japan somewhat. England is very resistant. This culture is widespread in France, and Norway, Sweden.

JJ: I understand there was a wonderful French anthology put together on the beat movement. Have you seen that?

AG: Yes, a number of them. I have seen them. And also, really influential, most influential in Italy. A whole generation there. Not only the poets and writers but also painters and intellectuals. So I would say probably the presence—

not the presence, but the influence of the beat generation is probably stronger now than it ever was, because in the late 1950s and early 1960s it was "notorious": what they were getting was a media-packaged Frankenstein version of people with berets and cockroaches and eyeglasses and bongo drums. Out of *Time* magazine and the CIA version, rather than the original literature.

JJ: And the cultural movement that it became in a way. Would you call it a movement?

AG: Well, a movement in the sense that it had elements that led to the Greens.

JJ: Yes.

AG: To ecological, psychedelic politics.

JJ: The name of John Clellon Holmes has not come up in our talk so far.

AG: Holmes was a very nice guy.

JJ: Was he a sort of Boswell of the movement?

AG: No, no. He was a good, close friend of Kerouac and a very good, close friend of mine. Back in the 1940s and early 1950s. I don't think he was as great a genius in prose as either Kerouac or Burroughs, or even Hubert Selby Jr. [author of *Last Exit to Brooklyn* (1964), *The Room* (1971), and others], who I like. There's still a little, a slightly middle-class American novelist prose style. It isn't an invention. Holmes was very advanced in cultural appreciation, but I think the most important thing is the actual texture of prose; basically the beat generation is a movement of people who began working together in the ivory tower, purely for art's sake. The reason it had a social fallout is that it's close to an Einsteinian "art for art's sake" wherein the subject is *the nature of the mind itself.* Candor! Whitman's word for what he asked from future poets was "candor." So in examining the texture of consciousness, the psychedelic aspect of the contemplative, a Buddhist aspect, naturally everything else rises—all the contents of the mind. Nothing human is alien: erotic, ecological, political, and whatnot.

One thing I forgot was that with the trials of *Howl, Naked Lunch,* and the Grove Press's efforts to legalize *Lady Chatterley's Lover* and Henry Miller, we were part of the liberation of the word. I would say what happened in the 1940s and early 1950s was a spiritual lib, late 1950s liberation of the word, legally, in America; breakdown of censorship. The last big censorship trial was *Naked Lunch* in 1966. After that the floodgates were open to anything! From that you have many different kinds of liberation; like women's lib, gay lib, even to some extent, black lib. You might know Abbie Hoffman and Tom Hayden went south to Birmingham to help blacks gain the vote and begin desegregation of races in the early 1960s with copies of *On the Road* in their pockets. There was some beat influence; it wasn't the main one; but it was a substantial breakthrough that made people look around at America and begin to examine the texture of American life and society in stasis at the end of the 1950s. So from "spiritual lib," I would say, to progression of language lib, it would have, as a fallout, other social liberation movements: the gay lib, sexual revolution, sex lib, to women's lib to some black lib and old folks lib, Gray Panther Lib, and then minority lib and then appreciation of American Indian liberation and appreciation of the quality of indigenousness; and individuality rather than homogeneity.

JJ: Did the black poets like Bob Kaufman, LeRoi Jones, or Ted Jones spontaneously join the whole movement in its spirit, or would they bring something that was new, additional?

AG: Well, we were social companions. And literary companions by the late 1950s. See, LeRoi Jones wrote me in Paris when I was living with Burroughs asking for material for *Yugen* magazine, which he'd just started. His *Yugen* magazine (1958–1960) was one of the great magazines of that time. I would say three or four were: *Black Mountain Review*, which in its last issue carried the signal pages of Burroughs's *Naked Lunch*; Philip Whalen poems; Kerouac's "Brakeman on the Railroad" and his "Essentials of Modern Prose"; my own poem, "America"; and Herbert Huncke's story "Elsie." All those were in the last issue of *Black Mountain Review*.

JJ: And *Floating Bear*?

AG: *Floating Bear* was edited by LeRoi Jones and Diane di Prima. Also *Evergreen Review* and *Chicago Review* to *Big Table*; and maybe one or two other mimeograph magazines, like *Combustion*, edited by Ray Souster, a disciple of Williams's from Toronto. Also, LeRoi Jones had the grand "salon"—literary salon in the late 1950s at which you could find all the contributors to *Yugen*. Three blocks away from here on Fourteenth Street, I saw at one party, in one room, at one time, Langston Hughes, Don Cherry, Ornette Coleman, Cecil Taylor, Franz Kline, Kerouac, myself, Orlovsky, Corso, A. B. Spellman, other blacks that I didn't know at that time; Frank O'Hara, maybe Frank's friends, Larry Rivers and Arnold Weinstein; maybe intersecting with Kenneth Koch, John Ashbery, and others; Robert Creeley, Charles Olson —Olson wasn't there until Creeley was around New York.

JJ: This was an amazing combination.

AG: It was a real mad combination— "All American." The later jazz all based on spontaneous wisdom. The abstract expressionism, free jazz, open form poetry, or spontaneous mind poetry. Jones even went to visit a Buddhist teacher as well. And *Yugen* also had material by Snyder and Whalen. So there was an era of good feeling from the late 1950s—and there was Peter Orlovsky; the poets Paul Blackburn, Joel Oppenheimer, and Ray Bremser would all be there, part of LeRoi's *Yugen* salon. There were some parties where we were all together, some beautiful moments. That was the cultural cresting of the beat generation. It was also a joining culturally of black and white. Eldridge Cleaver and Jones appreciated Kerouac's appreciation of black culture. For that Kerouac was really putdown by neoconservative whites—these ideologues called him a white chauvinist. Actually, Kerouac noticed that black culture was "mis-noticed" in America. That was his phrase—"mis-noticed" (very delicate phrase)—by the white culture. You know the passage in *On The Road* where he passes a porch, and he sees wild, happy, funny blacks enjoying the jazz and the last sunshine. It's dusk on the porch. Eldridge Cleaver read that paragraph in jail and admired and thought it was great. But Norman Podhoretz, a neoconservative critic blind to Kerouac's prose beauty, cites it as an example of Kerouac's ignorance and white chauvinism. Blacks liked his élan in those days as being signs of sympathetic companionship and liked that particular passage in *On The Road.*

JJ: Yes, well, that explains what one always feels, even from a distance. I think there was more of black and white being seen apart from within America than there is from the distance of, let's say, Europe.

AG: Maybe Kerouac as French-Canadian had a more European vision. Kerouac had a lot of experience in Harlem in the early 1940s. He witnessed the development of bebop with Esoteric Records, with recording engineer Jerry Newman and Seymour Wyse, Kerouac's Horace Mann High School friend; when he was a student he went out and heard jazz at Minton's and saw in person Charlie Christian, "Bird" Parker, Lester Young, Roy Eldridge, Gillespie, Coleman Hawkins, Illinois Jaquete, Bud Powell, and others; so Kerouac had a great immersion in black bop culture. He would listen to bebop all the way, all night. Sometimes we listened in 1944–1948 to Symphony Sid's radio broadcasts; Sid was a very famous guy. He was really a disc jockey and was broadcasting the new bebop classics then.

So there was some mixture of cultures all along. I would say that it was like a confluence. A lot of black poets then and now by hindsight attribute to me or Kerouac a kind of breakthrough in poetry which empowered them to write in their own cultural idiom again, or reinforced their own values.

JJ: Right. It must be gratifying.

AG: At least—that's what I heard recently from Audre Lorde, June Jordan, and many of the African American poets here who appreciated what we had done as a kind of liberation of language and a feeling, so that they could manifest their private world and not to imitate the academic white.

JJ: I think it's only fair and justified, I'm sure. That's the way we've seen it from the distance . . .

AG: And that's the way I see it, as a confluence.

JJ: Have we explained the name of Lawrence Ferlinghetti in our talk?

AG: Now, that's right. Ferlinghetti played a very strong role as publisher, appreciator, and old bohemian. There's a certain melancholy Old World quality in his poetry that's inimitable and very valuable.

JJ: He's also the French connection, is he not?

AG: Yes, for [Jacques] Prévert and his Sorbonne education. Because of his surrealist interests, Philip Lamantia's also a larger French connection, with [André] Breton. Yes, he definitely had that French café sense; Ferlinghetti is a champ. His poetry, though, seems a little too referential, dependent on puns, on atmosphere and French mood rather than on the kind of precision that Ezra Pound or Williams would, uh . . .

JJ: Ask for.

AG: Ask for. Yeah.

JJ: And Philip's? Philip Lamantia's?

AG: He's very valuable, particularly in the late 1950s, his *Collected Poems* from City Lights. I understand he's had several books out since, all good. He was very ill for a while. He kept switching back and forth between surrealism and Catholicism and junkyism and whatnot, now finally bird ecology. But he's always had an interesting career. When I went to China to teach I brought his texts as exemplary postwar American poetry with a genuine surrealist flavor.

JJ: When was that?

AG: In 1984 or 1985—I was there two and a half months, and I taught in the Foreign Language Institutes in Beijing, and in various colleges in Tunming, Suchow, Hangchou, and Baoding, and Shanghai's Fudan University.

JJ: Had there been any knowledge of your work and the beats in general?

AG: Yes, I found that in the Chinese anthology of twentieth-century prose, volume two, used by the elite foreign-language students, who study English and come to MIT, the largest single selection of prose was Kerouac. Printed in China! With a very appreciative and very intelligent, understanding essay on it. Better than I've ever seen in America.

JJ: That's very surprising.

AG: Very funny. Also, Snyder and I had been influences on the recent "misty" or "obscure" school of post–Cultural Revolution Chinese poetry.

JJ: So what did you teach in China? What was the message you wanted to convey?

AG: I had to decide what was the essence of American poetry that I would want them to experience. So what I brought was a bit of Pound, several poems by Charles Reznikoff, a lot of W. C. Williams: "the pure products of America go crazy"—that's always in his poems; then I jumped to contemporaries. And I presented some brief prose by Burroughs, some of Kerouac's "Mexico City Blues," and a few prose sketches from *Visions of Cody*. Philip Lamantia—a few poems of his; Gregory Corso's "Bomb" and "Hello" and "Gasoline"; a long poem by Kerouac that had not been published on Mao Tse-tung. A few poems by Orlovsky, particularly one on recycling of human manure in Chinese rice fields. John Wieners—two or three poems by Creeley. So of the contemporaries it was Wieners, Creeley, a little Olson, Gary Snyder, Philip Whalen, Lew Welch, Lamantia, Peter Orlovsky, David Cope, Michael McClure, and one or two that I've forgotten. That was what I thought was the essence. With a copy of the Don Allen anthology *New American Poetry, 1945–1960*.

JJ: Did you try Nanao's [Nanao Sakaki's] poetry on them?

AG: Yes, I brought one or two poems of Nanao. As part of the Snyder selection—a dozen poems. Those are not the standard American anthology, but the Chinese students really appreciated it.

JJ: Did you teach poetry in this country before you taught in China, or is the current appointment at Brooklyn College the first one in the academic world?

AG: I had been teaching at Naropa Institute since 1974, and what I taught was, for four terms, line by line, the complete works of William Blake, from beginning to end. Up to the seventh book of the Vala, the seventh night. By then all the students had gone on and I could start all over again. I also taught a course on William Carlos Williams.

JJ: There?

AG: Yes. Some of it's been published in *Composed on the Tongue* — you'll find several lectures on Williams there. And I taught a course on the English lyric from Pound's "Seafarer," up through Corso. Lyric. You know, Thomas Wyatt and Eliot, Pope, Dryden, Christopher Smart, Campion, all the way up. I taught a course in Sapphic poetry. And classical meters—quantitative meter as distinct from stress meter. Then I taught a course in nineteenth-century American poetry geniuses—Poe, Dickinson, Melville's poetry, and his prose from *Pierre*, and Whitman. Then I taught a series of courses called Literary History of the beat generation. Those are being transcribed to be edited as a book.

JJ: As for the teaching, however, do I understand correctly that the Naropa students would be people already motivated and interested primarily in studying poetry?

AG: Right.

JJ: Well, that would make them a different lot from the students at Brooklyn College, wouldn't it?

AG: No. I'm teaching the MFA Poetics program there, primarily.

JJ: And what about the current course in Afro-American Poetics?

AG: This "Black American Literary Genius" is a volunteer course I invented for my own pleasure and to make a bridge to the students there and stir things up culturally, make a bridge over the alienation between the different cultural-social groups.

At Naropa the students attend (1) the Jack Kerouac School of Poetics; (2) the Naropa Institute Buddhist Contemplative College; and (3) summer programs with myself, Gregory Corso, William Burroughs, Anselm Hollo, Kenneth Koch, Robert Creeley, Diane di Prima, and Anne Waldman; those are the people that come and teach. What we've done is codify the same gang as in *Yugen* magazine and the *Black Mountain Review*. We've codified that as an institution for transmission from generation to generation, which is something I don't think other generations of poets have done so well. The American "fugitives" did it with Vanderbilt in the South and Kenyon College. There was some of that with Eliot, but it didn't come to much poetry really, more for academic teaching and criticism— whereas we combine poetics with the discipline and classicism of Tibetan Buddhism and Zen; we literally have Tibetan lamas and Zen masters coming there to teach. Connected with Burroughs, myself, and joining each other with a great deal of respect. So these are historically very interesting complementarities. Like the American beatnik and black and now the American beatnik black post-beat connection with the Tibetan—with the East. You see, Eliot studied Sanskrit and had some Himalayan wisdom, but I don't think he knew Zen masters and Tibetan lamas directly. Whereas we're actually working in conjunction, experiencing the actual texture of the mind with the originators of the Himalayan tradition. Yeats had a deal with third-hand theosophy derived from Himalayan transmission gone through the Golden Dawn Society, Madame Blavatsky, and what mish-mash! Eliot had a "mélange adultère de tous." We have a more direct transmission. Also many of us actually went to India—the Whitmanic "Passage to India" was made literal in our generation.

JJ: Whereas for Whitman it was a daydream?

AG: Yes, a very intuitive and brilliant daydream. We had the chance to actually embody, manifest that.

JJ: I was going to drop this question, but now that you mention the Buddhists, the Zen and all that, someone, I think it was Carolyn Cassady, said that the beat movement was much more than is generally believed a religious movement. Would you agree with that?

AG: Yeah, in the sense that it was mystically religious, yet practical and artistic. Kerouac spoke of it as "the Second Religiousness," a phrase he took from Spengler who points out that in a time of declining empires, a second religiousness arises. Kerouac's adaptation of the phrase. You should take a look at his great essay "The Origins of the Beat Generation." It's a brilliant thing, very definitive.

JJ: One footnote question: the essay by Norman Mailer "The White Negro"—was it of particular importance for the movement?

AG: I don't think Kerouac dug it, because I think he thought it was relatively "ideological," it's clear. It probably was very intelligent, though, because he, Mailer, had a good grasp or glimpse of the great apocalyptic goof that middle-class white culture was making. You know, he had some sense of an apocalypse or transcendence, beyond ideology, some transcendent change of consciousness. So I think he's tuned in properly there. Except that Mailer, unfortunately, has, to some extent, "out-Hemingwayed" that macho business of thinking that "the cool psychopath" was more macho and more honest than a delicate artistic fairy like me, you know. Mailer has some sort of boxing-Hemingway-macho element that Kerouac was much too sophisticated to settle for. Kerouac, as a football player, didn't have to worry about that, you know, about physical boxing (or mental boxing). So that I think Kerouac disliked Mailer's and [John Clellon] Holmes's interpretation of beat as "criminal" and "psychopathic" flavored, because Kerouac saw beat as Christlike; the Lamb, the emergence of the Lamb, not the emergence of the grand criminal savants. So he thought Mailer had it inside out.

JJ: On the terminology now, "beat" and "hip"—what is the connection and what is the development of, let's say, the legacy of one into the other?

AG: Well, both words, etymologically, were introduced literarily by Herbert Huncke to us about 1944–1945.

JJ: They were? So what is true about the word that Bob Kaufman introduced "beat"?

AG: Kaufman came on the scene—well, I met him only in the late 1950s, 1959, in San Francisco, though he was around before, but you know . . .

JJ: Barbara Christian, a black female critic, maintains it was Kaufman who invented that term and cited that as another example of blacks not being recognized for their contributions in America.

AG: No. John Clellon Holmes in 1952 had this article, "This Is the Beat Generation," in the *New York Times*. Kaufman came to prominence later literarily, you know, San Francisco in the late 1950s. And lived upstairs from me on 170 East Second Street in the Lower East Side and took psilocybin then in my apartment, with Kerouac, when Timothy Leary visited, 1960.

JJ: So it *does* come from Huncke?

AG: Oh, yeah. Our introduction is 1944–1945–1946 from Huncke. Ten years—really—fifteen years earlier, 1945. Huncke around Times Square.

JJ: And "hip"?

AG: He used that word also.

JJ: Could you specify the differences between the terms?

AG: Now, the beat generation was, so to speak, a literary group. It was only later, by hindsight, called the beat generation in the *Times*. On the basis of a conversation with Kerouac. Kerouac was *un*naming generations, saying it's not a generation; it's no "lost generation," it's just a beat generation. Everybody's too beat to be a generation. So Holmes then thought this was an interesting phrase. And then in the *New York Times* magazine wrote, "This Is the Beat Generation," 1952. But again defining it with a side overtone in terms of violence and juvenile delinquency, that is, mindless protest. So that was pasted on Kerouac by Norman Podhoretz later, that beat folk were all ignorant criminals. But Kerouac was religious and talking about the Lamb of Jesus and spontaneous Buddhist mind.

JJ: Right.

AG: And I was having visions of Blake in 1948; we weren't illiterate "barbarian" psychopaths.

JJ: And you were also cleansing of all the middle-class stuff, is that right?

AG: I don't think we were concerned with the middle-class values.

JJ: No?

AG: That's a middle-class paranoia. The middle-class writer people in *Time* magazine thought we were rebelling.

JJ: So the beatniks were not rebels?

AG: Caught up by William Blake, you don't have to worry about cleansing yourself of "middle-class values."

JJ: All right, I am trying to understand.

AG: It's a minor matter, the "middle-class values" in this context. That's like a relatively primitive Marxist notion, you know, "bourgeois" and "middle class." That's some hangover from class war. Kerouac's whole point was that beat went beyond the old Marxist ideological battle of class warfare and into some *practical* attitude of transcendence. Practical had to do with, I mean, like dropping LSD or learning meditation techniques. It's like the bomb, you know. It's not cleansing yourself of the middle class, it's *cleansing the doors of perception themselves*, in which case middle-class notions and ego notions and everything else gets cleansed—personal identity as well as national or class or race chauvinist identity.

JJ: And the materialistic orientation?

AG: Yes, as in the Zen view or way. REAL is real. As well as simultaneously dreamlike. MIND goes beyond ideology. To me, it always did, and to Kerouac. It was the secondary explainers, such as Lawrence Lipton, who put a Marxist trip or spin on the beat ethos. Or Todd Gitlin, an academic historian. Many ex-communist Stalinist turncoats who became CIA agents, or political-hangup people like Norman Podhoretz—who was once a liberal and then became a right winger—wrote all this babble gobbledygook, about "middle-class co-option" and all that. That's their trip. It's an intellectual, ideological trip, rather than a spiritual one involving an alteration of perception, a basic turning about at the root of consciousness.

JJ: I dig your point, I think.

AG: Alteration of the source, the ground of perception. An examination, not of the ideas in the mind, but the texture of thought itself. Follow?

JJ: Follow. The working of consciousness?

AG: Yes, the texture of consciousness. So that back in the 1940s—1944, 1945, and 1946—Kerouac and I were talking about the "new vision" or "new consciousness." By 1948 both Snyder and myself and others had had some kind of actual change of awareness. You couldn't quite call it visionary or mystical experience, but it was some experience a little more profound than the later psychedelic experience with acid. It's a natural experience: the deconditioning from hyper-rationalistic, hypertechnologic monotheistic heavy-metal bureaucratic homogenized hierarchical aggression in thought processes—unnatural to begin with—that create planetary ecological chaos, totalitarian monopoly of power, over-rigid centralized authority, and police-state conditions in response to the degeneration of the natural environment.

JJ: And back to the term "hip" . . .

AG: Well, then, by the 1960s there was the Frankenstein image of the beatniks. "Bongo drums! Man, that's cool! That's hip!" Then by the late 1960s it became politicized with the SDS [Students for a Democratic Society] and a somewhat ideological Marxist politicized mental thing laid down, rather than a change of consciousness. Change of ideas, rather than a change of soul.

JJ: So those were the lifestyles of the hippies?

AG: Yes, "lifestyle" and all that. It had some elements. The 1960s continued in a sort of lineage inheriting a lot of the beat material—like Abbie Hoffman and Tom Hayden going south with copies of *On the Road*.

JJ: And the projection of the new style into the appearance of those people?

AG: Some of it did. So that was what they called the hippie movement, I guess. And I see it as a historical lineage thereafter.

JJ: A projection, of a sort?

AG: I think it was a limitation of the original vision. The hippies still believed in "progress." Whereas we had already read not only [Oswald] Spengler, but also earlier [Arthur] Rimbaud, who did not believe in progress when he said, "La science, le progrès, la nouvelle nobilité, le monde marche; pourquoi ne tourne-t'il pas?" Remember that? From *Season in Hell*? He says, "Science, progress, the new nobility; the world marches on, why the fuck doesn't it turn around? Why the hell doesn't it go backward?" So, we already had that. We no longer believed in that sort of liberal, progressive notion of progress.

JJ: Not even in scientific terms?

AG: Oh, science has brought us to the end of the planet.

JJ: That's right, almost.

AG: The bomb, or planetary AIDS.

JJ: Did the active Vietnam protest movement unify various groups?

AG: Yes, everybody agreed here. Yeah, that's right.

JJ: And the civil rights movement?

AG: Yes, everybody agreed with that. There were noble pacifist Ghandian elements in the civil rights movement—I think the differences were that the progressive groups used subterfuge, manipulativeness, and a stereotype aggression to get its political effects, and that was kind of counterproductive. That's where Kerouac and I diverged mainly. When I was in Chicago I was in charge of mantra chanting, whereas Jerry Rubin was more in charge of rabble-rousing, so there's a difference.

JJ: In Walter Lowenfels's book *Where Is Vietnam? American Poets Respond*, however, many streams seem to have joined in the protest against the very existence of the Vietnam conflict, wouldn't you say so?

AG: Oh, sure. And, you know, Lowenfels was around at LeRoi Jones's. Lowenfels was at those parties, also. Yeah. And Langston Hughes.

JJ: This is a very surprising fact for a few reasons.

AG: I met Langston Hughes at LeRoi Jones's party one night when Ornette Coleman was playing music and everyone was dancing. That's the only time I met Langston Hughes. In 1959 or 1960. A great, touching moment in history. When Black Mountain poets and painters, beatniks, the abstract expressionists, the free-form jazz, the Harlem Renaissance, all met together in one room.

JJ: That's great.

AG: Isn't that marvelous?

JJ: I find it particularly marvelous, because I am personally interested in Jean Toomer's and Langston Hughes's work, you know. Have you read Langston Hughes since? Have you read more of him recently?

AG: No, not since that moment. I'm just beginning now. I've started reading a lot more now.

JJ: So you wouldn't have an assessment of him and the Harlem Renaissance writers?

AG: I knew him, Toomer, Claude McKay, and James Weldon Johnson, from the Untermeyer anthologies, mainly, and I didn't think much of them, because I didn't understand what they were saying. I never knew the great poem, that great poem—that national anthem called "The Black National Anthem" was written by James Weldon Johnson.

JJ: I am sure many more Americans did not know that.

AG: And I didn't know that Johnson was the head of NAACP [National Association for the Advancement of Colored People] as field director. Nor did I know that he worked with Du Bois. Nor did I know that he was an American consulate in Nicaragua when the marines arrived in 1912. Nor did I know that he wrote, "If you like-a me, like I like-a you, da da-da da-da da-da," et cetera.

JJ: With his brother, Rosamond.

AG: "One live as two, two live as one, under the bamboo tree." They didn't teach us that T. S. Eliot got his *Fragment of an Agon*'s "under the bam, under the boo, under the bamboo tree" from the darkies.

JJ: Modernism was never associated with ethnicity.

AG: That was rarely taught in white scholarship about Eliot.

JJ: James Weldon Johnson was quite a versatile man.

AG: Great man!

JJ: Yes. Though he pursued many exciting modern ideas, one feels that in his ways of practical writing he still was a man of the previous century.

AG: Well, you know, he was updated to the twentieth century in the work he did with his brother, Rosamond. The shows.

JJ: Of course. But also collecting all those spirituals and then collecting all the black music of the past . . .

AG: Yeah. Didn't he write, didn't he put together the first anthology of black poetry?

JJ: Yes, that's right.

AG: Also, he wrote a very important book which I haven't read yet . . .

JJ: Which one is that?

AG: *Black Manhattan.*

JJ: Right, he did, later in his life. It was published around 1930, I believe.

AG: And in the history of blacks in the United States—one fact is that it was the blacks who settled Greenwich Village first. Amazingly. So there's a very funny form from ancient days to now, there's a funny parallelism going on. It was basically black culture, African American bebop, hipness, marijuana, jazz, and blues improvisation that "turned on" the beat writers. Kerouac's *Mexico City Blues* poems and my "Howl" are white adaptations of jazz-blues saxophone's ecstatic improvised choruses. And Bob Dylan's stylistic guru for his songs is the great mysterious blues poet minstrel, the African American lyricist-guitarist-singer Robert Johnson—who died in 1938 aged twenty-six!

New York, East Village
17 May 1989

■ **Part II**

JJ: Allen, welcome to Palacký University, Olomouc. I am grateful that we can have our second interview here, in our liberated country. Although I hoped for it when we met in New York for the earlier conversation, more than four years ago, I was not convinced it would really happen. But, as a matter of fact, you are visiting our country and this campus for the second time since our Velvet Revolution of 1989. Which is wonderful and truly rewarding.

I would like to ask your opinion about the possible link between modernism from the early twentieth century, specifically in America and in American poetry, and the beat generation.

AG: By modernism, I assume we understand the literary movements that began before World War I, with Pound, James Joyce, Eliot, William Carlos Williams, Marianne Moore, Hilda Doolittle, Gertrude Stein, and others. The link is very direct in many ways. Almost all the poets that practiced open form in the beginning of the 1950s were picking up from the inheritance of the experimental writers and the writings of the modernists.

In many cases there was a direct personal connection. Robert Creeley, who was associated with the beat movement as a friend, from the Black Mountain school, worked with Charles Olson. And had a long correspondence with Pound as to how to run a literary magazine. Pound wrote him that he should feature the work of one or two geniuses, but then have incidental material, as the extra. The backbone of any issue of the Black Mountain Review, specifically, was then Robert Duncan, Charles Olson, and Robert Creeley himself. And then the poets of the Black Mountain and the painters, and in the last issue, myself as West Coast editor. Gary Snyder and Philip Whalen and Lou Welch connected with William Carlos Williams at Reed College in the early 1950s. As I did, in the early 1950s. So that Williams sorted out my poetry, edited it for me, and wrote a preface to the first book and the second book.

Olson himself was Pound's secretary when Pound came back to America. There was from Robert Duncan and the San Francisco scene and Kenneth Rexroth always a direct connection to the old writers of the modernist period. As far as stylistics is concerned—Pound, Stein, and Laura Riding. Philip Whalen, for instance, was very much influenced by Gertrude Stein as well as by meeting Williams.

So there was kind of a lineage, especially between the experimental open form as distinct from the later Eliot's return to English blank verse, and to conservatism, royalism, and political anti-Semitism, to some extent.

JJ: Initially, you mentioned Pound and Eliot together because they both represented the beginning of something new in a larger sense .

AG: Yes, the beginning specifically of the presentation of poetry as a record of discontinuity in consciousness. That is not an unhealthy thing, the natural discontinuity of jumping from one thought to another, rather than linear thought, you might say, a holistic, *gestalt* aspect of mind, taking many impressions at one time, or in succession, not in an Aristotelian logical way, but in a more holistic comprehension.

JJ: In the early decades of the century, above all in the 1920s, one could hear the views of a modernist poet, such as T. S. Eliot, along with the views of an anthropologist and folklorist, B. A. Botkin. And they saw, indeed, very differently what the presence of many ethnic groups would mean for the future of American culture, what multiculturalism would bring to American modernism. Botkin was quite optimistic, while Eliot was afraid of the consequences. Would you daresay that one or the other was closer to truth ?

AG: Well, I don't know about truth, but I know I am not interested so much in Eliot's attempt to base his psychology and art on a purely upper-class Western white, particularly monotheist, Christianity . . .

JJ: But is this not what he eventually came to be identified with?

AG: Yes. The monotheism, I think, is a problem. Particularly the location of his faith in the Anglican Church, or some variation of Catholicism.

JJ: While Botkin was Jewish.

AG: Oh, was he? Well, but the lineage of modernism in painting, for instance, includes African images in Picasso, and it also includes the importation of Oriental perspectives in painting and poetry. Pound using the Chinese written character as a medium for poetry, the visual aspect and the aspect of the presentation of discontinuous images, as connected but not abstract and logically explained. In painting the notion of a different kind of perspective, or even collage, as you might see in some Japanese prints, affected all painters of the late nineteenth century and early twentieth century, and all the poets, particularly through Japanese haiku and Chinese hieroglyphic, so to speak. Now, Eliot also grew from Eastern thought, studied Sanskrit and Buddhist philosophy, and he used a lot of Buddhist terms like *shantih*, the four activities of the Buddha at the very end of *The Waste Land*, to enrich, magnetize, destroy. In the end of *The Waste Land* there is a kind of paraphrase for the Buddha activities, which I'd have to look up to find out; it is to enrich, magnetize, destroy . . .

JJ: The source being identified, we can make a search later, if we need to.

AG: But Eliot finally drifted away from that orientation of the Buddhist nonthe-istic to the monotheistic, and I think that was a big separation point, be-cause then it was a closed universe, and a closed verse form again, whereas with the nontheistic and more experimental bohemian modernist it was an open universe and an open verse form, indicating an open mind.

JJ: More open also to the new ethnic and social elements in America?

AG: Well, there is a continuity among the radical, even leftist inclinations of William Carlos Williams, and [Charles] Reznikoff, George Oppen, and Carl Rakosi, who actually were communists, some of them. Williams was more sympathetic. But in any case, there was a rather complicated situation; Oppen and Rakosi quit writing because of thinking they were not worthy of writing, they were not proletarian enough. Reznikoff continued writing, but was not very well known and printed his own books and so went into ob-scurity until he was resurrected by my own generation, not only the beat group, but the Black Mountain and the San Francisco group. We all knew each other quite well, especially toward the 1960s. Reznikoff, Oppen, and Rakosi—the second generation of modernists, the objectivists—were quite friendly, in fact. Rakosi, who is the last still alive, still comes to the Naropa institute, to the Jack Kerouac School, and has read for me at Brooklyn Col-lege. So there is a continuity that is very nice. That's one of the better things, I think, about the beat generation. We did not reject the older generations; we chose among them that strand which went from Whitman through Williams, the democratic open form.

JJ: Recently I read Solzhenitsyn's article in which he argues that modernism cut the links with history, indeed severed the modern world from tradition, which I cannot see as fully justified. Do you?

AG: Oh, I don't know. It did sever some links but . . . it severed the link with . . .

JJ: The more immediate predecessors?

AG: I want to formulate it in more technical terms. It severed the link with nine-teenth-century poetic forms; but nineteenth-century poetic forms are not classical forms because the authors themselves severed the link with the real classical forms. The real classical forms are the kinds that Ezra Pound used, that is to say, in English quantitative verse. The attempt to approximate clas-sical quantitative verse, measure of the vowel length, the tradition of vocal-ization from Homer through Sappho which had fallen into disuse, except for very theatrical sort of things, in Oscar Wilde or something like that. And so, if you look at Pound, he was reestablishing links with the development of poetry, when it went from Latin into provincial languages, and continuing that development in American language and attempting to update and modernize; as Wordsworth did a hundred years earlier, he modernized the diction and rhythms of the speech. Then also you have to consider that African American forms, or African forms, are also classical. They are not

European classical, but they are multiculturally classical, they go back to very ancient times, as do Australian aboriginal cultural forms.

JJ: As probably do all ethnic forms, or most of them . . .

AG: So, in a sense we are reestablishing links that have been broken by the Christian imperium, cultures that have been scattered and destroyed. People like Picasso and Apollinaire and later the beat writers were picking up the threads of broken cultures and including them in our own heritage. So in that sense, I do not think Solzhenitsyn is really appreciative of the intelligence and of the classical continuity and fidelity of the modernist generations.

JJ: Would you find the term "ethnic modernism" a contradictable one?

AG: Well, I have not heard that term, actually, but obviously in a world where you can get on a plane and hop over to India, Australia, or Santa Fe, or Africa or New Orleans or Harlem or the Kennedy School in Cambridge. . . . People are tied more closely together and have more access to varying traditions and there are more mixtures and influences as the world gets mixed more and more. America is a melting pot, a multiracial community, and naturally the culture is going to be multiracial, as elements of African American or Chicano or American Indian or Polish or Czech and Slovak or English tradition have vogues, fads, popularities, or uses, socially. Right now, as a kind of medicine against the mechanization of popular music and disco, the rap music came on top of the disco and returned popular music to speech and language and poetry and rhyme, which was like an African American tradition—the griot, the rapping, the styling out, the dirty dozens, the signifying monkey tradition—putting human voice back into radio and into popular song.

JJ: You have mentioned African American culture and its tradition. Now, its impact is certainly not limited to the African American community anymore, as it has influenced America at large. Has it influenced the beat poets?

AG: I think African American influenced the whole world. I would say it was the African American tradition that ended the cold war, actually.

JJ: That is an interesting and daring remark.

AG: The white civilization tended to repress sexuality and the body and make it an abstract head trip. As Blake pointed out, Urizen (your reason) took over. And created the nuclear bomb. The older tradition of Africa included the unification, the unity of body and mind in ritual and dance and some grounding in the vulgar realities of life by the griot and songmen who were more realistic and down to earth. So when African dance, song, and story came to America, it evolved into some form of spirituals and jazz which involved the breath and the body, and call-and-response, and migrated from the South in the form of jazz and blues up to Chicago and out to New York and out to the whole world, ultimately taking over the world of white music in the form of rock and roll. The envisionary music, in a sense of bringing ecstasy, ecstasy through dance. So that now in Olomouc, if you go to the Palacký University disco club, you can see kids dancing to an African beat, moving their behinds. It is as if the African influence opened the muladhara chakra or the anal chakra and made the West come back into its body and shake its ass. I would say that the combination of blue jeans, appropriate for such a dance as rock and roll, African American rhythms, and a personal return to the body from an abstraction of ideology had more to do with ending the cold war and overthrowing the absolutist bureaucracies of the socialist countries than all of the military threats.

JJ: Well, that's why the totalitarian authorities were so afraid of jazz and later of rock, of course.

AG: All dictatorships were afraid of rock and roll and jazz. They thought it was degenerate art. Because it came from Africa. But it was exactly that kind of thing that influenced the highest culture in Europe, whether it is Berthold Brecht [and] Kurt Weill's [*Rise and Fall of the City of*] *Mahagonny* and *Dreigroschenoper*, the greatest operas of the century, or the slight influence on Stravinsky and the enormous influence on Paris and the modernists in the 1920s. Enormous influence later on the beat generation—during the era of bebop, the 1940s—in that Kerouac was hearing the musicians play and talk to each other through their horns, they were using rhythms of everyday speech on the street as a way of communicating to each other. Kerouac heard those rhythms, like "salt peanuts, salt peanuts," and began returning them to prose and poetry rhythms from spoken rhythm, the rhythms of spoken speech of African American culture, to the less regular rhythms of bebop, where the beat was more variable than in old-fashioned funky jazz.

Through Kerouac's hearing that and admiring those rhythms and trying to write them in prose you have a lineage of African American influence on American poetry toward open form. And a new refreshment of it. Plus the notion of spontaneous composition, which is an ethnic mix in various ways; there is the oriental influence, Milarepa, and the nonliterate poets that improvised, the American Indian influence, the African American influence, all of them involving spontaneous mind, spontaneous utterance, improvisation. So the whole world of American Indian dance and song, and African American influence, and Eastern thought—all involve improvisatory forms, oral forms also, and the awakening of the mind to present circumstances rather than imitating previous literary forms.

JJ: We know about the cultural influence and even the ideological relevance of jazz and rock music in our world, where freedom was missing for decades. But the impact of such music, as you have described it, could not be particularly welcomed by the American establishment either, right?

AG: At first the Americans resented jazz, they thought it was "nigger music" and lower-class music.

JJ: So it may have contributed to the end of the cold war on both sides of the divided world.

AG: In some respects. Certainly rock and roll was a part of the change in the American consciousness of the 1960s, I would say, and thereafter.

JJ: Thank you, Allen, for the interview.

Olomouc, Palacký University
November 1993

Printed in the United States
65577LVS00004B/160